PRESIDENTIAL
POWER

PRESIDENTIAL POWER

Unchecked and Unbalanced

MATTHEW CRENSON
AND
BENJAMIN GINSBERG

W. W. Norton & Company
New York • London

Manufacturing by Maple-Vail Book Manufacturing Group
Book design by Brooke Koven
Production manager: Julia Druskin

Library of Congress Cataloging-in-Publication Data
Crenson, Matthew A., 1943–
Presidential power : unchecked and unbalanced /
Matthew Crenson and Benjamin Ginsberg. — 1st ed.
p. cm.
Includes bibliographical references and index.
ISBN-13: 978-0-393-06488-9 (hardcover)
ISBN-10: 0-393-06488-3 (hardcover)
1. Presidents—United States—History.
2. Executive power—United States—History.
I. Ginsberg, Benjamin. II. Title.
JK511.C74 2007
352.23'80973—dc22
2006102366

W. W. Norton & Company, Inc.
500 Fifth Avenue, New York, N.Y. 10110
www.wwnorton.com

W. W. Norton & Company Ltd.
Castle House, 75/76 Wells Street, London W1T 3QT

1 2 3 4 5 6 7 8 9 0

In memory of
Frank Rourke and Harold Seidman

Contents

PRESIDENTIAL
POWER

Preface

Sometime in the second half of the twentieth century, the president moved into the driver's seat of our political system. This, at least, is the commonly accepted view among political observers both professional and amateur. The change is sometimes lamented, but its occurrence is hardly ever doubted, and yet never adequately explained. The emergence of the United States as a world power is occasionally invoked to account for the recent prominence of our presidents. National security issues and foreign policy have moved to the center of American politics, and these are matters in which presidents tend to enjoy the initiative. War and diplomacy can certainly contribute to the strength of the executive branch, but not consistently. The Vietnam War seemed, at least temporarily, to undermine the power of the White House, and the recent operations in Iraq may have a similar effect. Certainly, the loss of both houses of Congress represented a setback for the Bush administration, if not necessarily for the long-term expansion of presidential power.

Our book develops a fuller explanation for the expansion of presidential power. We argue that presidential aggrandizement follows, in large part, from the same decline in popular political engagement that we have attempted to explain in our previous book, *Downsizing Democracy*. Here we consider how the waning of citizen activism has affected the functioning of government. We approach the problem as we would if we were attempting to solve a crime, by considering the motives, means, and opportunities that have contributed to presidential aggrandizement.

Motive

Motive, we argue, has been shaped by changes in the country's system of presidential selection, changes that favor more aggressive and assertive candidates with bigger ideas for the country than Benjamin Harrison or Zachary Taylor had. Presidents of the past were often creatures of party. But parties were institutions of popular mobilization. The public's retreat from politics is both a symptom and a source of party disintegration, and it has changed the making of presidents. When parties governed, presidential hopefuls waited expectantly for the call of party, or unexpectedly received the summons, and parties propelled them toward the White House.

Today's candidates are self-propelled. The diminished role of party in elevating politicians to the presidency means a sharp increase in the effort required of presidential aspirants, their staffs, and sponsors. Successful candidates today are driven and ambitious competitors who often spend years or entire careers plotting to seize the nominations of their parties. What they lack in ambition, their supporters and campaign staffs often supply. Those who reach the White House aspire, not just to occupy the office, but to change history, an objective that usually drives them to enlarge the capabilities of the presidency itself.

Opportunity

The opportunity to enlarge presidential power has expanded as congressional power faltered. The same popular disengagement that accompanied the retreat of parties has also undermined the status of Congress, traditionally the most popular branch of government. Unlike the presidency, Congress lacks the means to carry its will into effect. It can articulate its collective intentions, but it does not command the armed forces or expert functionaries needed to implement them. It has relied instead on its authority as the voice of a large and vigilant electorate to bend the executive to its purposes. But its commands lost their efficacy as the electorate diminished and the citizens who composed it were converted into mere customers in the marketplace of public services. And, while the decline of party liberated presidents from a political encumbrance, it damaged the chief mechanism through which Congress called itself to order. Congress could no longer act as a coherent body able to stand up to the single-mindedness of a vigorous chief executive. The Democratic Congress elected in November 2006 appears to be having difficulty agreeing on anything but the need to conduct investigations of the Bush administration's programs.

Means

Finally, the means by which presidents enhanced their powers have been provided by the ongoing expansion of the bureaucratic state, which has supplied presidents with the mechanisms of unilateral government—executive orders, signing statements, national security findings, bureaucratic rule making, and other administrative arcana of the modern state. The result of this confluence of motive, means, and opportunity is, in our view, sufficiently illegitimate to warrant examination through an analytic lens usually reserved for criminal activity. A crime has been committed, not violently or abruptly, but unobtrusively and by degrees. We hope to get to the bottom of it.

THIS BOOK IS the product of a long and fruitful scholarly collaboration. According to academic mythology, scholars are happiest when exchanging ideas, and this is true up to a point. You can always find colleagues who are willing to hear about the book that you are writing—but not for long—and then you have to hear about theirs. Coauthorship helps to solve this problem. It means that there is always someone who is just as intensely interested in your book as you are and willing to discuss it at length. The result of our many lengthy discussions is a better book than either of us would have written on his own. And in spite of the fact that our perspectives on politics diverge sharply on some points, we are still on speaking terms. We hardly ever argued because we hardly ever expected to agree about anything in the first place. Before acknowledging anybody else, we would like to thank one another.

We also want to thank a number of colleagues, students, and organizations who did have the patience to listen to us while we were writing and paid enough attention to make useful suggestions. Portions of the argument advanced in this book were presented at Agnes Scott College, Hamilton College, Kalamazoo College, the Woodrow Wilson Center, and the Centro de Investigación Y Docencia Económicas in Mexico City. In addition, the *South Atlantic Quarterly* gave us the opportunity to clarify and condense our main argument in its special issue on the Bush presidency. We are also grateful to our hardworking research assistants, Tania Balci and Alex Ginsberg. Our editors at Norton, Steve Dunn and Ann Shin, struggled through the project with us through several title changes, footnotes corrupted by e-mail, and confused deliberations about which version of which chapter was the correct version.

As scholars, we owe a special debt to those who came before us. In this case, our most personal debt is to two former Hopkins professors, the late Frank Rourke and the late Harold Seidman, from whom we learned much about the purposes and ideals of politics and the business of the presidency. Accordingly, we dedicate this book to Frank and Harold.

Matthew A. Crenson and
Benjamin Ginsberg
January 2007

1

From Republican Government to
Presidentialism

IN OCTOBER 2002, both houses of Congress voted overwhelmingly to authorize the use of military force against Iraq. The measure originated with President George W. Bush and allowed him complete discretion to decide whether, when, and how to attack the regime of Saddam Hussein. The president had rejected any change in the resolution's wording that would impose the slightest limitation upon his prerogatives, and his legal advisers insisted that he did not need congressional authorization in any case. The decision to go to war with Iraq was the president's to make. The congressional resolution was simply a symbolic gesture of legislative approval without practical or legal significance, except that it could be used to embarrass members of Congress who later decided to criticize the war.

According to one administration official, the White House did not "want to be in the legal position of asking Congress to authorize the use of force when the president already has that full authority."[1] Scarcely any members of Congress objected to this apparent usurpation of their constitutional power to declare war, although West Virginia's Senator Robert Byrd—a consistent defender of senatorial privilege—remarked disgustedly that his colleagues might as well hang a "gone fishing" sign on the Capitol and close up shop.[2] Outside observers in the media saw an administration "contemptuous" of the Congress and a Congress "timorous" in the face of presidential demands.[3] Even congressional action to support the president's military initiative seemed to underline the irrelevance of the legislative branch. When France pointedly refused to join the preemptive strike against Iraq, Congress decreed that the menu in its dining room would no longer carry French fries or French bread, only "freedom" fries and "freedom" bread. The congressional nomenclature never caught on in the nation at large, and the French seemed not to notice.

Bush is hardly the first president to start a foreign war on his own initiative. James K. Polk claims that distinction. But the contrast between Polk's war and Bush's helps to reveal how drastically the dynamics of presidential power have changed. Polk achieved victory, but won no power. Bush has won power without victory. Even when presidents fail, the power of the modern presidency continues to grow.

Polk's war was with Mexico. Its ostensible objective was the annexation of the independent Republic of Texas, a goal that commanded widespread popular support. Polk's own support for the enterprise helped him to take the Democratic nomination from front-runner Martin Van Buren in 1844, and the same issue helped the dark horse candidate from Tennessee to defeat the renowned Henry Clay later that year. Days before Polk's inauguration, both houses of Congress passed resolutions calling for annexation. Polk himself had helped to fashion the compromise that carried a single version of the legislation to the desk of outgoing President Tyler for his signature.[4]

Since a majority of Texans supported annexation, Polk had a mandate to implement the standing policy. He might have done so with less bloodshed and political grief if he had fixed the southern boundary of Texas at the Nueces River, where the Mexican government itself seemed willing to draw it. Instead, Polk ordered General Zachary Taylor to take up a position 150 miles to the south, on the left bank of the Rio Grande. Mexican troops attacked a U.S. reconnaissance patrol there, killing or capturing about forty men. The news reached Washington on the evening of May 8, 1846. That afternoon, Polk and his cabinet had already decided to ask Congress for a declaration of war. Now they could justify the request as a response to the Mexicans' invasion of the United States to "shed American blood on American soil."[5]

Unlike Bush, Polk could not wage war without a congressional declaration—something no president has needed since December 8, 1941—and Polk got his declaration, but with it came a steady erosion of presidential influence. First-term Congressman Abraham Lincoln launched eight "Spot Resolutions," demanding to know whether the spot at which American blood was shed actually lay within the territory of the United States.[6] The House took no action on them, but Polk's implausible justification for the invasion of Mexico called up a chorus of dissent, some of it from members of his own party. Even his constitutional role as commander in chief was not secure. In an era of political generals, the Democratic Polk found himself trying to control two Whig commanders—Winfield Scott and Zachary Taylor. He suspected both of them of waging war as much to win the presidency as to defeat Mexico. Polk tried to get Congress to create a new lieutenant generalship so that he could place a Democratic soldier in command of his war. Congress declined. Polk dismissed General Scott, a step that cost the president the good will and support of men throughout the military.

He could not even control his own diplomatic emissaries. In an attempt to win peace by negotiation, Polk dispatched Nicholas Trist to Mexico. Trist was chief clerk of the State Department, and one of his principal qualifications for the mission, in Polk's view, was that he did not seem inclined to use his Mexican exploits to advance any presidential ambitions. But he was also not inclined to follow the president's instructions. The Mexican government rejected Trist's initial terms for ending the war. Polk ordered Trist home. Trist ignored him, went on negotiating, and achieved agreement with the Mexicans on the Treaty of Guadaloupe-Hidalgo. A friend carried it to Washington and presented it to an astonished President Polk. Polk had Trist placed under military arrest and escorted from Mexico City to Veracruz, where he was placed aboard a ship for Washington. But Polk was stuck with Trist's treaty, which the Senate ratified. Congress subsequently passed a resolution congratulating Zachary Taylor for his victory at Buena Vista, and censuring Polk for the war "unnecessarily and unconstitutionally begun by the President of the United States."

Presidents Polk and Bush have recently met up on the Internet, where some electronic journalists and keepers of Web logs have seen them and their respective wars as a matched set.[7] Perhaps they do share in common the conviction that America's destiny is to bring democracy to the world, but there is a profound difference between their war stories. Polk's war was a resounding success. The country gained California and New Mexico along with Texas. But in victory, Polk found no glory, only congressional censure and humiliation, and he added nothing to the power of the presidency as an institution. In Polk's day and for long afterward, the president was not allowed the power to start wars, not even successful ones. Today, on the other hand, presidential power seems undimmed by failure.

Bush's war, like Polk's, has had its critics. The abuse of Iraqi prisoners raised questions about the administration's adherence to the rules of war, and the 9/11 Commission disclosed a measure of executive inattentiveness before the attacks on the Pentagon and World Trade Center, and confusion after them. There were also indications of deliberate deception in the administration's earlier claims that Saddam Hussein was in league with Al-Qaeda and that he had stockpiled weapons of mass destruction so terrible that they made him an imminent threat to American national security.

Presidents of past generations have almost all faced ordeal by congressional inquisition, and the experience has been hurtful and damaging. Congress has used its investigative powers to drive one president from office and wound two others.[8] In January 2007, congressional Democrats were preparing to use their newly won control of Congress to launch investigations into the Bush administration's conduct on a variety of fronts. Such congressional counterstrikes are supposed to have chastened the "imperial presidency."[9] But the great paradox of the modern American presidency is that no matter what humiliations presidents undergo at the hands of commissions and committees, the institution of the presidency emerges with its powers enhanced. The political world of President Polk has been turned upside down. While presidents fail, the institution of the presidency flourishes.

As members of his own party in Congress sought to distance themselves from President George W. Bush and congressional Democrats called for investigations of his administration's conduct, Bush ignored Congress and used his executive powers to govern. Even after suffering an embarassing electoral rebuff in the 2006 contest for control of Congress, Bush continued to command. The president's only acknowledgment of his party's electoral setback was his decision to replace Defense Secretary Donald Rumsfeld, who was apparently designated as the official fall guy for the administration's mistakes in Iraq.

In the midst of the lurid scandal that brought him to impeachment, President Clinton refined the techniques by which presidents use executive orders and the processes of administrative regulation to circumvent the statutory powers of the Congress. Clinton was adding to a repertoire of executive initiatives developed in part by Ronald Reagan, while Congress was investigating his administration's misdeeds in the Iran-Contra scandal. Together, Bush, Reagan, and Clinton contributed to the onward march of executive power, carried forward by one beleaguered president after another, in the face of a Congress that seems to retain only the power to complain and harass. Louis Fisher, America's leading authority on the separation of powers, observes that the powers of Congress have suffered a "precipitous decline" for the past fifty years in the vital matters of national defense and the federal budget.[10] One might add that presidents of the twentieth century also expanded their powers of unilateral action in almost all matters by finding new uses for executive orders and new ways of overseeing bureaucratic regulation.

The Presidential Imperium

The development of executive autonomy occasionally advances forcefully in dramatic responses to war, terrorism, or nuclear threat, but its path runs more frequently through the fine print of public business. It leaves its tracks in the Federal Register, in the arcana of the budgetary process, and in subterranean struggles for bureaucratic control that never break the surface of journalistic attention, much less make the evening news.

The Budget

Consider, for example, the presidency of Warren G. Harding. He came to office in 1921 with the promise to return the country to "normalcy" after the dislocations of Wilsonian progressivism and World War I. Chief among those disruptions were the sweeping powers that Congress had ceded to the president to meet the exigencies of war in Europe. The National Defense Act of 1917 authorized the president to procure needed military hardware by any means necessary; and the 1917 Lever Food and Fuel Control Act gave the president the power to regulate the transportation, production, storage, and mining of wartime necessities, and the power to fix prices, to requisition needed materials, and to take over the operation of factories and mines.[11] At war's end, congressional leaders declared that the wartime powers of the president had been temporary adjustments, and they were to be relinquished as quickly as possible. In 1920, despite President Wilson's opposition, Congress repealed sixty of these wartime measures. The Republican presidential nominee, Warren Harding, pledged that he would abjure "executive autocracy."[12]

Harding, however, was not indifferent to executive power. His administration, in fact, achieved the most substantial enhancement of the president's budgetary powers since the ratification of the Constitution—the 1921 Budget and Accounting Act. With few exceptions, presidents prior to Harding had been ignorant bystanders in the budget-making process. Each executive department presented its own annual request directly to the congressional committee that oversaw its budget, and appropriations were the end product of bargaining and compromise between committees and agencies, in which the committees usually had the upper hand. Congressional appropriations committees scrutinized the agency proposals and drew up legislation that specified, to the last dollar, how funds were to be spent. In one of the appropriations acts for 1871, for example, the Department of Agriculture was authorized to spend $1,500 for the upkeep of horses, $250 for subscriptions to scientific periodicals, $250 for laboratory apparatus, and $100 for the collection of minerals and ores.[13] Congress—not the chief executive—maintained near-absolute control of the federal bureaucracy. As Woodrow Wilson observed in his doctoral dissertation, the government of nineteenth-century America was an emphatically congressional government.

There was no unified executive budget, no coordination to assure that overall spending would match anticipated revenues. But in 1910 a committee appointed by President Taft had recommended that the president be given the coordinating authority to prepare an overall "executive budget" to be presented to Congress each year. House Speaker "Uncle" Joe Cannon would not go along. The framers of the Constitution regarded the power of the purse as the principal political resource of the House, and Cannon regarded congressional budget making as a republican bulwark against "Prussian-style" militarism and autocracy.[14] Congress united behind its Speaker to strike down the president's presumed encroachment on congressional authority and republican government. They went further—to prevent Taft from interfering with the budget process, Congress prohibited agency officials from preparing any budget documents without a specific congressional mandate. Taft could not even request departments to prepare estimates for him. The president ordered agency heads to ignore the statute, but Congress refused to accept any budget documents formulated without legislative authorization.[15]

During World War I the budgetary pressures resulting from wartime spending forced Congress to reconsider the issue. President Wilson requested the authority to present a unified executive budget to Congress in place of the patchwork of agency budgets. Congress's response was the 1919 Budget Act, which provided for such a budget but also included a number of provisions designed to ensure continuing congressional control of the budget process. Wilson found the restrictions so onerous that he vetoed the legislation.

In 1921, Warren Harding succeeded where Wilson had failed. Out-of-control federal spending prompted Republican congressional leaders to reach an accommodation with the new Republican president. Congress agreed to a unified executive budget, but only if it were prepared by an agency distinct from the Office of the President. A new Bureau of the Budget (BoB) would be housed in the Department of the Treasury, which Congress regarded as the federal department most responsive to congressional influence.[16]

Although the 1921 Budget Act was not scheduled to take effect until 1923, Harding seized the opportunity to expand presidential control over federal spending and issued an executive order requiring agencies to submit their proposed budgets to the BoB for the 1922 fiscal year. He worked closely with General Charles G. Dawes, the BoB's first director, to enhance White House control over the executive branch. To this end, Harding and Dawes introduced the principle of central legislative clearance.[17] Agencies had to get BoB approval for all requests and recommendations submitted to Congress, not just budget requests. The agencies at first resisted this challenge to their independence from executive control, but after Harding's death in 1923, President Coolidge ignored congressional and agency objections and mandated a central clearance procedure. The president required agencies to obtain BoB clearance for all proposals with budgetary implications—in other words, almost everything. Congress, with no Speaker Cannon to rally its members, was unable to turn aside the presidential initiative. After the 1920s, Congress would no longer independently specify the Agriculture Department's allotment for the upkeep of horses or the State Department's allocation for newspaper subscriptions. Instead of making the budget, Congress would surrender that responsibility to the president and the Bureau of the Budget. It would respond to a unified executive budget prepared in the executive branch.

In 1939, President Franklin Roosevelt capped the New Deal era of executive aggrandizement with the creation of the Executive Office of the President, in which Congress voted to house the Bureau of the Budget.[18] Now under direct presidential direction, the BoB emerged as the institutional medium through which Roosevelt and his successors shaped the nation's policy agenda. The executive budget provided Congress with the starting points for setting priorities in taxing and spending. Congress, once the incubator of national legislation, now played the secondary role of fiscal kibitzer, reacting to presidential initiatives rather than developing programs of its own. The controls it once exercised over federal agencies now belonged to the Bureau of the Budget.

Congress, however, was no pushover. In 1974, after President Nixon blocked the expenditure of funds appropriated by Congress, it passed the Budget and Impoundment Control Act. The legislation embodied a comprehensive strategy by which Congress might regain at least parity with the executive in deciding how to take and spend the public's money. The act centralized Congress's own budgetary process and established the Congressional Budget Office (CBO), a congressional counterweight to the president's BoB, now renamed the Office of Management and Budget (OMB). Instead of simply reacting in piecemeal fashion to the president's budget, the new system called for a unified congressional budget resolution, just as comprehensive as the president's proposal. Rather than restore congressional stature, however, the rationalized congressional budget-making process revealed new congressional weaknesses and in some respects only increased the president's budgetary control.

It is one thing for the president to arrive at a unified executive budget, quite another for a legislative body composed of 535 independent members.[19] The situation tends toward congressional stalemate and executive victory. In 1998, for example, the Republican party controlled both houses of Congress. But partisan division, dis-agreements between House and Senate, and disputes among factions within parties prevented Congress from agreeing on a budget resolu-tion. President Clinton's budget prevailed as a result.[20]

The new congressional budget procedures served presidential power in a second way. The relatively decentralized procedures in force before 1974 meant that the president's unified budget might be nibbled to tatters by a horde of hungry interest groups operating through representatives in dozens of congressional committees and subcommittees. The process was so disjointed that it defied presiden-tial coordination and control. After 1974, the unified budget resolu-tion provided presidents with a single, distinct target. A chief executive with solid support in the House and Senate could control both sides of the budget process, legislative as well as executive, and hit the bullseye. This is what happened in 1981 when President Reagan used Congress's budget resolution to implement his own program of tax cuts, increased defense spending, and curtailment of domestic social spending—a program that led to the ominous budget deficits of the 1980s and 1990s. Reagan almost certainly would not have been able to bring about his "revolution" if his budget had been subject to incre-mental attack.[21]

The deficit reduction targets and spending caps negotiated by Congress and the president to cope with the budget deficits of the Reagan era played a further role in reducing congressional influence and strengthening presidential management of the economy. Fiscal policy—the power to tax and spend—is the principal instrument of congressional economic policy. Spending caps and pay-as-you-go (PAYGO) accounting rules prevent major changes in the balance between taxes and spending and restrict congressional opportunities to manage the economy. The fiscal discipline needed to reduce deficits meant that fiscal policy gave way to monetary policy—control of interest rates and the supply of money and credit. In the nineteenth century, monetary policy had been one of the salient issues of congres-sional debate and the dramatic focus of presidential elections. But the creation of the Federal Reserve System in 1914 and its subsequent development took monetary policy out of the hands of congressional politicians, though not entirely outside the sphere of presidential influence. The chairman of the Federal Reserve Board became a more important economic policymaker than the chairs of key congressional tax and budget committees. Congress's role in economic policy was further eroded by the tax cuts and high military spending of the Reagan and Bush administrations, which reduced the discretionary funds at the disposal of Congress.

Finally, the centralization of congressional budgeting has meant that Congress can no longer subvert the president's budget through the discreet death by a thousand cuts. Congress now confronts the president's budget with a budget of its own. Since presidents generally find it easier to speak with one voice than Congress, and to command media attention, presidents generally have the upper hand in such confrontations. President Clinton exercised it in his triumph on the fiscal 1996 budget.[22] His struggle with Congress led to a shutdown of some federal agencies for almost two months, provoking a public reaction that weakened congressional resolve. The experience, as Louis Fisher points out, has undermined congressional confidence in its own ability to enforce budgetary discipline, and as a result Congress has ceded even more power to the president, including the line-item veto.[23] Representative David Obey of Wisconsin, the ranking Democrat on the House Appropriations Committee, sees a Congress transformed into a spineless "jellyfish" by its surrender of budgetary authority to the White House.[24]

War

The president's war powers have expanded recently in much the same way as his budgetary powers. Attempts to curb executive authority have backfired. The War Powers Act of 1973 intended to prevent future presidents from carrying the country into the quagmire of some future Vietnam. In fact, it gave the president more discretion in the deployment of military forces than the Constitution itself had granted. Under the War Powers Act, the president on his own initiative, may commit American military forces to combat abroad for up to ninety days. But the Constitution allows no ninety-day exemption from congressional review, and as a practical matter, once American troops have been committed, both military and political considerations would make it difficult for Congress to pull them back. Presidents both before and after the War Powers Act have acted as though they did not recognize any limits to their war-making powers. In 1950, for example, President Harry Truman deliberately refused to ask Congress for a declaration of war before sending troops to Korea. Leaders of both houses volunteered to enact a joint resolution approving his action, and they assured him that Congress would pass such a measure. Truman did not take them up on the offer. Dean Acheson, his secretary of state, had advised him that it was best not to create the impression that Congress had anything to say about Truman's exercise of his powers as commander in chief.[25] Presidents since the passage of the War Powers Act have followed Truman's example.[26] Congress last exercised its constitutional power to declare war more than sixty years ago.

The congressional capitulation to President Bush's Iraq policy is one more chapter in its surrender of war-making powers to the presidency. Bush at least requested a resolution of congressional support, while announcing in advance that he did not need it. It was unnecessary, perhaps, because the Bush administration and its predecessors had learned the lessons of Vietnam. As expressed in the so-called Powell Doctrine, they comprised two imperatives: Never go to war without overwhelming force, and never go to war without the overwhelming support of the American people. The Bush administration, of course, ignored both of those principles. For the executive branch, the lessons of the Vietnam War were not embodied in the Powell Doctrine. Vietnam taught military planners in the Pentagon and White House that they had to redesign warfare to make it less vulnerable to political pressures originating outside the commander in chief's sphere of authority. Instead of mobilizing an army of politically troublesome conscripts, they fielded an all-volunteer army. Instead of assembling overwhelming force, they used heightened firepower, high-tech weaponry, and professionalization to make do with fewer soldiers on the ground. The formula may not work as a military strategy. But its political virtues were decisive.

Executive Unilateralism

No president has surpassed Franklin D. Roosevelt's record number of executive orders. His successors, however, have made more inventive use of executive agreements, findings, memoranda, reorganization plans, interpretations, announcements, proclamations, and national security directives, along with executive orders, to achieve their domestic and international policy objectives without consulting Congress or the electorate.[27] Executive orders became President Clinton's preferred instrument of governance after his party lost control of Congress in 1994. George W. Bush used them to prosecute a campaign against terrorists inside the country but outside the legal system and the Constitution.[28]

But executive orders are only the most elementary instruments of unilateral executive power. Beginning in 1970, under the Nixon administration, regulatory review emerged as an auxiliary mechanism of presidential legislation. All regulations proposed by agencies not legally independent of the president had to be cleared by Nixon's Office of Management and Budget. The independent agencies were presumably beyond presidential control. The members of independent regulatory agencies are appointed by the president, but the president cannot interfere in their decisions. During the Clinton administration, however, even the independent agencies were required to submit annual agendas of regulatory action to the OMB, and beginning in 1973, the mechanism of regulatory review was augmented by the regulatory "prompt." The OMB's Office of Information and Regulatory Affairs can notify an agency that a particular regulation is to be adopted.[29] By appropriating the rule-making powers of the federal bureaucracy, presidents can legislate without consulting the legislative branch.

The congressional response to executive regulation came in the Congressional Review Act (CRA) in 2000. The CRA requires agencies to submit proposed rules to Congress for its approval and establishes a procedure by which Congress can void regulations. The problem, of course, is that a congressional decision to invalidate a regulation could be vetoed by the president. The CRA therefore provides Congress with no sure way of restraining presidents determined to use the rule-making process to make national policy single-handed.

Taken together, the expansion of presidential war and spending powers, the increased prominence of executive orders and other presidential policy instruments, along with the introduction and expansion of regulatory review through the OMB represent a massive reallocation of political authority to the presidency from the other institutions of government. Under Franklin Roosevelt, the enhancement of presidential power was understandable. FDR was popular and his tenure was a time of domestic and international crises that demanded centralization. But the drift toward presidentialism has become a chronic tendency in American politics under presidents who suffered drastic losses of popularity after being elected and those who were barely elected in the first place. It has continued when the same party controlled both presidency and Congress as well as during periods of divided government. It has weathered Watergate, Vietnam, Iran-Contra, Monica Lewinsky, and Abu Ghraib. Early critics of the Constitution saw in the presidency the inherent threat of "monocracy." Perhaps they were right.

Congress, of course, still functions. But it seems to function at its best when it is tearing down rather than building up. In the 1980s and 1990s, Congress played a leading role in dismantling federal welfare and housing programs in favor of policy "devolution" to the states. Some critics suggest that devolution may have been Congress's way of shifting difficult decisions to state politicians.[30] And it is useful to remember those eerie weeks in October 2001 when key congressional office buildings closed because they had been contaminated with anthrax. The business of Congress virtually halted. But there was no crisis in government and nothing close to the uproar that Congress caused in 1995 when the conservative majority tried to shut down the executive branch. What Congress does, it seems, counts for much less than what gets done at the other end of Pennsylvania Avenue.

Perhaps the White House has emerged as the business end of American government because defense and foreign relations, the specialties of the executive branch, have recently accounted for so much of the government's business.[31] War generally strengthens presidential leadership, but in the wars of the past, presidential power receded once peace was restored. Nor does it take a war or an international crisis to put the president in the driver's seat. Presidential power has extended over broad expanses of domestic policy because presidents have seized the political initiative in budgeting, regulation, and bureaucratic control. The turn from Woodrow Wilson's congressional government to the presidential government of today originates in internal as well as international politics, and its beginnings were recognized by Wilson himself when he brought out the 1900 edition of his famous book.

Presidentialism and Popular Disengagement

Presidentialism has risen as popular participation in politics has declined. The political demobilization of Americans has been most pronounced in congressional and local elections, but it is evident in presidential elections as well, where turnout reached a peak in 1896 never again attained.[32]

Americans, in short, are no longer as much a part of American politics as they used to be. Their political disengagement is puzzling and disturbing. It is puzzling because current circumstances should stimulate popular involvement instead of depressing it. Political activism, for example, is associated with educational attainment and Americans are better educated today than at any time in the past, but most forms of political participation are in decline.

Party competition is supposed to raise voter turnout. Today's parties are closely matched and sharp ideological differences separate their elites. Voter turnout continues to sag.

Finally, organizations with political agendas can be expected to stir up the grass roots. The so-called "advocacy explosion" of the past forty years has given us a larger population of interest groups in Washington than ever before. But the population boom in advocacy groups does not seem to have provoked a proportionate increase in organizational participation.

Just why these trends are disturbing should be no puzzle. They hint at a severe erosion of democracy. The old sources of popular activism no longer seem to work. That is why scholars and journalists, ourselves included, have given so much thought to the reasons for popular disengagement, and of course we have generally agreed that it is a bad thing.

But there is another set of questions about declining participation that remains to be addressed, and it has to do, not with the causes of political disengagement but with its effects on government institutions. As one might expect, the passing of popular mobilization has affected the authority of different institutions differently. Stated in the simplest and most obvious terms, government institutions whose influence derives from popular mobilization have suffered politically. But institutions that do not depend on public participation in order to achieve their objectives have become more powerful by comparison. The implication is that the decline of popular political engagement has tended to diminish Congress while enhancing the presidency.

Representative assemblies like the U.S. Congress derive their influence from the support that they enjoy in civil society. That is what makes them representative. Presidents, of course, benefit from popular support as well, and political scientists whose image of the presidency was formed by the era of Franklin Roosevelt sometimes judge that the presidency is a more popular institution than Congress, with its seniority-bound committees run by linen-suited Bourbons from the Deep South, urban bosses, and smooth lobbyists.[33] The populist impression of the presidency is easy to understand by comparison.

Imagine, however, a hypothetical United States in which the public has completely withdrawn from politics, and neither Congress nor the president can count on any backing from the society outside government. Congress would represent no one and speak only for itself, and it would lack the means to carry out its will. But the president would still command soldiers and bureaucrats and the power to get things done. Now imagine a fully mobilized polity. In this United States, Congress can call upon political resources to counter presidential willfulness. If it commands popular support, it can unseat presidents. And if it can unmake presidents, it can also bend presidents to its will.

This is no abstract thought experiment. It approximates the calculations that the framers made when they tried to strike a balance between the executive and the legislature. They supposed that the power of Congress would depend less on "parchment" stipulations than on ties to politically active groups in civil society. These links would be forged within local constituencies and strengthened by frequent elections that would allow those constituencies ready access to Congress—especially the House of Representatives. These groups would regard their access to Congress as a valued political resource, and would for that reason support congressional claims to power against other branches of government, with which they had scarcely any contact. Popular support, according to Madison, would inspire Congress with "an intrepid confidence in its own strength."[34] The power of the chief executive, on the other hand, would depend most on what the framers called "energy," the president's ability to act quickly and decisively through the administrative and coercive institutions of the executive branch.[35] The president could never be indifferent to popular support, but the ultimate base of his power would be "the disbursement of the public moneys . . . the arrangement of the army and navy . . . [and] the administration of government."[36] The framers believed that the Congress's broad base of popular support would give it an advantage in institutional struggles and would probably make it the dominant institution of American government. They hoped, however, that the president's institutional power and unitary character would be sufficient to provide at least some check against what they feared would be "the propensity of the legislative department to intrude" upon the other branches of government.[37] Parchment—and the "energy" of political ambition—would be the principal ingredients of presidential power.

POPULAR DEMOBILIZATION AND INSTITUTIONAL POWER

For much of its history, the relationship between president and Congress confirmed the expectations of the framers, but there was also much that they did not anticipate. One blind spot was presidential selection. The Constitution provided for the Electoral College but specified no means for choosing its members and no process for nominating the presidential candidates from whom the Electoral College would pick the winners. Political parties are also unmentioned in the Constitution, but the "evils of faction" were very much on the minds of the framers, and the most thoughtful among them wanted either to avoid parties altogether or to neutralize their harmful effects.

Many of the framers would live to see an America in which parties were essential to the political mobilization of the public, and for that reason parties also became critical to the nomination and election of American presidents. With a few notable and obvious exceptions, the politicians that the major parties chose to elevate to the White House during the nineteenth century held views and ambitions that posed little threat to party dominance or solidarity. Parties also served as the organizational armatures that gave congressional majorities the unity and discipline that they needed to deal with the unitary presidency on equal footing—better than equal when presidents were chosen for their inoffensiveness.

Near the start of the twentieth century, however, presidential aspirants began to run for office on their own account instead of waiting to be called by their parties. A different sort of person came to occupy the White House. To make oneself president required a powerful, driving ambition rarely found in the politicians who waited for their parties to make them presidents. Self-made presidents have generally wanted something more than the title and the office. They have tried to use the office to make history. Their ability to break the parties' control of the presidential nominating process was a sign of party weakness, attributable in part to the introduction of the direct primary and other reforms in state and local politics, but aggravated by the new independence of presidential candidates. The gradual unraveling of party organization made it more difficult for congressional leaders to impose party discipline, and individual members of Congress needed little prompting to place their own political interests above those of their parties.

When powerfully ambitious presidents faced a Congress with a reduced capacity to achieve unity, the stage was set for a steady shift of power toward the executive branch. It occurred not just because presidents could act decisively while Congress struggled to gather its forces. The executive, unlike the courts or Congress, is the only branch of government that controls the means to carry out its own will, and an important aspect of presidential supremacy has been the effort to bring the executive branch under ever tighter White House control. The bigger the bureaucracy grew, the more presidents could achieve.

All this occurred against the background of generally declining public participation, especially in elections. The deterioration of parties was a factor in popular disengagement, but so was the growth of the federal bureaucracy and the emergence of litigation as an alternative to mobilization. Both provided organized interests—and some interests scarcely organized at all—with the means to get what they wanted from government without disturbing the political somnolence of the general public. Congress, the most popular branch, might have been expected to reanimate the public. But the interests of Congress as a whole are not necessarily the same as the interests of its individual members. They have been elected by the voters who are already mobilized. Mobilizing new voters may seem a risky gambit for incumbents facing reelection.

In short, the privatization of the American public has tended to make the presidency the central institution of American politics. But that is a conclusion that needs a great deal of explaining. For one thing, it is a conclusion that stands very much at odds with other persuasive views of the president as the tribune of the people or the popular chief of a political party. In other words, there is nothing self-evident in the idea that the presidency should flourish while political parties and popular mobilization decline.

THE PRESIDENT AS PARTY LEADER

Political parties have, in fact, helped to endow some of our greatest presidents with the capacity to achieve their most memorable accomplishments. Jefferson, Jackson, Lincoln, and Franklin Roosevelt all managed to reach at least some of their objectives and to enter the pantheon of presidential greatness because they were party leaders. Jefferson not only benefited from the support of a party but merits some claim to the distinction of having invented the first political party in the world, although he left most of the heavy lifting to others who created a network of Democratic Republican clubs and committees that carried Jefferson to the presidency and delivered a congressional majority congenial to his leadership. The Jeffersonian party organization, however, did not have sufficient grip at the grass roots to turn out a majority of the eligible voters for either of the elections (1800 and 1804) that carried the builder of Monticello to the newly constructed White House. There seemed no need for majority turnout. The Federalist opposition was disorganized and in decline. Only the electoral chicanery of the Republican vice presidential candidate, Aaron Burr, gave them a shot at the presidency. Perhaps Jefferson's chief strength as a party leader was the weakness of the party that opposed him.

Andrew Jackson was in much the same position, except that his party did manage to mobilize voters more effectively than the Jeffersonians. In 1832, Jackson, became the first president to win an election in which turnout exceeded 50 percent, but just barely. His Whig opposition was still trying to organize its forces and was never fully successful, but when it did manage to put together a spirited campaign with a popular candidate, it drove the Democrats from office, and most of the presidents elected during the ensuing struggle between Democrats and Whigs may be counted among the most for-gettable in American history.

Parties make presidents great, it seems, when the president's party is the only one in the field. The condition is usually met only with the emergence of a new party organization whose newly found coherence gives it a brief advantage that lasts only until the opposition forces have time for counter-organization. This rule appears to govern the extraor-dinary case of Abraham Lincoln. When he was elected in 1860, most of the opposition seceded, and for the remainder of his presidency, he headed a single-party state. But Lincoln's experience also illustrates the unreliability of party as a source of presidential power. When the supply of congressional Democrats diminished, the legislators of Lincoln's party turned much of their fire on him. To the extent that Lincoln depended on his party, he relied for the most part on Republican governors, not congressional Republicans, and his princi-pal political strength was probably the Union Army. He depended at least as much on his powers as commander in chief as he did on his influence as Republican leader. Occasionally, he used the two powers in tandem, as when he ordered his generals to furlough regiments whose votes were needed in critical state elections or used Union troops to supervise balloting. Lincoln's presidency was at its most imperial when he acted solely on the basis of his war powers, and sometimes carried out his will beyond the bounds of the Constitution.

Franklin Roosevelt was clearly a different sort of partisan president. In refounding the Democratic party during the New Deal, he orches-trated a vast extension of its electoral base, reaching out to constituen-cies of the dispossessed. Having won their votes, he sealed their loyalty to the party with hundreds of thousands of federal jobs and millions of dollars in loans and benefits. His reward was the landslide reelection of 1936.

Yet it was after this stunning victory, when FDR appeared to have constructed a party of his own, that he encountered Democratic oppo-sition. Congress, dominated by Democrats, rejected his first reorgani-zation plan for the Office of the President, a plan that would have extended his powers significantly. Conservative Democrats, not just from the South but from the Midwest and border states, declared themselves opposed to his new social policies. Roosevelt tried to purge the party of his most annoying critics during the congressional elections of 1938. The landslide victor of 1936 emerged from the 1938 elections a chastened loser. This failure to govern his own party, says Sidney Milkis, was the experience that turned Roosevelt away from party government. It made him a "presidentialist."

For presidents, the problem with American parties has been their decentralized structure. Federalism and the separation of powers have fragmented the American electoral system. Parties tend to be organized around elections. What seems to be a national party is usually just a confederation of powerful local and state political organizations. Collectively, they bear little resemblance to the more hierarchical parties formed in the unitary parliamentary systems of Europe. Party power in America generally comes to rest at the periphery of government rather than at its core. Only under exceptional circumstance have presidents been able to subordinate state and local leaders in order to achieve the consolidation of party control at the national level. Jefferson, Jackson, Lincoln, and Roosevelt were exceptional, but none of them was able to achieve an institutional fusion of party and presidency. They were all products of electoral upheavals, and when the voters came to roost once again, parties reasserted their power over presidents.

GOING PUBLIC: THE PRESIDENT AS GREAT COMMUNICATOR

After the rebuff of Franklin Roosevelt in 1938, says Sidney Milkis, FDR was "firmly persuaded of the need to form a direct link between the executive office and the public."[38] A number of presidents have attempted to make the same connection, although few have been so successful at it as Roosevelt. Speaking directly to the people, over the heads of Congress and party, has emerged as a favored tactic of presidential leadership in the age of television, but it had its beginnings even before the age of radio. William McKinley was the first occupant of the White House to set aside a room for the press, and he had run for office in 1896 as the candidate of "The People Against the Bosses," the bosses of his own party.

"Going public" is not the same as the popular mobilization by which some presidents have created or rebuilt political parties. Jefferson and Jackson, though great party builders, made few speeches or public appearances. Abraham Lincoln, en route from Springfield to his inauguration, stopped his train to greet the crowds along the way, but Lincoln spoke only briefly at each stop, saying that it would be inappropriate for him to offer public views on the pressing issues of the day.[39] All three of these "partisan" presidents held office during a time when it was considered bad form for presidents to address the people directly except on ceremonial occasions. Congress apparently regarded any more tendentious communication from president to people as an impeachable offense. Just such a charge was included in the bill of impeachment against Andrew Johnson.

Although McKinley may have begun to erode the prohibitions on presidential speech, they were not fully broken until the administrations of Theodore Roosevelt and Woodrow Wilson. Roosevelt made a personal appeal to the public in 1904 to achieve passage of the Hepburn Act, which prohibited railroads from offering discounted rates to large shippers and authorized the Interstate Commerce Commission to set maximum freight charges for railroads.[40] The bill had passed the House but was stalled in the Senate because members of the president's party, including Majority Leader Nelson Aldrich, opposed it. Roosevelt launched a presidential tour of the nation, making speeches designed to be covered in the local press in each city where he stopped and then picked up by the wire services. Roosevelt also pioneered the use of White House leaks, making sure that favored reporters and muckraking magazine writers got information and public documents damaging to the railroads and their political champions. The strategy succeeded. Roosevelt personally aroused public opinion to put pressure on Congress, and the effort brought a railroad regulation bill to his desk that included virtually every feature he had sought.

Woodrow Wilson refined Roosevelt's techniques for rallying the public around the president. Not only did he embark on speechmaking expeditions around the country; he also invented the press conference so that he could exercise similar influence without leaving Washington. After his election in 1912, Wilson met regularly with correspondents from major newspapers and invited them to ask him questions about political issues in the news. Sometimes he even provided friendly reporters with the questions that he wanted to answer.

Wilson was also the first president to make use of professional public relations consultants. After winning the 1916 election on the slogan "He kept us out of war," Wilson wanted to prepare public opinion to support the war efforts of Britain and France, a step opposed by influential isolationists in the Senate and much of the population. The president asked New York publicist George Creel to design a public relations campaign that would swing American opinion to the view that the country's interests demanded that it support Britain. When the United States finally entered the war, Wilson named Creel to head the new Committee on Public Information, whose mission was to mobilize, not just military volunteers, but the entire civilian population for the industrial and agricultural production essential to sustain the Allies' war effort in Europe. The Committee recruited its staff largely from major advertising agencies, and its assignment, according to Creel "was distinctly in the nature of an advertising campaign . . . our object was to sell the war."[41]

Wilson's last great effort to rally the public to his cause was his campaign to win Senate ratification of the Versailles Treaty and approval for America's membership in the League of Nations. When the Senate rejected the treaty, Wilson chose to go to the people instead of negotiating with the senators. He traveled eight thousand miles and delivered forty speeches whose purpose, he said, was to "purify the wells of public opinion."[42] The professorial president cast himself as tutor to a nation. A statesman, he said, "should act so as to educate." But Wilson's lectures did not move the Senate. His crusade, however, may have precipitated the stroke that left him incapacitated for his last year in office.

Wilson's crushing defeat hardly discouraged his presidential successors from making their own direct appeals for popular support against congressional recalcitrants or unfriendly interest groups or simply to lay the groundwork for reelection. Franklin Roosevelt's fireside chats on the radio during the 1930s made him a personal and welcome presence in millions of homes. In the 1950s, Dwight Eisenhower's press conferences—the first to be televised—convinced the public, according to Fred Greenstein, that Ike was "solid and full of common sense."[43] Kennedy's press conferences radiated wit and charm. Johnson and Nixon lacked his poise but made an impact with prepared speeches. Johnson used a televised speech to a joint session of Congress to frame his administration's response to a violent attack by Alabama officials on civil rights demonstrators in Selma. His address is credited with gathering sufficient public support for voting rights legislation to overcome congressional resistance.[44] Johnson also used television appeals to build public support for his War on Poverty. This time the campaign included, not only speeches, but televised visits between Johnson family members and the poor people who would presumably benefit from the program.[45]

Jimmy Carter and Bill Clinton both preferred the televised town meeting as a format for personal contact with the public. It was less formal than the prepared speech, but since the "town" included only invited participants, it was less likely to produce hostile, loaded, or querulous questions. Under Clinton the White House Communications Office assumed a role similar to Woodrow Wilson's wartime Committee on Public Information. Its job was no longer simply to respond to reporters' inquiries, but to mount a coherent communications strategy—promoting the president's policy objectives, responding to unfavorable media coverage, and projecting a positive image of the president across the country. The office continued to perform these positive, promotional functions under George W. Bush, whose first communications director, Karen Hughes, worked to keep her office "ahead of the news" by constructing stories that would dominate the headlines and preempt critical coverage.

Media mastery defined the presidency of Ronald Reagan, the "Great Communicator." Reagan himself once remarked, "There have been many times in this office when I've wondered how you could do the job if you hadn't been an actor."[46] Reagan's best efforts were carefully scripted. Public speaking was one of his greatest strengths. In 1981, for example, Reagan's budget and tax proposals were stalled in Congress. The president countered with a nationally televised speech before a joint session of Congress to mass public support for what was to be the signature measure of his administration. The performance— a "smash" according to Newsweek—triggered a tidal shift in public opinion that yielded thousands of constituent calls to Democratic members of Congress,[47] many of whom switched their votes. One Democratic member said of his colleagues, "They say they're voting for the president's budget because they're afraid."[48]

Tip O'Neill tried to hold his Democrats together against the Reagan tide by warning them that public opinion was fickle. He failed in the short term, but there was nothing wrong with his observation. Reagan's approval rating dropped by twenty-two percentage points between 1981 and 1983,[49] and his ability to overawe Congress declined along with his standing in the polls. The elder President Bush plunged from an extraordinary 90 percent approval rating at the close of the 1990 Persian Gulf War to electoral defeat in 1992.

Theodore J. Lowi has argued that declines in popular approval during a president's term in office are nearly inevitable and follow a predictable pattern.[50] Presidents generate popular support by making promises; their performance almost always falls short of the goals that they have set. The result is public disappointment and the collapse of presidential influence.[51] Public opinion provides no safety net for presidential power.

A second failing of the popular presidency is that dependence on public opinion imposes a simultaneous dependence on the broadcast and news media through which presidents reach the public. At least since the Vietnam War, however, the relationship between the White House and the media has been an uneasy and sometimes adversarial one. Broadcast and print media, after all, exist not for the president, but for their audience, and as their middle- and upper-middle class audience turned against the war in Vietnam, it became receptive to investigative coverage and adversarial journalism.[52] Watergate only reinforced this tendency. Newspapers and broadcasters have discovered that aggressive use of the techniques of investigation, publicity, and exposure allowed the media to enhance their autonomy and carve out a prominent place for themselves in American government and politics.

Willingness to attack the president and administration is sometimes moderated by the editorial leanings of particular newspapers or networks. Once a story breaks, however, they seem to put aside partisanship and ideology to join in the chase. The relatively liberal *Washington Post* and *New York Times* gave the sensational charges against President Bill Clinton just as much play as they received in the conservative *Washington Times*. The *Post* even turned against its own former reporter, Sidney Blumenthal, for having abandoned his journalistic independence to become a defender of President Clinton during the

Whitewater investigation.[53] The mass media value ideological consistency less than their credibility with the public, which they can occasionally reinforce by talking trash to power.

Journalists seldom have to look far to find damaging information about presidents. They can cull their material from the torrent of rumors, accusations, and facts that arrive in newsrooms by fax on a daily basis. Information comes from "think tanks," professional "opposition researchers," and public relations firms with a stake in bolstering or undermining the administration in power.[54] Faultfinding generally sells more papers than praise. No wonder presidents become mistrustful of the press. Long before Monica Lewinsky became a household name, President Clinton regarded the media as his adversary. "No matter what I do," Clinton told a reporter, "you guys take it and you say . . . what else can I hit him about?"[55] However warm the initial encounters between the president and the press, the relationship almost always sours as an administration moves through its term in office. In the end, presidential public relations offensives almost always shift toward defensive operations.[56]

Finally, presidents are not the only politicians who practice public relations. Congress has become almost as adept at connecting with the public as the White House is. The most effective of its countertactics is the technique that Ginsberg and Shefter have called "RIP"—revelation, investigation, and prosecution.[57] It begins with sensational revelations embarrassing to the president and his administration. Then comes a congressional investigation, often with live televison coverage, resulting in the appointment of a special prosecutor to bring the executive evildoers to justice. Watergate provided a blueprint for congressional assaults on presidential popularity.

Contemporary presidents are no longer secure in their mastery of public opinion. They have certainly not given up on "going public," but they do so more sparingly than in the past. Presidential prime-time television appearances have declined in frequency over the last four administrations.[58] Instead of going directly to the public to sell major policy initiatives, presidents have relied on the White House media relations apparatus to protect their public images and cast them in a favorable light.

Motive, Means, and Opportunity: The Presidency Today

The shortcomings of party leadership and public appeal as means of presidential leadership have led presidents, especially the most recent of them, to pursue their objectives through the administrative capabilities of the executive branch itself. To exploit this instrument of presidential power, presidents must realize the same three conditions that serve as criteria of criminal culpability in the courts—motive, means, and opportunity. The means are not always available to presidents, because they do not always command the executive agencies needed to achieve their ends. Just because presidents are chief executives does not automatically give them control of the executive branch, and the executive branch has not always represented a significant political resource. Presidents had to exert themselves to gain control of the budget process, administrative regulation, and mechanisms of unilateral policymaking such as executive orders.

The opportunity to exercise bureaucratic power depends on the ability or willingness of the other branches of government to resist presidential initiatives. Congress, as the most popular branch, tends to preempt presidential initiative in periods of broad public mobilization.

The motivation is not simply a matter of personal inclination. It is at least in part a product of unnatural selection. Changes in the methods for choosing presidents over the life of the republic have changed the kinds of people who can qualify for election. Perhaps the most striking effects of the selection process show up as variations in political ambition. Today's candidate-centered campaigns tend to favor presidential aspirants who are driven, aggressive, tenacious, and perhaps even ruthless. Conventional political wisdom holds that those who lack the requisite "fire in the belly" should not even apply for the job.

Today, the making of a president can take years. Raising millions, building a campaign organization, courting supporters, maintaining a positive presence in the public consciousness—all of this demands, not only time, but a candidate with an obsessive drive approaching Captain Ahab's. Not all presidents, of course, seem monomaniacal. Some are known for napping on the job or taking long weekends at their ranches. But recent presidents have demonstrated that a genial, relaxed manner is perfectly consistent with uncompromising tenacity, and in the era of the institutional presidency, the public personality of the president may serve as the smiling face of a relentless machine. Mounting a presidential campaign requires a gathering of "investors" who make enormous commitments of money, ego, effort, and organization to package and sell their brand of president to the country. They expect political returns commensurate with their considerable investments, and they expect the presidency to deliver.

The modern system for selecting presidents assures that they will come to office only after prolonged effort, during which they are likely to acquire ambitious agendas and massive obligations. We expect them to make history. Presidents of the past were created in an evening's deliberation at party conventions, and they were expected to make as little trouble as possible. Changes in the institutions and processes for choosing presidents go some distance toward explaining the kinds of presidents that we have had, and the ways in which they have governed. Selection does not explain everything, but it does contribute to an understanding of the construction of presidential influence. Understanding the presidency begins with a consideration of how politicians become presidents. The selection system bears in particular the motivations or ambitions of those who occupy the office.

2

Choosing Presidents

THE ERA OF GREAT presidents is over. That at least is the retrospective assessment of president watchers both inside and outside the discipline of political science. Theodore Lowi has argued that the decline of political parties has left presidential aspirants on their own to pursue the country's highest office. Unsupported by legions of party workers, they try to work themselves up to the grandeur of the White House with grand promises that they are rarely able to keep. And so they almost always disappoint us in the end.[1]

Marc Landy and Sidney Milkis offer a similar explanation for the loss of presidential greatness. Presidents, they suggest, used to mobilize popular constituencies through national party organizations. They were great not just because they did great things, but also because they transformed the political regime of the republic in concert with vast movements of partisan supporters. They persuaded Americans to see and embrace their presidential visions of what the country should become. But since Franklin Roosevelt, presidents have governed independently of party, and the great democratic tides that empowered Jefferson, Jackson, Lincoln, and Roosevelt no longer uplift our presidents to a realm of popular myth above mere history. Great presidents are creatures of popular folklore, and they cannot emerge independently of the populace that enshrines them.[2]

What these two explanations have in common, besides their disenchantment with recent presidents, is the contention that the dimming of presidential luster has something to do with the diminution in the president's base of organized popular support. The political parties that used to lift politicians to presidential greatness no longer play so important a role in powering the careers of our chief executives. Behind this shared supposition, however, there is a broader, simpler, and perhaps more useful observation: The kinds of presidents we get depend on the processes by which we get them. They used to be products of party politics and popular movements, but recently a different set of processes converts politicians into presidents.

Selecting a President and Presidential Character

Modes of presidential selection are not just mechanisms for choosing presidents. They also help to make presidents. The manner in which we choose presidents, in fact, may have implications that extend well beyond presidents themselves. The process by which politicians become presidents is likely to influence the conduct of everyone with presidential ambitions.[3] The members of this small but highly influential stratum of the nation's leadership struggle to align themselves and their reputations with the series of portals through which they must pass in order to take possession of the Oval Office. Those few aspirants who achieve success find that the process by which they have gained it defines their authority and the character of its legitimacy.

It follows that there may be a critical connection between historical changes in the selection of presidents and the character of American politics in general, especially executive politics. But the connection is rarely explored today. In political science, an academic division of labor has made the study of the presidency and the study of presidential elections the concerns of two largely separate groups of specialists. This disjunction would have puzzled the framers of the Constitution. Some of them, at least, were acutely sensitive to the ways in which political institutions might be shaped by the methods specified for choosing their leaders.

In the case of the presidency, Alexander Hamilton outlined the relationship between the selection process and presidential character in the *Federalist Papers*. In common with his coauthor James Madison, Hamilton argued that the extended scope of a national republic would help to ensure its political good fortune. He applied the same general argument to the presidency.

> Talents for low intrigue, and the little arts of popularity may alone suffice to elevate a man to the first honors of a single state; but it will require other talents, and a different kind of merit, to establish him in the esteem and confidence of the whole Union. . . .[4]

The higher the office and the wider its authority, the higher the character and talent needed to win it. But the loftiness of the office would also intensify the interests contending to control it. That was one reason for the Electoral College. It would temper the passions that might flare up in the struggle to reach the pinnacle of American politics. On the one hand, a small group of electors, picked by popular vote or state legislatures, would be able to conduct the complex, reasoned deliberations necessary to evaluate the fitness of presidential candidates. The electorate as a whole could never do that. On the other hand, the strictly limited and temporary purpose for which the electors were chosen would prevent them from becoming a power independent of the people. The task of electing the president would be committed, wrote Hamilton, "not to any pre-established body, but to men chosen by the people for the special purpose, and at the particular conjuncture."[5] In other words, choosing presidents through an electoral college was preferable to congressional selection, which would lend itself to intrigue and horse-trading while undermining the independence of an executive who needed to be strong enough to do unpopular things in the interest of national security and welfare. At the Constitutional Convention, James Madison had persuaded his fellow delegates that congressional selection of the chief executive would weaken Congress as well as the president, because it would "agitate & divide the legislature so much that the public interest would materially suffer by it."[6]

Finally, Hamilton thought that voting for electors rather then voting for presidents directly would be less likely to excite popular "tumult and disorder." "The choice of several to form an intermediate body of electors will be much less apt to convulse the community with any extraordinary or violent movements than the choice of one who was to be the object of the public wishes." The fact that the electors would meet separately in their respective states was another precaution against tumult and disorder. Hamilton suggested that "this detached and divided situation will expose them much less to heats and ferments, which might be communicated to them from the people, than if they were all to be convened at one time, in one place."[7]

The presidential selection process envisioned by the framers was a sober and deliberative one, and as passionless as possible. It was suited to a period in which it was positively unseemly to make a show of campaigning for the presidency. The "little arts of popularity" would do candidates little good, not only because the arena for the contest was too big to be won by backslapping and storytelling, but because the electors who actually did the selecting were people unlikely to be swayed by little gestures of respect or regard. Although the electors were not expected to be of the same standing as members of Congress, they would surely be substantial members of the community, not likely to be moved by "little arts" of any kind.

The candidates would have to be men of the same kind, but of much greater renown. To achieve presidential preeminence in the partyless early republic, one would have to be a figure of considerable personal repute. According to Joseph Ellis, the era's list of presidential prospects included no more than twenty or thirty names. To be eligible, one had to have played a distinguished role in the revolutionary business of building an independent American nation prior to the ratification of the Constitution.[8] In a sense, therefore, nominations for the presidency had been closed. Given the limited number of potential contenders, in fact, there was little need for a distinct nomination process, and the Constitution did not provide for one. Presidential nominations would become a matter of institutional improvisation and experimentation, one of the more changeable elements in American politics, and the process would produce notable changes in the characters of presidents and the presidency.

The framers had created a presidential selection system in which name recognition was everything, though they would not have recognized the term themselves. Since it was unseemly to campaign, candidates could not exert themselves openly to make themselves known.

46 / PRESIDENTIAL POWER

Since there were no grassroots campaign organizations, there were no institutions that their allies could use to help candidates to become known. They would have to achieve renown without any visible effort to do so. Presidential aspirants in the first years following the ratification of the Constitution would be measured against the standard of Washington, which permitted no visible ambition for the presidency; for, as Richard Shenkman points out, "to admit ambition for the office was to prove oneself immediately unworthy of it."[9]

The refusal to admit ambition, however, did nothing to diminish its strength. Perhaps the framers took so many precautions to dampen the "heats and ferments" of the presidential selection process precisely because they knew how powerfully driven presidential aspirants would be. Personal ambition had to be powerful, because no party organizations propelled candidates to public office. They had to be self-propelled, and the clash of ambitions among the early republic's presidential contenders made for vicious and intense conflicts. Because the currency of presidential politics was honor and reputation, the weapon of choice was character assassination. And since ambition could not be pursued openly, it had to be advanced by intrigue and conspiracy. Among the "founding brothers," there were notable tendencies toward fratricide.

Politics before Parties, and After

Even among the republic's revered founders and framers, therefore, presidential politics was a nasty business. It was nasty, not just because the founders were ambitious and passionate human beings, but because presidential politics rewarded nastiness, even made it necessary. And, as different as their time is from ours, the malice that so often taints the pursuit of the modern presidency seems a direct descendant of the country's ancient republican rancor.

Then as now, presidential aspirants ran for office largely on their own. Though campaigning at the turn of the nineteenth century was not the costly and elaborate affair it became by the turn of the twenty-first, it was conducted on the same candidate-centered model. Party organizations did not go trolling for presidential prospects—grooming, preparing, and promoting them for the ultimate election.

They did not suddenly discover dark-horse candidates in their ranks and elevate them to leadership. The contenders in both eras have had to be self-selected self-starters. Of course the presidential hopefuls of the republic's heroic age may not have set their sights on the office as early in life as today's candidates. When Adams and Jefferson began their political careers, after all, there was no such thing as the presidency. Now it is possible to spend an entire lifetime in pursuit of the office, and the quest may therefore have become more obsessive. But in both eras the quest has presupposed unusually intense commitment and ambition.

John Adams, at least, recognized early in life that he was a driven man, "anxious, eager after something." "I feel my own ignorance. I feel concern for knowledge. I have . . . a strong desire for distinction."[10] In his mid-seventies, after having achieved the presidency and retired from office, his ambition was still unfulfilled: "How is it that I, poor ignorant I, must stand before Posterity as differing from all the other great men of the Age?"[11] In one respect, however, he was no different from the others. They were all intensely ambitious; they were merely less candid about it than he. Adams seems to have come to terms with his own urge for distinction by attributing the same hunger to everyone else. In one of his more philosophical writings, he identified the "passion for distinction" as the animating impulse that governed all human beings; "whether they be old or young, rich or poor, high or low, wise or foolish, ignorant or learned, every individual is seen to be strongly actuated by a desire to be seen, heard, talked of, approved and respected."[12]

Thomas Jefferson was not as forthright as Adams in confronting his own ambition. For more than two years, in fact, he ostentatiously abandoned politics and his poisonous feud with Alexander Hamilton for the solitude of Monticello. John Adams naturally saw the move as a deviously self-serving step to advance Jefferson's presidential ambitions by posing as "a humble, modest, meek man, wholly without ambition or vanity." Adams was sufficiently perceptive, however, to suspect that Jefferson's bucolic interlude was designed to conceal his ambition not only from the country, but from himself.[13] James Madison, Jefferson's chief political agent, shared the same insight. He understood that "Jefferson's willingness to reenter the political arena depended upon sustaining the fiction that it would never happen." Madison was responsible not only for managing the "messy particulars" of his mentor's political resurrection, but also "for shielding his chief from the political ambitions throbbing in his own soul."[14]

Some ambition, of course, must throb in the soul of every presidential aspirant. But it is likely to reverberate more powerfully in some eras than in others, and its strength affects the intensity of competition for the White House. It undoubtedly takes more drive to be a presidential contender in periods when parties do not function effectively as institutions for the selection and sponsorship of the presidentially ambitious. And when candidates must go it alone, the personal character of their quest helps to define not only the severity of the struggle for office, but also the terms on which it will be waged.

Issues are important. In fact, they may hold greater importance now than they did when party identification was a far more influential factor in voting behavior than it is today. But the personal character of the candidates is just as weighty a consideration. It is likely to be raised by any candidate or faction whose issue-based appeal to the public seems to be faltering. The initial popularity of Bill Clinton's health-care initiative, for example, may have helped to animate the "vast right-wing conspiracy" that eventually led to the Paula Jones and Monica Lewinsky scandals, and impeachment.[15] His enemies turned to character assassination to counter a policy initiative that threatened to have widespread popular appeal.

Politicians who can survive the politics of character assassination without giving in to shame and disgrace are clearly different from ordinary human beings. Perhaps they are not quite human. Journalist Michael Kelly suggested, in fact, that most of our recent presidents have been moral monsters by reason of their ethical insensitivity. The common quality of the "monster-greats"—LBJ, FDR, Nixon, Clinton, and . . . John F. Kennedy—is that they were all maniacally driven men. They got the presidency, in large measure, because they wanted it so much that they were, in a sense, mad; they were great because they were monsters."[16]

But the "monstrosity" of modern presidents may be an illusion fostered by a press intoxicated by Watergate. Hardly anyone who had to undergo the scrutiny to which we subject contemporary presidents would emerge unsullied. Many Americans regard the modern politics of presidential scandal and personal vilification as a product of the modern mass media. In the past, the argument goes, many of our presidents did scandalous, even monstrous, things, but the press had the decency to keep quiet about the enormities of our executives.[17]

In fact, however, this is one of several respects in which today's competition for the presidency echoes the struggles of the early republic. Then as now, scandal and personal vilification were the stuff of politics. Membership in America's pantheon of nation-building heroes was no proof against vast conspiracies bent on character assassination. Washington himself was not immune.

Emblematic of the era—and its connection to our own—was the notorious publicist James T. Callender. He fled Scotland in 1793 to escape a charge of sedition. In the end, he was imprisoned here for a similar offense but pardoned by Thomas Jefferson. Convinced that he deserved better than mere freedom, however, he turned against his benefactor and publicized the liaison—recently confirmed by DNA evidence—between Jefferson and his bondswoman Sally Hemings. Between his escape from the Scottish prosecutors and his presidential pardon, Callender used his pen to smear some of the most illustrious figures of the Federalist elite. His disclosure of Alexander Hamilton's adulterous affair with Maria Reynolds, the young wife of a shady speculator, may have blasted Hamilton's presidential ambitions almost as decisively as Burr's bullet.[18]

But Callender's most venomous slanders were aimed at President John Adams, and they, like the attack on Hamilton, were backed financially by Adams' vice president, Thomas Jefferson, who denied his complicity until Callender published their correspondence. Callender's purpose—and Jefferson's—was to check the administration's supposedly hostile stance toward the revolutionary government in France and its perceived partiality toward Great Britain. To discredit the country's foreign policy, the journalist, prompted by Jefferson, sought to destroy the reputation of its author. Adams, wrote Callender, "is not only a repulsive pedant, a gross hypocrite, and an unprincipled oppressor, but . . . in private life, one of the most egregious fools upon the continent."[19] The abuse was eventually collected into two volumes entitled *The Prospect Before Us*, which earned Callender a $200 fine and a nine-month jail sentence under the Sedition Act.

Adams had not requested the legislation that allowed his administration to prosecute the journalists who defamed him, but he made vigorous use of the statute. His sensitivity to criticism was Nixonian in its intensity.[20] One by one the editors on his enemies list were clapped behind bars, and some of their Republican sponsors feared that they might soon be imprisoned too. But Republican opposition to the Alien and Sedition Acts did not mean that Republicans would hold back from similar measures themselves. In 1806, for example, Thomas Jefferson ordered the prosecution of four Federalist editors in Connecticut for seditious libel. Two clergymen faced similar charges for defaming Jefferson from their pulpits.[21]

The fraternal era of the founding brothers ended in the fratricide of presidential politics. During the election of 1800, in fact, the surviving founders came close to fracturing the political union that they had labored so hard to establish. While the president-centered conflicts of the more recent past have posed no such threat, they have generated crises that shook the political system to its foundations. We have seen one president resign and another impeached, both casualties of the politics of character assassination as well as their own deeds. The point is not that contemporary politics has returned to the patterns established in the years just after the founding, but that two eras so strikingly different in so many ways should converge toward such similar modes of political warfare.

Even James T. Callender has enjoyed a recent revival. Conservative columnist William Safire, one of the most prominent voices in the movement to eject Bill and Hillary Clinton from the White House, published a fictionalized, sympathetic account of Callender's career in the United States. It presents the notorious scandalmonger not as the Matt Drudge of his generation, but as a man of principle who turned against his republican patron when Jefferson, in his quest for power, departed from his principles.[22] *Harper's Magazine* editor Lewis Lapham senses other echoes between the Federalist era and our own. In the administration of George W. Bush, he sees a regime

> royalist in sentiment, "monarchical" and "aristocratical" in its actions, Federalist in its mistrust of freedom, imperialist in the bluster of its military pretensions, evangelical in its worship of

property. I don't think it mere coincidence that the official portraits of Adams, Washington, and Hamilton have been so flatteringly restored by those of our popular historians who see the story of the past reflected in the mirror of the present.[23]

The reflection also discloses some notable differences between present and past. The personal feuds that infected early competition for the presidency were expressions of the competitors' relations with one another. They were well acquainted; they had spent long stretches of time in one another's company, working together in the Continental Congress, the Constitutional Convention, on diplomatic missions, in warfare. Their contests for high office became personal because they knew one another too well. But that was not the only reason why personal honor and character figured so prominently in presidential politics. As Joseph Ellis observes, "Character mattered because the fate of the American experiment with republican government still required virtuous leaders to survive." Eventually the United States might develop into a nation of laws and institutions capable of surviving corrupt or incompetent public officials. But it was not there yet.[24]

It was a time when almost every presidential act might set a precedent or establish an institutional practice, when a president's personal character might make a profound impression on the attitudes of the public or the shape of their government. "I walk on untrodden ground," said George Washington. "There is scarcely any part of my conduct wh[i]ch may not hereafter be drawn into precedent."[25] Today the personal nature of the quest for the presidency once more gives prominence to considerations of character. The force of presidential ambition must be sufficiently powerful to sustain the long and arduous process of reaching the White House. Even if the candidates have no particular goals to achieve as chief executive—no vision—they must make policy commitments to supporting constituencies in order to assemble the personal campaign organizations and financial resources needed to propel them to the presidency. They reach the presidency with ambitious agendas. But having arrived at the triumphal culmination of the struggle, they find not the sweeping opportunities that faced the early presidents, but a constricted range of possibilities limited by the accumulated laws and entrenched institutions of a country more than two centuries old. One of the most striking features of the contemporary presidency is the tension between the intense drive and ambition required to become president under the current selection process and the restricted opportunities for action that face presidents once inaugurated. The disparity between ambition and opportunity is the central contradiction that drives contemporary presidential politics.

Electing the Electors: The Evolving Selection System

The framers of the Constitution prescribed a complex, indirect means for the election of presidents. They devised the Electoral College in an effort to insulate presidential contests from the baneful influence of faction and to preserve the executive's independence from Congress. But one of the central questions about the electors remained largely unanswered. Who would choose them? The Constitution left that issue to the discretion of the legislatures of the several states. In general, the legislatures adopted modes of selection that were variations on three basic themes—appointment by the legislature, direct popular election by districts, and statewide popular election of a so-called "general ticket" of electors.

For the first forty years following ratification of the Constitution, the state legislatures darted like water spiders from one kind of electoral system to another. An exasperated Senate committee of the period declared that it was "alike impractical and unprofitable" to conduct an orderly inventory of the state selection procedures "for they change with a suddenness which defies classification."[26] Massachusetts, in fact, never used the same selection process twice in a row from the first presidential election in 1789 to the eighth in 1824. Other state legislatures were only slightly more consistent in their schemes for choosing electors, and partisan manipulation was usually the purpose that drove change. When Federalists unexpectedly captured the New Jersey state legislature in 1804, for example, they repealed the law providing for the popular election of a general ticket of electors just three days before the voters were scheduled to go to the polls. The New Jersey legislators, not surprisingly, opted for legislative selection instead. In North Carolina, where the district system had been in effect since 1796, the republican legislature voted to replace it with legislative selection in 1811, despite widespread popular protest, so that the state's Federalist minority would not be able to capture any electoral votes in the presidential contest of 1812.[27]

States did not march inexorably from less to more popular modes of selection. In addition to New Jersey and North Carolina, a number of states returned to legislative designation of presidential electors after experimenting with direct popular election. Just before the closely fought election of 1800, for example, New Hampshire, Massachusetts, Pennsylvania, and Georgia all abandoned popular election for legislative appointment. The arrangement would make it possible for the legislature's majority party to name all the state's electors, maximizing the state's impact on the outcome of the presidential contest and minimizing the likelihood that any elector would defy party control.

But legislative selection was problematic. In the first place, it did not guarantee that a state would cast its electoral vote in a bloc for one candidate. In 1800, for example, Pennsylvania divided its electoral votes between Jefferson and Adams because its legislature was deadlocked. New York cast no electoral votes in the election of 1789 because its legislators were unable to resolve a deadlock.[28] Legislative selection also embodied a democratic contradiction. The legislators themselves were elected by popular vote, and the popular thing to do was to advocate popular election of the chief executive. Schemes for popular election of the electors gained ground by fits and starts—but usually on terms acceptable to state political elites.

Popular election by districts allowed for a more faithful reflection of public sentiment than either legislative selection or the general-ticket system. It meant that a state's political minority could win a minority of the state's electoral votes. This was the least desirable outcome for leaders of the state's majority party. Dividing the state's votes diminished its impact on the outcomes of presidential elections, thus undermining party leaders' claims to presidential favor. District elections also tended to undermine statewide political organization and reduced state leaders' control over the choice of electors. Little political coordination was needed for the voters of a single district to choose a single elector. The general-ticket system, however, presupposed a mechanism for assembling a statewide slate of electors pledged to a presidential candidate. It was a product of state political organization and a mechanism through which state party leadership could constrain voter choice.[29]

Statewide election of a slate of presidential electors—the system used by all but a handful of states today—was not so much a triumph of popular democracy as of political partisanship. It prevailed in spite of repeated attempts to pass a constitutional amendment that would make the district system universal. On four occasions the Senate approved such amendments by the necessary two-thirds vote, but in each case the proposal failed to achieve the required margin in the House, although it came within a few votes of success in 1821. In Congress, at least, majority sentiment favored the district system. Its proponents argued that the arrangement would minimize the interference of legislative caucuses and political factions in presidential elections and maximize the influence of the voters. The voters of at least one state—New York—endorsed the district method by popular referendum in 1828.[30]

Eight years later, however, Maryland was the only state that still chose its presidential electors by districts. When it abandoned the system in 1836, the option disappeared from presidential politics until Maine reintroduced it in 1972. District elections could not withstand the dynamics of political competition in a federal system. Winning the popular vote in a general-ticket state paid off more handsomely for presidential aspirants than winning in a comparable state that doled out its electors by districts. In the general-ticket state, the winner took all the electoral votes; in a state with district elections, the winner might get a majority of electoral votes, perhaps less than that if more than two candidates were in the race. Presidential aspirants were likely to address their appeals to states where their efforts tended to produce the greatest electoral returns—the general-ticket states. States that clung to the district system for choosing electors when other states opted for the general-ticket method were politically disadvantaged, and so were the presidential candidates who depended on their support. It was a disadvantage that Thomas Jefferson recognized in his close contest with John Adams in 1800. Virginia was one of a handful of states that had adopted the district system. Jefferson urged fellow Republicans in his home state to switch to the general-ticket method because it could not afford to risk splitting its electoral vote when the New England states dominated by Federalist majorities delivered their electors in solid blocs.[31]

In the end, neither Adams nor Jefferson won a majority of the Electoral College in 1800, and the task of choosing the president fell to the House of Representatives. The constitutional provision for this "auxiliary" method of electing presidents was considered a concession to small states. If the Electoral College failed to produce a majority for any candidate, the House would then choose among the five leading contenders for the presidency (reduced to three by the Twelfth Amendment). But each state's congressional delegation would cast only one vote at this stage in the selection process, and small states would therefore carry as much weight in the choice of the president as New York, Virginia, or Pennsylvania. This mechanism reintroduced an arrangement which had been explicitly rejected by the framers— congressional election of the president—and the allocation of one vote per state seemed to make this mode of selection arbitrary as well as unwise. Near the close of the Constitutional Convention, in fact, both Madison and Hamilton had attempted unsuccessfully to minimize the reliance on the auxiliary congressional system by introducing provisions that would allow for the election of candidates who had won the Electoral College with only a third or a mere plurality of the votes. Madison and Hamilton were apprehensive that a majority of the electors would rarely be able to agree on a single presidential candidate. Although the Revolution had produced a pool of national heroes with presidential stature, there was no certainty that the republic would continue to produce "continental characters" who commanded sufficiently broad support to capture a majority of electors. The electors might scatter their votes among favorite sons or regional candidates. In that case, the election would routinely fall to the House of Representatives, and under the rule that each state could cast one vote, it was distinctly possible that the winner could be the candidate least favored by the people. The president who emerged from this process might be the creature of Congress, without an independent mandate to govern or the legitimacy to act on behalf of the nation.[32] The expectation that the country would often have to resort to this secondary process of presidential selection was precisely what made it so appealing to the representatives of small states. They would carry far greater weight in presidential elections than their populations would seem to warrant.

After the deadlock of 1800, however, the House would intervene in a presidential contest only once. When states abandoned the selection of presidential electors by districts, they also tended to steer presidential contests away from the House of Representatives. The same general-ticket system that helped to frustrate the framers' hopes for presidential elections free of factions or parties also increased the likelihood that the Electoral College would be able to compose a majority for a single candidate. In states that conducted their presidential elections as winner-take-all contests, citizens might be reluctant to throw their votes away on minor parties and candidates. The emerging electoral arrangements tended to focus attention on the two leading contenders and to relegate lesser figures to the status of political distractions.

It would take more than a generation for the states to arrive at the procedure for electing the electors that prevails today. In 1800, electors were chosen by general ticket in only two of fifteen states. By 1824, twelve states of twenty-four used the general-ticket system.[33] This method obviously encouraged more popular participation in presidential elections than did the legislative appointment of electors, and the spread of general tickets among the states accompanied an expansion of the presidential electorate. By 1824, only three states retained property qualifications for voters. But even where citizens could vote directly for presidential electors, they participated at rates that were extremely low even by the unimpressive standards of present-day presidential elections.

Pennsylvania, for example, was one of only three states to adopt the popular election of a general ticket for the presidential election of 1792. But only 4000 residents bothered to vote, compared to 35,000 in the congressional elections just a month earlier. The presidential election of 1792, of course, was no cliff-hanger. Washington ran unopposed and won all the electoral votes. Since the only issue in play was the selection of the vice president, there was no reason to expect a groundswell of popular excitement. But the low turnout of 1792 was not exceptional. For more than a generation after the ratification of the Constitution, participation in presidential balloting generally ran a poor second to voting in state, local, and congressional elections. As Richard McCormick points out, "more voters were attracted to the polls by gubernatorial elections—or the election of sheriffs—than by presidential elections in this period."[34] The early presidents played for small audiences. Although the interested onlookers grew more numerous in time, a majority of the eligible voters would not turn out for a presidential election until 1828, when Andrew Jackson won his first term in the White House.

From the Visual to the Textual Presidency: Electors Shape Presidents

George Washington acted out his presidency before a much smaller constituency than Andrew Jackson did. The obvious differences between the two men, and among the intervening presidents, may have had something to do with the changing size and composition of the audience that had to be persuaded to elect them. In the case of Washington, scarcely any persuasion was needed. He was the towering figure in the pantheon of revolutionary heroes, the most prominent in a reservoir of presidential eligibles that would continue to supply the country with chief executives down to the time of James Monroe.

WASHINGTON AND THE VISUAL PRESIDENCY

America seems to have used up most of its great political personalities in order to bring itself into being. The founders' greatness was evident even before anyone knew what they were founding. "Times like these call up Genius," wrote one delegate to the First Continental Congress in 1775.[35] Washington himself sensed something providential in the events of independence. The citizens of America, he wrote, are "to be considered as Actors on a most conspicuous Theatre, which seems to be peculiarly designed by Providence for the display of human greatness and felicity."[36] Washington, of course, was the "conspicuous Theatre's" foremost figure of human greatness. From the distance of two centuries, however, it is not easy to understand what made him so great.

He was no orator. He eventually became a competent general, but no military genius. If England had sent more able commanders to subdue the colonies, we might still belong to the British Common-wealth. Nor did Washington win prominence with his pen. He deliv-ered his most memorable prose in his farewell address, originally drafted by Madison in 1792 when Washington was considering retire-ment, and then revised by Hamilton just before it was finally used in 1796. Washington, as Edmund Morgan points out, was not a man of many talents, and he was surrounded by fellow founders—Jefferson, Hamilton, Franklin, and others—whose range of brilliance far exceeded his own.[37] Yet even before they invented the presidency, these luminaries had chosen Washington to preside over them twice—once in the Continental Congress and later at the Constitutional Convention. Of course, they could actually see him and feel his pres-ence, and perhaps his greatness had to be seen to be fully appreciated. Maybe you had to be there.

In the small circle of founders and framers who emerged as presi-dential possibilities after the ratification of the Constitution, Washington stood apart. He made a deliberate effort to do so. He was the only representative in the Second Continental Congress who showed up wearing a military uniform. His biographer, Abraham Flexner, suggests that it was his way of asserting that the time for mili-tary action had arrived. But there are less charitable interpretations. Marvin Kitman contends that he was campaigning for the office of commanding general, letting the other members of Congress know that he already owned the outfit.[38]

Washington created a visible difference between himself and the common run of founders. It was a barrier that he maintained against the framers as well. By the time of the Constitutional Convention, he was already famous for his aloofness. Gouverneur Morris bet Alexander Hamilton that he could approach Washington at a recep-tion for delegates, slap him gently on the back, and say, "My dear General, how happy I am to see you look so well." When the moment came, Morris put his left hand on Washington's shoulder and compli-mented him on his appearance. "The response was immediate and icy. Washington reached up and removed the hand, stepped back, and fixed his eyes in silence on Morris, until Morris retreated abashed into the crowd." No one ever attempted such familiarity again.[39]

Washington had demonstrated that he was untouchable, and the nation's most likely contenders for the presidency had been eyewitnesses to the event. No one in sight would step forward to challenge his claim to the office. The founding brothers had created a republic of personal acquaintanceship, and Washington was acquainted with most of the people whose support was needed to make him chief executive. His power over them was less a matter of intellect or oratory than personal manner and bearing. Of course, only a small handful of citizens would ever see Washington. But in 1789, when most states chose their electors through their legislatures, it took only a few to seal his selection as president.

Washington's personal dignity and restraint were acquired by practice. As a young man, he had been an acquisitive dealer in land and "acutely eager for public esteem." He decided early to "push his Fortune in a military line," and he strenuously pursued the royal officer's commission that would satisfy his desire "to be distinguished in some measure from the common run of provincial officers."[40] His ambition was no secret, and while it never left him, he eventually learned that he could advance it most effectively by cloaking it in disinterested reserve, mild manners, and gravitas.

Washington succeeded, says Forrest McDonald, "because he was a consummate actor who had self-consciously been role-playing throughout his adult life." But he was no phony. He lived in an age when character was a kind of performance by which one struggled to rise above base instincts and natural vices. It was artifice in the service of virtue.[41] Contemporary presidents engage in similar feats of image construction when they hire media consultants to orchestrate their public appearances so as to produce presidential impressions. Washington was no different, except that he constructed his own image, without leaning on consultants, spin doctors, or such stage props as aircraft carriers, Mount Rushmore, the Statue of Liberty, or invitation-only "town meetings."

As president, Washington made a point of showing himself to the public. At his inauguration in 1789, he took the oath of office on a balcony of Federal Hall, where throngs of New Yorkers crowding the streets and rooftops could see him go through the motions. To deliver his inaugural address, however, he retreated inside to speak to the members of Congress alone. Speaking was not his strong point. In fact, one of the Pennsylvania congressmen in the audience commented critically on the president's delivery.[42] Washington also initiated the presidential practice of touring the country in order to show himself to the people. Public speaking, as Jeffrey Tulis points out, was a less important objective of these travels than public appearances—"seeing and being seen," as Washington himself put it. He had become a living embodiment of the nation, and by merely appearing he could strengthen the bonds that held it together.[43]

ADAMS AND THE TEXTUAL PRESIDENCY

Seeing and being seen were critical to political standing in the era of Washington. Vice President John Adams was acutely sensitive to the political significance of public appearances. As president he made no tours of the country like Washington, but he did hold weekly levees and tea parties to display himself to the public.[44] Unlike Washington, however, Adams was a gifted and prolific writer, and he gave powerful expression to the vital political role of visibility. It came in a series of essays that he wrote as vice president, when he may have had reason to be concerned about his own visibility.

> The poor man's conscience is clear, yet he is ashamed. . . . He feels himself out of the sight of others, groping in the dark. Mankind takes no notice of him: he rambles and wanders unheeded. In the midst of a croud [sic], in the church, in the market . . . he is in as much obscurity, as he would be in a garret or a cellar. He is not disapproved, censured, or reproached: he is only not seen. . . . To be wholly overlooked, and to know it, are intolerable."[45]

If Washington had been a visual president, Adams was more verbal. Before his vice presidential *Discourses on Davila,* he had published *A Defence of the Constitutions and Government of the United States,* and before that, as a representative to the Continental Congress at the very beginning of the Revolution, he had written his *Thoughts on Government,* whose views influenced Jefferson's draft of the Declaration of Independence. And before that, he had helped to conceive the Revolution itself when he published his *Dissertation on the Canon and*

Feudal Law in 1765 at the age of thirty. It advanced the view—
dangerous for the time—that government "was a plain, simple, intelli-
gent thing, founded in nature and reason, quite comprehensible to
common sense." He need hardly have added that what was accessible
to common sense might also be open to common people.[46]

Adams revealed himself to the public on the printed page. He
could convey his excellence to an audience that extended beyond the
range of eyesight. He did not have to be personally present in order to
demonstrate that he stood above the common order of human beings.
His personal presence, however, was hardly negligible. Adams was an
accomplished speaker and parliamentary debater. In the Continental
Congress, writes David McCullough,

> He would stand at his place, back straight, walking stick in
> hand, at times letting the stick slip between thumb and forefin-
> ger to make a quick tap on the floor, as if to punctuate a point.
> The "clear and sonorous" voice would fill the room. No one
> ever had trouble hearing what Adams had to say, nor was there
> ever the least ambiguity about what he meant.[47]

Adams's proficiency as a writer may help to explain why the
Continental Congress appointed him, along with Thomas Jefferson, to
the Drafting Committee responsible for composing the Declaration of
Independence. Jefferson arrived at the Congress with a shorter bibli-
ography than that of Adams. He was known primarily for a pamphlet
that he had published in 1774, *A Summary View of the Rights of British
North America.* Adams would later recall that Jefferson came to
Philadelphia with "the reputation of a masterly pen . . . , in consequence of a very handsome public paper which he had written for
the House of Burgesses, which had given him the character of a very
fine writer." Jefferson's pamphlet probably explains the Drafting
Committee's decision to assign him the task of writing the first draft of
the Declaration. He had done little else to distinguish himself at the
time. Unlike Adams, he was hopeless as a public speaker. During the
debate on his draft, he remained silent and sullen while the delegates
did violence to his prose. In later life, Adams and Jefferson would have
different recollections about how the younger man came to be the

author of the Declaration. The likely answer, as Joseph Ellis suggests, is that Adams was needed to lead the debate on the Declaration. Jefferson was not cut out for oratory. He became the draftsman.[48]

JEFFERSON AND THE MODEST PRESIDENCY

Twenty-five years later, at the peak of his political career, Jefferson would be "one of the most secluded and publicly invisible presidents in American history." In his administration, the work of government would be conducted almost entirely in writing. Washington the visible president and Adams the verbal president were succeeded by the "textual presidency" of Jefferson.[49] The republic of personal acquaintanceship, run by notables, was expanding. It had become the republic of the written word, the reading republic.

Political reading material had hardly been scarce before the administration of Thomas Jefferson. As feuding cabinet members under George Washington, Jefferson and Alexander Hamilton had sponsored rival newspapers, whose editors threw some of the first punches in the fiercely partisan press brawls that would accompany presidential politics for more than a century. In 1789, John Fenno received the patronage of Hamilton's Treasury Department—legal notices and printing contracts—to support the publication of the pro-Federalist *Gazette of the United States*. In 1790, Jefferson and Madison responded by persuading Philip Freneau, the poet of the American Revolution, to move to Philadelphia, where he became a translator in Jefferson's State Department. The annual income of $250 as a government employee supplemented the subscription and advertising revenues that Freneau could earn as editor of the newly founded *National Gazette*, which Madison expected to "be some antidote to the doctrines and discourses in favor of Monarchy and Aristocracy. . . ."[50] Madison, a major contributor to the early issues of the paper, defended the new venture in journalism as a step toward the creation of a sovereign and national public opinion that would help to solidify the bonds of union newly formed under the Constitution, but he also used the pages of the paper to discuss the "party issues" before the nation.[51] In short, the rise of a partisan press preceded the formation of party organizations. In the beginning, there were only words.

Words, however, were sufficient to provoke the Alien and Sedition

Acts of 1798. The legislation sharpened doctrinal divisions between the two emergent parties, with the Jeffersonian Republicans arguing for state sovereignty against the Federalist claims of a central power to protect the nation against subversion. Behind the doctrines, organizations began to form. James Madison edited Jefferson's draft of the 1798 Kentucky Resolution while it was in transit from Monticello to the legislature at Frankfort. Jefferson thought it best if this first bolt of Republican thunder against the Sedition Act came from a state other than his own. A year later Madison, a member of the Virginia House of Delegates, drafted a Republican manifesto for the legislators' approval and helped to convince his colleagues to enact the change in Virginia's selection of presidential electors from district elections to the general-ticket method, which was expected to give all the state's votes to Jefferson. The Commonwealth's Republicans wasted no time in convening to choose their slate of electors. At the same time, they formed a five-man central committee "to communicate useful information to the people relative to the election . . . [and] to keep up regular intercourse" with subcommittees in every county of Virginia. Madison paid dues of one dollar to the central committee and became the chairman of the Orange County subcommittee.[52] Virginia had a party organization.

Jefferson won a majority of the Electoral College in 1800, but his margin of victory might have been more comfortable had Maryland and North Carolina not chosen their electors under the district system. Both split their votes. In Pennsylvania, where Republican partisans were organized and active, the legislature chose presidential electors. Unable to resolve a deadlock, the lawmakers divided Pennsylvania's electoral votes between Adams and Jefferson, effectively canceling out the impact that the state might have had on the outcome of the election. When the balloting was over, Jefferson led Adams by eight electoral votes.

John Adams, however, was not yet defeated. Neither was Aaron Burr. Burr's reward for engineering Jefferson's victory in New York was his designation as Republican candidate for vice president. The Constitution as it stood in 1800 did not distinguish between presidential and vice presidential candidates. Each member of the Electoral College had two votes, one for each of two candidates residing in different states. The candidate receiving the most electoral votes became president. The second-place finisher became vice president. Jefferson and Burr received exactly the same number of votes, and the contest moved to the House of Representatives, where each state delegation was to cast its single vote for one of the three leading candidates—Jefferson, Burr, and Adams. On the thirty-sixth ballot—less than two weeks before Adams' presidential term ended—enough Federalist representatives abstained by casting blank ballots to give Jefferson ten states and the presidency.[53]

The election of 1800 was a close thing, and not just in vote totals. The prolonged stalemate generated rumors of a political coup, threats of secession, and intimations of armed force. The Twelfth Amendment, ratified in 1804, would remove at least one source of political anxiety about the presidential succession. Henceforth the electors would no longer cast separate votes for president and vice president. The vice president would no longer be the second most popular candidate, as Jefferson had been in the Adams administration. He would be a candidate chosen to maximize the electoral prospects of a presidential aspirant, not a presidential candidate himself. The first vice president chosen under the new system was Governor George Clinton of New York, "an old man who is too feeble to aspire to the Presidency."[54] The president would now occupy a commanding position in relation to the vice president.

Jefferson, however, would set strict limits on his capacity to command. Popular tradition has it that after moving from Monticello to the White House, the champion of limited government would abandon his Whiggish principles and make the most of presidential power. In fact, Jefferson made only modest use of those powers and exercised forbearance and self-restraint when he might easily have justified executive action. His most memorable legacy—the 1803 Louisiana Purchase—seemed to express an expansive conception of the president's unilateral discretion. But this assessment overlooks the fact that Jefferson was being urged to take Florida and New Orleans by force, and Congress had authorized him to raise an army of 80,000 for the purpose. Jefferson urged patience and a continuation of James Monroe's negotiations with Napoleon to purchase the territory. The course he chose was not only wiser than the alternatives being urged upon him but also made more modest demands on executive energy. Even so, Jefferson still harbored constitutional qualms about the purchase, and until his advisers persuaded him otherwise, he wanted to draft a constitutional amendment making the Louisiana Territory part of the United States.[55]

A modest presidency, sensitive to the prerogatives of the people, the states, and the Congress and scrupulous about constitutional restrictions, was the predictable result of Jefferson's republican suspicions concerning governmental authority, and especially executive power. A majestic president was perilously close to a king, and the republican crusade of 1800 had been animated in part by the suspicion that the Federalists had royalist ambitions. It was fitting that the Jeffersonian presidency should be meek and mild.

The meek and mild, however, are seldom presidential candidates and even less likely to win elections. They succeed only when they have party organizations behind them, congregations of political promoters willing to promote them when they were too modest, or simply unable, to do it themselves. The nascent Jeffersonian party, though hardly a machine, was an important ingredient in the construction of the Jeffersonian presidency. The Federalists, the party of "executive energy," were much less concerned about party organization than the Republicans. Perhaps they had less need for it. Noble Cunningham suggests that their control of the federal government and its patronage may account for their limited efforts at organization building.[56] But Federalist presidential candidates may also have been less dependent upon organized party support because they were not hamstrung by doctrines of presidential self-denial. They could present themselves as men of action, elevated above the common run of citizens, because their idea of the presidency demanded neither quietism nor humility.

Washington's practice of majestic self-display was not for Jefferson. He dispensed with the weekly levees and receptions that his predecessors had introduced. He sent his State of the Union messages to Congress in writing instead of delivering them in person. The ceremony seemed an unhealthy echo of the King's opening of Parliament. In only one respect did Jefferson's conception of the presidency seem politically assertive. He regarded the president as the equal of the Supreme Court in interpreting the Constitution. But he claimed the power to speak for the Constitution primarily to set limits on his power to exercise the veto. Jefferson held that the president could veto legislation only if it were unconstitutional. Mere policy considerations could not justify a president's decision to overturn an act of Congress.[57] A president's reading of the Constitution therefore defined the limits of his veto power. In any event, Jefferson never exercised the veto power during his eight years in office.

Selecting the Electable: The Invention of the Presidential Nomination

James Madison was the first president to be chosen by a congressional caucus. Jefferson had been endorsed by the Republican caucus in 1800, but there was no choice. He was the only candidate considered, and he was nominated unanimously. Until 1808, the business of the caucus was to nominate vice presidents.[58] Madison's succession to the presidency, however, encountered intense resistance within his own party. His fellow Republican James Monroe had been embraced by the so-called Old Republicans, or "Quids," who thought that Jefferson and Madison had moved further toward the Federalists than was prudent. Monroe himself was peeved because President Jefferson and Secretary of State Madison had rejected a treaty that he had negotiated with England, refusing even to send it to the Senate. New York Republicans, tired of playing second fiddle to Virginians, backed their own George Clinton. His supporters insisted that his age and infirmity did not disqualify him for the presidency, since the president had "in fact few details of office to perform"[59]—an assessment that reflected the recessive status of the Jeffersonian presidency.

Nomination by caucus would diminish the status of the office even further. At a time when most presidential candidates came from the president's cabinet, congressional influence over nominations helped to diminish the president's control over the executive branch. As James Ceaser observes, ambitious department heads were as likely to take their cues from Congress as from the chief executive, because courting the members of the caucus helped to advance their presidential aspirations.[60] Aside from weakening the presidency, the caucus had weaknesses of its own. Madison, for example, emerged from the 1808 caucus with eighty-three of its eighty-nine votes, plus ten absentee ballots cast by congressmen not on the premises. But the overwhelming endorsement was less solid than it seemed. The New York Republicans and Virginia "Quids" had both boycotted the caucus. Madison in fact had the support of only 93 of the 150 Republicans in Congress.[61]

Congressmen and candidates were prepared to ignore the caucus if it served their purposes, because the caucus never established its full legitimacy in the process of presidential selection. It had no standing in the Constitution. It was a political improvisation. In fact, presidential nomination itself was a subject that the framers never addressed. They were familiar with the idea of nomination. Writing in his diary in 1763, John Adams described the operations of a Boston "Caucus-Clubb" that met in the home of a local militia officer, where "Selectmen, Assessors, Collectors, Wardens, Fire Wards and Representatives are regularly chosen before they are chosen in the Town."[62] Gubernatorial candidates were often nominated by factional caucuses in state legislatures. Faction, however, was precisely what the framers were determined to avoid, and the nomination of competing presidential candidates presupposed the existence of factions or might call them into existence. It was to avoid factionalism that the Constitutional Convention decided not to vest the choice of the president in Congress. James Madison had warned that the responsibility would "agitate & divide" the legislature. An additional consideration, perhaps, was that the delegates to the Constitutional Convention anticipated no need for a nominating process to select the first president. He was already in plain sight, presiding over their deliberations. After the close of the convention, one of the former delegates remarked that the powers granted to the president under the proposed Constitution would not have "been so great had not many of the members cast their eyes toward General Washington as President, and shaped their Ideas of the Powers to be given to the President, by their opinions of his virtue."[63] In the short term, at least, the presidential questions had already been resolved.

Because he was chosen by acclamation rather than nomination, Washington was a president above faction. He was the living embodiment of the new nation, the Father of His Country, whose very presence would reassure his people that they were one. It was from this elevated status that Washington weathered the conflicts within his own cabinet, all the while denouncing the spirit of faction. Eventually the generality of the denunciation would narrow until it was aimed primarily at the "Democratic Societies" and their Jeffersonian supporters. Washington's alarm was understandable. The French Revolution provided a backdrop for the formation of the Democratic Societies. Given the context, it was easy to mistake opposition for insurrection, an attack on the political order itself and not just the policies of the current government. The Constitution, the argument went, had established representative institutions for the people, and they made "self-created societies" unnecessary. Committees of correspondence and other opposition groups were all very well when the people faced a monarchy. But America had become a republic, and the warrant for such factional organization had therefore expired. Washington's idea of government without parties seemed to come from the Constitutional Convention itself—the country's best men gathered in secret to deliberate until they composed their differences, finally emerging with a consensual decision to offer to the people for their approval.

Washington failed to acknowledge that the more fiercely he denounced partisanship, the more partisan he became himself. Convinced that he stood above party, however, he expected that his policies should be regarded as nonpartisan and therefore immune to factional criticism. John Adams was just as suspicious of parties as Washington, but he also saw that they were unavoidable in a republican government and that political clubs had to be permitted in a free country. He was even prepared to concede that a parliamentary opposition might serve a useful function, but only so long as it did not extend beyond parliament.[64] The trick was to check the influence of faction, and Adams thought that this was the role of the president himself—a role that required the president to remain absolutely independent of party.

Adams was "the archetypal illustration of a president without a party."[65] His organizational isolation was a matter of choice. He conceived of the presidency as an institution created to strike a balance between the few and the many. The job required complete impartiality and freedom from factional entanglements. The president had to blunt the aristocratic aggressions of the Hamiltonian Federalists while curbing the democratic excesses of the pro-French Republicans.

Parties had no role in making Adams president, and his image of the presidency held no place for party attachment, because the president had to function as the antipartisan force in the American system of government.[66]

MADISON: THE FIRST PARTY PRESIDENT

James Madison was the first president who stood in a party rather than above party. Jefferson may have been the rallying point for the Jeffersonians, but it was Madison, more than Jefferson, who assembled the coalition that made his mentor president. He was leader of the Jeffersonian minority in Congress, while Jefferson, as secretary of state under Washington, found it expedient to deny or conceal his partisanship, and Madison continued the work of party construction during his older colleague's "retirement" to Monticello.[67]

More than most of the framers, Madison was intellectually prepared for partisanship. Like Adams he conceded that factions were inevitable, but he did not see the presidency as a force above party that kept the parties in check. His famous argument in *Federalist 10* made factions safe for democracy. The remedy for faction would be the proliferation of factions. If the president were a partisan, other partisans would try to defeat him and his measures. Party was an extragovernmental extension of the Constitution's checks and balances. Madison may not have been ready to argue that parties were essential to a democratic system, but he saw virtues in party competition.

His own party, however, was fragmenting. Parties had scarcely established a presence in American politics before they began to disintegrate. Federalist opposition withered. The Republicans splintered. The fractiousness of the Republican majority in Congress may explain why Madison exercised the presidential veto power more frequently than Jefferson—seven times—but he followed Jefferson in restricting the use of the veto to legislation that departed from the Constitution, not just from presidential policy.

He also modeled his conduct in office on Jefferson's nonregal conception of the presidency. If Jefferson was "one of the most secluded and publicly invisible presidents in American history," then Madison must have been one of the others. Like Jefferson, he was a writer, but almost everything he wrote was published anonymously or pseudonymously. His notes on the secret proceedings of the Constitutional Convention stayed secret themselves, and his role in shaping the Constitution remained largely unknown during his lifetime. As president, says Garry Wills, Madison "did not like to put himself forward—he let his larger and louder wife act as his surrogate in many personal relationships."[68] Under Dolley Madison's management, the White House became the social center of Washington, until the British burned it down. Her Wednesday evening levees attracted the best people in town, but her husband did not seem to enjoy them. After attending one of the White House receptions, Washington Irving wrote, "Mrs. Madison is a fine, portly, buxom dame, who has a smile and a pleasant word for everybody . . . but as to Jemmy Madison—ah! poor Jemmy!—he is but a withered little apple-john." Another guest thought the President a "pale-visaged man of rather a sour, reserved and forbidding countenance. He seems incapable of smiling. . . ."[69]

Madison violated the presidential legacy of Jefferson in only one important respect—he made war. Jeffersonians had an understandable suspicion of the military, and the role of commander in chief seemed positively un-Republican. It implied a degree of centralization, hierarchy, and governmental activism that did not comport well with Jeffersonian principles. Jefferson, of course, had sponsored his own military adventure against the Barbary pirates in 1803. But Jefferson's war was small and far away—the perfect Jeffersonian war—and conducted under such strict constitutional standards that naval commanders were instructed not to engage in aggressive action until Congress issued a formal declaration of war in response to the declaration of the Bey of Tripoli.[70]

By contrast, in 1812 Madison fought a major power on American soil, but he was not as singleminded in his determination to initiate hostilities as Henry Clay, Speaker of the House and leader of the War Hawks in Congress, who saw war with Britain as an opportunity to seize Upper Canada. Clay had an ally in Madison's cabinet—James Monroe, who had reconciled with Madison after challenging him in the election of 1808, and was now secretary of state. Monroe had not abandoned, but only postponed, his presidential ambitions, and the cultivation of congressional leaders was critical so long as Congress dominated presidential nominations. According to Robert Remini,

"Monroe provided Clay and his friends with an ear and a mouth into the inner workings of the Madison administration." Madison himself, hoping for a second term, was susceptible to congressional pressure for the same reason as Monroe. He had a potential Republican challenger in DeWitt Clinton, and the War Hawks hinted that they would desert Madison if he failed to initiate a declaration of war.[71]

James Monroe was the last of the revolutionary generation to run for president. Hero of the Battle of Trenton, wounded in action, he had been almost constantly in public service since 1776. The country had finally exhausted its supply of leaders whose eligibility for the presidency had been validated by service as founders or framers. As their generation died off, so did the partisan division that had set its members at odds with one another. Monroe could adopt the disinterested pose of earlier presidents, forswearing political ambition, because there was no need to campaign. Once through the congressional caucus, he could glide into the presidency. In office he declared that he was leader of the nation itself and not just head of a party. The country would dispense with partisanship if everyone belonged to the same party. The one-time partisan reverted to the antiparty stance of the founders, and like Washington, made grand tours of North and South to conciliate the surviving handful of Federalists and invite them to join the great mass of Americans in the "country party," the party of the entire nation.[72]

In a one-party system, the presidential nominating process assumed an enhanced importance. To be nominated was to be elected. As long as the congressional caucus dominated the nominating process, presidents desiring reelection and cabinet members with presidential ambitions needed to build networks of congressional allies. The consequence was that President Monroe "placed the greatest reliance on the utilization of the contacts of the members of his cabinet with senators and representatives, having learned from his own experience in the Madison administration the value of this approach." He therefore relied on his cabinet not for advice, but for their political support and their ability to sway their friends in Congress. Building a consensus within the cabinet became the means for overcoming obstructions in Congress.[73] The system for nominating presidents helped to shape the political tactics of the chief executive and the internal politics of the executive branch.

The electoral debacle of 1824, however, would transform the nominating process and the presidency itself. It produced more candidates than any previous election, perhaps because the old standards of eligibility had evaporated. Since the country could no longer call on founders or framers, it was no longer clear who was entitled to consideration. The field suddenly opened to a new generation of aspirants. Not surprisingly, most of the leading competitors were those who had favorable prospects in the Republican congressional caucus. Three of them had been officers in Monroe's cabinet—William H. Crawford, John Quincy Adams, and John C. Calhoun. Henry Clay and William Lowndes were both members of the House and therefore in a position to call on their colleagues for support. There were two congressional outsiders. One was the governor of New York, DeWitt Clinton, and the other was Andrew Jackson, the hero of New Orleans and the only candidate who could take credit for military deeds comparable to those of the revolutionary generation. Before the balloting began, Lowndes died, and Clinton and Calhoun withdrew.

Since the would-be presidents all identified themselves as Republicans, the Republican caucus would be the only one to put forward a candidate. One-candidate elections may have been acceptable for George Washington, but the contenders of 1824 were no George Washingtons. They faced opposition. The caucus might be able to make a president, but it might not be able to make him legitimate in the eyes of the citizens. He would be regarded not as the choice of the people, but as the hand-picked crony of a congressional clique. Henry Clay, for one, declared that "the Cause of the Caucus is on the decline." He doubted, in fact, whether a caucus would convene.[74] In the short term, at least, Clay was mistaken. The caucus did convene in 1824. But in a larger sense, he was right—the caucus was finished.

As a nominating body, the caucus had been unpopular for some time. But in the 1824 election, one portent of its imminent displacement was the number of state legislatures that took it upon themselves to nominate presidential candidates. The Tennessee house declared for Andrew Jackson in 1822 and followed up with an official denunciation of the congressional caucus. Missouri, Ohio, and Kentucky went for Clay the following year. Maine and Massachusetts named John Quincy Adams as their favored candidate at about the same time.

South Carolina recommended Calhoun.[75] Political parties were creatures of state politics in the process of extending their sway over
national politics.

The only candidate who abstained from the scramble for state
endorsements was William H. Crawford, whose broad support in
Congress was expected to win him the Republican nomination. As secretary of the treasury under Monroe, he had used the extensive patronage
at his disposal—in customhouses and revenue districts—to win favor on
Capitol Hill.[76] But when the caucus convened in February 1824, only 66
of 261 congressmen showed up. Crawford's stock plummeted. His agents
opened negotiations to get him the vice presidential spot on the Adams
ticket. Even at this early stage in the election cycle, candidates were promising cabinet posts to gain support or buy off the competition[77]—antici-
pating the "corrupt bargain" that would win Adams the presidency in
return for making Henry Clay the secretary of state.

The four candidates who remained standing when the electoral
votes were cast had pursued sharply different political strategies, a sign
that the rules of the game were unsettled. Crawford played the party
loyalist, insisting that his unimpressive victory in the Republican caucus validated his status as the party's true candidate. John Quincy
Adams repudiated both party and caucus. His course seemed to follow
the old-fashioned rules that required presidents to be above party, to
betray no public ambition for the office, and to trust that the public
would honor them for their past services to the republic. In fact, as the
only candidate from the North, he hoped that his southern and western opponents would undercut one another while he stood quietly on
the sidelines. Henry Clay's campaign represented the boldest departure from past practice. He ran on a program. He outlined his platform on the floor of the House. It was the "American System," using
the tariff to finance internal improvements, economic development,
and expansion.

Andrew Jackson was the first Washington outsider to present himself as a candidate for the presidency. He followed traditional form in
denying any ambition to be president: "The Presidential chair is a situation which ought not to be sought for, nor ought to be declined when
offered by the unsolicited voice of the people."[78] He relied on his victory over the British at New Orleans to win the favor of the people. It

was all very much like Washington. But Jackson added something new. He was, according to M. J. Heale, "the first presidential candidate who acknowledged that the people had a right to question him on his views." Jackson used a letter of inquiry from a citizen of North Carolina as the occasion for composing a comprehensive statement of his political principles, and he granted permission to publish his reply.[79]

Jackson was the only candidate who seemed to have extensive popular support outside his own region, and he received more electoral votes than any other candidate, but not a majority, and the election passed to the House of Representatives. There the 1824 "corrupt bargain" was struck. The candidate favored in the Electoral College was denied the prize by the machinations of Washington insiders Adams and Clay. Adams felt sufficiently uncomfortable about the circumstances of his victory to allude to them in his inaugural address. Jackson's sense of injustice and outrage at having been dealt out of his victory would transform presidential politics.[80]

The Pictorial Presidency and the New Mass Party

In 1824 New York Senator Martin Van Buren had supported William H. Crawford, the standard bearer for the Old Republicans, or "Quids," who were concentrated in the South. But Crawford had suffered a disabling stroke and was unlikely to be a presidential contestant again, so Van Buren turned to Jackson, whose performance in 1824 proved that he had popular appeal. That popularity would serve as the attractive force in the formation of a new, national political party organized largely under the supervision of Van Buren. Jackson, out to avenge the wrong done him by the corrupt bargain of 1824, gave the enterprise his blessing and organized a kind of central committee in Nashville to coordinate the national effort on his behalf. The effort would depart from earlier ventures in partisanship because of the change in the nature of the electorate. Between 1824 and 1828, all but two states abandoned legislative selection of electors in favor of popular election, and the number of potential voters soared as states removed the last remaining property requirements for voting. It followed that the party organized by Jackson and Van Buren would not be a replica of the one created by Jefferson and Madison. The Jeffersonian party, as Moise

Ostrogorski points out, "had no need of rigid structure for the reason that the number of voters was generally limited by the qualifications for the suffrage . . . [and] because in American society, especially in New England, there was still a ruling class, . . . groups of men who, owing to their character, their wealth, and their social position, commanded the confidence of their fellow citizens and made them accept their leadership without a murmur."[81] The hierarchical society of 1800 required no elaborate party organizations because the society organized itself for political purposes, and because the politically active citizens were few.

The Jacksonian party, however, had to deal with multitudes of voters who belonged to a fluid society in motion. It would not be a party of notables meeting in caucus, but a party of farmers and mechanics meeting in local clubs. Mobilizing on such a scale required not only more organization, but also considerably more money than earlier parties. The election of Jackson to the presidency would cost about a million dollars. Mobilizing the poor required wealth.[82]

The idea of party was also changing. Van Buren's ingenious justification held that party imposed a curb on factional excesses and personal ambition. In the absence of party organizations, personal factions crystallized around presidential candidates who were usually members of Congress or members of the administration with followings in Congress. The contest among men was usually transformed into conflict over measures. The campaign would begin almost as soon as a newly elected president took office and a new Congress convened. Debates on policy would be contaminated by considerations of personal electoral advantage. Issues became the servants of presidential ambitions—even issues like the Missouri controversy of 1820 that threatened to fracture the republic. While the president lost control of the national agenda, the contestants for his job pursued the presidency without restraint and without regard for public good. Party, thought Van Buren, would impose a restraint that was missing from the politics of nonpartisanship. If politicians owed their election to a party, they would not go so far as to destroy the very institution that put them in office. They would stop short of an extremism that would imperil party survival or success.[83]

Parties would stand for principles, not candidates. The principles, of course, could not be too narrowly drawn lest they alienate potential supporters. And they had to be flexible.[84] After Jacksonian partisans won control of Congress in 1826, for example, they enacted a precisely drawn tariff—the "Tariff of Abominations" to its critics—calculated to please westerners who wanted protection for raw materials and agricultural products and southerners who opposed protection for manufactured goods. The losers were the manufacturers of the North, where Adams and Clay had their strongest support.[85]

Jackson himself aligned his conduct with the sentiments of his supporters. He declared his support for a "careful Tariff" that pursued a "middle and just course." Jackson followed the same careful, middle course on almost all issues save one. He would "purify the Departments." He would remove from office all those "who are known to have interfered in the election as committeemen, electioneers, or otherwise," along with "all men who are appointed from political considerations or against the will of the people and all who are incompetent."[86] Left unsaid was the obvious inference that the federal miscreants' jobs would be distributed among Jackson's supporters, another inducement for loyalty to the General. Apart from his preview of the spoils system, Jackson did not telegraph any of the other great principles that would guide his administration—not his opposition to the U.S. Bank, or internal improvements, or his policy of Indian removal. And his position on states' rights gave no hint of his subsequent stand in the 1832 Nullification Controversy when South Carolina asserted a veto power over the application of federal law within its boundaries.

Like the earlier generation of political parties, the Jacksonian party relied heavily on the press to communicate its cause to the people. But under President Jackson, editors actually entered the administration. Amos Kendall, Isaac Hill, and Francis P. Blair were members of the Kitchen Cabinet, insiders who gave advice to the president. Duff Green, editor of the *United States Telegraph*, received lucrative government printing contracts, until he became a pro-Calhoun heretic.[87] But words alone were not sufficient to forge Jackson's bond with his people. As political party organization grew downward toward the grass roots, the "textual presidency" of Jefferson had evolved into the "pictorial presidency" of Andrew Jackson.

Even before becoming president, the hero of New Orleans and Spanish Florida had wanted people to see him. But the politically relevant population was now too large for him to present himself in person like George Washington. Jackson resorted to pictures. During one three-month period in 1819, he sat for three portraits, two of them by members of the Peale family. In 1828, Jackson became the first presidential candidate whose image was carried on campaign buttons and also on jugs and plates. He became the first occupant of the White House to retain a portrait painter in residence with his own "painting room" in the executive mansion, who augmented his income by converting his portraits into engravings to be disseminated among the masses.[88]

The words and the pictures taken together were tokens of a new politics of presidential image construction. Jackson's partisans of 1824 had invented the full-length campaign biography. His enemies had painted him as a violent, autocratic hothead who fought duels, engaged in brawls, and executed militiamen whose only crime was trying to go home when their enlistments had expired. His friends made an unusual case for him, one that nearly inverted the claims made on behalf of earlier presidential aspirants. Jackson was the candidate who knew scarcely anything of the capital city. As preparation for his second bid for the presidency, he had served a brief term in the Senate, where his chief aims were to show that he was not a backwoods barbarian and to heal old animosities—with William H. Crawford, whom he had once challenged to a duel, and with Thomas Hart Benton, with whom he had tangled in a tavern brawl. Now, however, he was the sober citizen who knew nothing of Washington intrigue, who had never distributed patronage as a member of the cabinet. Among his qualifications for office were the fact that he was "never in Europe" and "never the HEAD OF A DEPARTMENT." "The very features which had seemed to disqualify Jackson for the presidency," as M. J. Heale observes, "were thus at a stroke transformed into assets."[89] Old Hickory was the first candidate for Washington's highest office who ran against Washington itself. He could afford to do so because the new Jacksonian party organization gave him a political base external to Washington.

Jackson's conduct as president was shaped by the processes and institutions that put him in office. His predecessors, some of them products of the congressional caucus, had been deferential toward the legislative branch. Jackson, who came to office in opposition to the caucus system, vetoed more pieces of legislation—twelve—than all previous presidents combined. And, in an even sharper departure from presidential precedent, he advanced a new doctrine of the veto power. Unlike Jefferson, Jackson claimed the power to kill not only unconstitutional legislation, but also acts of Congress that were inconsistent with the administration's policy positions, as he did most famously in his veto of the recharter of the United States Bank and in the Maysville Road veto, blocking federal financing of internal improvements.[90]

Independence from Congress also meant independence from the cabinet. Since the caucus was dead, presidential hopefuls in the cabinet had less reason to cultivate cliques in Congress. Jackson did not depend on his cabinet for their congressional influence. Most were men of such limited influence that they could not challenge the president's control of the executive branch. The new relationship with the cabinet secretaries erupted into public view in the cabinet purge of 1831, occasioned by the Peggy Eaton scandal. Jackson, in a "lunatic crusade," drove from his administration three cabinet members whose spouses declined to mix socially with the bride of Secretary of War John Eaton, a woman whose history was too savory for polite society. His vice president, John C. Calhoun, fell decisively from favor during the affair. His banishment from Jackson's inner circle, however, was due not only to spousal snubbing of Mrs. Eaton, but also to his differences with Jackson on the issue of states' rights and the revelation of the vice president's role in criticizing Jackson's seizure of Spanish Florida during the Monroe administration, when Calhoun had been secretary of war. Eaton and Secretary of State Van Buren resigned as well to lighten "the burden of dismissing the other members of the cabinet."[91] Having dismissed one secretary of the treasury in the Peggy Eaton affair, Jackson dismissed two more during the Bank War until he got one who was willing to obey the president's command to remove government deposits from the Bank of the United States.

As he demonstrated his independence of his cabinet, Jackson relied more heavily on the informal "Kitchen Cabinet." It was, as Richard P. Longaker has correctly observed, not a true cabinet. What it amounted to was an embryonic White House staff, "a group of personal aides providing the President with a variety of services. The staff includes policy advisers, lobbyists, liaison people, publicity experts, speech writers, and friends."[92] The "publicity experts" were the editors who helped Jackson write his speeches and project his image in the press.

Outside the Kitchen Cabinet stood the executive departments, housed in buildings at the four corners of the White House grounds, just a stone's throw from Old Hickory's office. Far beyond them were the customhouses, post offices, and public land offices scattered across the country and stretching toward the frontier. Altogether about eleven thousand clerks, auditors, collectors, and surveyors worked for the federal government. Jackson's spoils system would not make a clean sweep of them, but approximately one thousand were "proscribed" out of their jobs, most of them in the first year of Jackson's presidency. Jackson loyalists generally replaced them.[93]

To civil service reformers of the later nineteenth century, Jackson's policy would seem a retrograde step, an invitation to incompetence and corruption. Jackson may also have seen it as a backward step. His stewardship of the executive branch, he wrote to some Tennessee supporters, would endeavor to restore "the government to its original simplicity in the exercise of all its functions." To do so, apparently, meant that Jackson had to root out all those public employees among whom "office is considered as a species of property, and government rather as a means of promoting individual interests rather than as a means created solely for the service of the people."[94] Of course, the timeservers proscribed were also the most experienced public servants in the federal government. Jackson, the reformers would later argue, was sacrificing professionalism to politics. But Jackson had a response for these critics: "The duties of all public officers are, or at least admit being made so plain and simple that men of intelligence may readily qualify themselves for their performance. . . ."[95]

The spoils system, as Lynn Marshall has pointed out, marked the first stirring of an impersonal government in which "individuals could be placed or replaced without upsetting the integrity of the whole. Men were fitted to the system, not it to men. It was the administrative counterpart of the interchangeability of machine parts."[96] Jackson and the civil service reformers of a later time may both have seen his regime as a backward step for public administration—for good, or for ill. But it was also a step toward a bureaucratic future. Making administration "plain and simple" was one way of saying that it would be sufficiently faceless and anonymous to accommodate periodic infusions of inexperienced newcomers while continuing to function. In short, the Jacksonians began to convert the executive branch into a bureaucracy.

This bureaucratic blossoming would not become fully evident until Jackson's second term as president, when his office and department heads turned attention from dismissals and appointments to the organization of their agencies. The very idea of reorganization implies an element of depersonalization. It presupposes a capacity to distinguish the structure and functions of an agency from the human beings who make it up. Prior to the Jackson presidency, administrative reorganizations had been infrequent and relatively insignificant. During his presidency, however, two of the biggest federal agencies—the Post Office Department and the General Land Office—would undergo sweeping structural change. Partial reorganizations occurred twice in the War Department and three times in the State Department. Comprehensive reorganization plans were drawn up for the Treasury Department and the Navy Department but never enacted by Congress.[97]

The supposed frontier rustics who served under Old Hickory took most of the essential steps needed to convert the executive branch into a bureaucracy:

> What was informal became formal. Administrative jurisdictions and responsibilities were explicitly defined (in many cases for the first time). . . . In the process, administrative agencies were converted into organizational abstractions with an existence independent of the particular human beings who worked for them.
>
> Generalists became specialists. . . . [T]he various functions of government agencies were sifted out from one another and assigned to different internal divisions or offices.
>
> As a result, administrative hierarchies became both more formal and more elaborate. . . . In several agencies, bureaucratic executives no longer attempted to exercise control over their subordinates simply through personal supervision; they relied instead on complicated accounting and information systems. . . .[98]

The transformation of presidential selection that followed the construction of the Jackson party gave the chief executive a political base independent of Congress while making his cabinet dependent upon him. There was no longer a congressional caucus capable of making secretaries into presidents, and the combination of the spoils system and administrative reorganization made the president commander in chief—not just of the armed services but of the civilian bureaucracy as well.

By 1832, the Jackson party itself had undergone a measure of depersonalization. The Jacksonians had taken to calling themselves Democrats. The party's program had also become better defined than it had been in 1828. Jackson's vetoes and the stand he took in the 1832 Nullification Controversy had given stark definition to his position, and "streamlined" the heterogeneous congregation that had backed him in 1828.[99] They had also moved his enemies to paint him as "King Andrew," the imperious, impetuous president who was no Thomas Jefferson. The nascent Whig party made presidential restraint one of its articles of faith. Oddly enough, after Jackson's retirement in 1837, Democratic presidents would actually practice a restraint almost as consistent as that of the Whigs.

The party organization that emerged under Jackson acquired an existence independent of him or his personal popularity. That had been the intention of Martin Van Buren, who shared with Jackson the labor of building the Democratic party and who succeeded him in the presidency in 1836. Van Buren envisioned party as a force that stood above personal ambition, even presidential ambition. The Democrats' adherence to a strict constructionist view of the constitution was in itself a limit on presidential power. It elevated states' rights to a theological principle, limiting both federal and presidential authority and making diversity a basis for unity. The Democrats pledged to leave one another alone. They would not impose any national schemes of internal improvements or construct any national banks. They would be tolerant—even of slavery. The one thing that the party would not tolerate was disloyalty to the party. Unity stood above self-interest.[100]

National Party Conventions

The national party convention afforded a new instrument for achieving that unity. The Democrats held their first in 1832, but it was not the first of its kind. The short-lived Anti-Masonic Party had held a presidential nominating convention in 1831. Since there were no members of Congress elected as Anti-Masons, the party could not assemble a congressional caucus. Nominating conventions were already common in states and localities, and the Anti-Masons imported the institution into presidential politics. They employed it not just to choose a presidential candidate, but also to proclaim their party's principles to the country in an "Address to the Nation" read to the assembled delegates in its entirety on the last day of the convention, even though this forerunner of the party platform took more than an hour to recite.[101]

The Democrats and the National Republicans (Whigs) followed suit. In the case of the Jacksonian Democrats, the abandonment of the congressional caucus was not a matter of necessity, but of retribution. Congress was the body that had insulted the party's champion by the corrupt bargain of 1824. The convention, however, operated under one disadvantage in relation to the caucus. The members of the congressional caucus were elected officials who had been chosen according to constitutionally specified procedures. Convention delegates were members of a nongovernmental assembly who had usually been chosen by similar assemblies in the states, whose members had been chosen in turn by methods ranging from local conventions to self-selection and co-optation. The convention's irregular constitution meant that its legitimacy would be open to challenges such as the one that John Calhoun and his partisans launched against the Democratic convention prior to the election of 1844. They objected to the practice by which a state's convention delegates were chosen in a bloc by a state convention and instructed to vote as a unit for one candidate. Calhoun's supporters argued that delegates ought to be chosen in district meetings and cast individual votes for the party's presidential nominee. The advocates of statewide selection argued that their method mirrored the procedure for choosing presidential electors. In every state but South Carolina, electors were chosen in a bloc under the general-ticket system and all cast their votes for the same presidential candidate. Calhoun withdrew his name from presidential contention with the retort that conventions constituted in this way tended "irresistibly to centralization—centralization of control over the presidential election in the hands of a few of the central, large states, and finally in political managers, office holders, and office seekers. . . ."[102]

By the time Calhoun voiced his complaint, the Whigs had matched the Democrats in organizational development. In 1836, they had been less a party than an antiparty. They expressed disdain for the Democrats' fetish of party loyalty ("degrading subserviency") and their presidential nominating convention (a "packed 'office-holders' convention").[103] The position made it awkward for the Whigs to hold a national convention of their own, and the party was so factionalized that it would likely have failed to organize one if it had tried. Instead the Whigs ran a series of regional candidates with local followings, the most successful of whom was William Henry Harrison. The party would lift him from political obscurity to the pinnacle of government. When he first attracted notice in 1836, Harrison was a castoff of the political system. He was best known for his generalship in defeating native Americans under Pontiac at the Battle of Tippecanoe. But that was in 1811. Later he would be appointed governor of the Indiana Territory and serve in Congress. But in 1836 he was Clerk of the Court of Common Pleas in Hamilton County, Ohio.[104] Four years later an animated, national Whig organization would make him president.

One of Harrison's possible assets as a candidate was precisely that he had been politically invisible during the most divisive controversies of the Jackson years and had therefore missed the opportunity to alienate too many voters to get elected. The all-too-visible Henry Clay, with his bold, programmatic political strategy to become president, was too divisive to nominate in 1840 and too controversial to win in 1844. Americans were not ready for the "American System." Harrison forthrightly endorsed key elements in Clay's program—federally financed internal improvements, for example—but hardly anyone paid attention. The campaign was not sharply focused on issues. It was barely literate. The pictorial turn that Andrew Jackson brought to presidential politics took flight in the election of 1840 and became flam-

boyantly picturesque. The campaign was an affair of banners, illumina-
tions, marches, rallies, songs, political doggerel, and visual symbols
like the log cabin. Harrison enthusiasts painted giant leather balls with
anti-Democratic slogans and rolled them across the countryside. In a
call for party unity after the convention, Henry Clay insisted, "Not
men, but principles are our rules of action." But the Whigs in the
streets sang

> *Mum is the word boys,*
> *Brag is the game;*
> *Cooney is the emblem*
> *of Old Tip's flame.*[105]

In other words, Harrison's partisans were to boost their candidate, but
to remain cannily quiet about issues and principles.

Clay may have inflated the importance of principles, but he was
closer to the mark in his contention that the Whigs were not actuated
by men, at least not by presidents. The obtrusive presence and power
of party diminished the presidency. The Democrats entered the 1840
campaign unified behind Van Buren, but his administration had been
dogged by national economic problems, and he was unable or unwilling to exercise Andrew Jackson's executive initiative to meet the Panic
of 1837 and the recession that followed two years later.[106] He was the
creation of the party that he had helped to create. It had elevated him
to the presidency even though he was "associated with no great public
measures, had written no major treatises and prepared no major bills,
and his career in federal office had been unspectacular." He was
known primarily for intrigue and had risen by virtue of party service.
Instead of expecting the party to defer to him, like Jackson, Van Buren
"scrupulously deferred to the party."[107]

He was one in a succession of antebellum executives who seemed
to grow progressively more obscure as the country divided more
fiercely into sections and the slavery issue grew too volcanic to be
resolved within the bounds of the Constitution. Once the country had
looked for presidents among the great men of the republic, men
whose deeds testified to their excellence. The nation had not run out
of great figures. Calhoun, Webster, and Clay were widely admired and

known to harbor presidential ambitions. None could be elected, even though all three were more prominent than any of the presidents of their era. The achievement of party was to make lesser men—undistinguished men—into presidents.

The parties had developed a preference for obscure candidates or, in the case of the Whigs, candidates whose political principles were obscure. The need for dark horses was more urgent in the case of the Democrats. Their convention rules required a two-thirds vote for nomination, and determined minorities could therefore veto the candidacies of leaders who espoused policies that they found objectionable. Objections tended to become more numerous as antebellum politics became more bellicose. The remedy was to seek out inoffensive nominees—candidates, for example, who came from one region of the country but took up positions attractive to another section. Franklin Pierce and James Buchanan fit that formula, both northerners with a high regard for the political sensibilities of slaveholders. Martin Van Buren was cut from the same cloth, but his distinctive virtue was the fact that he had been anointed by Andrew Jackson.[108]

JAMES K. POLK, DARK HORSE PRESIDENT

James K. Polk was a dark horse of a different color. He became president much as Martin Van Buren had, by party service, and was nominated by the same Democratic convention that denied Van Buren his chance for a return to the presidency. Polk came to the convention hoping for the vice presidential nomination on a Van Buren ticket. He was hardly an unknown, having served as Speaker of the House and governor of Tennessee, but his fortunes had taken a downturn. He had lost two gubernatorial elections in a row. Before leaving Tennessee for the convention in Baltimore, he spoke with Andrew Jackson, his political mentor, who suggested that Polk might offer himself as a presidential prospect if the party were deadlocked. He was a loyal Van Buren man, but unlike Van Buren, he favored the annexation of Texas. It was an issue that divided the Democrats but aroused the country. On the first ballot, Polk made no showing at all. Van Buren received a majority, but not the two-thirds vote needed for nomination. Polk became the nominee on the ninth ballot, when the delegates, "swept away on a tide of delirious celebration," unanimously chose Polk as their standard-bearer—"overwhelmed with ecstatic astonishment at their miraculous delivery from the fatal deadlock which . . . had seemed to doom their party to certain defeat and possible dismemberment."[109] Unable to unify behind its most prominent leaders—Van Buren or Calhoun—the Democrats had joyfully settled for a nobody.

"Who is James K. Polk?" became the Whigs' campaign cry. Against this nonentity, they could offer the voters Henry Clay, one of the great men of the age. But Polk defeated him in 1844 in the closest presidential election since the ratification of the Constitution.

The dark horse had won the presidency by a nose, and there was reason to expect that he would be a cautious president deferential to the party that had elevated him. He was certainly faithful to the Jacksonian creed, as Jackson himself acknowledged. But he also followed Jackson's model of executive assertiveness. Perhaps it was precisely because he was not a famous figure like Jackson or the founders and framers of the early republic. Polk had not become president because he was great. The presidency was an opportunity to become great, a once-in-a-lifetime chance "to build a national reputation. . . ." He was "determined to use his party's power as aggressively as he could to realize great national achievements."[110] In a letter written shortly before his inauguration, he announced, "I intend to be myself President of the U.S." And he followed through. He demanded that each of his cabinet members, as a condition of appointment, abandon all personal political ambitions and devote himself completely to the effectiveness of the Polk administration. He invented the executive budget. Until Polk, the various federal departments submitted their estimates directly to Congress without presidential review. Polk required that all the budgets be submitted to him first. He reviewed and occasionally revised the estimates and sent a consolidated budget on to the legislative branch.[111] The practice would not be repeated until the 1920s.

His greatest achievements, however, were in international relations rather than domestic administration. He orchestrated the greatest expansion in U.S. territory since the Louisiana Purchase. To the consternation of many northern Democrats, he added Texas to the country through war with Mexico. Oregon and California became states. Aggressive negotiations with Britain achieved a settlement of the disputed boundary with Canada in the Pacific Northwest. His administration succeeded in getting Congress to enact a new tariff, which generally lowered rates, but less drastically than many protectionist Whigs had feared, and attracted widespread public support. Polk also managed to win approval for an Independent Treasury, a pet measure of bank-shy Jacksonians, because it provided a place other than a national bank in which to keep the federal government's money, and without distributing the funds among politically favored "pet banks" in the states. Martin Van Buren had managed, with three years of effort, to get a similar measure passed. It was the only major legislative accomplishment of his administration, and it was repealed after he left office. Polk added the measure to his list of accomplishments, even though it deprived him of the potent patronage that could be distributed through the manipulation of federal bank deposits.

He seemed similarly self-denying in his use of federal appointments. In spite of Democratic hopes that he would make a clean sweep of Whigs in the federal government, Polk retained those who had demonstrated administrative efficiency, and his appointments of Democrats succeeded in alienating some of the most influential and troublesome factions within the party.[112] He had pledged himself to a course of neutrality among the Democratic party's many factions. He "insisted that the impartial bestowal of offices to all groups increased his popularity with the masses."[113] Since he had already pledged to serve only one term in order to get the nomination, however, it is difficult to credit his sensitivity to mass opinion. In the process, he sacrificed the support of key leaders, almost none of whom was satisfied with his faction's share of patronage. Polk expressed distaste for the business of distributing jobs but refused to surrender the responsibility to his cabinet members. To maintain control of his administration, he had to control appointments. To preserve his independence, he could not afford to show excessive favor to any one of the many factions into which the Democratic party had resolved itself.

Polk's conduct is open to varying interpretations. Norman Graebner sees it as a case of simple "political ineptness and surprisingly little knowledge of party structure. . . . Polk's policy . . . overlooked the basic requirement of presidential loyalty to key politicians."[114] But it seems unlikely that a politician of Polk's experience and skill could be so ignorant of party structure. He had been able to manage his relations with the Democratic factions and their leaders through a nominating convention and a presidential campaign. Stephen Skowronek offers a more subtle interpretation. Polk, Skowronek suggests, was playing a complex but ultimately unworkable game. While remaining within the framework of the Jacksonian political regime, he was attempting to establish his own autonomy from it. His pledge to practice justice in doling out patronage among the factions and leaders of his party was a cagey attempt to advance his personal ambitions while maintaining the appearance of political neutrality—a loyal party man at the service of the organization in its entirety. The ploy was designed to enable him to escape control of any faction but only succeeded in alienating all of them. Polk was not only a dark horse, but a lame duck, because of his pledge to serve only one term. He could be defied.[115]

If so, the most remarkable feature of the Polk administration is that it accomplished so much with such dim political prospects. The reason, perhaps, is precisely that Polk detached himself from the organizational component of the Jacksonian regime while remaining faithful to its programmatic principles. It was subservience to party organization that crippled executive initiative. It put sectional chieftains in charge of agencies and policies. The cabinet, once installed, would use departmental patronage to feed the factions they represented, mortgaging the administration to a dozen or more irreconcilable tribes and principles. By declaring himself a lame duck, Polk liberated himself from the fetters of party. Although members of Congress visited him with repeated pleas to make himself available for a second term, he steadfastly refused. He refused to yield even when importuned by delegates from the Democratic convention itself, who crowded his office, pleading that he reconsider his one-term pledge: "These expressions of approbation are, of course, gratifying to me, but I have firmly maintained the ground I have heretofore occupied of not being again a candidate. . . ."[116] It was the price he paid for power.

Unlike Polk, the Whig nominees did not need the presidency to achieve greatness. On the one hand, there was Henry Clay; on the other, a rank of renowned generals, two of whom had won their military reputations under Commander in Chief James K. Polk. Generalship was William Henry Harrison's only claim to fame. Zachary Taylor and Winfield Scott had staked their claims in the Mexican-American War. They were famous, but they were also unknown. The great merit of military men was that they had rarely committed themselves to positions on the polarizing issues of the era such as slavery, internal improvements, the tariff, or states' rights. The Whigs needed candidates of renown because the level of organization in their party was deficient by comparison with the Democrats, and they needed candidates with popular appeal, but candidates who would unify the party and win some non-Whigs besides. They were, after all, the minority party.[117] Doctrinal diffuseness was attractive in a candidate. It might enable the party to stretch its support without losing its base. Occasionally, the candidates did not cooperate. In 1836, William Henry Harrison was more communicative about his political views than some Whigs thought was prudent. Nicholas Biddle advised, "Let him say not one single word about his principles or creed, let him say nothing, promise nothing. . . . Let the use of pen and ink be wholly forbidden as if he were a mad poet in Bedlam."[118] When General Zachary Taylor emerged as a presidential prospect after his victory at the battle of Buena Vista, New York Whig Thurlow Weed suggested to the General's brother that Taylor should write no letters dealing with politics and should discuss no political issues. It was not clear at the time that Taylor was actually a Whig or whether he had ever voted. Taylor nevertheless insisted on writing letters. Most of them proclaimed his nonpartisanship. When Whigs began to bristle at his detachment from their party, he conceded that he "was a Whig, but not an ultra Whig," and if elected would not be the "mere President of a party."[119]

Whig presidents might have been able to define their positions more clearly after election if they had survived their full terms, but both Harrison and Taylor died in office. Harrison was succeeded by Vice President John Tyler, a lapsed Democrat who relapsed after assuming the responsibilities of president in 1841. Like Polk, Tyler demonstrated that antebellum presidents who slipped the bonds of party tended to be more assertive than those who could not. Tyler's succession set precedents, not just because he was the first vice president to take the place of a president who died in office, but also because the Constitution simply says that the duties of a dead president shall "devolve on the Vice President." It did not say that Tyler could assume the title of president and serve out the remainder of Harrison's term. Ignoring cautions from Congress, Tyler had a judge swear him in as president soon after learning of Harrison's death, and within ten days he had taken up residence in the White House. He proceeded to veto most of the Whig domestic program conceived along the lines of Henry Clay's American System. His veto of a Whig tariff bill prompted the first effort in history to impeach a president. Like Andrew Jackson, he invoked the right to exercise the veto not just to kill unconstitutional legislation, but also on grounds of policy differences with the Congress. He also set the country on the path that led to the annexation of Texas and the Mexican-American War.[120]

The presidents produced by the antebellum party system were generally not men of towering ambition. James Polk left Tennessee for the Baltimore convention hoping that he might be considered for the vice presidency. In 1852, New Hampshire Democrats placed the name of Franklin Pierce, a former senator, before their convention as gubernatorial nominee to replace a previously named candidate who had died. Their expressed intention was to give him a position from which to reach the vice presidency at the national convention to be held later that year. But Pierce, a reformed alcoholic, was fearful that the vice presidency might reawaken his old vice. So was his wife. He wrote a friend at the convention that the introduction of his name "would be utterly repugnant to [his] taste and wishes." His presidential prospects were later advanced by others who ignored his expressed wishes because they expected to gain office if he were elected. Pierce may have known of their efforts and approved. His one concession to presidential ambition was that he declined to tell his wife that he was in the race for president until notified that he had won the nomination from a deadlocked convention.[121]

Not all antebellum candidates were as diffident as Pierce. James Buchanan had connived at becoming president for over a decade. He was so cagey that it was difficult to determine where he stood. Beyond a few statements of general principle, writes Michael Birkner, "he became known for talking so circumspectly that it was often difficult to grasp his point."[122] Perhaps the habit of concealing his views finally prevented him from forming any. Once president, he seemed unable to do anything with the office.

Would-be presidential candidates could vacillate like Pierce or speak vacuums like Buchanan, because election did not depend on aggressive self-promotion, clear position-taking, or personal renown. Victory depended on party organization. As a result, the pursuit of the presidency was not the fratricidal quest that it had been among the founding brothers. When the era of "continental characters" was over, party organization propelled the politically obscure to the Oval Office.

Presidential Selection from Ratification to Rebellion

From the election of George Washington to the eve of the Civil War, the Constitution's silences concerning the issue of presidential selection were filled in with the pandemonium of popular campaigns and party conventions. The state legislatures moved by fits and starts toward the popular election of presidential electors, but it was popular choice within constraints imposed by party. The general-ticket system promoted—and was promoted by—state party organizations. They were needed to construct statewide slates of electors, and by constructing slates, they extended their influence across their states. The introduction of a winner-take-all presidential contest at the state level helped in turn to diminish the likelihood that presidential elections would wind up in the House of Representatives. A candidate who failed to win a majority of a state's popular vote got no electoral votes. State political factions would therefore tend to consolidate behind candidates who seemed capable of winning a majority, and in the process helped to avoid the splintering of the electorate that would throw the election into the House.

The construction of state party organizations also provided a presidential base of power outside Congress. Andrew Jackson was the rallying point for a new political order that eclipsed the Jeffersonian system of the early republic and the congressional caucus that vetted its presidential candidates. By mobilizing untapped reservoirs of popular power, Jackson expanded the range of presidential action, achieved an unprecedented measure of autonomy from Congress, dominated his cabinet and the executive branch more forcefully than his predecessors, and erected a new ideological orthodoxy for those who followed him. His successors were not as free to innovate because they were bound to the party and the political creed that he had established.

In several respects, the evolution of the presidency in the Jacksonian and antebellum eras seems to reflect the unfolding of political time as calibrated by Stephen Skowronek.[123] Presidents like Jefferson, Jackson, Lincoln, and Franklin Roosevelt constructed new political regimes. In the process of creating a new kind of national politics and destroying an old kind, says Skowronek, they expanded the scope of presidential action and authority. Their successors, however, exercised only the power of "affirmation." They were bound to the ideology and the political coalition that sustained them and defined the regime in which they operated. Finally, as a regime deteriorates, the presidents who govern within it become increasingly constrained. They have a longer and more complex record to defend than their predecessors; the coalition that supports them is likely to have become factionalized and reduced in strength. The line of descent from Jackson into presidential passivity and mediocrity seems to reflect the passage of "regime time" as Skowronek describes it.

The antebellum system of presidential selection did not produce results entirely consistent with Skowronek's account. The most notable exceptions were John Tyler and James Polk. By different means, they extracted themselves from party and became more assertive than other presidents of their era. Skowronek does not neglect them. He regards Tyler as a case of "preemptive leadership," an attempt to find a middle way between the dominant party coalitions by combining elements from both. Such leaders pursue a "mongrel politics" that challenges the existing political divisions. The power of preemptive presidents is typically volatile, and they are usually repudiated by their successors.[124] As president, however, Tyler did not attempt to practice a mongrel politics that placed him between the two parties. After Harrison's death, he abruptly abandoned his Whig friends and moved rapidly toward the southern Democrats, and while it is true that he did not survive beyond the term won by Harrison, he exercised his presidential powers quite vigorously as long as he held the office. Perhaps the most decisive consideration in Tyler's case is that he sidestepped the customary presidential selection process. He was nominated for the vice presidency by a party other than his own in order to give a southern tilt to a ticket headed by a candidate whose principal strength was in the Northwest. He did not owe his election to the Democrats, and he was prepared to desert the Whigs.

James Polk was a classic product of the antebellum selection process—a Democratic dark horse who emerged from a deadlocked convention paralyzed by its two-thirds rule. Like other Democratic candidates, he reduced resistance to his nomination by promising to serve only one term if elected. Unlike the other candidates, he took advantage of the political opportunities arising from the fact that he did not have to worry about reelection. Declaring his neutrality with respect to the many Democratic factions won him a measure of independence from all, although he did incur the disapproval of Martin Van Buren. Polk's presidency drew its strength not from party, but from the executive branch itself, where he dominated his cabinet and exercised personal control of the budget, patronage, and military operations. In fact, the Mexican-American War gave him opportunities for executive leadership that a peacetime president might not have enjoyed.

Polk's presidency also shows that "regime time" cannot neutralize history. Wartime presidents such as Woodrow Wilson frequently exhibit unexpected strength. Generally, political time runs the risk of overlooking political issues. The partisan selection system that produced dark horses and politically unknown generals was, at least in part, a response to seismic rifts between sections of the country, and slavery was the issue that could move the ground under the feet of politicians and party managers. Obscure politicians of ambiguous leanings were indispensable not just for winning elections, but also for keeping the country in one piece, and the campaign hoopla and humbug of the antebellum era were the tokens of a politics of avoidance. In the end, of course, the schism could not be avoided, and another wartime president would begin a new regime cycle.

The idea of regime cycles is a useful one, but it cannot transcend history, including the history of the presidency itself. Changes in the nature and powers of the office make it difficult to compare presidents across generations, even though they are similarly placed in the arc of a presidential cycle.[125] Among the factors that help to transform the office and its occupants are the features of the presidential selection system. Often, changes in the selection system signal deeper changes in American society or culture. Sometimes, however, the selection system develops its own dynamic that exerts an independent influence upon the kinds of presidents we get. And, occasionally, presidents themselves have used the "disruptive force"[126] of their office to change the mode of presidential selection so as to advance their own fortunes and reshuffle the political calculations and prospects of the politicians who come after them.

3

War and Peace and Parties

THE CIVIL WAR STARTED with a presidential election. Even before the electoral votes had been officially counted, South Carolina had seceded. Six more states left the Union before Abraham Lincoln could deliver his inaugural address, because they could not abide his victory in the presidential contest of 1860. It had delivered the White House into the hands of a candidate and a party pledged to prohibit the expansion of slavery to the territories. Southerners envisioned a future in which the slave states were doomed to become a shrinking minority in a political system that consistently elected free-soil presidents, and they suspected that Republican opposition to the expansion of slavery was a mere cloak for outright abolitionism.

In other words, the Civil War began, not just as a conflict about union and slavery, but as a dispute about presidential selection. On the surface, of course, no changes had occurred in the selection process. The candidates were still nominated by party conventions in 1860, as they had been since 1832. The Electoral College still chose the president, and the electors were still chosen by popular vote under the general-ticket system everywhere but in South Carolina, the only state whose legislature continued to choose its contingent in the Electoral College.[1]

The legacy of the Jacksonian era, however, was a presidential selection system structured by political parties, and the parties had changed. The two major parties of the antebellum era had expended much of their energy in the effort to straddle a sectional schism that divided the nation into two cultures, two economies, two political systems. They were exhausted. The Whigs, in particular, had never been more than a "pseudo-party, never quite attaining the coherence or the ideological clarity of the Democrats."[2] The Democratic party was not much more substantial. The "so-called 'presidential synthesis' of American politics," according to Don Fehrenbacher, greatly exaggerates the organizational integrity of both antebellum parties. It obscures the "decentralized, diverse, mutable character of political association at the state and local level. There the insurgent, the bolted convention, the splinter group, the improvised coalition, and the call for a new party were virtually routine aspects of the political process." The Whig and Democratic organizations unraveled somewhere just above the grass roots. Town and county caucuses were sparsely attended or never met. The delegates chosen by them frequently failed to show up at state conventions. The local operations of the parties were conducted by a small handful of residents, often no more than one or two percent of the local population.[3]

The Republican party that nominated Lincoln and carried him to the White House was a different sort of organization than the ones that had gone before it. The Republicans, unlike the Whigs and the Democrats, made scarcely any attempt at all to bridge the country's most important sectional division. They were the northern party pure and simple. In 1860, southerners who cast their ballots for Lincoln numbered less than two thousand, most of them living in the vicinity of Wheeling, Virginia (now West Virginia). In the border states, Lincoln did only slightly better. Kentucky, where he had been born, gave him barely one percent of its popular vote. More than any other candidate in 1860, Lincoln was the champion of a region. Even John C. Breckenridge, the voice of southern states' rights, received more than 278,000 votes in the North, although he carried no state above the Mason-Dixon Line. Democrat Stephen Douglas's total popular vote was second to Lincoln's, but he won only twelve electoral votes to Lincoln's one hundred and eighty. His popularity was spread too thin to register in the Electoral College. He placed second in fifteen states, but second-place finishers get no electoral votes.[4]

Lincoln enjoyed a critical advantage under the general-ticket system for choosing presidential electors in the states. Even if the Democrats had been united in 1860, Lincoln would still have won the presidency in the Electoral College while losing the popular vote. In fact, Lincoln received a smaller percentage of the popular vote than any other successful presidential candidate in the nation's history—a little less than 40 percent. With few exceptions, even presidential losers have outpolled Lincoln.[5] The Lincoln presidency owed more to the nation's peculiar indirect method for choosing its chief executives than any other administration in American history.

To preserve the Union, many were prepared to abandon the method of presidential choice, or even Lincoln himself. The New York *Herald* urged Lincoln to release his electors, relinquish the White House, "and invest his name with an immortality far more enduring than would attach to it by his elevation to the Presidency."[6] Others proposed changes in presidential selection that would protect the South's vital interest in the perpetuation of slavery. A North Carolinian recommended the abolition of the Electoral College and the direct election of the president—with southern votes weighted in proportion to the population of unenfranchised slaves. Others suggested that the president be elected from one section and the vice president from the other. Every four years, the presidency would shift from North to South or back again. No bill could become law unless signed by executives from both regions.[7]

The proposals for electoral reform were tokens of a more general determination to divert the South from its secessionist course. Unionists from all sections hoped in vain that some change in the way presidents were chosen would help to preserve the republic. They tried with little success to extract some reassuring statement from the president-elect that would reduce southern anxieties about the future of slavery. Lincoln, like most presidential aspirants of the antebellum period, generally kept his silence both before and after the election. The *New York World* declared it the tamest presidential election since 1820. According to David Potter, in fact, Lincoln "had waged one of the most laconic campaigns in history . . . he had probably indulged himself in public utterance less than any other aspirant to the Presidency except, perhaps, Zachary Taylor."[8]

Lincoln, however, had done most of his speaking before the presidential campaign began. He was a relatively obscure politician from the hinterlands who talked his way into national prominence through 175 speeches delivered between 1854 and 1860. Perhaps appropriately, his first important speech, delivered before the Springfield Young Men's Lyceum in 1838, addressed the subject of political ambition. The country's founders and framers, he said, had been greatly and properly ambitious. Powerful ambitions were suited to the monumental scale of the work they had to perform. The drive for personal distinction could express itself in the creation of an independent nation and the formation of the fundamental law that secured its freedom. But those revolutionary times were past, and the heroic ambitions that made them so momentous were now a threat to the very same free institutions for which the founders had contended. Now it was vital to guard against the "towering genius" whose thirst for greatness could be satisfied only by pulling down the institutions that embodied the greatness of the founders. American politics no longer held a place for those who came from the "family of the lion, or the tribe of the eagle." Such men burned for distinction, and they would gain it "whether at the expense of emancipating the slaves or enslaving freemen."[9]

Lincoln was speaking as a Whig, alluding to the autocratic inclinations of Andrew Jackson and the Democrats who condoned them. But he may also have been addressing his own personal ambition, the "little engine that knew no rest," according to his law partner.[10] Still, it was only a little engine, operating within the confines of state politics. In Illinois, Lincoln was emerging as a skillful leader of his party, a member of the "Springfield Junto" that struggled to exercise influence over the selection of Whig candidates for statewide offices, usually in the absence of a statewide convention. But the Junto had little control over county and district contests, where the Whigs were often unable to field any candidates at all or produced several independent aspirants who succeeded in splitting the vote and losing to Democrats. The Republican party with which Lincoln allied himself in 1856 was a more coherent organization than the party he was leaving. Though only a few years old, it was on its way to developing a sophisticated organizational apparatus founded on the intense loyalty and widespread participation of its members. Lincoln himself recognized that his new party would succeed only if it resisted "the temptation to lower the Republican Standard in order to gather recruits . . . such a step would be a serious mistake—would open a gap through which more would pass out than pass in." The point, in other words, was to accentuate the division that separated the Republicans from the welter of ex-Whigs and Douglas Democrats, not to become another polyglot confederation. The Republican party was the kind of political organization that Martin Van Buren had envisioned when he was laboring to assemble the Jacksonian party in the 1820s—a party whose coherent collective interests were supposed to take precedence over personal ambition.[11]

One sign of Republican solidity was the close correlation between the party's national, state, and local votes. Whig electoral participation had varied sharply in Illinois between national and state elections. The Whigs seemed to be able to rouse themselves only when the presidency was at stake. But Illinois Republicans turned out with machine-like regularity for elections at all levels of government, and in much larger numbers than the Whigs had.[12]

The state party that produced Lincoln had the organizational depth needed to propel a mere political functionary to the presidency. As Stephen Skowronek points out, Lincoln could not match James Polk's legislative record or Franklin Pierce's military record. He was the darkest of dark horses. His "identity as a presidential candidate was fully submerged in the collective identity of his party, and even after his election to the presidency, he never achieved more than a modicum of acceptability within its ranks." He held little personal authority, but "extraordinary systemic power."[13]

First President of a New Party

Like Andrew Jackson, Lincoln was the embodiment of a new party. In Old Hickory's case, however, the role of political innovator had seemed to unleash a surge of executive energy. Breaking free of an old political regime and creating a new vehicle for political mobilization liberated the presidency from traditional strictures about the exercise of the veto power and deference toward Congress and cabinet. But Lincoln was no Jackson. Whereas Jackson had been autocratic and impetuous, Lincoln seemed cautious, deliberate, and deferential.

Jackson was famous for his veto messages. Lincoln rarely exercised the veto power, and almost always with respect to bills of little importance. He played hardly any role in shaping the major legislation passed during his tenure. Congress took the initiative on the tariff, created a Department of Agriculture, established land-grant colleges, passed the Homestead Act, instituted the first national income tax, and erected the legislative framework that would lead to the construction of a transcontinental railroad. Lincoln contributed little more than his signature. He allowed his cabinet secretaries broad discretion in the management of their departments. David Donald has attributed his restraint to Lincoln's Whiggish political origins. The party of his youth had taken shape in opposition to the executive highhandedness of Andrew Jackson. The Lincoln presidency, says Donald, reflected the same Whiggish restraint. One of his greatest political assets was his passivity. His gift for inaction drew the southern hotheads to fire the first shot of the Civil War, and so they also drew the blame for starting it. Since any actions would offend someone, according to Donald, Lincoln took as few as possible.[14] Lincoln himself declared that his policy was to have no policy. "I claim," he said, "not to control events, but confess plainly that events have controlled me."[15]

David Donald's Lincoln sounds nothing at all like the president who unilaterally suspended the right of habeas corpus, spent public money on private military recruiters without congressional authorization, or issued the emancipation proclamation—again without consulting Congress. On the basis of such acts of executive usurpation, Stephen Oates has challenged the portrait of Lincoln as a passive president who played by the rules and deferred to the will of Congress. Lincoln, he argues, had abandoned his Whiggish principles when he embraced those of the Republican party. "No Republican," writes Oates, " was more committed to the principles of free labor, self-help, social mobility, and economic independence, all of which lay at the center of Republican ideology, of Lincoln's ideology." Above all, Lincoln was committed to the preservation of the Union, not simply for its own sake, but to preserve the possibility of popular government everywhere. The disintegration of the American nation would vindicate the confident predictions of European conservatives and some southern reactionaries who argued that democracy was simply a prelude to anarchy and rebellion. Perhaps the determination to prove such predictions wrong prevented him from backing down in the face of the southern threat to secede, and later provoked him to wage war against the secessionists. Lincoln's measures grew in boldness as the conflict evolved into precisely the "remorseless revolutionary struggle" that he had initially tried to avoid.[16]

In fact, the inconsistencies in Lincoln's conduct as president probably had less to do with Whig or Republican ideologies than with the nature of the office that he occupied and the tasks that he faced. When he exercised the presidential war powers, he acted with a bold autonomy reminiscent of Andrew Jackson, and he interpreted his war powers broadly to give him maximum latitude in such political matters as reconstruction. There was no Whiggish way to save the Union or to rebuild it. In other matters, he was more circumspect. His deference to the legislature was less a remnant of Whiggish belief than a prudent regard for the Republican organization that had elevated him from obscurity. Like the nineteenth-century presidents who would follow him, Lincoln was a creature of party. Jackson had made the Jacksonian party, but Lincoln had joined the Republicans when they were already a going concern, and they had made him. He made war, and so long as he did his status as commander in chief gave him a source of authority and executive energy that was largely independent of party. Lincoln marked a clear departure from the string of deferential presidents who followed Jackson. The obvious explanation for his exceptional character is the Civil War. What the war obscures is the extent to which he followed in the footsteps of his colorless predecessors. He was a president made by party, and in matters unrelated to war and reconstruction, he allowed Congress to take the initiative.

Parties at Peace

The conditions for presidential autonomy in the nineteenth century were too dependent on the war to outlast it. Although the loss of Lincoln deprived the executive branch of a gifted tactician, even he would have been compelled to come to terms with Radical Republicans in Congress to reconstruct the South. Congress, after all, had the power to decide whether it would accept members from the states of the former Confederacy. Lincoln's failed attempt to win Louisiana's readmission to the Union on his own terms after the 1864 elections foreshadowed the limits of the postwar presidency. Congress would no longer play second fiddle.[17]

Congress almost unmade the presidency of Andrew Johnson. According to Brooks Simpson, he enjoyed greater freedom of action than any of the Reconstruction presidents, even though he succeeded to the White House by assassination rather than election. From the time of Lincoln's death to the reconvening of Congress in January 1866, Johnson followed his own course in rejoining the South to the rest of the Union. In the short run, his bewildering mix of forceful speech and modest action led every Republican faction and most northern Democrats to claim him as one of their own. But the ambiguity of his policies gradually evaporated as it became apparent that he was far more willing to reinstate the voting rights of former Confederates than to grant the vote to former slaves or to black veterans.[18] Johnson was a fluke. He came to office outside the ordinary system of presidential selection. In a sense, he was a genetic mutation in the evolution of the presidency, a misfit. His irregular accession to the presidency helps to explain both his political assertiveness and his political downfall. He was out of step with his time and its institutions.

Perhaps he hoped to bring southern states back into the Union swiftly enough to blunt the demands of Radical Republicans in Congress and to supply the political base needed to elect him president in his own right. But the strategy of the Radical Republicans ran exactly counter to Johnson's, and theirs trumped his. Before the war, southern representation in Congress had been based on the region's free population plus three-fifths of its slaves. Now that blacks were no longer in bondage, however, defeated Confederates would return to Congress in numbers increased to reflect one hundred percent of their former slaves. In losing the war, the South and their northern Democratic allies might gain Congress. Republicans rose up to prevent the defeated Confederates from returning to the Capitol in triumph.

Johnson's struggle with the congressional radicals turned on the definition of the southern electorate. Would it be composed so as to elect a conservative president or a radical Congress? Bills to extend the life of the Freedmen's Bureau, an organization established by the federal government in 1865 to assist the newly freed slaves and protect the civil rights of southern blacks, were the first steps to carry former slaves to full citizenship, supported by moderate as well as radical Republicans. Johnson vetoed both and embarked on the course that would lead to his impeachment.

The post–Civil War republic was not kind to presidents. It was an era of assassination as well as impeachment. Three times presidents came to the office without having been elected to it, and even some who earned the presidency by election began their administrations with feeble mandates or unformed missions. Ulysses S. Grant plotted his path from generalship to presidency to avoid taking sides in the controversy between Andrew Johnson and the Radical Republicans in Congress. The military commander who rarely hesitated to commit his troops became a politician committed to very little at all. According to one of his biographers, "There was, in fact, no issue he cared about deeply; no cause in the furtherance of which he sought the presidency."[19] He would give the members of his administration few purposes to think about besides private gain. Grant himself had not even bothered to vote in the nation-breaking election of 1860, although he had favored the candidacy of Stephen Douglas, and he had voted for the Democratic candidate in 1856. But at the Republican convention of 1868 he marched unchallenged to the presidential nomination.[20] He became president not to advance any personal ambition or political agenda, but because the Republican party anointed him.

Like Grant, all post–Civil War Republican presidential candidates were Civil War military officers, with the exception of James G. Blaine. Blaine lost, although his military record was not the only liability that defeated him. Just as the country's creation had brought forward a generation of founding heroes to govern its early development, so the war to preserve the Union had given the nation a new pantheon of potential presidents. But no one would mistake them for the founders and framers. James Bryce looked them over and asked why great men were not chosen as presidents.[21] Presidents were propelled to the White House less by heroic reputations or personal ambition than by masses of party activists, and the mobilizing experience of war itself lived on in the Republican party as a rallying remembrance to arouse the faithful. Waving the bloody shirt was one of James Blaine's rhetorical specialties. Other Republican candidates had little else to recommend them.

In contrast to Grant, for example, Rutherford B. Hayes did not stride unopposed to his party's nomination. He began near the back of the field, and won the nomination on the seventh ballot largely because of the personal and political handicaps of the frontrunners.[22] But he had a clear understanding of his party. "Nothing unites and harmonizes the Republican party," he had written to Senator John Sherman in 1871, "like the conviction that Democratic victories strengthen the reactionary and brutal tendencies of the late rebel states."[23] Hayes, however, was no radical. In fact, part of his appeal to other Republicans was his bland moderation on just about everything. His margin of victory was so moderate that he probably would have lost if members of his own party had not controlled the counting of the votes.

Hayes' election was not the only presidential contest whose outcome was tainted. In fact, the stature of the presidency itself suffered following the Civil War because the legitimacy of the selection process was questionable. In the Republican party, dozens of convention delegates came from "rotten boroughs" in the South where there were scarcely any Republican voters and no Republican officeholders because the black Republican electorate created by the Fifteenth Amendment had been systematically driven from southern politics by menace and murder. The Republican presidential candidates usually won their nominations through the large-scale purchase of delegates from the former Confederacy. Delegates to Democratic conventions may have been accountable to real voting constituencies, but the candidates they nominated entered the general election with the virtual assurance that they would win every southern electoral vote. The same racial disenfranchisement that cheapened the Republican nomination also debased the election of Democrats.[24]

Of course, the circumstances that distorted presidential selection persisted well into the twentieth century, but they receded from consciousness into thoughtless custom. So long as the "stolen" election of 1876 remained fresh in southern memory, however, it made the South's electoral outrages seem righteous, at least to southerners. And a glance southward provided Republican machines of the North with more than enough justification for the buying and stealing of votes, if justification was needed. The presidency stood atop a pyramid of partisan fraud.

A large part of being president in the Gilded Age of the late nineteenth century consisted of maintaining the party organization that helped to elect presidents. During his first eighteen months in office, Benjamin Harrison spent four to six hours of each day on the distribution of patronage.[25] As the first Democrat to win the presidency since James Buchanan, Grover Cleveland was besieged by a party starved for federal jobs. The onslaught of office seekers so overwhelmed him that he issued a statement pleading that the limits of his own endurance and a "due regard for public duty, which must be neglected if current conditions continue . . . oblige me to decline . . . all personal interviews with those seeking appointments to office. . . ."[26]

In the golden age of patronage, the power to appoint might have made the president supreme, but the president generally did not appoint on his own initiative. He usually followed the recommendations of his party's members of Congress. For President Grant, at least, deference to Congress was a matter of custom and good sense. In retirement, he explained the practice to one of his traveling companions on his postpresidential world tour:

> It has become the habit of Congressmen to share with the Executive in the responsibility of appointments. It is unjust to say that this is necessarily corrupt. It is simply a matter of custom that has grown up, a fact that cannot be ignored. The President very rarely appoints, he merely registers the appointments of Congress. In a country as vast as ours the advice of Congressmen as to persons to be appointed is useful, and generally for the best interests of the country.[27]

Congressional influence over presidential appointments was both symptom and cause of the localized character of party organization in the United States. It was a period, says Robert Marcus, when "Presidents and cabinet members complained that patronage created loyalties to the man who recommends, not the administration that appoints."[28]

In presidential elections, at least, parties had strong incentives to overcome parochialism and internal fragmentation. At the national level, the two major parties were more evenly matched than one might guess from the outcomes of late nineteenth-century presidential elections. Although Republicans dominated the White House, Republican presidential candidates failed to win a majority of the popular vote from Grant's victory over Greeley in 1872 until McKinley defeated Bryan in 1896. In only five of the same two dozen years did Republicans control both houses of Congress. Close competition and the importance of access to presidential patronage were powerful reasons for achieving party unity, but political parochialism made it difficult to build unity around politically prominent candidates. Prominence made enemies.

Plumed Knights and Dark Horses

James G. Blaine was a case in point. He commanded support on the floor of every Republican convention from 1876 to 1892. Blaine was probably the most consistently popular politician in his party—its "Plumed Knight"—but his popularity carried a price. One of the standing jokes of the era was that Blaine drove men insane in pairs, one for and one against.[29] When he finally won his party's nomination in 1884, it was only to lose the election to Grover Cleveland. In an era of closely matched parties, a presidential aspirant could not afford to alienate any portion of his party. Blaine had alienated plenty. In 1882, for example, feuding between his New York supporters and the state's other Republican factions had contributed to his party's loss of the governorship to the Democratic candidate—Grover Cleveland.[30] Blaine's partisans had placed Cleveland in a position from which he could seize the Democratic presidential nomination in 1884 and defeat their own champion.

Stephen Grover Cleveland was a large, conscientious plodder with a photographic memory. A hardworking attorney, he found the energy to live a second life as a "roystering blade" in the saloons of Buffalo, where he was known as "Big Steve." His rocket-like rise to national prominence had begun late in 1881 when he happened to have dinner in the same restaurant where a committee of Erie County

Democrats was meeting to pick a candidate for mayor of Buffalo, a solidly Republican city. Cleveland had last run for office a decade earlier when he won a three-year term as sheriff, a post in which he insisted on honest value from the contractors who supplied the county jail, and in spite of moral qualms, served as hangman on two occasions instead of hiring a substitute, because he regarded executions as one of his official responsibilities. His record for integrity and devotion to duty won him election as mayor in 1881. A year later, a schism among the New York Democrats gave the gubernatorial nomination to the political novice from upstate, and the schism among the Republicans gave him the governorship itself. Two years later he was one in a crowded field of aspirants for the Democratic presidential nomination.[31]

Cleveland had several advantages over his rivals. He had the best chance of carrying New York's thirty-six electoral votes, in spite of the opposition of New York's Tammany Hall political machine. More important, perhaps, he was prominent without being well-known. Cleveland had been politically visible for only three years. He had never been to Washington. But he had compiled an honorable record as mayor and governor. During his first term in Albany, he had reached across party lines to the minority leader of the State Senate, Theodore Roosevelt. The two had formed an alliance to pass civil service legislation and a program of administrative reform for the government of New York City. His record won him the support of a distinguished contingent of reform Republican "Mugwumps"—including Carl Schurz, E. L. Godkin, Henry Ward Beecher, and George William Curtis—who were disgusted with their party's conservative "Stalwarts." He took his party's nomination rather easily, but won election by fewer than 24,000 votes.[32]

Evenly matched and internally fragmented parties preferred inoffensive candidates for the presidency because they were unlikely to alienate any of the multifarious interests necessary to compose a winning coalition. They did not have large personal followings that might tempt them to act independently of party. Inoffensive candidates came from the rear ranks of party leadership, and they took the nomination by surprise, sometimes even to themselves. They were not men who had long burned with ambition for the presidency, such as James

Blaine. They were not apt to have any personal political agendas. They were not programmatic partisans.

James Garfield, for example, was managing Senator John Sherman's presidential campaign when he was nominated from the floor of the Republican Convention in 1880. He immediately demanded that he be recognized on a point of order and objected that he had given no one permission to place his name in nomination. He was overruled. Garfield was aware that there was support for his candidacy, but the movement on his behalf was so obscure that its existence was not generally known until long after his assassination, and his embarrassment at running against his own candidate for the nomination was genuine. He carried the convention on the thirty-sixth ballot, conscious that his victory might be undermined by the charge of treachery toward Senator Sherman. Two of his supporters tried to make amends by paying Sherman's campaign expenses.[33]

In 1884 Cleveland, unlike Garfield, was no dark horse. He won nomination on the second ballot. But his public career had been brief, and his views were sufficiently obscure so that he could accommodate a party platform that papered over most of the differences that divided Democrats. The differences were numerous and wide. As the opposition party for most of a generation, Democrats were united only in their enmity to the Republicans and in the conviction that they had been robbed in 1876. The platform straddled almost every issue of significance.[34]

From Military to Merchandizing Campaigns

As president, Cleveland forfeited most of the assets that had helped him to win the office. His championship of the gold standard alienated Democratic silverites, and his vetoes of private military pension bills provided Republicans with political ammunition that only became more explosive when Cleveland signed an order returning captured Confederate battle flags to the South. Perhaps most damaging was Cleveland's attempt to "educate" the country about the tariff. In 1887, he devoted virtually his entire State of the Union message to the subject. Protective tariffs, he explained, not only made for higher prices but generated more revenue than was needed to run the government. The accumulating surplus was an invitation to "schemes of public plunder." Five years earlier, in fact, Congress had earned national outrage when it carved up a substantial portion of this surplus by passing the most extravagant piece of pork-barrel legislation since the founding. This infamous "Big Divide" was a bipartisan orgy of expenditure. Mugwumps applauded Cleveland's determination to prevent a recurrence by the selective reduction of duties on imports. But the tariff was an issue that tended to divide Democrats while unifying Republicans. Since the presidential election was still almost a year away, the Republicans would have ample opportunity to exploit the issue.[35]

Cleveland carried his quest for tariff reform into the campaign of 1888. The loyalists in the clubhouses were unacquainted with issue-based appeals, and many Democrats, especially in the East, were not as hostile to protectionism as were the agricultural interests of the South and West. While Cleveland won the popular vote in 1888, it was by a margin of less than a thousand, and he lost the presidency in the Electoral College to pious, colorless Benjamin Harrison, who in turn lost to Cleveland four lackluster years later.[36]

Cleveland's triumph and defeat were both omens of change in presidential selection and in presidents. His appeal to the Republican reformers represented a break in party ranks that no dark horse could have managed. His issue-based campaign of 1888 was a break with the "militaristic" mode of campaigning that had prevailed since antebellum contests for the presidency and a move toward what Richard Jensen has called the "merchandizing style." Military campaigning was a matter of marshalling the faithful for torchlight parades and rallies where they chanted slogans and waved placards as they marched past politicians who waved back. The party was a quasi-military organization. Its aim was not to convert the opposition to the true faith, but to triumph and take no prisoners. "The election," says Jensen, "was conceived as a great battle pitting the strength of two opposing armies and the genius of their generals, with the spoils of victory being patronage positions and the seats of power."[37]

The Democratic party under Cleveland took the first steps to demilitarize presidential campaigns, but the drawbacks of the army-style campaigns were already evident to members of both major parties. Army-style electioneering could misfire. One danger, according to an Ohio Republican, was "that when you go into the enemy's strong-hold you only arouse his soldiers to vigorous action." The Democratic party chairman in Wisconsin agreed that rallies and parades "stir up the other side almost as much as their own. The trumpet that sounds the note of battle not only inspirits its friends, but awakes its enemies." He advised voter education as an alternative, and Cleveland agreed. His tariff-centered campaign was, he wrote, "one of information and organization. Every citizen should be regarded as a thoughtful, responsible voter, and he should be furnished the means of examining the issues involved in the pending canvass for himself."[38] The merchandizing campaign had been born. The presidential election would be transformed from a battlefield into a marketplace. The voters would be informed, individual political consumers, with minds of their own, shopping for candidates and policies.

In 1892, for the first time since Grant, both parties reached agreement about their presidential candidates on the first ballot. Presidents Benjamin Harrison and Grover Cleveland were dull, but not dark horses. Cleveland's nomination, in particular, suggested a change in the relationship between candidate and party. He was not the creation of the party, not a nominee who had been elevated from the ranks only after many ballots and compromises. For the moment at least, he was the leader, if not the master, of the Democrats, and some of them resented him for it. While a thunderstorm raged outside the hall, the Tammany machine's orator of choice, W. Bourke Cockran, took the rostrum to charge Cleveland with "personalism." He was, said Cockran, a man with politically independent friends. It would be preferable to nominate a Democrat "who will not raise up against us any active hostile force within our own ranks."[39]

The circumstances of party politics were changing. Margins of victory became more decisive. In the congressional elections of 1890, the Democrats handed President Harrison the worst defeat experienced by the Republican party since the Civil War. In 1892, Cleveland opened up his victory in the popular vote from the hairsbreadth margins of the previous two elections to almost 300,000—still no landslide, but a sign that many former Republicans had deserted their party. Off in the distance, agrarian anger over indebtedness, tight money, high interest rates, and low agricultural prices gave the newly gathered Populists the biggest third-party vote since the founding. A sizeable portion of the electorate had come unhitched from their parties. A new generation of voters, born after the Civil War, was entering the electorate. They did not share the memories that made their fathers steadfast Democrats or Republicans. Success would come more frequently to parties that drew in the doubtful and less to those who simply aroused the old and faithful.

Cleveland's fate in his second term demonstrated just how volatile the electorate could be. After going heavily for the Democrats in the congressional elections of 1890 and electing a Democratic president in 1892, the voters swung even more heavily to the Republicans in 1894. No party in possession of the White House has ever suffered a greater repudiation in a midterm congressional election. The chief reason for Cleveland's misfortune was the Panic of 1893 and the extended depression that followed it. He may have made matters worse because of the very qualities for which he was admired—manly courage, steadfastness, stolid determination. He had the confidence of his convictions, but they may have been the wrong convictions. Tight money in a depression seldom restores prosperity, and calling out the troops to put down labor unrest, as the president did in the Pullman strike of 1894, rarely restores real peace. By 1896, Cleveland could not control his own party, much less the country.[40]

The Politics of Personal Ambition

Grover Cleveland and Benjamin Harrison were poles apart in personal temperament—Cleveland the saloon carouser and Harrison the pious Presbyterian. But as presidents, they were peas in a pod. Both men immersed themselves in detail. The presidency, as they understood it, was primarily an administrative office.

When Cleveland's secretary received word of the president's renomination for a second term in 1888, he found his boss in the White House library examining the textbooks used in government schools on Indian reservations. After glancing at the telegram, he turned back to the books. Cleveland did not hesitate to exercise the veto power, but he resorted to it most frequently with respect to private pension bills, which he examined with the scrupulous care of an attorney to determine whether the pensioners' claims were consistent and justified. Harrison busied himself with new styles of penmanship used by government clerks, filing methods in the Pension Bureau, and the development of armor plate for warships. Both men worked hard at the job, but they held extremely limited views of its scope. In response to a plea for presidential action, Cleveland once responded, "I did not come here to legislate." Harrison was only slightly more assertive. He held office during the hyperactive "Billion-Dollar Congress," but he stood on its sidelines. The Sherman Antitrust Act significantly expanded the powers of the executive branch. Harrison played little if any part in its enactment. He signed it without objection but made no effort to enforce it. His attorney general neglected to send any instructions regarding the new law to U.S. district attorneys for more than a year after passage. The McKinley Tariff of 1890 embraced the principle of reciprocity and granted the president unprecedented powers to negotiate trade agreements with other nations. The Republicans lost control of Congress before Harrison sent any treaties to the Capitol for ratification.[41]

Presidential ambition was more intense outside the White House than inside. At first, it seemed to animate only presidential losers—James G. Blaine and William Jennings Bryan. Neither ran his campaign from the stationary stolidity of a front porch. In 1884, Cleveland gave two speeches, in Newark and Bridgeport, while pretending to be preoccupied with his gubernatorial responsibilities in Albany. Blaine was everywhere. Had he not sought exposure so avidly, he might also have avoided the principal gaffe of his campaign. He had finished a speech to a gathering of Protestant clergymen in New York when a Presbyterian minister who shared the platform with him condemned the Democrats as the party of "Rum, Romanism, and Rebellion." Blaine had not been quick enough to repudiate the characterization, and it probably lost him the support of the Irish voters whom he had previously cultivated, aided by the fact that he was married to a Roman Catholic. The blunder, coming in New York late in the campaign, served to undermine Tammany's efforts to sink the reform-minded Cleveland. It sent droves of infuriated Irish Catholics to the candidate of their party and the enemy of their machine.

Blaine's struggle with Cleveland was arguably one of the foulest in the history of the presidency. Its concentration on character assassination recalled the contests of the early republic, but with some notable differences that reflected changes in the properties of the presidency itself. Most sensational was the revelation that bachelor Cleveland had fathered a child out of wedlock. In response to the taunt "Ma, Ma, where's my Pa?" Cleveland did the unexpected. He owned up to his responsibility, and when an investigating committee of clergy dug out the whole story, it showed that Cleveland had been scrupulous in acknowledging all obligations of paternity short of marriage. "In a perverse way," writes H. Wayne Morgan, "scandals unified the party and covered its weaknesses. . . ."[42] James G. Blaine's misconduct had the opposite effect among Republicans. He had tried to talk his way clear of a shady railroad stock transaction that reflected on his probity as a member of Congress. Among Republican Mugwumps, reformers, and independents, the difference between Blaine and Cleveland seemed clear:

> We are told that Mr. Blaine has been delinquent in office but blameless in private life, while Mr. Cleveland has been a model of official integrity, but culpable in his personal relations. We should therefore elect Mr. Cleveland to the public office which he is so well qualified to fill, and remand Mr. Blaine to the private station which he is admirably fitted to adorn.[43]

In public perception, at least, a distinction had begun to emerge between the office of the presidency and the person of the president.

Like Blaine, William Jennings Bryan was his party's perennial champion and its consistent loser. Like Blaine, he campaigned actively for the presidency, instead of waiting for it to be delivered to his front porch. But Blaine had made a banner of the bloody shirt. He rallied the faithful by appealing to old loyalties. Bryan rose as a Democrat in predominantly Republican Nebraska. He could triumph only by converting unbelievers. His drive for the presidency reflected a new conception of the electorate implicit in the "merchandising" campaign. Party identification was no longer a matter of cultural identification—a commitment that spanned generations and penetrated as deep as religion.[44] Political convictions could be changed by campaigning. That was the purpose of Bryan's magnetic oratory and his contribution to the business of presidential selection. Presidential candidates had good reason to risk the unseemliness of stump speeches and whistlestop oratory if such exertions could actually change the voters' minds.

The election of 1896 was one of the great mind-changing contests in the evolution of presidential elections. It turned on the color of money—silver or gold. An alliance of silverites, the American Bimetallic League, had pushed the issue to the top of the electoral agenda. The organization's existence and vigor was one portent of a new alternative to political parties—organized interest groups. "What was novel in the late nineteenth century," writes Elisabeth Clemens, "was the intent *and* organizational technologies to link 'lobbying' to significant numbers of voters who would be guided by associational ties rather than by partisan loyalty." The emergence of organizations with mass membership advocating reform outside the framework of political parties "represented the distinctive contribution of popular associations to the weakening of the party system." The bimetallists were aggressively antiparty. Newspaper reporters, barred from the meetings of the league, got close enough to the meeting hall so that they "overheard all established parties, including the Populist, being 'cussed.'" At its 1893 convention in Chicago, a measure designed to assure equal representation of all parties on the league's resolutions committee was shouted down with the cry, "We want no party lines!"[45]

The candidates of 1896 ran against their own parties in order to win nomination. Although William McKinley and Marcus Hanna are remembered as embodiments of the Republican establishment, their march to the White House pitted them against the party insiders. McKinley's Republican rivals were Thomas Reed, powerful Speaker of the House, and Senator William Allison of Iowa. Both chose party functionaries as their campaign managers—one the chair of the Republican Executive Committee, the other the Iowa representative to the Republican National Committee and former president of the National League of Republican Clubs. Marcus Hanna, by contrast, held no official position within the party. His counterparts, writes Stanley Jones, "were established political leaders who knew the right bosses, the right businessmen, and all the tricks of their craft. They conferred with the powerful bosses, with the influential businessmen, and set up the traditional machinery only to discover that in 1896 none of the familiar tactics worked." The rallying cry of the campaign that Hanna managed was "McKinley against the bosses," later amended to "The people against the bosses."[46]

Hanna and McKinley were discreet insurgents. They spent eight years setting up their shot at the presidency, and took pains to keep it from going off prematurely. At the 1892 Republican convention, incumbent President Benjamin Harrison had first claim on the nomination, but McKinley's floor support was sufficiently strong to present the danger that he might surface as a challenger to the anointed candidate. McKinley and his operatives managed to keep the groundswell under the surface, but with difficulty. Enthusiastic devotees, for example, insisted on carrying McKinley on their shoulders from his carriage to his hotel. After adjournment, Hanna is said to have remarked, "My God, William, that was a damned close squeak!"[47]

William Jennings Bryan posed a far more audacious challenge to his party's establishment. In 1892, while Hanna and McKinley were trying to avoid an open break with their party's leadership, Bryan publicly repudiated Grover Cleveland, the presumptive nominee of his party. He declared that he would not serve as a delegate to a national convention dominated by a gold Democrat, and as a member of the resolutions committee of the Nebraska state convention, he introduced a measure favoring the free coinage of silver. It nearly succeeded.[48]

Bryan the orator is the unacknowledged advance man for the so-called "rhetorical presidency." He did not introduce speechifying into American politics. But until Bryan tried to preach his way to the presidency, Congress had been the principal theater for political oratory. The president spoke, but said little. The antebellum chief executive was, in M. J. Heale's phrase, the "mute tribune." As the embodiments of national unity and power, presidents seldom permitted themselves to say anything controversial or partisan. They spoke only of patriotism or sectional harmony or republican principles. After the Civil War, when sectional harmony and patriotism stood in need of restoration, presidents spoke more frequently than previously, but scarcely any nineteenth-century presidents ventured beyond the safe ground of sacred union. The notable exception was Andrew Johnson, whose inflammatory verbal assaults on his congressional enemies figured among the impeachment charges that nearly drove him from office before the expiration of his term.[49] His path to the presidency was as unusual as his conduct.

The transition from the military to the merchandising campaign changed the role of presidential rhetoric. Its purpose was no longer just to enunciate familiar themes and mobilize old adherents, but to persuade and convert. In a sense, the new electoral regime meant that presidential candidates had a hand in choosing the voters who supported them. William Jennings Bryan chose a Democratic party entirely different from the one that had elected Grover Cleveland four years earlier.

As he approached the Democratic convention of 1896, Bryan turned cautious and stealthy. When the Nebraska Democratic convention instructed its national delegates to vote for him, he persuaded them to rescind their support. If he were a declared candidate, custom would prevent him from attending the national convention as a delegate. Meanwhile, he was soliciting other states, not for delegates committed to him, but for uninstructed delegates who might rally to his cause once they convened and succumbed to his oratory and charisma. A poll of the Democratic delegates at the start of the party's convention in Chicago showed that he still ranked seventh among the seven prospects whose names had surfaced as potential candidates for the presidency.[50]

McKinley and Hanna came out in the open for their final drive toward the Republic nomination. The effort was unconcealed and aggressive. They formed a thoroughly candidate-centered campaign organization. Instead of enlisting state political leaders as members of a nominating confederation, their principal strategy was to capitalize on McKinley's personal popularity to snatch the states from beneath their leaders.[51] "The people against the bosses" was not just a campaign slogan. The *New York Herald Tribune* predicted that if McKinley won, he might "owe his success to the underlying and deep-seated hostility of the mass of Republican voters to the dictation and domination of a boss oligarchy." A Wyoming senator, describing himself as "not much a McKinley man," conceded that "McKinley is in it with the masses in nearly every state in the Union. . . ."[52]

Both candidates, in short, secured their nominations by personal popularity rather than party organization. McKinley had a distinguished Civil War military record, having risen from the ranks to become a major. The title would stick with him for life. He built public support during an equally distinguished congressional career, in which he emerged as the leading advocate of the tariff. Bryan had a more abbreviated congressional tenure, in which he starred as a spokesman for silver and agrarian causes, and then sixteen months out of office to travel the country giving speeches while writing articles and newspaper editorials. His "Cross of Gold" sermon at the Democratic convention was only the oratorical capstone of a long and carefully engineered campaign to make himself and his party the champions of the bimetallist creed. Some at the convention believed that if the vote were taken immediately after the famous speech, Bryan could win on the first ballot. Bryan knew better and decided to wait. His managers needed time to gather in the delegates moved by his address but committed to other candidates. Even after a night of consultations in hotel lobbies and corridors and a day of concerted persuasion on the floor of the convention hall, it still took five ballots for Bryan to accumulate the two-thirds majority required for the Democratic nomination, and it might have taken more if eastern Democrats opposed to the party's pro-silver platform had not chosen to abstain. The party was no longer theirs.[53]

Many Populists, on the other hand, found a new home among the Democrats. Bryan's support within his own party was strongest in states where Populists presented a significant challenge to Democratic politicians. During his months of preconvention campaigning, Bryan had served as intermediary between prosilver Democrats and the silverites of other parties, whom he tried to win over by insisting that principle was more important than party. He was convincing enough to win the Populists' presidential nomination as well as the Democrats'. Many conservative Gold Democrats from the East deserted to McKinley, and some formed a new party, the National Democratic, to express their alienation from the regular Democrats' platform without going so far as to endorse the Republicans.[54]

A handful of Republicans had also deserted their party on the issue of silver, but McKinley provoked no such schism in his party as Bryan and the Democratic prosilver platform had elicited. McKinley sought no nominations but the Republican one, and it was his even before the convention was called to order. Whereas Bryan was an insurgent candidate bent on reconstructing his party, McKinley had seized control of his party and sought to hold it together. The convention was orchestrated, down to the smallest detail, from the Major's home in Canton, Ohio. As chair of the credentials committee, Mark Hanna screened out the dissenting delegates, including the lieutenants of party bosses like Maine's Reed and New York's Platt.[55]

The presidential campaign that he managed seemed to echo the militaristic mobilizations of the past. McKinley conducted it from his front porch, just as Benjamin Harrison had. Delegations of faithful Republicans numbering about 750,000 made the pilgrimage to Canton where they stood in McKinley's front yard to hear him equate American patriotism with sound money and a stiff tariff. But the front porch campaign was not as homebound or homespun as it seemed. Days before a delegation arrived, a telegram would reach Canton with a dossier of information about the group's membership, their political attachments and inclinations, the community from which they came, and its locally revered residents. When the train pulled into Canton, a mounted company of uniformed volunteers would conduct the visitors from the station to the specially constructed arch at the end of the Major's street, where they would be halted until the preceding delegation had exited through the arch at the opposite end of the street. Railroad companies had discounted their fares to Canton and modified their schedules so that one contingent would leave town as another arrived. Delegation leaders were expected to discuss the texts of their speeches with McKinley in advance, so that there would be no slipups like "Rum, Romanism, and Rebellion." By the time the visitors arrived, McKinley could greet some of them by name, mention absent family members, allude to matters of strictly local interest.[56]

Behind the campaign's personal touch was a businesslike campaign bureaucracy with headquarters in Chicago and New York. Matthew Quay, Pennsylvania's Republican boss, was given nominal control of the New York office but little real authority, and he retired to Pennsylvania as the political struggle was reaching its climax. The campaign organization was not a creature of the Republican party or its chieftains. It was centered on McKinley and dominated by his intimates—Mark Hanna, Charles G. Dawes, and William Osborne,

McKinley's cousin. From Chicago, freight cars packed with McKinley campaign literature rolled out to paper the nation, part of an educational effort that included a speakers' bureau with 250 representatives in twenty-nine states. Five million families received McKinley material weekly. Theodore Roosevelt remarked that Hanna had "advertised McKinley as though he were a patent medicine." Special divisions of the campaign organization appealed to a variety of interest groups. There was a women's department, a "Colored Bureau," a German department, a traveling salesmen's bureau, and a division to appeal to bicycling enthusiasts.[57]

Dawes, who ran the Chicago office, chose his staff from business, not politics. He introduced competitive bidding for printing and supply contracts. Members of the office staff received regular salaries. Mark Hanna, a businessman before he was a politician, endorsed every step toward organizational efficiency while he solicited political contributions from the captains of banking and commerce. In the end, the McKinley campaign consumed between three and four million dollars, not counting the funds expended by state organizations. Most of the money came from New York.[58] Businessmen, business money, and business methods transformed the campaign into a kind of corporation.

Candidate Bryan broke with political precedent just as sharply as McKinley, but his campaign was also sharply different from his opponent's. While McKinley waited for the trains that brought his supporters to Canton, Bryan took to the railways to reach his audiences and convert them into supporters. Between the July convention and the November election, he traveled 18,000 miles and delivered at least 3,000 speeches. At first, he rode scheduled trains with the other passengers and carried his bags from station to hotel. But in October the Democratic National Committee provided him with a private car. It carried not only Bryan, but also stacks of campaign literature, which were dropped off at every stop.[59]

The McKinley campaign outspent Bryan's by at least ten to one. Bryan's organization operated on only $300,000 in contributions. State and local committees may have collected a similar amount. Bryan's populist message did not bring out the generosity of people with money to contribute to political campaigns. Few newspapers endorsed him.[60]

The presidential campaign had become a strenuous contest of endurance, money, and large-scale organization. The antique fiction that candidates waited quietly for the call of the people had been decisively abandoned. The Republicans had the money and the organization; Bryan had the endurance, a manifestation of a political drive that dominated his life. After 1892, he never won an election, but he never left politics. He was sustained by his political causes rather than by political victories, and his causes were so ambitious that they survived him to be adopted by successors in later generations. According to Lewis Koenig, Bryan's crusade not only anticipated the Progressive Era, but also survived after his death in the programs of the New Deal.[61]

Kevin Phillips makes a similar claim for the winner of 1896. McKinley, he argues, opened the Progressive Era. His assassin prevented him from building on the beginning that he made in his first term. But it was McKinley, says Phillips, who

> put in place the political organization, the anti-machine spirit, the critical party realignment, the cadre of skilled GOP statesmen who spanned a quarter of a century, the expert inquiries, the firm commitment to popular and economic democracy, and the leadership needed from 1896 through 1901 when TR was still maturing.[62]

Owning the White House

McKinley may not have had the opportunity to mature into a full-fledged progressive himself, but he clearly represented a break with the presidents who had preceded him. None of those who reached the White House after the Civil War contributed as much to their own victories as he had. Party organization undoubtedly helped to produce the record voter turnout of 1896, but McKinley's corporation-sized campaign was an organization of his own making. He would make the presidency his own as well.

Unlike Grover Cleveland, McKinley did not regard legislating as off-limits for presidents. Much of his agenda, even before the outbreak of the Spanish-American War, revolved around foreign policy. One of his first initiatives was the annexation of Hawaii over the opposition of many members of Congress, including Republican Speaker of the House "Czar" Reed. Lacking the two-thirds majority needed for ratification as a treaty by the Senate, the annexation was packaged as a joint resolution. It required only a simple majority of both houses. Reed's attempt to stop it failed. He left the chamber during the vote to avoid the humiliation of being present while the House repudiated his leadership and "raged at the cheers that greeted annexation."[63]

McKinley redefined domestic issues as international ones. His concession to the silverites was "international bimetallism." The United States would reintroduce silver coinage if it could persuade England, France, and Germany to monetize silver. His efforts to do so were not strenuous, but he was energetic in his attempts to negotiate reciprocal trade agreements. Among other things, the selective lowering of tariffs was a means to control the monopoly power of the trusts by exposing them to international competition. It was to deliver a major speech on reciprocal trade—"the most important one of my life," according to the President—that McKinley went to the Pan-American Exposition at Buffalo in September, 1901, where Leon Czolgosz would assassinate him.[64]

By that time, McKinley had established himself as the nation's first internationalist president. Even before his inauguration, Senator Henry Cabot Lodge found him ruminating at his home in Canton about Hawaii and Cuba. Lodge wrote Theodore Roosevelt that the president-elect was "entirely prepared to face the responsibilities at the earliest possible moment and to deal with them." Over the course of his presidency McKinley came to embrace the so-called "large policy" articulated in the Republican platform. It was expansionist and international.[65]

Against his will, McKinley also became a wartime president. Under intense congressional pressure to go to war with Spain, he insisted that the conduct of foreign affairs was an executive power in which Congress could not interfere. Grover Cleveland had made similar declarations, but when Spanish intransigence and the explosion of the *Maine* finally changed McKinley's mind, he went to war on his own terms. He demanded an appropriation of $50 million with no congressional debate and no restrictions on his discretion in spending it. The bill passed less than a week later. There was no immediate "presidential" request for a congressional declaration of war. McKinley feared that pro-Cuban congressmen would include a provision to recognize the establishment of a Cuban republic. Congress passed a joint resolution in 1898 endorsing American intervention in Cuba but left the conduct of the war completely in McKinley's control and mentioned only Cuban "independence," not its status as a republic. When the war ended, McKinley would get Congress to give him just as much control over the Philippines, America's first colony. The legislative branch would have nothing to say about the government of the islands. They fell under the authority of the president as commander in chief.[66]

McKinley made war with a freer hand than Lincoln had, partly because McKinley was spared the awkward problem of making war against his fellow Americans. In fact, he regarded the war against Spain as an exercise in national unity that would further heal the lingering sectional animosities of the Lincoln era. But McKinley had also arrived at the presidency by a different route than Lincoln had followed. Lincoln was the product of his party, and it had made him its president. McKinley had created a personal campaign organization that seized his party from its bosses—the presidency was his.

McKinley did not neglect domestic politics. In the midterm election of 1898, he took the unprecedented step of touring the country to campaign for Republican congressional candidates.[67] The trip helped him to preserve safe Republican majorities in both houses, but it was also one expression of a presidential determination to exercise leadership in Congress. McKinley could not hope to control the legislative branch so long as its membership included congressional party leaders like Reed, Aldrich, Cannon, Hoar, and Lodge—politicians who could command popular support of their own. He may not have made himself master of Congress, but he had generally secured its cooperation. "Not since the presidency of Thomas Jefferson," writes Wilfred Binkley, "had there been achieved such an integration of the political branches of the federal government and such consequent coherence and sense of direction in its functioning."[68]

In his management of Congress, McKinley enjoyed the assistance of Garret Hobart, an able politician from New Jersey and former senator, who consented to serve as his vice president. As its presiding officer, he kept watch over the Senate and often gathered the votes needed to approve McKinley's legislative proposals and treaties. Hobart also helped the president with his cabinet, using his charm to cope with ticklish problems of interpersonal relations that McKinley could not resolve for himself. Hobart died before the close of McKinley's first term. The new political stature that he had given to the office of the vice presidency was one of the inducements used to persuade the ambitious Theodore Roosevelt to accept second place on the 1900 Republican national ticket.[69]

The Turn of a Century

For approximately half of our history since the ratification of the Constitution, American political practices and institutions discouraged the active pursuit of the presidency. In a country whose people believed that any boy could grow up to be president, self-conscious striving for the office seemed somehow unfair to the other boys. Egalitarian sentiment reinforced a wariness of executive power that probably began with the colonists' resentments about the exactions of royal governors. In time, however, these cultural biases merged with institutional interests. Political parties—locally based and led by legislators—tended to select presidential candidates who were likely to challenge the eminence of neither party nor legislature. More often than not, parties chose standard-bearers of modest political repute who espoused no big plans and had no itch to make history. In any case, powerfully ambitious politicians were unlikely to find many attractions in the office of the presidency. Except in wartime, it did not amount to much.

The campaign fought by William McKinley and William Jennings Bryan not only triggered a critical realignment of the electorate, but turned the political system toward a new way of contesting presidential elections. Both had set a course for the presidency long before the election of 1896. Neither made a secret of his interest in the office. Neither waited patiently to be anointed by a party convention. Both successfully challenged the leadership of their respective parties to win nomination, and after winning McKinley began to make something of the presidency.

There have always been ambitious people in American politics, but the presidency has not always been accessible or attractive to the politically ambitious. The volatility of the national electorate between 1890 and 1894 may have given Bryan and McKinley the encouragement needed to pursue presidential ambitions. Both men had lost congressional seats in the sharp partisan shifts of midterm elections— McKinley in 1892 and Bryan in 1894. The swings signified that some voters, at least, had detached themselves from their party loyalties, and they proved in the most tangible way possible that congressional careers might not be as secure as they were when the Gilded Age glowed its brightest.

Neither candidate, of course, was running for the sake of job security. Of the two, Bryan was more clearly animated by a cause as well as personal ambition. In his famous sermon at the Democratic convention, he claimed to stand for "a cause as holy as the cause of liberty— the cause of humanity." The struggle for the presidency, he said, was "not a contest between persons." His strength came not from his personal abilities, said Bryan, but from the cause that he served.[70] McKinley's cause, apparently, was the full dinner pail, the symbol of economic prosperity.

Bryan spoke of cause where earlier candidates might have invoked party, and his candidacy reflected the extent to which the causes of national politics had become detached from the two major parties. Popular causes had drifted off into third parties like the Populists or the Prohibitionists. They had been taken up by organized interest groups, one of the political innovations of the late nineteenth century, shortly to become one of the dominant political institutions of the twentieth. Cause had become the rallying call in Bryan's personal quest for the presidency, one that embraced both the Populist and Democratic parties. Selfless devotion to cause could also justify the personal pursuit of high office as something other than an expression of private ambition. In the meantime, the causes left to the two major parties were losing their magnetism as the electorate came to include more and more voters for whom the Civil War was just history and not a memory.

Perhaps Grover Cleveland's earnest but unsuccessful championship of tariff reform in 1888 had been the first break with the traditional politics of the presidency. But Bryan brought purpose-driven presidential politics to full maturity. And the voters who found it frightening were swept up by the efficiently managed, "merchandizing" campaign of William McKinley.

Presidents and presidential candidates still needed party organizations, and voters were still attached to parties. But for a growing segment of the electorate, party identification was no longer a lifetime commitment. A would-be president who could command the support of these moveable voters could show up at his party's convention with a claim on the nomination independent of the party organization or its bosses. Parties continued to dominate presidential politics, but they no longer monopolized it.

The First Roosevelt and His Party

William McKinley had shown that it was possible to win the presidency without much reliance on party bosses, but he had not demonstrated that the construction of a personal campaign organization was the only way to win. Parties could still make presidents, and Theodore Roosevelt knew this. Although he was almost constantly at odds with the leadership of his party, he would not desert it until it denied him the presidential nomination in 1912. In 1884, like other Republican reformers, he fought through his party's state and national conventions to prevent scandal-tainted James G. Blaine from becoming a presidential nominee. But unlike many other Republican "independents," he remained with the party when the cause was lost. He sullenly refused to second a motion that Blaine be nominated by acclamation, but he would not bolt. He announced that he had "no personal objections to Blaine," and then took off for the prairie to play cowboy rather than participate in the campaign.[71]

Roosevelt was propelled by such boundless energy and ambition that he was unlikely to have become president by the usual route. He alarmed his own party's leadership. The idea that he should be nominated for the vice presidency on McKinley's ticket reportedly provoked Mark Hanna to snap, "Don't you realize that there's only one life between that madman and the White House?" When TR's nomination became accomplished fact, Hanna wrote a letter to President McKinley: "Your *duty* to the country is to *live* for *four* years from next March."[72]

As a vice presidential candidate, Roosevelt would conduct no front-porch campaign. His role was to make stump speeches across the country while McKinley remained in Canton to receive visiting delegations in his front yard. Roosevelt's speech-making abilities and the popularity he enjoyed in the West by reason of his camping and cowboy adventures had been points in his favor when he was nominated for the vice presidency. In the prairie and mountain states, he was expected to match William Jennings Bryan oration for oration.

Roosevelt privately hoped that he would be able to move from the vice presidency to the presidency, but if he succeeded, he would be the first vice president in American history to make the jump. As it was, assassination made him president, not political skill or popularity. But possession of the White House did not give him leadership of his party. That belonged to the man who had thought him mad. Mark Hanna saw his nightmare scenario come to life.[73]

Roosevelt, the former U.S. Civil Service Commissioner, astutely manipulated presidential patronage in one state after another to tilt the Republican party against Chairman Hanna. He was organizing his forces to achieve election in his own right. In 1904, his only speech was to accept the nomination, but he converted the White House into a campaign headquarters, firing off directives to Republican party operatives all over the country. He sensed that Methodists were lukewarm to his candidacy and asked campaign manager George Cortelyou to see what could be done to rouse their enthusiasm. He bombarded state party officials, suggesting what they should do with the Bohemians in Chicago, the Germans in Indiana, and the Italians in New York. He wrote letters to veterans' groups simply to send his best wishes. He tried to intervene in an intraparty feud that divided Maryland Republicans.[74]

PRESIDENT AS ARBITER

When Roosevelt spoke to the people, the institutional intermediaries between president and public evaporated. In a tour of New England during the summer of 1902, he looked out at the crowd on a village green in Massachusetts and declaimed, "The government is us . . . you and me!"[75] His conduct in office echoed Andrew Johnson's populist conception of the president as the tribune of the people, but

TR carried it off without being impeached. While he clearly enjoyed his popularity, he placed an even higher value on the power that it gave him. He used it to intervene directly in American society to restore an equilibrium upended by industrial concentration and corporate power.

With the approach of cool weather in 1902, a strike of anthracite miners threatened one of the country's principal sources of winter warmth. For five months, the mining companies refused to meet with John Mitchell, president of the United Mineworkers. There had been murders, assaults, eye-gougings, attempted lynchings, and riots in Northeastern Pennsylvania. Instead of sending in the troops, as Cleveland had done in the Pullman strike, Roosevelt summoned the interested parties to Washington to see if he could work out their differences. Political parties had been the traditional institutions of interest aggregation and accommodation; conflict resolution had been the business of the courts. Now Roosevelt reached past both institutions to project the power of the presidency into the midst of the contending groups in an attempt to achieve a balance among them that would benefit the public at large. In the event of a deadlock, Roosevelt held in reserve a force of ten thousand federal troops prepared not to subdue the strikers, but to seize the mines from their owners and reopen them under government auspices. Roosevelt confided his plan to a shocked Republican congressional leader who raised the most obvious objections: "What about the Constitution of the United States? What about seizing private property with no due process of law?" Roosevelt grabbed him by the shoulder and shouted, "The Constitution was made for the people and not the people for the Constitution."[76]

Roosevelt never doubted that he was one with the people—the decent, right-minded, hard-working people at least—and he managed to achieve a meeting of the minds with mine owners and mine workers. The union and the owners agreed to the appointment of a presidential Coal Strike Commission, and the mines began to produce coal again. He was praised by the London *Times* for having acted in "a most quiet and unobtrusive manner" to do "a very big and entirely new thing. We are witnessing not merely the ending of the coal strike, but the definite entry of a powerful government upon a novel sphere of operation." "Roosevelt," says John Morton Blum, "envisioned an equilibrium of consolidated interests over which government would preside." He took "special pride in asserting and extending the power of the federal government."[77]

TR: THE CAUTIOUS CRUSADER

Yet beneath his irrepressible and impetuous energy, Roosevelt concealed self-doubt and guarded caution. Though he would win the 1904 election in a landslide, he confided to close associates the expectation that he would lose. A few months before the Republican convention, he told a British friend that the presidency "tends to put a premium on a man's keeping out of trouble rather than upon his producing results." An aspirant with a "strongly accentuated career normally drives more enemies to the other side than draws friends from it. In consequence, the dark horse, the neutral-tinted individual, is very apt to win against the man of pronounced views and active life."[78] TR was counting himself out of the nomination. When the nomination was secure, he fretted that the Republican candidate for the governorship of New York might be defeated, and that the loss of his home state would undermine his national popularity and lose him the presidency.[79] His frenetic and, to some, unseemly efforts to direct his own campaign from the White House seemed to arise from an undercurrent of worry about the result.[80]

On the night of his victory, he announced that he would not seek another term. He would later explain, "I don't think that any harm comes from the concentration of power in one man's hands, provided the holder doesn't keep it for more than a certain, definite time, and then returns to the people from which he sprang."[81] As president, Roosevelt was sensitive to the limits of his power, at least in domestic politics. He had served three-and-a-half years of the term that McKinley had won, and now he faced another four years in office. He feared that the case for seeking a further term would seem to be grounded upon an assassination and a technicality. The American people might regard it "with a feeling of disappointment."[82] Roosevelt was a curious combination of confident ambition and worried self-restraint.

Roosevelt observed a similar restraint in some of the most important policy decisions of his second term. Railroad regulation and tariff revision were two of his top priorities after his election in 1904. John Morton Blum argues that Roosevelt threatened Republican conserva- tives with the prospect of reduced tariffs so that they would go along with his proposal for railroad regulation—the Hepburn Act—which would permit the Interstate Commerce Commission access to the accounts of the railroads and limited authority to set shipping rates. Having secured the Hepburn Act, Blum argues, the president dropped tariff reform from his agenda. But there is a simpler explanation for the president's abandonment of the tariff issue: Tariff reform was bad politics. In 1905, the administration issued a directive mandating that building materials for the Panama Canal should be purchased abroad, because they were cheaper than the tariff-protected products of the United States. The announcement came at a time when the Senate Committee on Interstate Commerce was considering Roosevelt's rail- road legislation, but the order was rescinded three days later in response to complaints from high-tariff Republicans. If it was an exer- cise in intimidation, hardly anyone was intimidated, and Congress adjourned soon afterward, before the Senate had taken any action on the Hepburn Bill.[83]

When the railroad legislation came before Congress again in 1906, Roosevelt made no mention of the tariff issue. The reason, he wrote, "is that there are large parts of the country which want no tariff revi- sion, and of course their representatives are hostile to any agitation on the issue. . . . I am going to make every effort to get something of what I desire . . . ; but I shall not split with my party on the matter. . . ."[84]

Roosevelt the president was still Roosevelt the party loyalist. He had captured the party through the distribution of presidential patronage, and he was not about to destroy the foundation of his power. He had made a speaking tour of the nation to stir up public support for the Hepburn Act, going over the heads of the Congress. But the speech that probably pushed the legislation through the Senate was the one he made when laying the cornerstone of a new House office building. It coupled a plea for railroad regulation with an attack on a recent "muckraking" article, "The Treason of the Senate," which accused the members of the upper house of corruption and illegal relationships with special interests. Roosevelt needed to gain the sympathy of the Senate, where the Hepburn bill faced stiff opposition. He won progressive railroad legislation by defending Republican conservatives and party bosses.[85]

PARTY PROBLEMS

Matthew Josephson has dismissed the Hepburn Act as camouflage for capitalist domination of railroad regulation. It was certainly less radical than William Jennings Bryan's demand for government ownership of railways. Given the resistance of powerful senators like Rockefeller son-in-law Nelson Aldrich, however, it was probably the most that TR could achieve under the circumstances. And if the significance of the legislation is judged by the enemies that Roosevelt earned by it, the Act could hardly have been a comfort to capitalists.[86]

The Hepburn Act was probably the most important domestic policy to emerge from the Roosevelt administration, its most controversial and extensive interference with the operations of the free market. The president could also take credit for the Pure Food and Drug Act, the National Reclamation Act, the creation of a Department of Commerce and Labor, and some major prosecutions under the Sherman Antitrust Act. He was a restlessly ambitious president who recognized the limits of his power. Although he won by a landslide in 1904, he was accompanied in victory by a strong Republican majority in Congress. It followed, says Edmund Morris, that "whatever reforms he intended would have to be accomplished within the bounds of party orthodoxy." Roosevelt himself said as much: "I have a very strong feeling that it is a president's duty to get on with Congress if he possibly can, and that it is a reflection on him if he and Congress come to a complete break.[87]

Roosevelt would later confess in his *Autobiography* that his relationship with Congress grew more strained as he approached the end of his presidency. He and the Republican leaders of Congress, he says, struggled resolutely to get along with one another, but with increasing friction, Roosevelt "pushing forward and they hanging back. Gradually, I was forced to abandon the effort to persuade them to come my way, and then I achieved results by appealing over the heads of the Senate and House leaders to the people. . . ."[88]

Roosevelt discovered that going over the heads of the Senate and House was only one of the ways to get around them. In 1907, western congressmen attached an amendment to the Department of Agriculture appropriation that would have prevented the administration from setting aside as park or wilderness areas any public lands in six western states. Before signing it, Roosevelt issued executive orders creating twenty-one new forest reserves in those same states and enlarging eleven others. There was no statutory basis for the president's action. William Howard Taft would later get congressional authorization to set aside public lands as reserves. Roosevelt dismissed the measure as having given "the President the power which he had long exercised, and of which my successor had shorn himself."[89]

Roosevelt's political ambition is undeniable. But as long as it operated within the territorial and political limits of the United States, it was also a self-denying ambition. As president, he rarely overreached. But in the presidential campaign of 1912, President Roosevelt, the Square Dealer, was transformed into candidate Roosevelt, the New Nationalist. John Morton Blum suggests that the only thing new about New Nationalism was the label; Roosevelt was simply summing up views that he had expressed in bits and pieces while president. He declared himself for regulation of monopolies rather than trust-busting and for progressive income and inheritance taxes and workmen's compensation. He laid it all out in a 1910 speech at Ossawatomie, Kansas, commemorating a battle between John Brown and proslavery raiders from Missouri.[90] Richard Hofstadter concedes that TR may have struck some new notes in his speech and purged his views of qualifications and reservations, but suggests that he was merely a stalking horse for Republican standpatters who wanted to squelch the candidacy of the progressive Robert La Follette in 1912. His new progressivism, in short, was not the genuine article.[91]

Roosevelt's close friend Elihu Root also held doubts about the authenticity of TR's political rebirth, but found his newly expressed views unfamiliar and shockingly radical. "Theodore," he wrote, "has gone off on a perfectly wild program most of which he does not really believe in, although of course at this moment he thinks he does. He has a tremendous following of Populists and Socialists in both parties. . . ."[92] But instead of returning to the mildly reformist politics of his patrician friends, Roosevelt moved further away. He had already denounced the Supreme Court as an obstacle to progress, and then recommended that state judicial decisions be subject to popular recall. He fell in with the activists of the women's labor movement and the Consumers League, endorsed female suffrage, spoke out against child labor. During a speaking tour of the South, he described himself as a "radical," and then wrote a long antilynching article. The New Nationalism had rapidly evolved into something genuinely new, and Roosevelt was on the verge of contesting the Republican nomination in 1912.[93]

BULL MOOSE PRIMARIES

He could not win the nomination as he had in 1904, by the distribution of presidential patronage. For the first time, direct primaries would contribute significantly to the selection of delegates to the party conventions. In 1912, about a dozen states had provided for the direct election of delegates to the two major party conventions. A few had presidential preference primaries in addition to those for the selection of delegates, and three gave state parties the option of holding primaries. One-third of the Democratic delegates and more than 40 percent of the Republicans would be chosen by direct primaries.[94]

Roosevelt's strategy was to make the most of the primaries. Since William Howard Taft now controlled both party and patronage, the primaries were Roosevelt's only route of return to the White House. His task was to demonstrate to the party leadership that he was more popular than Taft. But the New Nationalism was unlikely to endear him to the party regulars. Its public debut at Ossawatomie, where Roosevelt first referred to the New Nationalism, may have contained little that he had not already said as president. But saying it all at once in the form of a manifesto was something that he had never done as president, and it came as a shock to his friends and former political associates. Roosevelt had not yet broken decisively with William Howard Taft and become a candidate for the presidency. But the clear, systematic statement of his political creed was precisely what the primary campaign demanded. The electorate would have to hear something new. The New Nationalism was Roosevelt's attempt to give it to them. Fully developed, it would supply most of the underlying assumptions for the welfare state, and it advanced a new conception of the presidency. Roosevelt announced it at Ossawatomie: "This New Nationalism regards the executive as the steward of the public welfare."[95]

On the Republican side, the election of 1912 approximated a natural experiment on the implications of presidential selection. After an uncertain start, Roosevelt had overwhelmed Taft in the thirteen states where there were Republican primaries, but Taft overwhelmed Roosevelt in the Republican convention. In other words, the primaries produced a candidate with an ambitious, new political agenda while the party convention produced a candidate who had never really wanted to be president in the first place.

Roosevelt himself seems to have changed along with the mode of presidential selection. In 1904, he had won nomination by distributing party patronage in order to control the Republican convention. Dispensing patronage did not provide much occasion for issuing ideological manifestos. The presidency that followed was energetic but politically cautious. In 1912, Roosevelt sought the nomination through direct primaries, and emerged as a radical ready to construct a centralized state. The Roosevelt of 1904 was the president of the Square Deal. In a world of monopolies and trusts, his job was to ensure fair treatment for consumers and competitors. The Roosevelt of 1912 was the candidate of the New Nationalism. He saw the state not simply as arbiter but as an active instrument for social welfare. He told the crowd at Ossawatomie that he stood "not merely for fair play under the present rules of the game, but . . . for having those rules changed so as to work for more substantial equality of opportunity and of reward for equally good service."[96]

Changes in popular attitudes and personal sentiments undoubtedly figured in Roosevelt's ideological transformation, not changes in the system of presidential selection. But the presidential primaries provided a venue in which Roosevelt could promote ideas about the presidency and public policy that would scarcely have gotten a hearing in the Republican convention. In fact, Roosevelt and his supporters bolted their party's convention precisely because it seemed so unfairly stacked against them and so unreceptive to their political principles.

Academic Politics

Woodrow Wilson represented another consequence of the primary system. In 1912, he had held public office for only two years. The primary campaigns provided an opportunity for the New Jersey governor, a newcomer to national politics, to introduce himself to the country at large. It was true that the party conventions of the nineteenth century had also transformed political newcomers and unknowns into presidential candidates, but these politically obscure candidates had succeeded by remaining obscure. If they campaigned at all, they did it from their front porches or, like Grover Cleveland, from the governor's office in Albany. Wilson stood for something new in presidential candidates—a fresh political face with something to say.

His brief political career did not mean that he was short on political ambition. In fact, Wilson had been discussing a run for the presidency with potential backers since 1906, and he had daydreamed about a political career as an undergraduate at Princeton. He went to law school in Virginia because he thought that legal practice would be a prelude to politics in his native state. But his law degree led instead to a law partnership in Atlanta, where Wilson found few clients and no political opportunities. He decided to become a political scientist.[97]

The first political kingmaker to see a president in Wilson was George Harvey, editor of *Harper's Weekly*. He and other prominent New York Democrats were looking for an attractive conservative candidate to purge their party of Bryanism. Wilson was the president of Princeton, a southerner, an articulate opponent of government regulation of business who exalted the virtues of individualism against government paternalism. In a 1904 speech before the New York Society of Virginians, Wilson had argued that what the country needed was not "a party of discontent and radical experiment" but "a party of conservative reform, acting in the spirit of law and ancient institutions." Harvey introduced Wilson to wealthy contributors and influential editors who liked his tolerance of trusts, if not his view of the presidency, which he outlined in a lecture at Columbia in 1907: "The President is at liberty, both in law and conscience, to be as big a man as he can.[98]

Harvey was well acquainted with politics in both New York and New Jersey. He had covered the state for the *New York World*, then served as a staff member to New Jersey's governor, who gave him the honorary title of Colonel and appointed him State Insurance Commissioner. Harvey had also worked briefly for a newspaper owned by former Senator James Smith, the Democratic boss of Essex County.[99] In 1910, with the joint sponsorship of Smith and Harvey, Wilson won the

Democratic nomination for the governorship of New Jersey.[100] He made his political debut, in other words, under the auspices of Wall Street capitalists and a big-city political machine.

Within months of taking office, Wilson turned against the political machine that had helped to make him governor. It took him just that long to reinvent himself as a progressive. The legislative reforms that he pushed through the New Jersey legislature during his first year as governor helped to alienate most of the Wall Street backers who had financed his campaign. Of his early supporters, only Colonel Harvey remained, and he began to waver when Wilson opened his presidential campaign with an attack on the "Money Trust." The governor finally told Harvey that his support and the endorsement of *Harper's Weekly* were damaging Wilson's presidential prospects in the West. He could not understand why the Colonel was offended.[101]

WILSON AND THE "OUTSIDE" STRATEGY

Wilson entered the primary season as the frontrunner for the Democratic nomination, and suffered for it. He won more primaries than any other Democratic candidate in 1912—six of thirteen contests—and got more votes, but did not live up to expectations. He lost his native state of Virginia to Alabama conservative Oscar Underwood, chair of the House Ways and Means Committee. He campaigned energetically in Illinois, but lost its delegates to Champ Clark, Speaker of the House. Two other delegate-rich states, Massachusetts and California, went for Clark as well. Clark was also the favorite of the party professionals and big-city bosses in the North, and went to the Baltimore convention with most of the delegates who had been selected in party caucuses and state conventions. Weeks before the convention, Wilson wrote, "I have not the least idea of being nominated. . . ." Vote-counters gave Champ Clark a majority of the delegates, but not the two-thirds majority required for the Democratic nomination.[102]

Clark was the kind of candidate that party conventions had produced for most of the nineteenth century. He was "a docile, unthreatening figure," the Democratic counterpart of William Howard Taft. "Of all his utterances," said the *New York Times*, "only the things he never ought to have said are remembered."[103] Other newspaper editorials warned that the nomination of such an unimpressive candidate might give the presidency to the Republicans. In addition to the support of the press and the more progressive Democrats, one of Wilson's assets was the convergence of his short-term political interests with those of William Jennings Bryan. Bryan had given his blessing to both Wilson and Clark. But Bryan also wanted the chance to make a fourth run at the presidency himself. To that end, he would try to deadlock the convention, and since Clark was closest to victory, Bryan would try to prevent him from achieving it. Wilson stayed in step with Bryan until the end of the convention, when he had a majority of delegates, but not enough to win. The obstacle to victory was now Wilson's identification with Bryan, who had made himself intensely unpopular. Wilson's managers arranged for one of the delegates committed to him to mount the speakers' platform for a vicious attack on Bryan. On the forty-seventh ballot, Wilson reached his goal.[104]

If it demonstrated nothing else, Wilson's drive for the presidency showed how much he was ready to sacrifice for the White House. Ideology, friendships, political alliances and loyalties were all expendable. President Taft regarded him as "an utter opportunist." But Taft was not a factor in the politics of 1912. He hunkered down in Washington and refused to campaign. Wilson, on the other hand, was a moving target, and his conservative past combined with his progressive policies to enable him to appeal to Democrats of almost every stripe. Since the Bull Moose Republicans had walked out on their party, Wilson could win simply by preserving unity among Democrats, and Louis Brandeis came up with the common denominator that would unify Democrats against Roosevelt. Whereas Roosevelt promised to regulate industrial monopolies, Wilson promised to break them up. "Ours is a program of liberty," Wilson declared; "theirs is a program of regulation." Unlike Roosevelt's New Nationalism, Wilson's New Freedom did not look forward to a time "when the juggernauts are licensed and driven by commissioners of the United States."[105] It was a message that appealed to progressives alarmed about economic concentration and conservatives wary of state power.

NEW NATIONALISM, NEW FREEDOM, NEW PRESIDENT

The scheming of William Jennings Bryan may have failed to win him the Democratic nomination, but the presidential campaign that followed the conventions carried his signature. Like his crusade in 1896, it was about causes. Both candidates professed them. Roosevelt's departure from the Republican party meant that he could not rely on party identification to attract voters. His substitute for party identification was the New Nationalism—a body of principles and objectives that showed what he stood for. As a substitute, it failed. Roosevelt acknowledged as much when the returns were in. "The strength of the old party ties," he said, "is shown by the fact that, although we carried the primaries two to one against Taft . . . about as many Republicans voted for him as for me."[106] Wilson, of course, could not have known this while the campaign was in full swing, and he matched Roosevelt's creed with one of his own. A candidate of the gaslight era might have kept quiet and let the party organization do the work of mobilizing and motivating. But Wilson was not the candidate of the party organization. His campaign, according to Jeffrey Tulis, "was the first of the now normal 'outside' strategies that attempt to form a party around the candidate, rather than to capture a nomination by successful appeal to party leaders inside a preexisting organization."[107]

The contest between the New Freedom and the New Nationalism left much of the electorate unmoved. Fewer than sixty percent of the eligible voters bothered to cast ballots in 1912—the lowest turnout since 1836. Perhaps the differences between TR's progressivism and Wilson's version were too subtle for the public to grasp. Perhaps Republican party activists threw in the towel because the desertion of the Bull Moose Republicans seemed to put victory out of reach. Perhaps Wilson's candidate-centered campaign undermined the exertions of the Democratic party's organizational base. But perhaps the drop in participation marked a change in the structure of political struggle itself. The increased activism of the federal government stimulated the activities of organized interest groups for whom "voting and the electoral process were less important than the ability to influence legislation and to protect their interests by lobbying and otherwise applying direct pressure on political leaders."[108] Getting elected and governing had begun to separate from one another. The first required control of a party that could mobilize popular support. The second rested on achieving an equilibrium among organized interests.

WILSON, PARTY LEADER

Although his campaign had operated outside the bounds of party organization, Wilson's party became his principal vehicle of policymaking. But Wilson's Democratic party was not the party of ward leaders and clubhouses; it was the party in Congress. A month before his inauguration, Wilson announced that he intended "to be the leader of his party as well as the chief executive officer of the government. . . . [The president] must be the prime minister, as much concerned with the guidance of legislation as with the just and orderly execution of the law."[109] His "ministerial" conception of the presidency would lead Wilson to violate traditions of executive conduct that were ancient, at least by American standards. He was the first president since John Adams to address Congress in person, and he would be the first president since Grant to confer with members of a congressional committee at the Capitol. A prime minister, as parliamentary leader, would be expected to stand before the legislature to explain the policies of the party he led. Presidents had avoided such appearances because they recalled the king's opening of parliament, or because executive intrusions into the Capitol seemed to violate the separation of powers, or because of apprehensions about executive demagoguery or dictatorship.[110]

Barely a month after his inauguration, Wilson addressed a joint session of Congress concerning tariff reform legislation. The House readily voted to invite him to the Capitol. (No president would show up uninvited.) But the Senate was more resistant to the innovation. Written messages from the president, one Senator argued, "were more in accord with American republican institutions" than an address delivered in person "with its pomposities, and its cavalcadings. . . ." The objections only served to make Wilson's speech seem more historic and newsworthy.[111] Later he would meet in the President's Room at the Capitol to discuss his tariff reductions with members of the Senate Finance Committee, and after that, for the first time in living memory, the Senate Democratic Caucus would convene to work out an agreement on the tariff.[112]

Once Wilson got the tariff legislation he wanted, he returned to Capitol Hill a month later with legislation to establish the Federal Reserve System, then the Clayton Antitrust Act, and the establishment of the Federal Trade Commission. Wilson had come to Washington with an agenda. Administration initiatives expanded the Agricultural Extension Service, created the Department of Labor, regulated child labor. He proceeded systematically, unlike Theodore Roosevelt, pursuing one legislative project at a time. According to Marshall Dimock, "No other President in American history has so clear an idea of what legislation he wanted. . . ." Dimock suggests that Wilson may have been developing his agenda since his days as a graduate student at Johns Hopkins. Republican legislators felt the pressure of his ambition. Iowa's Senator Cummins complained:

> The influence which has been exerted by the President upon members of Congress, an influence so persistent and determined that it became coercive, is known to every intelligent citizen of the United States. . . . The President of the United States . . . has laid the heavy hand of his power upon a branch of the Government that ought to be coordinate, but which, in fact, has become subordinate.[113]

When Wilson spoke to Congress, of course, the press and the public were listening. That was not enough for him. Wilson invented the presidential press conference as a way of institutionalizing presidential communication with the public. Theodore Roosevelt had developed the background briefing, which permitted him to disclose his own point of view to reporters without being identified as the source. His executive secretary, William Loeb, also gave press briefings. But Wilson did it himself once a week. It was actually a means to limit his exposure to the press. During the interval between election and inauguration, he had grown impatient with the journalists who always seemed to be hovering around him and his family. The weekly press conference was a device for structuring reporters' access to the president.[114]

Whereas Theodore Roosevelt had been impetuous and spontaneous, Wilson was systematic and methodical. The press conference was a way of routinizing access to the president. His legislative agenda was planned in advance and ran on a schedule. The formation of a legislative proposal, then a speech to a joint session of Congress, culminating in a Democratic consensus, succeeded by another legislative project—it all followed a presidential timetable driven by executive objectives. Wilson was ambition rationalized.

He also extended presidential ambition through reliance on government bureaucracy. Four years before he reached the White House, Wilson wrote, "There are no more hours in the President's day than in any other man's. If he is indeed the executive, he must act almost entirely by delegation, and is in the hands of his colleagues." As president, he not only left the running of the executive departments to his cabinet secretaries, but permitted them considerable discretion in policy formation. The Smith-Lever Act, the most significant piece of agricultural legislation of Wilson's first term, was the work of Agriculture Secretary David F. Houston, who designed the bill in discussions with members of Congress and only very general direction from the Oval Office.[115] The result was the Agricultural Extension Service. It was the nationwide counterpart of a proposal that Wilson had introduced when governor of New Jersey. Wilson's plans were so big that he had to rely on bureaucrats and agencies to realize his ambitions.

The extent to which Wilson himself augmented executive power has been obscured by the vast concentration of presidential and bureaucratic authority that resulted from the country's entry into World War I. His success in mobilizing public opinion has been shadowed by his great failure in rousing sufficient support to force Senate approval of U.S. membership in the League of Nations. Although his nomination in 1912 was something of a fluke, the introduction of primaries as elements in the presidential selection system was essential to Wilson's elevation to the White House. If there had been no primaries, he might not have been a presidential presence at the Democratic convention. A majority of his delegates had been won in primaries.[116] Without them, he might not have been able to stop Champ Clark from seizing the nomination. On the other hand, primaries tended to recruit presidential candidates with sufficient stamina and motivation to make themselves presidential nominees instead of waiting for the party to designate them as potential presidents. Primaries opened the presidency to candidates of ambition who did not want the encumbrances that came from bargaining one's way to the presidency, and who were sufficiently self-propelled and confident to weather the rigors of a primary campaign.

4

From Normalcy to Primacy

THE PROMINENT ROLE that the direct primary played in 1912 had virtually evaporated four years later. In 1916, Theodore Roosevelt and Charles Evans Hughes were the most popular Republican candidates, but neither would permit his name to be entered in any of the Republican primaries. Hughes was an associate justice of the Supreme Court, a position that removed him from partisan politics, and he did not resign from the Court until after the Republican convention gave him its nomination. His positions on war and military preparedness, farm policy, and female suffrage—all important issues in 1916—were unknown. Until accepting the nomination, he had never actually declared his candidacy. The best evidence that his hat was in the ring was his failure to respond to a letter from former President Taft urging his candidacy. His silence was taken as proof that he did not reject the idea. For his part, Roosevelt felt out of step with the electorate, and his contesting of the primaries would revive memories of the unpleasant schism that had contributed to the party's loss of the presidency four years earlier. Although more states held presidential primaries than ever before, most of the Republicans who entered them were favorite sons or long shots, not believable candidates. In the Democratic primaries, Woodrow Wilson was the only believable candidate. Turnout was low.[1]

Primaries had become politically marginal mechanisms of presidential selection. Worse, they forced members of the same party to run against one another and supplied needless occasions for the aggravation of party schisms. The presidential primary was going out of fashion along with progressivism itself. A third of the states that had direct primaries in 1916 had abandoned them by 1935. During the same period, only one state—Alabama—adopted the primary system for selecting delegates to the national party conventions. Some states retained presidential primaries but legally prohibited the delegates from specifying which of their party's presidential candidates they preferred. In others, a favorite son candidate, usually the governor, would tie up a state's delegates, so that they would go to their party's convention under the control of state party leaders. In one way or another, state party organizations managed to reassert their primacy in the presidential nominations. Even so, primaries faced persistent challenges because they generated low turnout and added to government expense, and because so many presidential candidates avoided them.[2]

In effect, the country was operating under two competing systems of presidential selection—the party convention and the direct primary—and the party conventions were winning. They gave the country Harding and Coolidge, presidents of limited ambition with achievements to match. Primaries would not produce another president until Herbert Hoover's successful campaign in 1928, and Hoover was already the favorite before the primaries began.

Normalcy

In 1920 Warren G. Harding entered only three primaries, lost two, and won the Republican nomination anyway. The former Ohio newspaper editor was just finishing his first term in the U.S. Senate and was wavering between a presidential bid and reelection to the Senate. He seems to have been propelled by his cagey campaign manager, Harry Daugherty, who finagled an arrangement with the Ohio Republican State Committee that would allow Harding to run for reelection to the Senate in 1920 if his presidential bid failed. In that case, his presidential candidacy would serve merely to enhance his political stature and improve his chances for reelection to the Senate. Harding actually filed for reelection to his Senate seat while the Republic convention was in progress and its outcome still uncertain. The prospect of the presidency made him nervous. Shortly after declaring his candidacy, he had written to a close friend in Texas that the "only thing I really worry about is that I am sometimes very much afraid that I am going to be nominated and elected. That's an awful thing to contemplate."[3]

Harding had won fewer delegates in the primaries than any of the other Republican aspirants. But a deadlock among the leading candidates left an opening for his hard-driving campaign manager, who persuaded delegates to make Harding their second, third, or even fourth choice for the nomination. He emerged as almost everyone's compromise candidate. Harding was an amiable peacemaker who could help the party heal the divisions that remained from 1912, and he came from Ohio, a state that had been lost to the Democrats under Wilson. The Republicans wanted it back.[4]

Indecisiveness clouded Harding's presidential agenda. Unlike Wilson, he developed his administration's legislative program only after lengthy consultations with his cabinet, congressional leaders, and prominent figures in business and finance. The results took Congress by surprise. Harding called them into a special session, which he opened with a wide-ranging and ambitious speech that called for tariff and tax changes; federal promotion of aviation, highways, and the U.S. merchant fleet; aid to farmers; regulation of radio and cable communications systems; the creation of a federal public welfare department; and an executive budget-making process that would establish control over government expenditures. Then the president sat back and waited for Congress to work out the details of his program and enact it. He did not think it proper for the executive to meddle in the business of the legislative branch.[5]

Harding's administration, however, was more active than Harding himself. Its achievements, now largely forgotten, were the work of cabinet members and bureaucrats. The Washington Disarmament Conference was forced on the administration by Senator William Borah, and the treaty that resulted from it was the work of Secretary of State Charles Evans Hughes. The Budget and Accounting Act had been worked out during the course of the Taft and Wilson administrations, and it was given life by Charles G. Dawes, the first director of the Budget Bureau. Commerce Secretary Herbert Hoover took the first

144 / PRESIDENTIAL POWER

steps toward the regulation of aviation and radio and promoted agricultural cooperatives and foreign trade. Treasury Secretary Andrew
Mellon designed a tax policy. Harding backed all of them. So long as
his advisers agreed with one another, he could be decisive, even
assertive. But when they diverged, his resolve dissolved. To his speech-
writer, he confided, "I can't make a damn thing out of this tax problem. I listen to one side and they seem right, and then—God!—I talk
to the other and they seem just as right."[6]

Calvin Coolidge, who succeeded to the presidency at Harding's
death in 1923, was less susceptible to advice.[7] He may not have been as
silent as his nickname suggested, but he was clearly a minimalist when
it came to public policy, and he needed no one to advise him how to
stand pat. "Silent Cal" won a full term as president with only modest
exertion, although his prospects at first seemed dim. Congress had
shifted sharply to the Democrats in 1922, and the disclosure of official
corruption in the Harding administration hurt Republican prospects.
Many politicians expected that the election of 1924 would return the
Democrats to the White House. That prospect may explain the intensity of the Democratic struggle for the nomination. On one side was
William G. McAdoo, "a more sophisticated version of William Jennings
Bryan," who spoke for rural and small-town drys, or supporters of
Prohibition, in South and West and enjoyed the support of the Ku Klux
Klan. His rival was Alfred Smith, the champion of Catholic, big-city
immigrants and wets of the Northeast. The cultural, religious, and ethnic divide that separated them made compromise almost impossible,
and antagonism between the two sides had deepened during the sharply
fought primary contests between Smith and McAdoo. Resolution finally
came on the 103rd ballot, when the delegates discarded the frontrunners and settled for Wall Street lawyer John W. Davis, whose probusi-
ness conservatism made him almost indistinguishable from Coolidge.
Progressive candidate Robert M. La Follette was one beneficiary of the
Democratic deadlock. Although he was a third party candidate, he outpolled Davis in eleven states.[8]

Coolidge, of course, was the most conspicuous gainer. The only
obstacle between him and election as president was Republican progressive Hiram Johnson, the vice presidential remnant of Theodore
Roosevelt's Bull Moose ticket. Lacking control of federal patronage and

the Republican party organization, Johnson could win the nomination only through a primary fight. Coolidge showed how easy it was for an incumbent president to control the primaries. The Alabama primary produced a contested outcome. But Coolidge controlled the committee that decided such disputes. Johnson was strong in Michigan. So Coolidge operatives discovered an elderly Michigan resident named Hiram Johnston and put him on the ballot. Coolidge's control of local party organizations defeated Johnson everywhere but in North Dakota. In the general election that followed, Coolidge's vice presidential candidate, Charles G. Dawes, did most of the campaigning.[9]

No great policies animated the Coolidge presidency. The president told one audience that the country already had too many laws, "and we would be better off if we did not have any more. . . . The greatest duty and opportunity of government is not to embark on any new ventures. . . ."[10] Coolidge's greatest innovations were limited to presidential public relations. Radio gave this supposedly silent president one of the most widely heard voices in the United States. Within his own administration, however, he faced vigorous competition for public attention. Secretary of Commerce Herbert Hoover made his previously obscure department one of the most heavily publicized in the federal government. Under Hoover, it had its own press room and a full-time press officer. Assigned by President Coolidge to head a rescue and relief operation following serious flooding in the Mississippi Valley, Hoover took a survey trip through the flooded area and arranged to float down the river accompanied by an armada of photographers and newspaper reporters. One Republican senator observed that the 1927 flood had ruined the South but made Hoover president. Coolidge, upstaged by his commerce secretary, began to refer to Hoover as "the wonder boy" or "the miracle worker."[11]

The Great Engineer of American Society

Hoover was one of three cabinet members from the Harding administration whom Coolidge had retained. He seemed out of place. In an administration that made a virtue of government inactivity, Hoover's department was always in a bustle. It issued so many reports and surveys that it became the biggest customer of the Government Printing

Office. The secretary's endless stream of causes and projects frequently carried him beyond the bounds of commerce. He was known
as the secretary of commerce and "undersecretary of everything else."
When President Harding offered him the cabinet position in 1921,
Hoover laid out his conditions for accepting it: "I must have a voice on
all important economic policies of the administration. I stated that this
would involve business, agriculture, labor, finance and foreign affairs.
. . . I stated that, if I accepted, I wanted it made clear to the other
departments from the very beginning." Even those who found Hoover
congenial worried about his too-obvious ambition. One State Department official wrote that although he liked Hoover personally, "politically
. . . I am desperately afraid of him." Within the Coolidge administration,
he thought, Hoover was engineering a campaign aimed at "making him
the great figure in American life, the one man in the administration
who has completely at heart the good of the American people . . . ," but
his relentless self-promotion revealed instead a man who was "insanely
ambitious for personal power."[12]

Hoover launched his campaign for the presidency without the
blessing of Coolidge. The president had announced his intention not
to seek reelection at the end of summer in 1927, confounding the
pundits who predicted that he would run for another term. Hoover
announced his candidacy two weeks later. Republican regulars continued to press Coolidge to concede that he would be receptive to a presidential draft. Hoover, as one Kansas City stalwart complained, "does
not speak the language of the politicians or the delegates." He had
never run for elective office, and he was laying claim to the top nomination in a party that regarded him with suspicion. He had supported
the renegade candidacy of Theodore Roosevelt in 1912 and then
accepted appointment as wartime food administrator in the Wilson
administration. His name had even surfaced as a possible Democratic
presidential candidate in 1920.[13]

The presidential primaries offered Hoover an opportunity to show
the party regulars that he was popular with the Republican rank and
file. He entered most of them, even where he had to compete with
favorite sons. He won only where he did not face a local candidate, but
since the favorite sons had been expected to win anyway, their victories
did not undermine Hoover's status as the presidential front-runner.

He went to the convention with a majority of the delegates, won the nomination on the first ballot, and defeated Al Smith in a landslide.[14]

His presidential honeymoon was brief, and he would go down in popular memory as the unbending conservative who preached the virtues of rugged individualism while the families of the unemployed went hungry. If he was not actually responsible for the crash and the Depression that followed, he was guilty of not doing enough to salvage the American economy. Among historians, however, Hoover generally earns a more appreciative assessment. There is no denying that he came to the presidency with big ideas and abundant energy.

He began under the best of circumstances. Congress was solidly Republican. He had won the presidency with 58 percent of the two-party vote. The country was prosperous. He called Congress into special session to act on agricultural relief and tariff revision. The Speaker of the House had predicted that the special session would complete its business and adjourn in only a month. But there was trouble almost immediately, and the fractious session floundered on for almost seven months.[15] Hoover first clashed with the congressional farm bloc on the kind of aid that the federal government should give to agriculture. Hoover wanted to provide loan funds so that farmers could organize cooperatives to help them produce and market their crops more efficiently. Congressional representatives of the farm bloc wanted federal subsidies for farmers forced to sell at reduced prices on the international market. Senators of his own party helped to defeat Hoover's proposal, and it was months before a compromise could be arranged—without the intervention of the White House. It provided for a Federal Farm Board that could purchase agricultural surpluses to sustain prices. In the meantime, Congress took up Hoover's proposal that he should have the authority to change tariff rates by as much as 50 percent on the recommendation of an expert Tariff Commission. When the special session finally closed, just one month before the opening of Congress's regular session, there was still no decision on the tariff, and the Hawley-Smoot Tariff that Congress finally approved was nothing like Hoover's proposal.[16]

Hoover's relationship with Congress, even when it was controlled by his own party, was inharmonious. Unlike Woodrow Wilson, Hoover did not see himself as a prime minister who led his party in the legislative branch. In his *Memoirs*, he describes the president merely as an "adviser to the Congress on the state of the nation . . . proposing social and economic reforms made necessary by the increasing complexity of American life." He was uncomfortable with politicians, awkward, incapable of making small talk. "No activist president" of the twentieth century, writes Martin Fausold, "kept his distance from the Congress as did Hoover. . . ."[17]

Hoover saved his activism for the executive branch. Ten days after his inauguration, he directed the Treasury Department to disclose the names of those taxpayers who received large refunds from the federal government. Then he instructed the Justice Department to do the same with respect to the identities of people who had lobbied for the appointment of federal judges, a step designed to disclose any undue partisan pressures, or perhaps to discourage those who would play politics with the judiciary. He launched a comprehensive program of reform in the overcrowded federal prisons. He intervened to head off a strike against the Texas and Pacific Railroad. He launched a reform and reorganization of the Bureau of Indian Affairs. By executive order he forbade the sale or lease of government oil lands, to avoid future scandals like the infamous 1922 Teapot Dome affair and also to conserve oil supplies, and he added two million acres of public lands to the federal reserve. All of these actions came before the stock market crash, in the first eight months of Hoover's term, along with an announcement that he would ask Congress to enact a general reduction of the income tax, favoring earners in the lower brackets.[18]

Hoover's preferred mechanism of executive policymaking was the fact-finding commission. One of his first as president was the White House Conference on Health and Protection of Children. Like most of his committees and commissions, its activities were supported by private funds rather than congressional appropriations, in this case a $500,000 grant from the American Relief Association. The ARA held the surplus funds left over from Hoover's food relief activities in Belgium at the end of World War I. Conferences like this one, widely publicized, were supposed to elicit citizen action—perhaps more conferences and commissions at the state and local levels—which would eventually result in voluntary remedies or state and local legislation. By his own count, Hoover initiated thirty-eight commissions or committees while in the White House. At one point he had twenty-six of them operating simultaneously.[19] Hoover, the Quaker president, seemed to be attacking the country's problems by leading it toward a national "sense of the meeting."

It was a meeting, however, to which Congress was seldom invited, especially after the stock market crash in the early months of the Depression. Conferences and committees proliferated, but Hoover issued no calls for legislation. The resolution of the country's economic problems would come out of the economy itself, not from Congress. We could no more "legislate ourselves out of a worldwide depression," said Hoover, than we could "exorcise a Caribbean hurricane by statutory law."[20] What was needed was the voluntary cooperation of the people and institutions that made the economy work. Hoover convened a series of economic stabilization conferences in the cabinet room at the White House. They included the leaders of major industries and labor unions, railroad and construction executives, governors and mayors. The governors and mayors were persuaded to expand public works projects to boost employment. The industrialists were urged to maintain their payrolls even as they curtailed production, so that workers would not be idled or forced to accept wage reductions. At Hoover's request, the president of the U.S. Chamber of Commerce created a central committee of business executives, the National Business Survey Conference, "for the purpose of systematically spreading into industry as a whole the measures which have been taken by some of our leading industries to counteract the effect of the recent panic in the stock market." Organized labor, for its part, agreed to refrain from demanding wage increases.[21]

Hoover envisioned a society of voluntary, self-regulating trade associations, agricultural cooperatives, and labor organizations coordinating their efforts to serve the interests of society as a whole, a benign and voluntary corporatism.[22] But in fact, Hoover was creating pseudo-legislatures based in the executive branch, little parliaments of experts and executives who, with the aid of data generated by government, would sort out the country's problems. Today, the participants would be called "stakeholders," and something like Hoover's approach to policymaking survives in the contemporary federal bureaucracy. It brings the executive branch into direct engagement with the institutions of the American economy and society.

As the Depression darkened, however, the hopeful talk of Hoover's conferences lost its persuasive power. The National Business Survey Conference was dissolved eighteen months after its formation. Its "pioneer work," said a White House spokesman, had been completed, and other agencies would carry on its functions.[23] Its counterpart for banking and financial institutions—the National Credit Corporation—had an even shorter life. Hoover had persuaded the country's leading banking and financial executives to form a voluntary organization of banks in the late summer of 1931, while Congress was not in session. Member banks put up two percent of their deposits to join the corporation. In return, they could qualify for stabilization loans to keep themselves afloat. It took only two months for Hoover to realize that the bankers were too stingy with their loans to save other banks. The Reconstruction Finance Corporation, supported by federal funds and bonds, would take the place of the private voluntary organization. It would make loans to banks, railroads, and agricultural cooperatives.[24]

Hoover's philosophy of voluntary associationism had taken a beating, and now, after the 1930 midterm elections, he faced a Democratic House and a Senate with a one-vote Republican majority. Rather than abandon his faith, he encouraged the organization of a citizens' committee to combat hoarding. Anxious consumers had taken a billion dollars out of the nation's economy in the expectation that things would get even worse.[25] They did get worse. Hoover was impelled to make more departures from his vision of voluntary cooperative action to reinvigorate the marketplace. Step by step, he accepted and supported measures that increased the role of federal authority in the economy. In the end, he acquiesced to the Emergency Relief and Construction Act. It was signed just after Franklin Roosevelt had won the Democratic nomination, and it represented the opening act for the New Deal's WPA and CWA. Relief—even work relief—was something that Hoover had always rejected out of hand. It would unbalance the budget and undermine the socially responsible individualism that he had preached since he was a member of the Harding administration.[26]

In his 1922 book *Individualism,* Hoover had advanced the encouraging idea that America would escape the revolutionary disruptions that other societies suffered following World War I because the country's distinctive creed of individualism would make it immune. American individualism, according to Hoover, had "long since abandoned the laissez-faire of the Eighteenth Century. . . ." No society could survive "solely upon the groundwork of unrestrained and unintelligent self-interest." American individualism was tempered by equality of opportunity and by "instincts of kindness, pity, fealty to family and race; the love of liberty; the mystical yearnings for spiritual things; the desire for full expression of creative faculties; the impulses of service to community. . . ." American individualism sought self-expression more than self-advancement. But the development of the country's distinctive individualist values depended in turn "upon the ever-renewed supply from the mass of those who can rise to leadership." Our progress was "almost solely dependent upon the creative minds of those individuals with imaginative and administrative intelligence. . . ." Modern communications enabled these rare leaders "to spread their influence over so enlarged a number of lesser capable minds as to have increased their potency a million-fold."[27]

Hoover's quintessential American individualist was an organizer, not a solitary, and organization was progress. Our spiritual life had been enriched by the "vast multiplication of voluntary organizations for altruistic purposes. . . ." The modern economy was marked by "an extraordinary growth of organizations for advancement of ideas in the community for mutual cooperation and economic objectives—the chambers of commerce, trade associations, labor unions, bankers, farmers, propaganda associations, and what not." These groups were valuable, not just because they provided opportunities for individual self-expression, but because they represented a "field for training and the stepping-stones for leadership." These developments helped to explain why "business organization is moving strongly toward cooperation. . . . Cooperation in its current economic sense represents the initiative of self-interest blended with a sense of service." Finally, the role of government was to preserve the conditions for cooperative individualism—to regulate the economic concentrations that interfere with equality of opportunity, but to abjure the public production of goods and services itself.[28]

Herbert Hoover's drive for the presidency was animated by something more than a mere policy agenda. He wanted to realize a vision of

American society based on voluntary cooperation and in the process to create new and better Americans. Behind the commissions, conferences, and committees, there was a plan for American society. It emboldened a man who by all accounts was diffident, thin-skinned, and shy to risk the public exposure, hurts, and humiliations of high political office. The millionaire mining engineer had gone as far as he could in his profession. Living in London in 1912, he told a visiting friend that he was "as rich as any man has a right to be." But "just making money wasn't enough." He was interested in getting "into the big game somewhere"; "interested in some job of public service—at home of course."[29] Hoover drove himself into the public sphere against his private nature, because it was the only arena large enough to accommodate his vision. He no doubt saw himself as one of "those individuals of imaginative and administrative intelligence" who emerged out of the mass and led those of "lesser capable minds" toward a society of cooperative individualism.

President of the Party

Herbert Hoover rose to presidential prominence outside the framework of the Republican party organization, a fact that may have been responsible for his troubled relationship with Congress. Sidney Milkis has argued persuasively that Franklin Delano Roosevelt left his party behind him as he pressed forward toward governmental reorganization and economic reform. FDR's New Deal eventually "resulted in the development of a modern presidency and administrative apparatus that makes party government unnecessary."[30] But it is quite unlikely that Roosevelt had this result in mind when he was elected in 1932. His quest for the presidency was an exercise in party politics and party mobilization. Like McKinley, Wilson, and the first President Roosevelt, he sought to control his party so that he could make use of it, and to that end, he worked to enhance the organizational and political coherence of the Democrats.

In 1921, shortly after his unsuccessful campaign for the vice presidency, FDR wrote to the Democratic National Committee urging the establishment of a full-time party bureaucracy with a national headquarters and periodic conferences of party activists to discuss issues and party ideology. His purpose was to unify his party around a common creed, one that clearly distinguished it as a liberal alternative to the Republicans. The DNC ignored his suggestion. The need for unity could not have been more apparent after the disastrous Democratic convention of 1924, when McAdoo and Smith had fought their way to a 102-ballot stalemate. Roosevelt renewed his proposal, which the Democratic National Committee once again dismissed. FDR followed up with a letter addressed not to the committee, but to three thousand Democratic activists, including all the delegates to the grueling convention.[31]

The party that FDR envisioned was not the Democratic party as it stood in the 1920s. It was a national party, clearly more centralized and ideologically coherent than the one that fractured along regional and cultural lines at the 1924 convention. Roosevelt had been there on his crutches at Madison Square Garden to plead for party unity and to nominate Al Smith, the "happy warrior." His physical handicap may have been a political asset. At the time, it seemed to put an end to his ambition for high office. He could command the trust of his party's political rivals because he was no longer a rival himself. He was, says Frank Freidel, "a premature 'elder statesman' trying to bring harmony among quarreling Democrats."[32] He stood apart from the feuding Democratic factions.

Meanwhile, Roosevelt and his faithful agent Louis Howe were maneuvering to make FDR governor of New York in 1932. By then, FDR expected to have made more progress against his disability, and perhaps the Republican era would play itself out in time for Roosevelt to take a shot at the presidency in 1936, an objective on which Howe had set his sights since 1912. Al Smith's presidential nomination in 1928 induced them, reluctantly, to accelerate their political schedule. Smith was vacating the governor's office and wanted Roosevelt to take over in Albany. Roosevelt resisted, but eventually gave in to Smith's argument that, by running for governor, FDR would help Smith to carry New York. Smith, as Conrad Black observes, never considered what would happen if Roosevelt won the governorship and Smith lost the presidency; perhaps he believed that with an invalid and political dilettante in the governor's mansion, he could continue to orchestrate state politics. Smith, says Black, "couldn't tell an indolent mama's boy from a man with a casual exterior who was fanatically determined to become president of the United States." Driven by that determination,

Roosevelt had "risen up from paralysis, rebuilt his body, virtually invented a new method of locomotion, and convinced the world that although half of him had atrophied . . . he was only 'lame.' "[33]

In 1932, Smith stood with Roosevelt's Democratic enemies, the conservatives who controlled the party's organizational apparatus. They were united in their determination to prevent FDR from winning the nomination. The stop-Roosevelt forces were organized around the party's chairman, John J. Raskob, who had been a Coolidge Republican until 1928, when Al Smith, as presidential nominee, chose him to head the Democratic National Committee. He was a wealthy executive of the DuPont Corporation and, since DuPont held a majority stake in General Motors, he was also a major figure in the automobile industry, the creator of the General Motors Acceptance Corporation. The principal bond between Raskob and Al Smith was Prohibition. They were both against it.

So was Raskob's boss, Pierre S. du Pont. Prohibition was a symbol of intrusive, activist government that made businessmen uneasy. Du Pont had also been riled by the heavy taxes that Woodrow Wilson had imposed on high personal incomes and corporate profits to finance the country's participation in World War I. Some of these burdens continued after the Armistice. During the 1920s, du Pont had concluded that the legalization of beer would reduce taxation of the rich. Prohibition had placed an important revenue source beyond the reach of the federal government. In 1927, the Association Against the Prohibition Amendment estimated that a tax on legal beer would generate $1.3 billion annually—enough to cover a 50 percent reduction in income and corporate taxes. Raskob and the Du Ponts decided to contribute half a million dollars a year to the anti-Prohibition association. The Democratic party was another organization in need of financial support. The election of 1924 had left it heavily in debt. Raskob and the Du Ponts became heavy contributors and lenders, as did many of the wealthiest donors to the Association Against the Prohibition Amendment. In 1928, the party could back its presidential candidate with more than seven times the funds that it had laid out for John W. Davis in 1924.[34] In the Republican party, Raskob and his Du Pont associates would have been just one more band of economic royalists. Among the Democrats, they held the money bags.

Al Smith, the moderately progressive governor who had supported state welfare programs in New York, became a firm friend of business as a presidential candidate in 1928. He abandoned the traditional Democratic opposition to the tariff. Republican financial and trade policies seemed to have made the country prosperous. Smith embraced them. Roosevelt told his friends that Smith was making "a grave mistake," but he grudgingly consented to head the campaign's Division of Commerce, Industry, and Professional Activities. He sent out letters suggesting that Smith would impose fewer regulations on business corporations than Hoover, because letting "businessmen look after business matters is far safer for our country." Raskob, in a letter to one of the Du Ponts, could plausibly claim that the only remaining difference between the Democratic and Republican parties was the distinction between wet and dry.[35]

FDR faced formidable opposition in the Democratic establishment. By 1932, his opponents had new allies and a grand strategy. Al Smith tied up delegates in the urban Northeast. House Speaker John Nance Garner did the same for the South and West. When Roosevelt's drive stalled, they brought forth Newton Baker, once the progressive mayor of Cleveland and Wilson's secretary of war, but now an attorney for private utilities and an anti-labor proponent of the open shop. In early 1932, he even disavowed his support for American membership in the League of Nations, although he had been Woodrow Wilson's faithful acolyte in the drive to achieve it.[36]

To the dismay of many Wilsonians, FDR had also repudiated the League, arguing that it was no longer the organization that it had been in Wilson's day. Roosevelt was developing his own grand strategy, shifting his political base from the Northeast, where Smith and Raskob were strongest, to the West and South, where Democratic delegates had once mobilized behind William McAdoo, now a senator from California who was closely allied with the isolationist William Randolph Hearst. Roosevelt wanted to win both McAdoo and his supporters. His record as New York's governor included policies that might appeal to Democrats in the country's heartland. He courted the upstate agriculturalists by abolishing New York's land tax and financing rural road construction with gasoline taxes and general funds. He sponsored a reforestation program that was designed to raise farm prices by reducing acreage under cultivation. His support for the public control and distribution of hydroelectric power echoed the strongly held convictions of western progressives.[37] The man who backed the "happy warrior" against McAdoo in 1924 was trying to switch sides.

But the urbane squire of Hyde Park had trouble convincing the dirt farmers and drought-blasted ranchers of the nation's interior that he was one of them, and Democratic progressives were uneasy about his tolerance of Tammany, his support of Repeal, and his disavowal of the League of Nations. Roosevelt made friends in these quarters by attacking the conservative Democrats who controlled the national party organization. He embarked on a hostile takeover aimed at capturing the party itself, and in the process, successfully convinced many members of the party's progressive wing that was not in league with the northeastern conservatives.[38]

Roosevelt had been cultivating Democratic activists ever since his campaign for the vice presidency in 1920 had put him in touch with the party's workers in almost every state. Louis Howe kept up correspondence with them, although the letters seemed to come from Roosevelt himself. After winning New York's governorship in 1928, his correspondence took a turn against J. J. Raskob. It expressed misgivings about the party's dependence on large contributions (Raskob had lent the DNC $370,000 between 1929 and 1931). FDR's letters objected to the high-tariff plank in the 1928 platform and the party's "silly" attempt to win favor with big business. Raskob made himself an easy target in 1930 after Democratic congressional victories, when he and two of the party's congressional leaders joined the three unsuccessful Democratic presidential candidates of the 1920s to issue a "Cooperation Statement." It pledged on the party's behalf that the Democrats would not use their new legislative strength against President Hoover or pursue "rash policies," but work with the administration to achieve economic recovery. The statement aroused such widespread criticism among Democrats that Roosevelt could profit from it while maintaining a "discreet silence."[39]

But he spoke up forcefully early in 1931 when Raskob convened a meeting of the Democratic National Committee to endorse the repeal of national Prohibition in favor of state and local regulation of liquor. Roosevelt astutely avoided the merits of the proposal, but argued that the DNC had no right to issue major policy endorsements on behalf of the party as a whole. That power was reserved to the party convention where the delegates constructed and approved the platform. The New York State Democratic Committee passed a resolution to that effect, and FDR had copies of it sent to all the members of the DNC, but not to Raskob. Under attack from western and southern members of the DNC, Raskob retreated and withdrew his proposal. In his ongoing correspondence with Democratic activists, Roosevelt took credit for the outcome.[40] Although he had already declared himself for repeal, Roosevelt managed to side with the drys of the heartland to embarrass the conservative party leaders of the Northeast.[41]

In 1931, Jesse I. Straus, president of R. H. Macy and Company and a strong Roosevelt supporter, commissioned a series of polls to demonstrate his candidate's commanding lead in the race for the nomination. The first was a survey of all the delegates and alternates at the 1928 Democratic convention. Others covered persons listed in *Who's Who in America* and a survey of Democratic business executives and professionals. The Roosevelt polls not only received extensive coverage in the press, but also prompted newspapers to conduct polls of their own. A nationwide Scripps-Howard survey showed FDR leading the other Democratic prospects and capable of defeating President Hoover. Roy Peel and Thomas Donnelly, writing not long after FDR's inauguration, claimed that the polls were decisive to Roosevelt's nomination. Support for Roosevelt, they argued, "was not merely revealed by the surveys; it was largely created by them."[42]

The evidence of popular sentiment seems not to have deterred Roosevelt's opponents, especially Al Smith. Smith reacted with particular vehemence to a radio speech in which FDR had called for national recovery plans "that build from the bottom up and not from the top down, that put their faith once more in the forgotten man at the bottom of the economic pyramid." At the party's Jefferson Day dinner, Smith, his face flushed with anger, proclaimed that he would take off his coat and vest "and fight to the end any candidate who persists in any demagogic appeal to the masses of working people of the country to destroy themselves by setting class against class and rich against poor." The only sound hope for the unemployed, Smith claimed, was the return of prosperity to private employers.[43]

The fight was out in the open. Roosevelt had taken over William McAdoo's role as leading critic of the northeastern conservatives who gathered around Al Smith and held the party's headquarters. But McAdoo himself could not be drawn to FDR's side, even though the two men had converged in support of positive government committed to economic reform and recovery. Roosevelt had nevertheless won much of McAdoo's political constituency. James Farley, the New York State party chairman, had combed the country to collect delegates for his governor in the South and West. Notwithstanding Farley's optimistic reports, however, FDR lost the primary in California to John Nance Garner, who had McAdoo's endorsement, and the Texas convention committed its delegates to Garner as its favorite son. Smith prevailed in the conventions of Connecticut and Rhode Island and the Massachusetts and New Jersey primaries and split Pennsylvania's delegation with FDR. Roosevelt's critical task at the Chicago convention was to prevent the Garner and Smith camps from joining forces against him. Smith met with McAdoo in an attempt to reach across the residue of bitterness remaining from their marathon standoff in 1924, but nothing came of it. In the end, it was Smith's stubbornness that gave FDR the nomination. Southern and western delegates were so determined to prevent Smith from becoming the nominee that they clung to Roosevelt as the candidate most likely to trump the Happy Warrior. Had Smith withdrawn, they might have shifted to Garner. Since they did not, McAdoo and Garner marched their delegates into the Roosevelt camp. Deadlock would only turn the convention toward Newton Baker, who was perceived to be the candidate of the private utilities and financial interests. McAdoo and Garner had nowhere else to go, and FDR had promised McAdoo that he would be consulted on major cabinet appointments and California patronage. Garner received the vice presidential nomination.[44]

THE FIRST NEW DEAL

Roosevelt belonged to the same presidential species as McKinley, Wilson, and cousin Theodore. Each made himself president by taking on his party's leadership and displacing it. As a way of becoming president, seizing control of one's party clearly demanded more strenuous exertion than the nineteenth-century practice of disavowing presidential ambitions until being called to candidacy by the convention of one's party. But a president in command of his party also had to acknowledge restraints upon ambition, the most important of which were imposed by the need to maintain party unity. Immediately after defeating Al Smith, Roosevelt was referring to Smith as his "old friend Al," and Raskob as his "very good and old friend John Raskob."[45] The prepresidential Roosevelt had petitioned the Democratic National Committee to adopt an ideological profile sufficiently distinct from the Republican position so that voters could tell the difference. After winning the nomination, FDR emphasized the DNC's function as a mechanism for enhancing intraparty harmony, not ideological clarity.[46]

In seizing their parties, presidential aspirants had to be sufficiently aggressive to make enemies and, if necessary, ruthless enough to turn against friends. Once in control they had to embrace their adversaries. In the struggle for possession of the parties, would-be presidents generally emphasized the differences between themselves and the party leadership. In victory, they needed the gift of equivocation or ideological suppleness to make the differences invisible.

Roosevelt, even during the whirlwind of the first hundred days, had to trim his policies to fit his party. Congress, as Frank Freidel points out, was no rubber stamp. New Deal legislative proposals did not pass intact from the White House to the statute books. After submitting the first pieces of emergency legislation to shore up the banking system, FDR consulted with the leading Democrats in Congress and responded to their advice. Even progressive Republicans like Hiram Johnson and George Norris got access to the Oval Office. Congressional leaders "provided the impetus and concepts for key pieces of legislation. Others in Congress did much to shape and sometimes improve the bills before them."[47] The adaptation of New Deal policy to Democratic party sentiment was built into the Rooseveltian practices of policymaking. FDR established a clear division of labor between those who developed policy ideas and those who sold the policies to Congress, the party, and the public. The first job was for the policy experts of FDR's "Brain Trust"; the latter, for political professionals like Jim Farley and Ed Flynn, Democratic boss of the Bronx. The party operatives were there to make sure that the policies advanced by the administration did not offend Democratic sensibilities. Strong party organization, Roosevelt thought, was the foundation of good policy. "You have to have the votes first," he told Brain Truster Samuel Rosenman, "then you can do the good work."[48]

Even after FDR had accumulated enough votes to make himself president, his good work was surprisingly modest. He seemed to scale back his aspirations during the presidential campaign itself. He began with a flourish. His acceptance speech broke with precedent because he flew to the convention in Chicago to deliver it. Nominees had previously waited for a party delegation to inform them of the convention's decision. Roosevelt told the delegates that they "must be a party of liberal thought, of planned action, of enlightened international outlook, and of the greatest good to the greatest number of our citizens." At the Commonwealth Club in San Francisco, he declared himself in favor of economic regulation and an economic bill of rights, including the right to make a comfortable living. But after Hoover attacked the radicalism and collectivism of Roosevelt's proposals, FDR turned moderate, promising a minimum of government interference with business, and attacking Hoover for his profligate spending and deficits. A Roosevelt administration, he promised, would balance the federal budget.[49]

As the campaign progressed, the differences between Roosevelt and Hoover seemed to grow dim, and the early New Deal did not make them much clearer. As historians have reexamined the transition from Hoover to FDR, many have found the continuities more prominent than the disjunctions. Early portrayals of Hoover and Roosevelt cast them as polar opposites—FDR the optimistic and pragmatic activist, Hoover gloomily rigid and ideologically hidebound. But by the late 1940s, Broadus Mitchell was ready to make the case that Hoover's policies, "explicit and implied, came closer to the program of the New Deal than has been generally recognized." Hoover's Farm Board anticipated Roosevelt's Agricultural Adjustment Administration. The Reconstruction Finance Administration was conceived under Hoover and adopted by the New Deal. After FDR's inauguration, officials of the Hoover administration worked with Roosevelt's administrators to fashion a response to the crisis in banking.[50]

Herbert Hoover emerges as an uncertain quantity in presidential history. Should we regard him as the last president of an old era or the first of a new one? Carl Degler insists that although Hoover served both Harding and Coolidge, he "was not of their stripe." He belonged to the progressive wing of the Republican party. He stood the same ground as George Norris, Hiram Johnson, and Robert La Follette, Jr., all of whom would eventually support the New Deal in Congress. Hoover, it was true, balked at federal relief programs for the unemployed, but almost half a year before the 1932 election, he authorized the Reconstruction Finance Corporation to provide financial backing to states whose own relief funds had been exhausted.[51]

John D. Hicks, historian of the Republican ascendancy in the 1920s, credits Hoover with starting the New Deal. It was Hoover, he says, "who first accepted as a governmental responsibility the task of defeating the depression."[52] But Hicks also acknowledges that Hoover was handicapped by ideology in his attempts to grapple with the economy. He was "the prisoner of his economic views; his strong convictions on the subject of what the government had no right to do greatly narrowed the field of his possible activities."[53] The experimentalism of the New Deal was alien to his temperament. Others see even more striking gaps between Hoover and the New Deal. He was not the precursor of government intervention in the economy, but a defender of old institutional relationships. Given the "vast array of New Deal policies, the assumption and concentration of power in Washington, the new intrusion of the federal presence in the everyday life of farmers, businessmen, bankers, and others," one historian finds the assertion that Hoover anticipated Roosevelt "staggering." Stephen Skowronek, on the other hand, acknowledges that Hoover's response to the Depression was, in many respects, a preview for the New Deal, but the same crisis that made Roosevelt a great leader established Hoover as a symbol of failure. He was handicapped by his place in political time. He belonged to a political era whose time had passed, and "he was inextricably tied to the governmental commitments that events were calling into question."[54]

The political commitments of the past may have been less damaging to Hoover than his own persona. According to Mount Rushmore visionary Gutzon Borglum, "If you put a rose into Hoover's hand, it would wilt." Roosevelt brought a sunny buoyancy to the White House; he made people feel good. In the few days after his inauguration, half a million Americans wrote to him. He had renewed their spirits. "It seemed to give the people, as well as myself, a new hold upon life." "People are looking to you almost at they look to God."[55]

The distance between the New Deal and Hoover's New Era would eventually widen, and the change in mood from one administration to the other was sudden and striking. But the differences between late Hoover and early Roosevelt were constrained and incremental. FDR's inaugural imprecations against the "money changers" who had "fled from their high seats in the temple of our civilization" had led some to expect nationalization of the country's banks. But the banking legislation he sent to Congress just five days after taking the oath of office was a disappointment. It extended government assistance to bankers so that they could reopen their banks. It had in fact been drafted by bankers. His economy message went to Capitol Hill two days later. It cut veterans' pensions by $400 million and slashed another $100 million from the salaries of government workers. Then he asked Congress to legalize 3.2 beer. After the success of his ten-year campaign to liberalize the Democratic party, he seemed to embrace the agenda of the business-friendly oligarchs whom he had vanquished. "In his circumspect treatment of banks," writes William Leuchtenberg, "in his economy message, in his beer bill, Roosevelt had summed up the program of the archconservative du Pont wing of the Democratic party. . . ."[56]

NEW DEAL: SECOND ROUND

Roosevelt's programmatic timidity left ample territory in which more radical political movements could fume and roar. In California, there was Dr. Francis Townsend whose scheme for a guaranteed pension for every elderly American was garnering much support. In the Senate, there were the progressives of the Midwest and the Plains— Burton Wheeler, George Norris, Gerald Nye, and Robert La Follette, Jr. After the elections of 1934, the congressional radicals would grow more numerous. Public intellectuals Charles Beard, Reinhold Niebuhr, and John Dewey all declared that FDR's misguided attempts to reform capitalism were only propping up the very system that had plunged the nation into the Depression. Further afield, the Communist party courted converts.[57]

But it was conservatives who propelled the Roosevelt administration toward the progressive wing of the Democratic party. A conservative Supreme Court tore up most of the recovery legislation that had been drawn to solicit the cooperation of business and the stabilization of agriculture. In April 1935, the convention of the U.S. Chamber of Commerce was taken hostage by conservatives who declared war on the gospel of economic planning that business had embraced only two years earlier. Roosevelt had nowhere to go but left.[58]

He had left the way open. His legislative agenda for 1935 had included work relief and social security programs, but Roosevelt had allowed Congress to take the lead in organizing support for them. A third piece of legislation that would become part of the liberal Second New Deal was Senator Robert Wagner's National Labor Relations Bill, from which the president had at first distanced himself. He gave the bill a lukewarm endorsement just a few days before the Supreme Court struck down the NRA, with its Section 7(a) guarantee of collective bargaining. Roosevelt's enthusiasm for the Wagner bill suddenly intensified. In addition, he proposed and won a new tax measure that was not included in his January State of the Union message. It imposed or sharply increased levies on estates, gifts, corporate earnings, and high personal incomes.[59]

The president entered the year of the 1936 election year more fully attuned to the liberal Congress that had won office two years before. His own victory four years earlier had left the Republicans with majority support in only six states. Roosevelt stood at the head of a Democratic party in which the South figured less prominently than at any time since the Civil War, and the party's nation-spanning spread set the stage for a momentous change in the system by which it chose its presidential nominees—the abandonment of the two-thirds rule. It had been in force since the first Democratic convention in 1832, an assurance that the South would be able to impose its peculiar interests upon the party's nominees. Roosevelt took pains to avoid offending southern sensibilities. The adoption of a simple majority rule for choosing the party's presidential candidates was harnessed to a change in the allocation of delegates that awarded seats on the convention floor in proportion to the size of a state's Democratic vote. The solid South stood to gain representation, but it had lost its de facto veto in the nominating process, and the need to win only a simple majority of the delegates helped to make Democratic presidents and presidential candidates less dependent on their party.[60]

The new Democratic alignment transformed the party's finances too. The Raskobs and Du Ponts no longer held the party for ransom. Organized labor made up for much of the financial support that the party had lost from bankers and industrialists. Unions contributed almost three-quarters of a million dollars to the Democrats during the campaign of 1936. Attorneys and other professionals also became major investors in the fortunes of the New Deal.[61]

The overthrow of the two-thirds rule detached the Democratic party from its regional base in the South and transformed it into a more fully national institution. The party's new sources of financial support detached it from the business interests whose influence and support had made it difficult to discriminate between Democrats and Republicans. Roosevelt, in his acceptance speech at the Democratic convention, lashed out against the "economic royalists." The president had declared war upon entrenched privilege.[62] It was not the first time he had done so. His acceptance speech in 1932 called for a Democratic party of "liberal thought and planned action," and his address to San Francisco's Commonwealth Club later in the same campaign proposed a new conception of the social contract under which government assumed a positive role in the regulation of the economy and the protection of its citizens' livelihoods.[63]

But Roosevelt in 1932 was the candidate of a party that still included John Raskob and the Du Ponts along with the embittered Al Smith, who would soon become a founder of the Liberty League, and the Democratic center of gravity still lay south of the Mason-Dixon Line. FDR trimmed his sails. In 1936, however, Roosevelt's party had come into alignment with his politics. It was the party of labor and liberals. As he had told Sam Rosenman, one had to have the votes before it became possible to do the "good work." He now had the votes.

The election of 1936 completed the voter realignment that resulted in the New Deal coalition. But it was a realignment produced less by the conversion of Republicans into Democrats than by the entry of new voters into the electorate, voters who had not been immunized by prior party attachments. In other words, their political identifications were still fluid and unformed. The number of potential voters grew substantially during the 1920s, but many did not immediately enter the electorate. Women—especially immigrant women—hesitated to take advantage of their voting rights under the Nineteenth Amendment. The children of the immigrants who had arrived during the two decades on either side of 1900 were coming of age politically in the 1920s, but not necessarily voting. During the 1920s and 30s, these potential voters became actual voters. Between 1920 and 1936, the total presidential vote grew by 70 percent, much more sharply than the growth of the voting-age population. Citizens with weak party identification or none at all were forming their political commitments and expressing them in the nation's polling places. In 1936, however, first-time voters flooded the electorate in unprecedented numbers, and the Democratic party gathered in the great multitude of them.[64] Although many of them would become longtime Democratic adherents, they entered the electorate in response to Roosevelt, and they were his people. The president had called up a mass of supporters who were probably more closely attached to him than to his party, and they were bound to him not just by the force of his personality, but by bureaucratic bounty. For the first time in American history, the federal government had emerged as a major source of actual or prospective benefits for its people. The WPA and Social Security were directly administered by the federal government; public welfare and unemployment insurance were run by the states, but with significant federal financial support and administrative supervision. Along with these individual benefits, the federal government would also extend low-cost electricity to rural America, as well as paved roads, irrigation, and flood control.[65]

Roosevelt had started to create not just a national party with a coherent liberal creed, but an "executive democracy" whose dependence on party had been sharply attenuated. As his aide Benjamin Cohen would later observe, Roosevelt's approach to the 1936 election had been to project a "suprapartisan" image to the public. Although Republican converts might play a small part in the composition of the New Deal coalition, Roosevelt sought to make Democrats of progressive and liberal Republicans. They would help him transform the Democratic party into the liberal force that he had envisioned since his 1920 run for the vice presidency. Moreover, there were parts of the country—Pennsylvania, for example—where victory required Republican converts, and it was in 1936 that black voters converted en masse from the party of Lincoln to the party of the New Deal. "The record of the New Deal," according to William Leuchtenberg, "enabled the President to seek votes less as the Democratic nominee than as the leader of a liberal movement that cut across party lines." He courted Progressives and Farmer-Laborites and snubbed conservative Democratic candidates in favor of Republican liberals such as George Norris. He even encouraged the creation of the American Labor Party in New York to accommodate socialist friends of the New Deal.[66] In his effort to refashion the Democratic party, Roosevelt passed beyond the bounds of party itself.

THE "THIRD" NEW DEAL

Franklin Roosevelt's success in liberalizing the Democratic party and his overwhelming victory in 1936 might have been expected to place him in a decisively commanding position with the Congress that convened in January 1937. He had received a larger percentage of the popular vote than any president since James Monroe. There were so many Democratic members in the new Senate that there was insufficient room to seat them all on the Democratic side of the chamber.[67] But Roosevelt himself recognized that his party's lopsided majority in Congress represented a problem. Without strong Republican opposition, the Democrats in Congress might fall to fighting among themselves. The expansion of the party's congressional majority had also made it more heterogeneous, and the southerners who had lost their veto power at the party convention still held leadership positions and seniority in Congress. The party's expansion threatened their political status, and its new ideological inclinations were alien to most southerners in Congress.[68]

Two of Roosevelt's initial proposals to the new Congress allowed conservatives to portray him and the New Deal as threats to constitutional government. In January 1937, the president transmitted an executive reorganization plan to Congress. It would have expanded the White House staff, strengthened presidential control over the budget and personnel management, and integrated previously independent agencies and commissions into the cabinet departments that reported to the president. The following month, Roosevelt loosed his court-packing plan on Congress without giving advance warning to his own party's legislative leadership. It would have empowered the president to add one member to the Supreme Court for every justice over the age of seventy but set the maximum size of the Court at fifteen. Roosevelt's plans frightened even his congressional allies. Taken together, they seemed to open a campaign of executive aggrandizement at the expense of Congress, the Court, and the Constitution.[69]

Both proposals for institutional restructuring were stopped dead in Congress. A third major proposal, the Wages and Hours Bill, nearly came to the same end. It had been designed to replace the minimum wage and maximum hours provisions of the NRA codes declared unconstitutional by the Supreme Court. Unlike the court-packing and executive reorganization proposals, the wage legislation was almost sure to win approval if it came to a floor vote, but a coalition of southern Democrats and conservative Republicans bottled up the bill in the House Rules Committee. A second attempt in the following session led to the same result, but the issue spilled out of Congress and into the Florida Democratic primary, where the incumbent New Deal loyalist, Senator Claude Pepper, was challenged by Congressman James M. Wilcox, an opponent of the Wages and Hours Bill. FDR departed from his established practice of avoiding open involvement in congressional primaries. He threw the administration's resources and his son James's personal endorsement behind Pepper, who won with 70 percent of the Democratic vote. Three days later, the Rules Committee allowed the Wages and Hours Bill to reach the House floor, where it won overwhelming approval.[70]

According to Sidney Milkis, the Administration's successful intervention in the Florida primary helped to prompt Roosevelt's disastrous effort to purge his party of anti–New Deal Democrats. It was one thing to defend a faithful incumbent; another, to oust the unfaithful. The New Dealers succeeded in dislodging only one of the hostile members of Congress whom they targeted in 1938, a congressman from New York City. In the South, where the New Deal's Democratic antagonists were concentrated, the purge failed completely, frustrated by the decentralized, localized structure of party organization in the United States. In states like Maryland and Georgia, Roosevelt's attempt to create a centralized party responsive to national leadership was rejected as outside interference. Although FDR did not completely abandon his longstanding mission to create a national party "of liberal thought and planned action," his attention shifted to administrative reforms along the lines of his 1937 executive reorganization. Their purpose, writes Milkis, was "to help him govern in the *absence* of party government." After the profitless purge, Roosevelt would govern more as chief executive than as chief of party, and the administrative state, rather than party organization, would mediate between president and people.[71]

The Neustadt Presidency

One of the most controversial commonplaces about American politics holds that the modern presidency began sometime during Franklin Roosevelt's years in the White House. The controversies arise from uncertainty about what it means for a president to be modern and from the claims to modernity advanced on behalf of FDR's predecessors.[72] Lewis Gould, for example, gives priority to William McKinley as the progenitor of the modern president. McKinley, says Gould, addressed the public directly concerning the retention of territories won during the Spanish-American War, circumventing both Congress and party. He built an executive staff in the White House. He installed telephones there. The new technology allowed him to keep his words off the written record and freed him to speak his mind. He accommodated the White House press corps, called on the expertise of special commissions, flexed his war powers during the Boxer Rebellion.[73] McKinley's modernity, in short, seems to consist in his contribution to the development of a president-centered polity in which the White House became the principal node in a network of political communication, administration, and policymaking.

McKinley's modernism often escapes notice because his assassination prevented him from completing the transformation he had begun, because his colorful successor Theodore Roosevelt stole his spotlight, and because the modern presidency went into hibernation from Harding to Hoover. The administration of Franklin Roosevelt, on the other hand, marks an irreversible change in the American presidency and in the political system more generally. To a remarkable degree, he defined the office for those who followed him, even for those like Ronald Reagan who would try to undo FDR's works while invoking his name and memory.[74]

No one has shaped our conceptions of the post-Roosevelt presidency more fundamentally than Richard Neustadt, whose ironic understanding of modern presidents emphasizes the political limitations inherent in the vastly extended powers of the office. Like Stephen Skowronek, Neustadt recognized that FDR was a modern president because he "tackled specifically modern concerns like managing the organized interests of industrial society or rationalizing a bloated federal bureaucracy" and "met with frustrations that would prove commonplace among his successors."[75] The growth in presidential powers, in other words, has been matched by an accumulation of presidential burdens. After Roosevelt, writes Neustadt, "the exceptional behavior of our earlier 'strong' Presidents has now been set by statute as a regular requirement." Law made the president a leader, but without necessarily giving him the capacity to lead. In rare instances, statute alone may invest a president with the power to command. But the power to command is a blunt instrument, and its exercise can be costly. For those reasons, perhaps, Neustadt suggests that such formal powers were usually invoked only as a last resort.[76]

Neustadt's president used formal powers as resources for persuading others to recognize how their own interests intersected with presidential objectives. This meant that presidential power was usually exercised through bargaining, not command. The bargains, however, were not isolated episodes in presidential politics. Current bargains were linked to those of the past and the future. Actual and potential bargainers are close observers of presidential behavior. They anticipate what the president can do to or for them in the future. Their expectations are based in part on their assessments of how effectively the president has used his powers of persuasion in the past. The president "guards his power in the course of making choices,"[77] because today's choices will help to determine the range and impact of the choices that he will be able to make in the future.

Within the formal powers of the office, the president tried to develop personal political capital. For Neustadt, in fact, presidential influence was decidedly personal. One person uses it to affect the behavior of other persons. Methodological individualism was one of the traits that Neustadt shared with the behavioral movement that was reshaping the political science discipline in which he worked. Another was the determination to look behind the formal structure of political institutions to examine the "real" behavior that was housed within them.[78] But the sources of Neustadt's perspective were less methodological than political. The personal nature of presidential power was rooted in the politics of the era when Neustadt observed presidents in action. It was a time that transformed politics as usual:

> In comparison with what was once normality, our politics has been unusual. The weakening of party ties, the emphasis on personality, the close approach of world events, the changeability of public moods, and above all the ticket splitting, none of this was usual before World War II.[79]

What had become normal in the politics of the modern presidency was the mutability of presidential influence. It no longer rested on a solid foundation of party regularity or public loyalty. It could not rest secure from disruptive events originating outside the sphere of presidential control. The president had to be ceaselessly at work protecting, investing, and augmenting his influence. No one else could do the work on his behalf. Although his office had become an institution, it could not protect him. Institutionalization was one aspect of the modern presidency to which Neustadt seems not to have attributed any decisive political importance. Presidential influence might not be a simple reflection of presidential personality, but it was a personal creation, not an institutional projection.[80]

Neustadt, however, saw the restless pursuit of presidential influence as occurring within an institutional framework. The expanded powers and responsibilities of the postwar presidency compelled the president to seek influence and helped him to acquire it. Neustadt does not consider whether the ordeal of reaching the White House after World War II tended to increase the likelihood that only the most deft and driven entrepreneurs in the influence industry were apt to survive it. The more powerful the presidency, the more attractive the job becomes to politicians of unusual ambition. The more ambitious the aspirants, the more strenuous the struggle for the office. The ceaseless pursuit of power that Neustadt saw in his presidents might be a continuation of the quest for the presidency itself.

The president-centered polity emerged along with the candidate-centered campaign. Long before a majority of the delegates to party conventions were chosen in presidential primaries, party dominance of presidential selection had begin to waver. Candidates for the presidential nomination had campaigned against their own parties' leadership at least since McKinley. Their purpose was not to defy or destroy the party but to take possession of it. Theodore Roosevelt took the Republican party away from Mark Hanna, although he had the distinct advantage of doing it from the White House. Wilson had defeated Democratic insider Champ Clark in 1912, aided by the imperishable presidential ambitions of William Jennings Bryan. FDR mounted his own campaign to oust the northeastern conservatives who ran the Democratic party as it carried him to the White House in 1932. But by 1940, according to Sidney Milkis, his presidential victory was more personal success than party triumph.[81] Although he faced heated opposition among Democrats themselves, they could not conceive of a way to unite the party and hold the White House without him. The party had become prisoner of a personality. The Republican party simultaneously experienced the onset of candidate-centered politics. Wendell Willkie, who had never before campaigned for public office, launched an advertising and mass media campaign designed to win popular support while courting influential Republican opinion leaders. The techniques that enabled him to win the nomination over Robert Taft and Thomas Dewey would later figure in the movement to nominate and then elect Dwight Eisenhower. The first indications of comprehensive change in the system for presidential selection were present by the early 1940s and widely recognized by the 1950s. By 1960, the transformation was sufficiently evident that political scientists thought it demanded an explanation. They suggested that "the combined effect of the primaries, the public opinion polls, and the mass media of communication" had given us the candidate-centered campaign.[82] While sensible and not necessarily incorrect, this explanation overlooks one obvious alternative: Candidates gave us the candidate-centered campaign.

The institutions of presidential selection are themselves products of presidential politics. The rules and procedures that governed the conduct of nominating conventions were subjects of dispute and revision over the course of a century and more. The unit rule, the Democratic party's two-thirds rule, the tradition that the party should approve its platform before nominating candidates—all were the results of factional struggles to influence the selection of candidates or the kinds of campaigns that they could run. The displacement of the convention by the presidential primary is supposed to have been engineered by the McGovern-Fraser Commission's attempt to rebuild on the ruins left by the Democratic convention of 1968. McGovern resigned as commission chair in 1971 to pursue the presidency under the new system that he had helped to fashion. But in fact the revival of the presidential primary began long before his commission put the finishing touches on candidate-centered campaigns. At first, primaries could not make presidential candidates, but they did unmake them. Wendell Willkie tried to use the primaries to recapture the Republican nomination in 1944. His appalling defeat in the Wisconsin primary put an end to his hopes. Harold Stassen, perhaps the most famous nonpresident in American history, made a valiant effort to ride the primaries to the presidency in 1948. He failed to win the nomination, but at least he succeeded in forcing Thomas Dewey to contest the primaries as well. While Stassen wasted his time trying to defeat Robert Taft on his Ohio home ground, Dewey campaigned for three weeks in Oregon and achieved the victory that was necessary to salvage his drive for the nomination.[83]

Dwight D. Eisenhower was the first successful candidate whose campaign seems to have followed a path to the presidency that skirted party organization. By some accounts at least, he is the first president who arrived at the office by means of an "outside strategy"—a direct appeal, not just to rank-and-file members of his own party, but to independents and disaffected Democrats.[84] The strategy was not entirely his own creation. Chapters of Citizens for Eisenhower and "Ike Clubs" began to form in the summer of 1951, months before he consented to be a candidate and after his repeated denials of presidential ambition.

But his own brother, Edgar Eisenhower, did not believe him. Close friends urged Eisenhower to issue an irreversible rejection of presidential overtures after the pattern of General Sherman, but he never did. In September 1951, Senator Henry Cabot Lodge visited Eisenhower at the Supreme Allied Commander's headquarters in Paris and urged him to allow his name to be entered in state primaries and authorize campaign professionals to take charge of the Eisenhower clubs. Later the same month, New Hampshire Governor Sherman Adams announced at a national governors' conference that Eisenhower's name would be entered in his state's primary, and expressed confidence that Eisenhower would not demand its withdrawal. Eisenhower said nothing about the New Hampshire primary until January 1952, when he announced that he would not ask to be relieved of his military post in order to campaign for the nomination but conceded that his supporters had a right to place his name on the New Hampshire ballot and confirmed that he voted Republican. In March, without campaigning in person, Eisenhower won 50 percent of the New Hampshire vote, more than Taft and Stassen put together.[85]

"In some respects," says a 1960 text on party conventions, "the primaries may be said to have come into their own for the first time in the Republican campaign of 1952." Eisenhower's participation in them showed that he could win votes, and when he began to campaign in person, "it proved that Eisenhower himself was willing, however reluctantly, to take on the burdens of political leadership—to associate with working politicians, to accept the rules of the game, and to work for his own nomination and election."[86] But Eisenhower would also change the rules of the game in two ways. First, says Theodore Lowi, he delivered "a telling blow to the legitimacy of party leader control of delegates to the nominating convention." At the opening of the convention, Eisenhower's managers challenged the credentials of many Taft delegates who had been chosen, they said, autocratically and over the protests of Eisenhower supporters. When the credentials committee proved unsympathetic, the Eisenhower forces took their fight to the convention floor, where their "fair play" resolution passed, and the Taft delegates with the doubtful credentials were not seated and not permitted to vote on the measure that decided their status.[87]

Having antagonized party leaders, Eisenhower proceeded to run a campaign independent of the Republican National Committee. The Citizens for Eisenhower, with financial backing from wealthy Republican businessmen and the leadership of campaign professionals, mobilized workers nationwide in Eisenhower's cause. State and national Republican party organizations were not idle. The candidate-centered campaign organization may not have displaced the party organization, but it played a vital role in Eisenhower's electoral success.[88]

In the case of John F. Kennedy in 1960, the personal campaign eclipsed the one orchestrated by the Democratic party organization. The true campaign organization was the one headed by the candidate's brother Robert, and its key operatives included the senator's most faithful Massachusetts cronies along with a number of his relatives by blood and marriage. The urban political organizations of the Northeast and Midwest would prove essential to Kennedy's victory, but he first had to prove himself in the primaries, where state party organizations occasionally dissolve in family brawls and candidates present themselves directly to the voters. "Not until he showed primitive strength with the voters in strange states," says Theodore White, could Kennedy "turn and deal with the bosses and brokers of the Northeast who regarded him fondly as a fellow Catholic but, as a Catholic, hopelessly doomed to defeat."[89] In West Virginia he would prove himself among Protestants. He did not seek delegates in the primaries, and in that respect his campaign differed from those that followed the reforms of 1972. Kennedy used the primaries to demonstrate to delegates and party leaders that he was a winning candidate. But there was little difference between campaigning for effect in primaries and campaigning for delegates in primaries.[90] Intraparty elections tend to produce candidate-centered organizations with their own finances and personnel. In fact, intraparty struggles of any kind seem to have the same effect. In 1964, Barry Goldwater concentrated his preconvention campaign in nonprimary states where he mobilized "a personal 'grass roots' organization to capture delegates," and, says James Ceaser, pursued a "candidate-oriented strategy . . . in a domain that had usually been controlled by the regulars."[91]

Four years later came the calamitous Democratic national convention that led to the transformation of conventions into formulaic rites.

The most riveting convention of the television age stimulated the reforms that helped to make conventions too dull for television. The first signals of the sweeping change to come emerged at the 1968 convention itself, when the Rules Committee barred the use of the unit rule that bound delegates to vote as the majority of their state delegations did. The rule usually worked to enhance state party leaders' control over their delegates, but it often forced delegates to cast votes that did not reflect their own presidential preferences.[92] The McGovern-Fraser Commission, created after the chaotic convention in Chicago, successfully persuaded the party to adopt eighteen rule changes whose collective purpose was to assure that the delegates could express their presidential preferences, and to increase the extent to which the delegates represented the presidential preferences of Democratic voters.

Polsby and Wildavsky point out that in its attempt to achieve this end, the commission would "take control of the presidential nomination away from state and local party officials, as well as from national officeholders, and give it over to party activists attached to candidates and elected through primaries with safeguards to assure representation of those deemed insufficiently represented: women, youth, racial minorities."[93] The McGovern-Fraser guidelines did not actually require primaries, but meeting those guidelines would have required state Democratic parties to make radical changes in the way they constituted the caucuses or conventions that handled matters other than presidential nominations. The solution for a number of states was to continue business as usual, except for the selection of delegates to the national convention, which the voters would do in a state-administered primary. The number of Democratic delegates selected in direct primaries rose from 40 percent in 1968 to about 70 percent in 1976, and where there were Democratic primaries, the Republicans would also have them.[94]

In effect, a number of state party organizations simply bowed out of the process for nominating presidential candidates. Rather than represent the party as an organization, delegates would now be committed to presidential candidates. Even though the Democrats reintroduced party leaders and elected officials to conventions as "superdelegates" after 1980, the primaries continue to be the principal arenas for contesting presidential nominations. Since these primaries are mechanisms for delegate selection and not just "beauty contests," candidates incur risks by skipping any of them. But running in most or all of them, as Leon Epstein points out, means that "a successful nominating campaign needs a large and well-funded candidate-centered organization." Along with Richard Neustadt, however, he sees the new shape of presidential campaigns as the product of gradual change, driven in part by candidates seeking the best openings for the pursuit of their ambitions.[95] The spread of primaries after 1968, in other words, may have advanced a process of change that was already in motion. Perhaps Richard Nixon's self-destructive reelection campaign in 1972 is the strongest indication that candidate-centered campaigns are not merely by-products of the primary system. An incumbent in command of his party and unopposed in the primaries, Nixon abandoned his party and struck out on his own with the Committee to Reelect the President. The Republican stalwart of 1960, who had assiduously cultivated party leaders and officeholders while vice president, disconnected his political interests from those of his party and flew solo to his victory and later, his humiliation.

The candidate-centered campaign is the creation of the candidates themselves. Candidates use television to reach the electorate directly, without relying on organizational intermediaries. Opinion polling is the campaign's reconnaissance patrol. It influences tactical planning, and serves as a public demonstration of strength to sway donors and delegates. But sample surveys and media exposure are simply instruments that ambitious candidates exploit, like the primaries themselves, to clear the path toward the presidency. The ambition that drives these personal campaigns, however, is not simply personal, not just the candidate's. "There is an axiom in politics," writes Theodore White, "that a candidacy for any office is not simply an expression of individual ambition—any great candidacy is that gathering place of many men's ambitions."[96]

In effect, the need to feed and finance a national, candidate-centered campaign organization helps to socialize ambition. The drive that propels the campaign is not the candidate's alone. It is as though Mark Hanna has multiplied into an institution. In the case of a losing presidential candidate, the life of the institution may be brief. But the transformation of the campaign reflects the development of the presidency itself. In Neustadt's portrayal, presidents trade on the formal powers of the presidency to generate personal influence. But the same drive that animates candidate-centered campaigns also motivates presidents and their staff assistants to expand the formal powers and administrative resources of the presidency. In the process, they bring into being an institution with a structural interest in defending and expanding executive authority. In effect, the intensified presidential motive creates new presidential means. Political ambition is institutionalized.

5

Making the President Imperial

T
HE CANDIDATE-CENTERED campaigns of the past fifty years
tend to start early in the presidential election cycle and take off
at high velocity, especially when non-incumbents are running. Making
a good showing in the early primaries and open caucuses helps to
build the essential momentum that attracts news coverage, contributions, enthusiastic activists, and a loyal professional staff. To assemble
such a campaign and to stand at its center is no job for self-effacing
politicians who await the call of their party. It is not for the likes of
James Garfield or Benjamin Harrison. If nineteenth-century candidates had the "fire in the belly" that is supposed to motivate today's
presidential aspirants, they had to conceal it. Visible ambition was a
political liability. Active campaigning was bad form. But today the
rules are different, and today's candidates are a different breed.
Sometimes even the presidency itself is not big enough for them, and
they have repeatedly attempted to expand its powers and increase its
political autonomy.

They have usually pushed ahead on four fronts. Since Franklin
Roosevelt, presidents have tried to expand the reach, power, and size
of the Executive Office of the President (EOP). The EOP staff, in turn,
has been the president's principal means of advancing along three
other dimensions of White House influence. First, the White House
staff can enhance presidential influence over Congress. Second, it can
establish and extend White House control over the federal bureau-

cracy. Finally, the EOP staff helps to expand the sphere of direct presidential governance through executive orders, the regulatory process, and a variety of other devices invented in the cause of unilateral, presidential policymaking. The result has been a striking gain in the political autonomy of the White House—a capacity to make and execute policy without venturing outside the executive branch to consult Congress or even to heed public opinion. Presidents are most likely to resort to this "inside" strategy precisely when they cannot win congressional approval or public support for their policy objectives. FDR turned to it after he failed to win support for his Court-packing plan and was frustrated in his attempt to purge Democrats disloyal to the New Deal.

He was not the first to try to make policy on his own. When ordinary politics failed him, Abraham Lincoln called on the army to carry out his will. Theodore Roosevelt held an expansive view of presidential power, and while his appointment of the Keep Commission to recommend administrative improvements in the executive branch did not add immediately to the presidential imperium, it asserted the president's stewardship of federal administration.[1] The later Roosevelt would exploit the opening created by his cousin.

The Executive Office of the President

FDR received the report of the President's Committee on Administrative Management (the Brownlow Committee) while riding the wave of hubris that followed his landslide victory in the election of 1936—the same spell of brashness that produced the Court-packing plan and led to the fruitless party purge of 1938. In 1937, FDR proposed legislation based on the Brownlow report. It would have expanded the White House staff, strengthened the president's managerial and personnel powers, including the power to reorganize federal agencies, and ended the independence of the independent agencies. Like his other power plays of the "Third New Deal," this one foundered. In 1939, however, Congress agreed to a compromise proposal that gave FDR some of the powers he wanted. It authorized the president to appoint six administrative assistants and gave him, for a period of two years, the authority to implement reorganizations of the executive branch, subject to congressional veto. FDR used his new powers to issue an order establishing the Executive Office of the President. Public administration expert Luther Gulick called it an "epoch-making event in the history of American institutions."[2]

For most of that history, presidents had operated pretty much on their own. "If the President has any great policy in mind or on hand," Grover Cleveland complained, "he has no one to help him work it out." The president's attempts to form grand policy might be side-tracked by petty distractions. Cleveland's great plans, if he had any, could be interrupted by the White House doorbell or the telephone, both of which he often had to answer himself. He also kept track of the household expenses and wrote the checks to pay them. When it came to the budgets of federal agencies, however, the president exercised no such oversight. There was no executive budget. Estimates and appropriations were generally worked out between bureau chiefs and the chairs of congressional appropriation committees. The president was a mere bystander; any president who tried to intervene in the budget-making process would have been stymied by the insufficiency of presidential staff. Even President Grant, who had no great policies in mind, regarded the White House staff as inadequate. In 1868, the staff consisted of a private secretary, two executive clerks, a messenger, and a steward, all supported by an annual appropriation of $13,800. He supplemented his civilian staff with five high-ranking military officers reassigned from the office of the army's commanding general, William T. Sherman. Not until the administration of McKinley in 1897 would the president's helpers again be as numerous as they were under Grant.[3]

Even as it grew, the presidential staff remained overwhelmingly clerical. Harding's White House employed twenty-one clerks, two stenographers, a records clerk, an appointments clerk, a chief clerk, an executive clerk, and the secretary to the president. A few of the clerks and secretaries might actually serve as policy advisers, press officers, or in congressional liaison roles.[4] But members of Congress and other politically attentive Americans tended to regard the presence of these unofficial presidential aides with a measure of suspicion—like Jackson's Kitchen Cabinet or Wilson's Colonel House—a legally irresponsible and slightly disreputable power behind the throne.[5]

For that reason, perhaps, jobs on the nineteenth-century White

House staff did not seem especially desirable. Grover Cleveland's first choice as private secretary was Daniel Lamont, the man who had served him in a similar capacity when he was governor of New York. But Lamont wanted nothing of Washington. The exasperated president–elect finally broke his resistance by declaring, "Well, Dan, if you won't go, I won't." President Hayes noted that the first candidate to whom he offered the position as his private secretary not only declined the job but also expressed "hurt that I had suggested it to him." Although President Garfield thought that his private secretary was as important to the administration as the secretary of state, he had difficulty finding anyone to accept the position. He offered the post to John Hay, who had seen enough of White House work under Abraham Lincoln. He was not prepared for a second tour of duty: "The contact with the greed and selfishness of office-seekers and bull-dozing Congressmen is unspeakably repulsive. The constant contact with envy, meanness, ignorance, and the swinish selfishness which ignorance breeds needs a stronger heart and a more obedient nervous system than I can boast."[6]

Franklin Roosevelt's unofficial advisers were also the targets of abuse and suspicion. Thomas Corcoran and Benjamin Cohen showed up on the cover of *Time* at the peak of FDR's purge of his party, but not as men of the year. They were portrayed as shady characters who operated "beyond the rules" and were in fact "engaged in making them," even though no one had elected them.[7] Congressional approval for FDR's six assistants gave official recognition, if not legitimacy, to long-standing improvisation.[8] Unofficial advisers and staff borrowed from federal agencies continued to operate in the White House, but the president's official staff soon outgrew its makeshift alternative. The official employees now number nearly 400 who work directly for the president in the White House, along with another 1,400 staffing eight divisions of the executive office outside the White House.[9]

The executive order by which FDR created the Executive Office of the President enumerated five divisions within the organization. Aside from the White House office itself, the most important was the Bureau of the Budget (BoB), today called the White House Office of Management and Budget (OMB). It was conceived in the Taft administration, stillborn in the Wilson administration, and finally born again in 1921 under Warren Harding. To forestall direct presidential control of the bureau, Congress placed the new agency in the Treasury Department. But the president could appoint the bureau's director and assistant director without the Senate's approval.[10] Roosevelt's executive order relocating the bureau to the Executive Office of the President in 1939 was no great change, but FDR and his successors would add significantly to the bureau's powers. Since Harding, federal agencies had been required to get bureau clearance for all legislation that involved federal expenditures. Under FDR, all legislative proposals had to pass through the bureau before going to Congress, whether they had budgetary implications or not. The bureau also vetted all executive orders and proclamations and proposals for presidential vetoes. The growth of the BoB's responsibilities was reflected in its size. It expanded from a staff of 40 in 1939 to 500 in 1945.[11] In time, it would become the president's chief instrument for directing the federal regulatory process and an important vehicle for extending White House control over the federal bureaucracy.

The Bureau of the Budget and the workers in the White House provided President Roosevelt with two different kinds of administrative support. The staff in the White House, writes Stephen Hess, served the president by giving aid of "a personal, public relations, and political nature." The other staff, in the Executive Office Building, was responsible to the presidency, and its duties were "institutional in nature." Two kinds of executives—the president and the presidency—stood side by side in Washington. Until the start of World War II, the staff was driven primarily by FDR's idiosyncratic administrative style, with its overlapping jurisdictions and competing or incomplete grants of authority. The churning bureaucratic jumble emitted information useful to the president—more than he would have received from a neatly hierarchical arrangement—and it expanded the range of policy options that surfaced in the Oval Office. But the pressures of war and the failing health of the president necessitated delegations of authority to aides who made operational decisions in the name of the president. Harry Hopkins acted as the president's ambassador to the Allied powers, Admiral Leahy stood in as commander in chief, and Samuel Rosenman presided over domestic policy.[12] The presidency had begun to break away from the president.

The divergence may have been foreshadowed by the Brownlow Committee's dual conception of the EOP's functions. On the one hand, the White House staff would assist the president "in obtaining quickly and without delay all pertinent information possessed by any of the executive departments so as to guide him in making his responsible decisions," and, on the other, "when the decisions have been made," the staff would "assist him in seeing to it that every administrative department and agency affected is promptly informed."[13] What seemed to the Brownlow Committee a seamless flow of staff support might in fact call for sharply different sorts of administrative capabilities. The kind of organization that excels at obtaining intelligence for the president, as Bert Rockman points out, may not be suitable for assuring the implementation of the president's policies.[14] FDR's penchant for vague and inconsistent delegations of responsibility might increase the flow of political intelligence that informed the president's decisions. To assure that the decisions were carried out, however, a more ordered and single-mindedly hierarchical organization might prove more reliable.

The White House staff might also prove to be something more than a mere extension of the person of the president; it could help to compensate for presidential shortcomings. Harry Truman's limitations were magnified by the fact that he succeeded a president who had been a giant in life and a monument in death. He always came up short in comparisons with FDR. The press rated him as only fair at his job, and loyal New Dealers thought that "the administration was going to pieces" under Truman's undistinguished leadership. Even members of the president's staff expressed concern about his disorganization.[15] Truman's top staff members were so worried by the administration's lack of direction that they made it a practice to meet one evening a week at the apartment of a subcabinet official "to plot a coherent political course for the administration" in domestic policy. One of the participants, Clark Clifford, later recalled that he and the others "would try to come to some understanding among ourselves on what direction we would like to see the president take on any given issue. And then, quietly and unobtrusively, we would try to steer the president in that direction." Truman, apparently, was never aware that his staff had conspired to steer him.[16]

The presidency was bigger than the president himself, and during the Truman administration, it was the presidency whose powers grew. Congress added two important divisions to the executive office. The Council of Economic Advisors (CEA) became part of the EOP in 1946 and the National Security Council (NSC) was added in 1947. According to Milkis, some members of Congress saw these agencies as checks on the president's autonomy in military and fiscal matters.[17] The National Security Council had been conceived in 1945 as a means of bringing order to the ad hoc style of decision making by which FDR had directed the nation's defense and diplomacy in World War II. By the time Truman had taken office, the council had also become a quid pro quo for the creation of a unified Defense Department. The navy, although it would no longer have a seat in the White House Cabinet Room, would have a voice in the NSC, and the navy's political friends wanted to make sure that it was heard. The Bureau of the Budget, however, used its legislative clearance authority to make sure that the voices of the NSC would not be decisive. It insisted that the legislation creating the council should not grant it any statutory authority as a collective decision-making body, so that the president would have to adopt policies in and through the council itself. The NSC would be nothing more than advisory branch of the presidency with no independent authority.[18] The defense and enhancement of presidential power no longer depended simply on the president. The institutional presidency was a collective embodiment of presidential ambition. It would patrol the frontiers of presidential authority to guard against incursions and exploit opportunities for expansion.

The First Hoover Commission expanded the scope and made legitimate the status of the institutional presidency. Congressional Republicans created it to prepare the way for their party's expected return to the White House after the 1948 election. Chairman Herbert Hoover shared the legislators' misgivings about New Deal agencies and programs, but not their reservations about presidential power. The commission's proposals to increase the staff and executive capacity of the White House were intended to bring a coherence to the federal bureaucracy that reflected not Hoover the New Deal nemesis, but Hoover the Great Engineer, striving for administrative rationality and coordination. The same spirit animated the commission's insistence that democratic accountability demanded clear lines of authority over bureaucratic agencies, all converging on the White House. Because the recommendations originated with Hoover, they commanded the respect and even the endorsements of Republican newspapers and politicians.[19] The institutional presidency had become bipartisan.

So would the personal presidency. In an unusual preinauguration meeting of his cabinet-to-be at the Hotel Commodore in New York, Dwight Eisenhower announced that some members of his White House Staff would be "equally important with any Cabinet position that we have." They had to be able, he said, to walk into the office of any department head "and say 'Bill, this thing is wrong. We have got to do something.'"[20] In effect, members of the White House staff would be giving orders to cabinet members. A handful of presidential aides would exercise a measure of command over the federal bureaucracy. Staff members might enjoy the confidence of the president, but unlike the cabinet members, they had not been anointed by the advice and consent of the Senate. Chief of Staff Sherman Adams, national security assistant Robert Cutler, and congressional relations aide Wilton Persons would comprise a kind of shadow cabinet. Their job, stated simply, was to shadow the cabinet.

Midway through his first term, Eisenhower organized a formal cabinet secretariat to oversee the business discussed in the president's meetings with the assembled department secretaries. During his two terms in the White House, he held an average of thirty-four cabinet meetings a year—more than any other modern president—and the frequency of these meetings may account for Edward Corwin's conclusion that Eisenhower, "to a far greater degree than any of his predecessors, has endeavored to employ the Cabinet as an instrument of collective policy-making." The assessment is consistent with the once-popular impression of Eisenhower as a distant, uninvolved president, "reigning rather than ruling," golfing rather than governing. Fred Greenstein, however, sees Eisenhower's cabinet meetings more as a mechanism of presidential control than presidential dependence. Through his cabinet secretariat, Eisenhower pressed his department heads to expose their projects and plans to the criticism of their fellow department heads, intent on protecting their domains from the inroads of rival bureaucracies or supplying their expertise to advance administration policy. The cabinet meetings were deliberative assemblies, not decision-making bodies. Eisenhower, says Greenstein, sought the advice of his cabinet as a way of winning its support for his own decisions and coordinating the operations of the executive branch.[21]

Eisenhower used his cabinet secretariat and the White House staff to monitor the federal bureaucracy's implementation of his decisions. He also sought to make government organization more responsive to presidential authority. The president-elect announced the appointment of a Presidential Advisory Commission on Government Organization (PACGO) at the same time that he named his nominees for the cabinet. A further token of its importance to him was its membership—his brother Milton, Nelson Rockefeller, and Arthur Flemming (member of the first Hoover Commission and future secretary of health, education, and welfare). The commission was to operate out of the Executive Office of the President. Only three months after Inauguration Day, the commission had already submitted twenty reorganization plans to the president. Congress approved ten of them during Eisenhower's first year in office and six more in his second.[22]

PACGO represented a marked departure from earlier attempts to reorganize the executive branch. It would not go out of existence after delivering a final report. Instead, it would function continuously until the end of the Eisenhower administration. Its membership did not include independent experts on public administration, just the president's men. PACGO, however, had to share the field with a second Hoover Commission—Congress's entry in the Republican endeavor to reshape the federal bureaucracy inherited from the New Deal. Eisenhower tried to divert the new Hoover Commission from issues of reorganization into a review of federal policies, and he managed to delay its formation until PACGO was well under way.[23]

As chairman of his new commission, Hoover abandoned his Great Engineer persona for an unfettered assault on the bureaucratic spawn of the Roosevelt administration. The commission was particularly preoccupied with government management of water resources and public power generation. It generally favored the private sector. That was also its preference with respect to government medical services for veterans and military dependents. Even more controversial were its recommendations on legal services, one of which would have centralized all the adjudication functions of federal regulatory agencies in a single administrative court.[24]

Most of the commission's recommendations reached Congress only after the elections of 1954 had returned both houses to Democratic control, and most of the controversial recommendations were rejected. Many of those not requiring congressional approval were never implemented. But PACGO did its work more quickly than the Hoover Commission, and with the support of the president. While the commission was still drafting its report on water resources, Eisenhower, acting on a PACGO recommendation, created a cabinet-level committee on federal water and power policy, an area in which responsibility was fragmented among a multitude of agencies. The president's cabinet secretariat was also the fruit of a PACGO plan, as was the appointment of a presidential national security adviser. One of PACGO's more notable successes in Congress was the creation of the U.S. Department of Health, Education, and Welfare.[25]

Although some of his bureaucratic reorganization measures would require congressional approval, Eisenhower brought reorganization planning more completely into the presidential orbit than any of his predecessors. But organizational restructuring was only one way to assert presidential direction of the federal bureaucracy. Control of staffing was also vital, and for this purpose the Eisenhower administration invented Schedule C. By executive order, Ike created a personnel classification within the executive branch allowing political appointees rather than career civil service workers to occupy "confidential" or policymaking positions below the subcabinet level. The selection of Schedule C appointees was usually left to agency heads, but the agency heads themselves were presidential appointees. Although its reach was indirect, the White House was extending its influence to the upper-middle ranks of the civil service. Eisenhower appointees also used transfers and reductions in force to sideline bureaucrats deemed politically unreliable. Washington had not seen a Republican administration for twenty years, and only 6.6 percent of federal civil servants knew what it was like to work for a Republican president. The Eisenhower White House understandably wanted to seed the bureaucracy with its own loyalists.[26]

John F. Kennedy was no more trusting of the federal bureaucracy than his predecessor had been, but instead of attempting to police the permanent government through a cabinet secretariat and a staff of specialists, Kennedy dismantled the management apparatus that had distinguished Eisenhower's White House from all previous presidents'. Kennedy became his own chief of staff. Presidential assistants no longer specialized by function or policy area. A few, like Robert Kennedy and Theodore Sorensen, moved freely between domestic and foreign policy. Interdepartmental committees were dissolved. Kennedy thought that a White House organization with clearly defined areas of responsibility and lines of command would be unreceptive to policy innovation. Organization bred conservatism.[27]

Kennedy's aversion to the federal establishment grew stronger after the failure of the Bay of Pigs invasion, which he regarded as a disaster manufactured by the stodgy incompetence of the government's foreign policy and intelligence establishments. He would not entrust his own policy initiatives to existing agencies, and his staff would scout the existing agencies looking for emergent problems, not trusting bureaucratic careerists to acknowledge or resolve them. The White House would deal with them directly. If necessary the president would appoint a task force of experts drawn from outside the government to address a major policy initiative. At the same time, the presidential staff expanded because the president was reluctant to trust anyone outside the White House to handle serious business.[28] Operations too big to be run from the White House itself, such as the Peace Corps, got their own independent agencies. Innovative programs did not belong in big, bureaucratic cabinet departments, where they would be borne down by the deadweight of unshakable routine and entrenched mediocrity. The Kennedy administration foreshadowed a new antibureaucratic consensus in the making, one that would unite conservatives with neoliberals and members of the new left.[29]

The Conquest of Congress

In one respect, however, the Kennedy White House expanded on the staff organization designed by Eisenhower. Congressional relations became a more prominent function under Kennedy than under his predecessors, and its chief, Lawrence O'Brien, became one of a handful of presidential aides with direct access to the Oval Office.[30] Kennedy's emphasis on congressional relations went against the advice of two prestigious advisers. During the presidential transition period, Richard Neustadt and Clark Clifford had counseled the president-elect not to make too much of congressional relations. Their caution may have echoed the reluctance of Presidents Roosevelt and Truman to create a legislative liaison office within the White House for fear that it might "infect the presidency with congressional goals."[31] Clifford suggested that the vice president should be used to buffer the president from congressional demands for presidential contact and favor. Neustadt warned that an "over-organized" White House liaison operation—like the one that Eisenhower built in his first term—"tends to turn Presidential staffers into chore-boys for Congressmen and bureaucrats alike."[32]

FDR had conducted his business with Congress almost entirely through its party leaders and committee chairs. He was his own office of congressional liaison.[33] Although Eisenhower created an Office of Congressional Relations, he continued to meet weekly with the congressional leadership. His legislative relations staff had been formed, at least in part, to buffer him from the clamor of congressional politics, and he expected the party leadership in Congress to do the same. They were supposed to consult with their less senior colleagues so that Eisenhower would not have to listen to them himself. Eisenhower, says Kenneth Collier, was showing his "respect for congressional autonomy and the stature of the congressional leaders of the day." Direct presidential intervention in the business of Congress threatened to violate the separation of powers. Ike's newly formed congressional relations staff seemed to be in an uphill struggle against the Constitution. Bryce Harlow, who became head of congressional relations in 1958, described his job as an effort to "uncheck the checks and imbalance the balances." The fact that the Democrats controlled Congress for most of the Eisenhower administration added political adversity to the constitutional obstacles. Harlow thought it prudent not to show himself on Capitol Hill.[34]

Lawrence O'Brien had no reason to hide. Some members of Congress, in fact, complained that Kennedy's legislative liaison staff were entirely too visible on Capitol Hill, that they were insufficiently deferential and downright pushy when advancing the president's agenda against legislative resistance. Instead of becoming "chore-boys," as Neustadt anticipated, O'Brien and his aides converted the Office of Congressional Relations from "a buffer device to an important tool of presidential leadership."[35] O'Brien did not add to the size of his office, but he did reach out to form a network of legislative liaison specialists in executive agencies and departments so that his effective force of operatives increased substantially.[36]

By dealing with Congress through its leaders, FDR and Ike conceded it a measure of institutional integrity. Kennedy's elevation of the Office of Congressional Relations gave the White House the capacity to bypass the legislative leaders and treat Congress not as a single institution, but as a collection of self-interested political entrepreneurs. The president's emissaries to Capitol Hill could overcome legislative resistance to executive initiatives by "dangling rewards, threatening sanctions, directing the troops, unsticking legislative deals with side payments." The Office of Congressional Relations, in short, could exploit the advantage of presidential unity over congressional disunity—a structural difference between the executive and the legislature that may have been accentuated by historical change. Samuel Kernell has suggested that an era of "individual pluralism" broke down the institutional and partisan loyalties that once made Congress a more cohesive body than it is today. Even if presidents wanted to communicate with legislators through their leaders, the leaders might not be able to command the attention or compliance of their members. Individual members of Congress may share a common interest in defending and expanding the authority of their branch of government, but this collective interest in institutional power prevails only when congruent with the individual interest in getting reelected. The political interests of individual presidents, on the other hand, are almost always aligned with the empowerment of the presidency as an institution. "Presidents," as Terry Moe has pointed out, "have both the will and the ability to promote the power of their own institution, but individual legislators have neither and cannot be expected to promote the power of Congress as a whole in any coherent, forceful way."[37]

The White House Office of Congressional Relations even recruited individual members of Congress to promote the power of the presidency. Under Lyndon Johnson, speechwriters were added to the office staff to prepare material to be used by legislators friendly to the administration so that they would be able to plead its case or advance its policies more effectively than they could on their own. But such expansions of the presidential staff may also have helped to undermine the very unity that was supposed to be the principal advantage of the White House in its transactions with Congress. The president might be single-minded, but the presidency could speak with more than one voice. Johnson himself contributed to the disarray by appointing Lawrence O'Brien postmaster general while insisting that he also remain in charge of congressional relations for the White House. The emergence of a domestic policy staff under Joseph Califano only aggravated the problem. Califano's policy specialists frequently worked directly with members of Congress, leaving the Office of Congressional Relations in the dark and out of the picture.[38]

President Johnson himself was one of the administration's most determined congressional lobbyists, and members of Congress generally felt more comfortable dealing with LBJ than they had with JFK. Johnson, after all, was one of them. He had been the Democratic leader of the Senate; Kennedy had never held a position of leadership in Congress and never seemed a member of the Senate "club." Johnson's skill in dealing with the legislators, his unique position as successor to a martyred president, and his landslide election in 1964 all contributed to his success with Congress, and to the torrent of Great Society legislation that ensued.

His Office of Congressional Relations was a full participant in his assault on the legislative branch. Johnson briefed his congressional liaison officers about every telephone call he made to a member of Congress, and he expected round-the-clock reports on legislative victories and defeats. The office kept a detailed "favors file" to keep track of benefactions asked and those granted. It even covered legislators' attendance at White House social functions and occasions on which they had been photographed with LBJ. An administration support score was calculated and continuously updated for every member of Congress. Near the end of the Johnson administration, the Office of Congressional Relations requested responsibility for coordinating all of the president's appointments with members of Congress. Harold "Barefoot" Sanders, who had finally succeeded O'Brien as director of congressional relations, explained the request to President Johnson:

> Why is this important? Because we are usually the people who are asking the Congressmen to help the Administration. But if we are not the people who do the favors—and a Presidential appointment is about the biggest favor that can be done for a Congressman—we are less effective when we ask for favors.[39]

Johnson saw the point immediately and gave the OCR authority to oversee his meetings with members of Congress.

Although Johnson's party commanded a congressional majority, he could not count on the support of many southern conservatives for civil rights and social legislation. He and his congressional relations staff did not hesitate to approach Republicans. By the end of the Johnson administration, the president approved a new policy under which friendly Republicans would be notified in advance if the White House was about to announce a grant or contract in their constituencies. The fortunate Republicans would then be positioned to earn some credit for the favor shown their districts.[40] In its aggressive effort to solicit the support of individual legislators, the White House undermined not only the institutional integrity of Congress, but also the cohesiveness of congressional parties.

The Johnson administration's ability to reach across the separation of powers diminished after Democratic losses in the congressional elections of 1966 made Congress less responsive to the president. The voters seemed to want a more independent legislative branch. The president himself was increasingly preoccupied with the Vietnam War, and the Office of Congressional Relations was less able to hold its own with West Wing rivals who chose to deal with Congress directly. But the office itself had survived three presidents and become a fixture of the White House staff.

Survival, however, did not necessarily confer power on the office. Beginning in 1969, the presidency of Richard Nixon marked the onset of an extended period of divided government when the Capitol and the White House would belong to different parties. Congressional relations became a problem too big for one office; it was a concern for the entire presidential staff. Even after Jimmy Carter's 1976 election, when Democrats commanded both branches of government, Congress did not give way willingly to presidential leadership. Carter had won the presidency by running against a Washington establishment drifting in the backwash of Watergate. As a campaign strategy, it made sense. But Congress was the keystone of the Washington establishment, and it did not get on well with a president who had promised to fight pork-barrel projects, the legislature's bread and butter. And Watergate itself had engendered a diffuse mistrust of presidential leadership. After a year and a half of legislative disappointments, President Carter set up special task forces to coordinate the administration's congressional lobbying on critical policy initiatives, and he created a public liaison office to mobilize support outside of government for key elements of his legislative program. Once aroused, various interest groups were encouraged to push Congress toward the president's legislative priorities. Congressional relations had become too big a problem to be monopolized by the Office of Congressional Relations or its successor, the Office of Legislative Liaison.[41]

Congress represented an even more malign presence when White House and Capitol were held by different parties. Richard Nixon was the first president since 1848 to take the White House while his party lost both houses of Congress. Congressional relations were consigned to the second circle of power in the White House. Although the Nixon administration brought Bryce Harlow back to head the OCR, his relations with the president grew distant. To the White House inner circle, Congress was enemy territory. Congressional liaison staff who tried to represent the views of Congress within the White House risked the implication that they were disloyal to the administration. Bryce Harlow resigned. William Timmons, who succeeded him, was a step removed from the Oval Office, and without regular access to the president, he could hardly claim to be the voice of the president on Capitol Hill. Congressional telephone calls to the White House began to bypass Timmons to reach presidential intimates like John Ehrlichman and Robert Haldeman. Perhaps the greatest obstacle to effective congressional relations was the president himself. "Richard Nixon," according to Bryce Harlow, "was the type of individual who wanted to be

President with the least possible interference from other actors in the political system."[42]

Governing by Decree

The presidency offers broad opportunities to govern without interference. Executive orders, national security findings and directives, executive agreements, proclamations, reorganization plans, signing statements, and a changing arsenal of executive powers enable presidents to legislate unilaterally without consulting any legislators.[43] In effect, these mechanisms represent substitutes for the conduct of congressional relations, and the reliance on these modes of presidential policy making may help to explain why the business of legislative liaison has never been restored to the prominence that it had under Kennedy and Johnson.

Executive orders have a long history in the United States and have been the vehicles for a number of important U.S. government policies including the Louisiana Purchase; the annexation of Texas; the emancipation of the slaves; the internment of the Japanese during World War II; desegregation of the military; the initiation of affirmative action; and the creation of the Environmental Protection Agency, the Food and Drug Administration, and the Peace Corps.[44] Wars and national emergencies have most often provided presidents with the occasions for issuing executive orders. Abraham Lincoln relied almost exclusively on executive orders during the initial months of the Civil War. He used them to activate federal troops, purchase warships, and expand the size of the military. To cover the expenses he incurred, he advanced funds from the Treasury without congressional approval.[45] In the face of the emergency, Congress had no choice but to accept Lincoln's decisions and subsequently enacted legislation ratifying most of the president's actions. Political history repeated itself between 1940 and 1945, when President Franklin D. Roosevelt issued 286 executive orders related to military preparedness and the prosecution of World War II.[46] Many had sweeping implications for the lives of civilians. They created such agencies as the National War Labor Board, the Office of War Mobilization, the Office of Price Administration, the Office of Civilian Defense, the Office of Censorship, the War Food

Administration, and the Office of War Mobilization.[47] Other orders empowered government to seize private businesses engaged in defense production.[48] As in the Civil War, Congress had no choice but to unite behind the president in the face of national emergency. Congress, in fact, authorized such seizures under the War Labor Disputes Act of 1943, which allowed the president to take over privately owned factories and mines needed to supply military needs. After a brief decline after the defeat of the Axis powers, the volume of executive orders spiked once again during the Korean war.

In peacetime, executive orders became less numerous, but mere numbers can be misleading. Recent presidents have issued directives that are not called executive orders but have the same legal force—presidential memoranda, executive agreements, national security directives, signing statements, and presidential determinations. Numbers also tell us nothing about substance. A mere enumeration of executive orders does not reveal how consequential their content may be.[49] Recent presidents have developed a variety of new mechanisms to transform themselves into lawgivers, and their unilateral decisions cover the entire range of governmental concerns. Direct presidential policymaking—once reserved for times of war or national emergency—has now become a routine affair, even in routine times. Under the permanent state of war precipitated by the attacks of September 11, presidential government has emerged as a state within the state.

In foreign policy, unilateral presidential actions in the form of executive agreements have virtually replaced treaties as the nation's chief foreign policy instruments.[50] In domestic policy, executive orders have frequently served as vehicles for national antidiscrimination and affirmative action programs. FDR used an executive order to create the Fair Employment Practices Commission. Via executive orders, Truman decreed the desegregation of the armed forces and Kennedy prohibited banks from engaging in discriminatory lending practices. Johnson's order 11246 mandated minority hiring by government contractors. In his Philadelphia Plan, Richard Nixon went a step further by ordering federal contractors to establish specific goals for hiring minority workers on projects financed by the federal government.[51]

It is true that the president's power to carry out executive orders must be grounded in authority granted by the Constitution or federal statute, and the orders usually specify the statutory or constitutional foundation on which they rest. The courts have struck down executive orders judged to exceed the statutory powers of the president. In 1952, for example, the Supreme Court ruled against President Truman in *Youngstown Co. v. Sawyer* and held that he had no constitutional or statutory power to seize the nation's steel mills during the Korean War, even though a threatened steel strike would disrupt production of essential military materiel.[52] In 1995 President Clinton issued an executive order prohibiting federal agencies from contracting with firms that replaced striking employees with new workers. A bill designed to achieve the same result had failed to pass the Senate in 1994. The District of Columbia Circuit Court struck down the president's order, ruling that it violated the National Labor Relations Act, which gave employers the right to replace striking workers.[53]

The limits imposed by law still leave considerable latitude for presidential decrees. The courts have held that the statutory authority for executive orders need not be specifically granted but may be simply implied. President Nixon, for example, instituted wage and price controls in 1971 on the basis of the Trading With the Enemy Act.[54] The courts have also held that Congress might approve presidential action after the fact or, in effect, ratify presidential action through "acquiescence"—simply keeping quiet—or by continuing to vote appropriations for programs established by executive orders. Federal judges have upheld presidential orders even when they lie in what Supreme Court Justice Jackson called the "zone of twilight," where Congress and the president might hold concurrent authority and no statute prohibits presidential action.[55] In 1981, the Supreme Court invoked the "twilight zone" to uphold orders issued by presidents Carter and Reagan prohibiting certain types of claims by American businesses against Iranian assets in the United States that had been frozen during the Iranian hostage crisis of 1979–80.[56] The courts have also designated some areas, notably military policy, as inherently presidential, and allow presidents wide latitude to use executive decrees in those areas.

In theory, Congress could overturn an executive order simply by enacting a statute to negate it. Of course, the bill would have to command a majority sufficient to override a presidential veto. Congress would also have to be alert to the potential for presidential aggrandizement that lies beneath the legal language of executive orders. When Louis Brownlow drafted the order creating the Executive Office of the President in 1939, his intentional obfuscation concealed the powers inherent in a new executive unit that the order left unnamed. It would later emerge as the Office of Emergency Management, and it gave FDR the power to create on his own authority the armada of agencies that would run the country during World War II. Brownlow likened his handiwork to "a rabbit stowed in a hat," and "the little rabbit . . . was so disguised in small print, with no capital letters that it occasioned" scarcely any comment at all.[57] The task of finding out what powers lurk within an executive order is especially difficult, because the issuance of orders is not covered by the Administrative Procedure Act that governs the rule-making process for all the other agencies of the executive branch. In other words, the president is not required to give advance notice of an order or to hold public hearings about its substance. The procedures for issuing executive orders are specified only by executive orders.[58]

Presidents have frequently employed executive orders to specify the means or procedures that the executive branch will use to carry out the intent of Congress. Since the administration of Richard Nixon, however, the will of Congress and the will of the president have frequently fallen out of alignment with one another, and in the era of divided government, presidents have become more apt to exercise their powers of unilateral action in order to circumvent or frustrate the will of Congress.

The signing statement now serves as an instrument that substitutes executive for legislative intent. Like veto messages, signing statements come at the end of the legislative process, when the president decides whether or not to concur with the will of Congress. Presidents have issued signing statements from time to time ever since George Washington, although many of them were unrecorded and never became part of the legislative record. Others were innocuous benedictions issued in anticipation of a law's benefits for the nation and its citizens. Occasionally, however, presidents have used the signing statement to call attention to provisions of a bill that they regarded as improper or unconstitutional, even though they were willing to approve the statute in general.[59] President Truman, for example, issued a signing statement when he approved the 1946 Hobbs Anti-Racketeering Act. It outlined his interpretation of ambiguous sections of the statute and indicated how the federal government would implement the new law.[60]

Ronald Reagan's attorney general, Edwin Meese, along with Samuel Alito, then a Justice Department lawyer and now a Supreme Court Justice, receive the credit for converting the signing statement into a systematic mechanism of presidential direct action that frequently overrides the intent of Congress. Meese argued that carefully drafted signing statements would provide a warrant for executive agencies to act on the basis of the president's interpretation of a statute rather than guess at congressional intent. Perhaps even more important, the statement would become part of the statute's legislative history when the occasion arose for the courts to rule on its meaning. To establish the place of presidential signing statements in the official legislative record, Meese reached an agreement with the West Publishing Company to have them included in its authoritative texts on federal law.[61]

President Reagan began to issue detailed and carefully drawn signing statements—prepared by the Department of Justice—to reinterpret the bills that reached his desk from Congress. When signing the Safe Drinking Water Amendments of 1986, for example, Reagan interpreted sections of the act that appeared to require mandatory enforcement so that they would allow discretionary enforcement.[62] In other cases, Reagan's signing statements simply nullified portions of statutes enacted by Congress. In approving the 1988 Veterans Benefits Act, he declared that sections of the bill would violate the integrity of the executive branch and would not be enforced.[63] In the same year, Reagan signed a bill prohibiting construction on two pristine Idaho waterways but declared that one portion of the bill was unconstitutional and would not be enforced.[64]

The signing statement stratagem did not always succeed. When signing the Competition in Contracting Act in 1984, Reagan declared that portions of the law were unconstitutional and directed executive branch officials not to comply with them. But U.S. District Court Judge Harold Ackerman upheld the act and ruled that the president did not have the power to declare acts of Congress unconstitutional.[65] The Ninth Circuit Court of Appeals later reached a similar conclusion when it decided that the president did not have the authority to "excise or sever provisions of a bill with which he disagrees."[66]

Unfavorable judicial rulings posed no obstacle to the continued use of presidential signing statements to reshape the bills enacted by Congress. When George H. W. Bush signed the 1991 Civil Rights Act, he asserted in a signing statement that one of its provisions might be unfairly applied to businesses. In effect, he intervened in the act's legislative history to give direction to administrators charged with carrying out the law. During the same year, Bush signed a bill requiring that contractors building the Superconducting Supercollider in Texas pursue affirmative action in their hiring practices. The president's signing statement asserted that there was no valid basis for affirmative action in this case—even though the courts at the time had held otherwise—and directed the Secretary of Energy to ignore the affirmative action requirements.[67] Bush had opposed the passage of the bill. Now he nullified it, but without giving Congress the opportunity to override a presidential veto.

Presidents Reagan and Bush used signing statements for mostly conservative ends—to limit the scope of affirmative action programs, to block business regulation, to reduce the impact of environmental programs, and to thwart new labor laws. President Clinton demonstrated that signing statements could just as easily serve progressive causes. Faced with Republican-controlled congresses for six of his eight years in office, Clinton used his signing statements to neutralize the conservative crusade proclaimed in the 1994 Contract with America. In 1996, for example, Congress enacted a Defense Appropriations Bill with a provision that required the discharge of any member of the military who was HIV-positive. President Clinton signed the appropriations bill but asserted that this provision was unconstitutional. He ordered the Justice Department not to defend the HIV ban in court if it was challenged, which in effect represented an announcement that the provision would not be enforced. For Democratic and Republican presidents alike, the signing statement has served as a weapon for frustrating congressional initiatives. The courts have added the weight of judicial opinion to presidential signing statements by referring to them when interpreting the meaning of statutes.[68]

Presidential use of signing statements to challenge legislative provisions has grown sharply during the George W. Bush years. President Reagan used signing statements to attack 71 legislative provisions, and President Clinton used signing statements to question 105 provisions. By the end of 2005, with three years still remaining of his second term, President Bush had already challenged 500 legislative provisions with his signing statements.[69] Ed Meese's contrivance has become a full-blown instrument of presidential power.

While useful to presidents, signing statements are reactive—responses to congressional initiatives. President Clinton, however, faced a conservative Congress that refused to act on his administration's legislative agenda in matters of environmental protections, support for organized labor, expansions of affirmative action programs, and government regulation. The legislators were also skeptical about Clinton's effort to shift the country's foreign policy toward a multilateralism that envisioned cooperation with international organizations like the UN and collegial relations with allies. According to conservative legal scholar Todd Gaziano, Clinton tried to enact his administration's legislative program by executive order, thereby avoiding the inconvenience of having to consult a hostile Congress.[70] Clinton himself seemed to acknowledge the shift toward unilateral action. In an interview given shortly after the Republicans took control of Congress, Clinton observed, "I had overemphasized in my first two years . . . the importance of legislative battles as opposed to the other things that the president might be doing. And I think now we have a better balance of both using the Presidency as a bully pulpit and the President's power of the Presidency to *do* things, actually accomplish things, and . . . not permitting the Presidency to be defined only by relations with Congress."[71]

Clinton would issue more than thirty executive orders relating to the environment and natural resources alone. Executive Order 13061 establishing the American Heritage Rivers Initiative was designed to protect several major river systems from commercial and industrial development, but also to override the land use powers of state and local governments. When Congress failed to approve the administration's Children's Environmental Protection Act, Clinton incorporated a number of its provisions into an executive order he issued on Earth

Day.[72] Another Clinton order, Environmental Justice for Minority Populations, required all federal agencies to show that their plans and projects took into account implications for environmental justice. An accompanying presidential memorandum held that existing civil rights legislation empowered federal agencies to revoke grants to state and local projects whose adverse environmental consequences disproportionately affected members of minority groups.[73] During his last days in the White House, President Clinton issued orders closing off millions of acres in ten Western states to residential and commercial development. The orders declared that the lands were protected national monuments under the 1906 Antiquities Act.

During the 2000 presidential campaign, George W. Bush denounced Clinton's high-handed seizure of western lands. But in 2003, when western conservatives challenged Clinton's executive order before the Supreme Court, President Bush sent his solicitor general, Theodore Olson, to defend the authority of presidents to issue such orders. Olson suggested, in fact, that the Court had no legal basis to question the orders issued by Clinton.[74] Clinton had demonstrated that an activist president with an ambitious policy agenda could achieve a substantial measure of success without a congressional majority. George W. Bush, elected by the thinnest of margins, did not want to surrender the presidential capacity to do the same.

President Bush issued more than forty executive orders during his first year in office. One of his first prohibited the use of federal funds to support any international family planning organizations that provided abortion counseling services. It also imposed limits on the use of embryonic stem cells in federally funded research. But the terrorist attacks eight months after Bush's inauguration gave his administration an intense new focus fired by anger, grief, and fear. By executive order, the president created the Office of Homeland Security and not long afterward issued another order authorizing the creation of military tribunals to try noncitizens accused of participating in terrorist acts against the United States. Other orders froze the American assets of those associated with terrorism, provided expedited citizenship for foreign nationals serving in the U.S. military, and ordered the CIA to use all means possible to oust President Saddam Hussein of Iraq, who stood accused of plotting terrorist strikes.

Some of President Bush's orders were issued and carried out in secret. Soon after the 9/11 terrorist attacks, the president issued national security directives authorizing the National Security Agency (NSA) to eavesdrop on Americans and others inside the United States who communicated via telephone or e-mail with persons outside the United States.[75] The NSA was authorized to engage in what is sometimes called "data mining," a process of sifting through millions of calls and e-mails searching for words and phrases that might signal terrorist involvement. Under the terms of the relevant statute, the Foreign Intelligence Surveillance Act, the government is required to obtain warrants from a special court, the Foreign Intelligence Surveillance Court, which holds secret sessions at the Justice Department. Normally, such a warrant would be sought by the FBI, not the NSA, which is authorized by statute to engage only in operations outside the United States. President Bush, however, decided to bypass statutory restrictions in order to make use of the NSA's superior electronic information-gathering capabilities. Encountering a firestorm of protest when the existence of the secret orders was leaked to the press in 2005, President Bush and his advisors asserted that the president had acted properly.

The president said he based his actions on Article II of the Constitution and Congress's 2001 resolution giving the president the authority to use "all necessary and appropriate force against those nations, organizations, or persons he determines planned, authorized, committed, or aided" the September 11 attacks against the United States. A 2006 Justice Department memorandum asserted that the president's constitutional position was supported by the *Federalist Papers*, numerous court cases, the writings of Republican and Democratic presidents, and many scholarly papers.[76] Critics, however, contended that the president's logic seemed to suggest that there were really no restrictions upon presidential power. Georgetown law professor Jonathon Turley said, "There's no limiting principle to that theory."[77] While the president denied that he was claiming unilateral powers, his own advisors painted a different picture. Presidential legal adviser John Yoo said in a 2001 memorandum that no statute enacted by Congress "can place any limits on the president's determinations as to any terrorist threat, the amount of military force to be used in response, or the method, timing, and nature of the response."[78] Yoo is widely believed to have written the legal justification cited by the president for his secret domestic eavesdropping orders.

Bush's executive orders were not confined to the national security arena. Unable to overcome congressional opposition to stepping up domestic energy exploration, the president signed an executive order, closely following a recommendation from the American Petroleum Institute, that freed energy companies from a number of federal regulations. Another executive order created a task force charged with expediting the issuance of permits for energy-related projects. Still another presidential directive effectively prohibited federal agencies from requiring union-only work crews on federally funded projects. Enforcement of the order was enjoined by the U.S. District Court, but the Court of Appeals held that Bush had the authority to issue the order.[79]

Like his predecessors, Bush used signing statements to undermine legislation that he was unable to block. For instance, in the course of signing campaign finance reform legislation in March 2002, Bush declared that the bill was "far from perfect," and implied that the provisions of the bill were "nonseverable," meaning that if the federal courts declared any portion of the bill unconstitutional, the entire bill would be rendered void.[80] The actual bill contains no such provision, but Bush was seeking to write his interpretation into the legislative history to increase the likelihood that if some future federal court is dissatisfied with any one portion of the law it will strike down the entire measure.

Other Bush signing statements were designed to thwart congressional efforts to intrude into the president's Iraq policies and his war on terror. In 2003, for example, in signing legislation creating an inspector general to oversee the U.S. administration governing Iraq, the president declared that this official should "refrain" from audits and investigations into matters involving intelligence and counterintelligence.[81] The legislation enacted by Congress contained no such limitation. That same year, when he signed the legislation creating the 9/11 Commission, the president indicated that, while the law contained requirements for the executive branch to disclose sensitive information, he would interpret this requirement "in a manner consistent with the president's constitutional authority to withhold information" for national security reasons. In other words, he would not feel compelled to disclose anything he did not wish to disclose.

In a similar vein, in 2004, Congress reorganized the nation's intelligence community and established rules governing the flow of information among intelligence agencies. When he signed the law, the president asserted that these rules were "advisory."[82] More recently, Congress enacted legislation prohibiting the cruel or inhumane treatment of prisoners held by the United States. This so-called "torture amendment," sponsored by Senator McCain, had been opposed by President Bush. Faced, however, with strong congressional support for the legislation, the president invited McCain to the Oval Office and announced that he planned to sign the bill "to make clear to the world that this government does not torture."[83] After he signed the bill, however, the president issued a statement asserting that the legislation would be interpreted "in a manner consistent with the constitutional authority of the president to supervise the unitary executive branch and as commander in chief and consistent with the constitutional limitations on judicial power." In other words, the president was asserting that the legislation would not prevent him from doing whatever he wanted. Senator Lindsey Graham (R-SC) pointed out that, "If you take this to its logical conclusion, because during war the Commander in Chief has an obligation to protect us, any statute on the books could be summarily waived."[84]

Congress is not entirely unaware of the manner in which presidents have been using signing statements to refashion the meaning of the legislation that it passed. This issue was repeatedly raised by Senator Kennedy during the 2006 hearings to confirm Judge Samuel Alito's Supreme Court nomination. And, as early as 2002, Congress attached a provision to the appropriation bill for the Justice Department requiring the president to notify Congress concerning the Department's nonenforcement of laws on the grounds that they were pronounced unconstitutional in presidential signing statements. President Bush signed the bill—and then issued a signing statement. It said that he would provide Congress with the information requested but only "in a manner consistent with the constitutional authority of the President to supervise the unitary Executive Branch and to withhold information the disclosure of which could impair foreign relations, the national security, the deliberative processes of the Executive Branch, or the performance of the Executive's constitutional duties."[85] A presidential signing statement restricted the full disclosure of signing statements.

Regulatory Review

Whenever Congress passes a law, the agency responsible for implementing it may have to write hundreds of regulations to carry out the will of Congress. A statute to improve air quality, for example, may delegate to the Environmental Protection Agency the power to draw up and enforce dozens of rules and regulations that will govern the actions of corporations, individual citizens, federal agencies, and units of state or local government whose conduct may affect the concentration of pollutants in the atmosphere. In making rules, federal agencies must follow a system of rules themselves. They require public notice of a proposed rule by publication in the *Federal Register,* public hearings, and appeals. Once the process is complete and the resulting rules are published in the *Code of Federal Regulations,* administrative rules carry the force of law and effect of law and will be enforced by the federal courts.

Some statutes are quite detailed and leave agencies with little discretion. Frequently, however, Congress issues a broad statement of legislative intent and leaves the details to an administrative agency.[86] A classic example is the 1914 Federal Trade Commission Act, which outlaws "unfair methods of competition," but fails to specify what is unfair. The Commission was left to define its own standards of fairness. In the words of administrative law scholar Kenneth Culp Davis, Congress typically says to an administrative agency, "Here is the problem: deal with it."[87]

Although Congress delegates discretion to administrative agencies, presidents have found ways to appropriate it and use it for their own ends. The invention of "regulatory review" during the Nixon administration and its subsequent expansion have given presidents a mechanism to engage in rule making without significant participation of the lawmakers in Congress. The immediate occasion for this expansion of presidential power was the creation of the Environmental Protection Agency in 1970. The new agency's regulations represented alarming increases in costs for American industry. Nixon responded to business concerns by establishing a "quality of life" review process within the newly renamed Office of Management and Budget. Nixon required the EPA to submit proposed regulations for month-long review prior to their publication in the *Federal Register*. OMB in turn circulated the proposals to other agencies for comment, mainly to allow the measures' adversaries more time to mobilize the opposition. In 1974, President Ford issued an executive order formalizing this review process. Ford required that the OMB subject proposed regulations to an "inflationary impact analysis" before their publication in the *Register*. President Carter issued a new executive order replacing this procedure with a requirement that the OMB analyze the cost of major proposed regulations, evaluate plausible alternatives, and approve the least cumbersome form of regulation.[88]

The Nixon, Ford, and Carter efforts fell short of full-blown presidential control of the rule-making process. Although agencies might follow the procedures mandated by the president, in the end they were not obligated to change their proposed regulations to comply with the president's policy goals. Congress paid little heed to the procedures for regulatory review because they seemed to be mere symbolic gestures to placate important constituency groups. But these initial presidential regulatory initiatives established precedents and prototypes for more determined efforts in the Reagan administration and its successors to bring federal regulation under presidential control. Congress itself unwittingly contributed to the expansion of presidential power in 1979 by enacting the Paperwork Reduction Act, which created the Office of Information and Regulatory Affairs (OIRA) within OMB. Congress was responding to business complaints that companies were spending too much time and money on the forms and records required by government regulations. Through OIRA, OMB was authorized to monitor and limit the impositions of regulatory agencies on the businesses and industries that they regulated.[89]

A month after taking office in 1981, Reagan issued Executive Order 12291 establishing a process for centralized presidential oversight of agency rule making. The order required that regulatory agencies use cost-benefit analysis to justify proposed regulations. Rules were not to be adopted unless the potential benefits to society outweighed the potential costs. To prove that they had complied with this mandate, agencies were now required to prepare a formal Regulatory Impact Analysis (RIA), which was to include an assessment of the costs and benefits of any proposed rule, as well as an evaluation of alternative regulations that might impose lower costs. OIRA was responsible for evaluating these regulatory impact analyses. Agencies were prohibited from publishing proposed rules without OIRA clearance, and they were required to incorporate OIRA revisions into the rules that they eventually published. OIRA could block the publication and implementation of any rule that it disapproved.

In effect, the Reagan administration used the statutory cover of the Paperwork Reduction Act to achieve a unilateral extension of White House power. The intention was not simply to reduce red tape for regulated business firms. OIRA became the instrument through which the White House seized control of the rule-making process, so that it could block or amend rules at will. Since rule making is essential to the implementation of virtually every statute, the presidential establishment had not only asserted its control of the rule-making process, but also enlarged on its constitutional role in the legislative process by dictating the way in which laws would be implemented. The administration quickly used the regulatory review process to curtail the impact of federal environmental and health and safety legislation. It blocked the promulgation of new rules by the EPA and the Occupational Safety and Health Administration (OSHA).[90]

During the eight years of the Reagan administration, an average of eighty-five proposed rules were returned to agencies each year for reconsideration or withdrawal.[91] While this figure represents only a small fraction of the rules proposed by federal agencies, the rejected rules naturally tended to be controversial and therefore politically important. Reagan's opponents in Congress denounced the president's intervention in the rule-making process but were able to wrest only minor concessions from the White House.[92] Administrators in the regulatory agencies raised few obstacles to the new regime in rule making. Under the Civil Service Reform Act of 1978, presidents gained greater control over the assignment of senior bureaucrats to the top positions in federal agencies, and the Reaganites had taken full advantage of this opportunity to fill strategic positions with administrators sympathetic to the president's objectives.[93] The clarity of those objectives left little room for bureaucratic improvisation, especially since agency compliance was regularly monitored.[94] Given presidential control over budgets, staffing, and the general quality of agency life, most career bureaucrats find cooperation more sensible than struggle with the White House.

In 1985, President Reagan further expanded presidential control over rule making. By executive order, he required every regulatory agency to report annually to OIRA its objectives for the coming year. OIRA would assess each agency's regulatory agenda for consistency with the president's program and notify agencies of modifications needed to bring their plans into alignment with the views of the president. This new order went beyond Reagan's initial regulatory review program. Executive Order 12291 had authorized the White House to review rules after they were proposed. Its sequel enabled the White House to intervene before rules were drafted.[95] Reagan's order forced agencies to take account of presidential goals and not just congressional intent when formulating the rules that carried legislation into effect. With the stroke of a pen, Reagan had expanded the White House role in rule making and enhanced its power to determine what the will of Congress would mean in practice.

President George H. W. Bush continued Reagan's practices, but shifted much of the responsibility for regulatory review from OIRA to the "Council on Competitiveness" headed by Vice President Dan Quayle. Shifting responsibility from a statutory agency to a purely presidential office further reduced the ability of congressional opponents to interfere with presidential control of the review process.[96] President Bill Clinton abolished the Competitiveness Council shortly after taking office in 1993, but instead of retreating from White House regulatory review, Clinton extended presidential control of regulatory agencies by directing OIRA to issue "regulatory prompts"—orders instructing agencies to adopt particular regulations. Whereas Reagan had used regulatory review to prevent the imposition of rules to which he objected, Clinton took the further step of requiring agencies to formulate rules that he wanted.[97] Elena Kagan, a law professor and official in the Clinton White House, explains that Clinton felt hemmed in by congressional opposition during most of his presidential tenure. Determined to make his mark in domestic policy, Clinton used the bureaucratic rule-making process to accomplish unilaterally what he was unable to achieve through Congress.[98]

In 1993, Clinton issued Executive Order 12866 to replace Reagan's two orders regarding regulatory review. Clinton preserved the essential components of Reagan's regulatory oversight system. He required agencies to submit major regulations to OIRA for review, and he extended the use of cost-benefit analysis for the evaluation of proposed rules. He also continued the annual regulatory planning process created by Reagan. But Clinton added two new elements to the regulatory review process. First, he extended regulatory review to independent agencies like the Social Security Administration.[99] President Clinton did not require the independent agencies to submit proposed rules for review, but he did order them to submit their annual regulatory agendas to OIRA, which reviewed them for their consistency with the president's priorities. Although Congress had placed the independent agencies outside the orbit of presidential power, Clinton was trying to bring them under presidential control.

More important in the short run, Clinton's new order asserted that the president had full authority to direct the rule-making activities of executive agencies, not just to block rules to which he objected, but to order the adoption of rules that advanced the administration's policy objectives. Clinton's order said only that conflicts between agencies and OIRA over proposed rules would be resolved by presidential decision, but soon after issuing the order, Clinton began issuing formal orders directing executive agencies to propose for public comment rules that the president had conceived. On 107 occasions, Clinton ordered regulatory agencies to publish in the *Federal Register* rules that originated in the White House. Presidential rule making covered a wide variety of topics. Clinton ordered the Food and Drug Administration to issue rules designed to restrict the marketing of tobacco products to children. The White House and the FDA then collaborated for several months on nearly one thousand pages of new regulations affecting tobacco manufacturers and vendors.[100] In other cases, the president devised rules for the Departments of Labor, Agriculture, Health and Human Services, Interior, and Treasury gov-

210 / PRESIDENTIAL POWER

erning water pollution, the inspection of imported foods, patients' rights, and assault pistols. In principle, agencies might have objected to these presidential directives and appealed to Congress for support, but Clinton did not mandate any rules that he expected the agencies to reject.[101]

Clinton thus avoided agency resistance and recourse to Congress. In the process, however, he was building a body of precedent that would empower the president to take full control of the regulatory process. After the Republicans captured Congress in 1994, Clinton turned more frequently to administrative directives to achieve his legislative objectives. Administrative rule making allowed him to legislate on matters of health care, parental leave, gun control, and environmental protection without the inconvenience of consulting a hostile Congress. Republicans denounced Clinton's actions as a usurpation of congressional power.[102] But after winning the White House in 2000, President George W. Bush went right on exercising the powers that Clinton had seized. In fact, Bush's OIRA administrator, John D. Graham, issued a memorandum announcing that the president's chief of staff expected federal agencies to "implement vigorously" the principles and procedures outlined in former president Clinton's Executive Order 12866.[103]

During the first seven months of Bush's presidency, OIRA returned twenty major rules to agencies for further analysis.[104] One was a rule drafted by the National Highway Traffic Safety Administration (NHTSA) to implement legislation enacted by Congress requiring tire pressure monitoring devices on new cars. The auto industry objected to the cost of implementing the NHTSA's proposal. OIRA, responding to the industry complaints, told NHTSA to study alternative rules and thereby blocked the will of Congress. At the same time Bush continued Clinton's use of presidential "prompt letters" instructing agencies to issue new regulations. Five such letters went out during Bush's first year in office.[105] One prompt encouraged OSHA to require employers to use automated external defibrillators to prevent heart attack deaths. Another told HHS to require that food labels disclose trans-fatty acid content.[106] Since both agencies were eager to adopt the presidentially mandated regulations, it appears that Bush is following the Clinton example of ordering agencies to undertake actions they favor in order to establish precedents that will legitimate the power of the presidential prompt. OIRA chief Graham may have been hinting at broader use of the president's regulatory powers when he announced that the administration would welcome suggestions from citizens and groups concerning the abolition of existing rules as well as proposals for new rules. The scope of OIRA's influence became evident in 2003 when several members of Congress, concerned with the expansion of presidential control of agency rule making, asked the General Accounting Office (GAO) to prepare an assessment of OIRA's role. The GAO examined eighty-five important rules adopted by federal agencies during the prior year. The study found that OIRA had exercised significant influence on the rules adopted by federal agencies in twenty-five of these eighty-five cases.[107] In several instances, representatives of interest groups affected by proposed rules had met directly with OMB and OIRA officials to press their cases, thereby circumventing the agencies and Congress. The lobbying community, ever sensitive to Washington's shifting political currents, apparently detected the new configurations of bureaucratic power.

Through the process of regulatory review, successive presidents have built up a significant capacity to reshape legislation and even to achieve significant policy goals without any congressional action at all. They have achieved this success with surprisingly little media scrutiny or public awareness. Few Americans have heard of the OIRA, and the media pay little attention to the agency. But the obscure office buried in OMB has added substantially to the power of the president.

The Unilateral Presidency

The Constitution intended that presidents should govern collaboratively, and for much of our history, presidents have been willing cooperators. They have foresworn the use of the veto for reasons of mere policy. Only fundamental constitutional objections would entitle them to assert their own convictions over the will of Congress. Nor would presidents counter Congress by appealing to the people over the heads of the legislators. In fact, they hardly ever discussed matters of policy with the public at large. Abraham Lincoln, addressing crowds from his train on the way to his inauguration, confined himself to expressions of good will and gratitude rather than speaking out on the issues that had carried the nation to civic rupture and the verge of sectional warfare. It would be inappropriate, he said, to offer his views on matters likely to require presidential attention.[108] In the ritual of inauguration itself, presidents act out their historical deference to Congress and courts. The Chief Justice intones the oath of office, and the president-elect repeats the words. The Capitol steps, not the White House, serve as the platform for the inaugural address. Originally the speech was delivered to Congress in its own chambers, not to the public out of doors.

The ceremony is an echo of a presidency that has passed. Since the turn of the twentieth century, presidents have routinely attempted to circumvent the constitutional check of an obstructive Congress by carrying their cases directly to the people, and a few have tried to mobilize party—an institution outside the Constitution—to tilt the balance among branches in their favor. Lately, however, presidents have chosen to go it alone rather than going public or going partisan. Executive orders, signing statements, regulatory review, and a miscellany of proclamations, presidential findings, and executive agreements have endowed presidents with a capacity for unilateral action unforeseen in the Constitution.

So long as he acts within the executive branch, the president is on home ground, where he is apt to meet little opposition and few surprises. Going public has become a chancy tactic, because it entails dependence on newspapers and networks that get some of their best mileage with readers and viewers from the exposure of wrongdoing in high places, presidential or otherwise. Besides, Congress has learned how to go public itself. In televised hearings, it has staged episodes of high political drama which usually culminate in the wreckage of a president or an entire administration. Reliance on party provides today's presidents with little security and scant leverage. It is precisely the decline of party that makes today's presidential campaign a candidate-centered trial by ordeal that demands larger-than-life egos and ambitions.

Going it alone—the executive strategy—is not fault-free. On a few occasions, the federal courts have vetoed presidents' unilateral initiatives. The Supreme Court invalidated Truman's seizure of the steel mills, and a lower federal court nullified Clinton's order barring the hiring of replacements for striking workers. In theory, Congress could overturn presidential orders by statute. But such things happen only rarely. The courts have generally deferred to presidents. They have upheld only a small fraction of challenges to executive orders, and although members of Congress may denounce presidential decrees, the lawmakers rarely step beyond rhetoric to reverse a presidential order. In 1999, Congress prohibited the Department of Education from carrying out an executive order to administer national education tests.[109]

In 2000, Congress went a step further. In response to President Clinton's aggressive regulatory review program, the Republican-controlled Congress passed the Congressional Review Act, which required federal agencies to submit all proposed regulations for congressional review sixty days before they were to take effect. One of the procedures created under the law allows the House and Senate to pass a joint resolution of disapproval, which not only voids the regulation but also prohibits the agency from subsequently issuing any substantially similar rule. The first test of the act came after Clinton had left office. In the early weeks of the Bush administration, Congress passed a joint resolution repealing an ergonomics standard that had been supported by the Clinton administration and adopted by the Occupational Safety and Health Administration (OSHA). President Bush, who opposed the standard, signed the resolution, and the ergonomics standard was voided. Congress was successful in this case only because Clinton was no longer president. Had he still been in the White House, he would almost certainly have vetoed the resolution. Indeed, one reason Clinton had been willing to sign CRA into law in the first place was that the president retained the power to veto any action taken by Congress under the statute's authority.

Perhaps Congress could respond more vigorously to the president's unilateral policymaking than it has so far. Certainly a Congress prepared to impeach a president should have the mettle to overturn his administrative directives. But the president has the initiative in such struggles, and Congress is on the defensive. The framers of the Constitution intended that "energy" should reside in the executive.[110] The president acts and Congress reacts. The president, moreover, acts single-handedly, while Congress must cope with its internal divisions. It suffers, as Terry Moe has observed, from a collective action problem.

Its members are likely to be more sensitive to the substance of a president's actions and its effects upon their constituents than to the general implications of presidential power for the long-term vitality of their institution.[111] Congressional leaders may have more reason than their followers to tend to the power of Congress as a whole, but today's legislative leaders coax and cajole more than they command their fellow partisans. Congress has yet to solve the problem of the administrative presidency. The president may not be able to govern in defiance of Congress, but he can govern without it.

In the early months of 2002, fears of bioterrorism forced the evacuation of Capitol Hill offices and put lawmakers out of business for several weeks. The president and his staff governed the country, issuing orders and decrees, while Congress stopped functioning. The situation was extraordinary, and Congress reasserted its prerogatives as soon as the anthrax scare subsided. But the weeks of silence on Capitol Hill may have been a portent of politics to come, when the president rules and Congress watches.

6

Presidential War Powers

I N WAR AND PEACE, the management of America's relations with the outside world stands at the heart of presidential power. Presidential power in foreign relations is derived from Article II of the United States Constitution, which makes the president commander in chief of the nation's military forces and gives the chief executive the power to negotiate treaties, to recognize foreign emissaries, and to appoint ambassadors and consular officials. As is often the case, the precise meaning of these constitutional powers has been defined through practice and precedent. The Constitution also gives Congress important military and foreign policy powers, including the power to declare war, to raise armies, to regulate commerce with foreign nations and, in the case of the Senate, the power to ratify treaties and concur in the appointment of ambassadors. The Constitution, as legal historian Edward Corwin observed, is "an invitation to struggle" for the power to control American foreign policy.[1] John Jay, however, observed in *Federalist 64* that the president has a number of advantages in this struggle. The president is a unitary actor, with better access to information and a greater capacity for secrecy and decisiveness than the Congress.[2] Over the course of more than two centuries, moreover, successive American presidents, beginning with George Washington, have labored diligently to make their office the dominant force in American foreign and security policy and to subordinate Congress's role in this realm.

In 1793, for example, Washington initially accepted the French ambassador, "Citizen" Genet, and then later demanded his recall. In both instances, Washington deliberately refrained from consulting Congress.[3] During the same year, Washington issued a proclamation of American neutrality when war broke out between Great Britain and France, again without congressional authorization.[4] In 1796, Washington refused to accede to congressional demands for documents relating to the negotiation of the Jay Treaty. He declared that, in his judgment, the papers were "of a nature that did not permit disclosure at this time."[5] Indeed, Washington was so determined to establish the primacy of the presidency in the realm of foreign policy that he objected vigorously to something as minor as a 1792 House resolution congratulating the French on their new constitution. Although the resolution was no more than a rhetorical gesture, Washington complained to his secretary of state, Thomas Jefferson, that Congress was seeking to "invade the executive."[6]

Washington's efforts to assert the primacy of the presidency in foreign policy were famously defended by Alexander Hamilton. In 1793, writing under the pseudonym Pacificus in a series of articles in the *Gazette of the United States*, Hamilton argued that the direction of foreign policy was inherently an executive function.[7] Hamilton asserted moreover that the federal Constitution gave the president the power of initiative in foreign policy. The specific grants of power in the Constitution and their logical implications, he wrote, gave the executive the right to "determine the condition of the nation . . . [and, if necessary] . . . to establish an antecedent state of things."[8] In other words, the president was free to undertake actions based upon his judgment of the national interest, and if he deemed it appropriate to confront the Congress and other governmental agencies with faits accomplis.[9] This is, as we saw in the previous chapter, not so different from the position taken by President Bush's legal advisors with regard to presidential power in the war on terror.

Indeed, the actions of subsequent presidents, from John Adams and Thomas Jefferson to Bill Clinton and George W. Bush, have often been consistent with Hamilton's vision of executive power. Thus, America's second president, John Adams, dispatched a peace commission to France in 1799 despite the opposition of Congress and even the disapproval of most his own cabinet members.[10] In a similar vein, America's third president, Thomas Jefferson, negotiated with France for the purchase of Louisiana and issued what today would be called an executive order consummating the bargain. Although Jefferson had previously condemned Hamilton's assertions of executive primacy in foreign affairs, as president Jefferson presented the Congress with a Hamiltonian fait accompli to which it gave its acquiescence.[11]

Nearly two centuries later in 1994, America's forty-second president, Bill Clinton, issued executive orders that provided Mexico with a $43 billion package of loans, including support from the International Monetary Fund and the International Bank of Settlements, to prevent the total collapse of the Mexican peso.[12] Congress had already rejected Clinton's request for a Mexican loan package. The president, however, believed that a Mexican economic crash would be disastrous for American economic interests and acted accordingly. In 2001, in the wake of terrorist attacks in New York and Washington, America's forty-third president, George W. Bush, issued executive orders that unleashed America's military might against the Taliban regime in Afghanistan, created secret military tribunals for the prosecution of suspected foreign terrorists, and froze tens of millions of dollars in foreign assets in the United States. Congress was barely consulted regarding any of these matters or the president's orders to the National Security Agency authorizing domestic eavesdropping. For its part, as we shall see, the U.S. Supreme Court has generally supported presidents' Hamiltonian view of their role in foreign policy. In 1936 Justice Sutherland, citing John Marshall, declared in the landmark *Curtis-Wright* case that the president was the "sole organ of the federal government in the field of international relations."[13]

Despite presidential efforts to monopolize foreign and security policy, from the time of the nation's founding, Congress also sought to play a major role in both areas. Writing in response to Hamilton's Pacificus letters, James Madison, using the pseudonym Helvidius, argued that the president's powers in foreign affairs were instrumental only. That is, it was Congress's constitutional role to determine the substance and direction of American foreign policy, while the task of the president was limited to implementing the will of the legislature.[14] The Constitution, as noted above, assigns to Congress specific powers in the realm of foreign affairs, including the power to declare war, the power to raise armies, and the power to regulate foreign commerce. On the basis of this constitutional authority, Congress has enacted numerous pieces of trade legislation; authorized the recruitment, training, and equipment of military forces; and on at least one occasion—the War of 1812—declared war over the objections of the president. Not unlike presidents, Congress has occasionally sought to use its constitutionally mandated powers to claim additional powers as well. For example, when Congress declared war against Spain in 1897, it included recognition of the independence of Cuba in its resolution, even though President McKinley was opposed to recognition of the Cuban insurgent government.[15]

Through its general legislative powers, moreover, Congress can exercise broad influence over foreign policy. Congress may, for example, refuse to appropriate funds for presidential actions it deems to be unwise or inappropriate. Thus, in 1796, the House of Representatives was asked to appropriate funds to implement the Jay Treaty. Opponents of the treaty demanded that the House be given all papers and records pertaining to the negotiating process—a demand rejected by President Washington. The House narrowly approved funding but accompanied its acquiescence with a resolution affirming its right to refuse appropriations for the implementation of any treaty to which a majority of its members objected.[16] On several occasions over the years, the House has indeed refused to appropriate funds needed to implement treaties negotiated by the president and ratified by the Senate.[17]

This power of the purse also extends to military action. Not only does Congress have the constitutional power to declare war, but under its general legislative powers it must appropriate the funds needed to support military activities. In *Federalist 69*, Hamilton argues that Congress's power of the purse provides it with an ultimate check on the president's power as commander in chief.[18] This principle was illustrated during the Reagan administration when Congress enacted the so-called Boland Amendment, which prohibited the president from using any funds to provide military support for right-wing "Contra" guerilla forces in the civil war then raging in the nation of Nicaragua. The administration's response was to seek funds from Saudi Arabia, the Sultan of Brunei, and even from private individuals. This attempt to circumvent Congress's authority sparked the 1986 congressional Iran-Contra investigations, which led to criminal convictions for several high-ranking administration officials. In 2007, congressional Democrats threatened to use their power of the purse\to gain some leverage over the Bush administration's Iraq policies.

If foreign policy entailed only matters of trade, recognition, international accords, and other peacetime pursuits, the constitutional struggle between the president and Congress might have gone on indefinitely without any conclusive resolution. Unfortunately, however, throughout the nation's history, war and military affairs have been central foci of American foreign policy. Although the United States has fought only five formally declared wars, American armed forces have been involved in hundreds of military actions and "small wars" in every corner of the world.[19] America's first small war, the 1801 naval campaign against the Barbary States, involved a handful of ships and generated few casualties. Other "small wars" have been quite large. American military action in Korea and Vietnam required the mobilization of hundreds of thousands of troops and resulted in tens of thousands of casualties. But, whether declared or undeclared, large or small, war has been the crucible of presidential power. During the nineteenth and early twentieth centuries, wartime expansion of presidential power tended to be temporary, generally limited to the duration of the war. In some respects, as we shall see, war mobilized the populace and empowered the Congress as much as it strengthened the presidency. Beginning with the Cold War however, and perhaps even more markedly in recent years, preparation for war has helped presidents to substantially reshape the constitutional balance of power among the major institutions of government.

The Double-Edged Sword

For much of American history, Congress has jealously guarded its foreign policy prerogatives. On more than one occasion, legislators have sought to implement their own foreign policy goals, even when these clashed sharply with those of the president. Examples are numerous. The War of 1812 was urged upon a reluctant President Madison by Henry Clay and his supporters in the Congress. In 1817, again led by Clay, Congress sought to compel President Monroe to extend formal American recognition to the South American republics that had recently proclaimed their independence from Spain. Monroe eventually acceded to congressional pressure and recognized the governments of Argentina and Chile.[20] In 1913, Congress enacted legislation, which presidents ignored, prohibiting the executive from participating in any international conference without specific congressional authorization. In 1919, the Senate refused to ratify the Versailles Treaty, thus blocking American membership in the League of Nations and thwarting President Wilson's most cherished postwar goal. In 1924, over the objections of the White House, Congress enacted legislation prohibiting further Japanese immigration to the United States. This act inflamed anti-American sentiment in Japan and undermined the president's diplomatic efforts in Southeast Asia. Between 1935 and 1939, Congress passed four neutrality acts designed to prevent American involvement in any European or Pacific war. The 1939 act, adopted after the outbreak of war in Europe, prohibited American aid to any belligerent nation and prohibited American ships from entering areas subject to naval blockades by any power. Any supplies provided to a belligerent might be sold on a cash basis only. This legislation was designed specifically to prevent President Roosevelt from coming to the aid of the democracies against Nazi Germany. In more recent years, Congress enacted the 1973 War Powers Act designed to delimit the ability of the president to deploy American military forces, as well as the 1980 Intelligence Oversight Act aimed at placing restrictions on presidential use of covert operations against the nation's foreign foes.[21]

As the foregoing examples suggest, Congress has not hesitated to assert its own foreign policy and security goals in time of peace. In actual wartime, however, Congress has generally deferred to the president's leadership. Indeed, Congress has often granted presidents significant emergency powers and acceded to presidential claims of authority under the Constitution's commander in chief clause that seemed to be justified by urgent wartime conditions. Expansion of presidential power during wartime was particularly manifest during the Civil War and during the First and Second World Wars.

THE CIVIL WAR

After the fall of Fort Sumter and the outbreak of the Civil War in 1861, President Lincoln issued a series of executive orders for which he had no clear legal basis. Without even calling Congress into session, Lincoln combined the state militias into a ninety-day national volunteer force, called for 40,000 new volunteers, enlarged the regular army and navy, diverted $2 million in unspent appropriations to military needs, instituted censorship of the U.S. mails, ordered a blockade of the Southern ports, suspended the writ of habeas corpus in the border states, and ordered the arrest by military police of individuals whom he deemed to be guilty of engaging in or "contemplating" treasonous actions.[22] Lincoln asserted that these extraordinary measures were justified by what he called the presidential "war power," which he saw as constitutionally implied by the president's role as commander in chief and his duty to ensure that the nation's laws were faithfully executed.[23] Lincoln's assertion of presidential war powers did not stop in 1861. During the course of the war, he instituted military conscription, suspended the writ of habeas corpus, and instituted trial by courts-martial throughout the nation for those accused of disloyal practices, and by presidential proclamation emancipated the slaves.

In almost every instance, Congress subsequently enacted legislation legitimating the president's actions. Thus, after the president ordered the expansion of the army and navy, Congress enacted legislation to that effect. Similarly, after the president instituted military conscription, Congress voted a draft law. And, after the president ordered the creation of military commissions to try those accused of treason against the United States, Congress enacted legislation governing the organization and conduct of such commissions. For its part, in the 1863 Prize cases the Supreme Court upheld the president's power to order a blockade of the Southern ports.[24] In the 1866 case of *ex parte Milligan*, however, the Court rejected the president's suspension of habeas corpus and indiscriminate use of military tribunals in areas of the nation that were not actually theaters of military operations. The Court, however, recognized the president's power to declare martial law and to suspend civil liberties in areas actually subject to military threat.[25]

WORLD WAR I

Unlike the Civil War, the First World War was fought far from American soil and under circumstances that permitted reflective rather than reflexive congressional action. In some instances Wilson, like Lincoln, claimed powers under the commander in chief clause without waiting for Congress to act. For example, the president created a number of new executive agencies including the 1917 Committee on Public Information, to disseminate government propaganda to the American public, without seeking specific congressional approval. For the most part, however, President Wilson sought legislative authority for his actions. And for the most part, Congress obliged by voting the president extraordinary powers, not only over the organization of America's armed forces, but also, on the theory that war required mobilization of economic as well as military might, over the nation's farms, mines, and factories. During a period of less than two years, Congress enacted legislation that gave the president discretionary authority to mobilize and organize the nation's manpower and productive capabilities.

The 1916 and 1917 National Defense acts authorized the president in time of war to place obligatory orders with any firm for any product or material needed for the nation's defense. The 1917 Selective Service Act gave President Wilson the authority to raise an army through nationwide military conscription, and the Espionage Act made it unlawful to interfere with military recruitment. The Lever Food and Fuel Control Act authorized the president to regulate the manufacture, mining, and distribution of all articles he deemed necessary to the war effort; the power to requisition food and fuel; the power to take over and operate factories, mines, pipe lines, and storage facilities; and the power to set prices for food and fuel. The Trading With the Enemy Act gave the president additional emergency economic powers and empowered him to censor all communications with foreign countries. The Priority Shipment Act gave the president authority to ration space for truck, rail, and ship cargo. Other statutes authorized the president to regulate foreign-language newspapers in the United States and to take over and operate the nation's rail and water transport systems, as well as its telephone and telegraph systems.[26] The Overman Act allowed Wilson to rearrange executive departments, their duties, and their jurisdictions without congressional approval. The president averred that such reorganization authority was needed to facilitate national mobilization for war, but even the act's proponents acknowledged that it came close to giving the president dictatorial powers.[27]

Under the authority of these pieces of legislation, President Wilson created a number of new executive agencies such as the U.S. Food Administration and the U.S. Fuel Administration, both established to implement the Lever Act. The Fuel Administration proceeded to implement fuel rationing plans including "heatless Mondays," while the Food Administration introduced price controls and distribution controls as well as rationing for major commodities such as beef.[28] Wilson used the Overman Act to reorganize agencies associated with wartime mobilization. His most important step was to separate an obscure agency called the War Industries Board (WIB) from the National Defense Council. Wilson made the WIB directly responsible to himself and gave it enormous power to regulate the economy. Relying on a mix of threats and negotiation, the WIB set prices in such major industries as chemicals, textiles, metals, and construction and represented one of the most comprehensive intrusions of government into the marketplace ever attempted in the United States.[29]

Also, nominally pursuant to the authority given to him by Congress, Wilson issued numerous executive orders aimed at both military and civilian functions. The president, for example, ordered the War Department to impose censorship on all telephone and telegraph lines, suspended civil service hiring rules for all government agencies, and discontinued the eight-hour work day for federal employees.[30] Among Wilson's most important executive orders was his proclamation of December 26, 1917, taking over the nation's railroads, whose operations he deemed to have been hobbled by labor strife, car shortages, and traffic problems. The president created a U.S. Railroad Administration, headed by Treasury Secretary William McAdoo, which operated the rail lines until 1920, when they were returned to their former owners.

In a series of cases decided after the war, the U.S. Supreme Court upheld virtually all the president's actions as well as Congress's decisions to delegate enormous powers to the executive branch. The Court upheld the constitutionality of the government's takeover of the railroads, imposition of censorship, and enactment of military conscription laws. "In war," said Chief Justice White, the scope of governmental power becomes "highly malleable."[31] Even the limits on free speech brought about under the Espionage Act passed constitutional muster, because, in the words of Justice Holmes, "When a nation is at war, many things that might be said in time of peace [are not] protected by any constitutional right."[32] Thus, for the Court as for the Congress, the exigencies of war justified an enormous expansion of the powers of the chief executive.

WORLD WAR II

The Second World War paved the way for an even more substantial expansion of presidential power than had occurred during the Civil War or World War I. As in the case of the First World War, Congress delegated substantial military and civil powers to the president. And what Congress did not give him by statute, President Roosevelt took by executive order. Even before the Japanese attack on Pearl Harbor brought America into the war, FDR sought to prepare the nation for armed conflict and endeavored to provide American support for Great Britain in its life-and-death struggle against Nazi Germany. As early as 1938, Roosevelt issued an executive order authorizing the army to sell older weapons to private contractors who would then be free to sell them abroad. This was a thinly disguised ploy to sell weapons and munitions to Britain. Little more than a year later, after the fall of France, the administration made use of the same order to send more than a half million rifles and other arms and ammunition to the beleaguered British.[33]

Still later in 1940, the president violated the recently enacted Neutrality Act, as well as several other federal laws, by ordering the transfer to Britain of fifty U.S. Navy destroyers in exchange for the lease of sites for naval bases. Roosevelt was responding to an urgent plea from British Prime Minister Winston Churchill, who informed the president that nearly half of Britain's destroyer fleet had been lost, crippling the kingdom's capacity to protect its shipping from German U-boats. Roosevelt knew that Congress would not agree to the sale but decided he must nevertheless proceed. When the deal was announced, Attorney General Jackson argued that despite its apparent illegality, the exchange of destroyers for bases was validated by the president's constitutional authority as commander in chief, which gave him the power to "dispose" the armed forces of the United States. Jackson construed the term "dispose" as including "dispose of."[34] In March 1941, Congress enacted the Lend-Lease Act, which effectively ratified Roosevelt's policy of providing material aid to Great Britain.

In another executive order issued in 1937, Roosevelt referred to an unnamed unit within the Executive Office of the President that would deal with unspecified emergencies. In 1940, the president issued a new executive order naming the unit the Office for Emergency Management (OEM). Roosevelt assigned the OEM major responsibilities for military preparedness and mobilization.[35] In the early years of the war, FDR used the OEM as the institutional base for the creation of dozens of new wartime agencies such as the Office of Civilian Defense, the War Labor Board, the Office of Censorship, and the Office of Production Management.[36] These agencies, all created by executive orders, gave the president enormous direct power over the civilian economy and the life of the nation.

In May 1941, with war looming, Roosevelt declared a state of national emergency and issued a number of executive orders designed to promote military readiness. The next month he issued an executive order seizing a North American Aviation plant in California, where a labor dispute threatened the production of fighter aircraft. Other plants threatened by strikes were subsequently commandeered.[37] Also acting on his own initiative, and without consulting Congress, Roosevelt sent American troops to garrison Greenland and Iceland in the spring of 1941 to thwart a possible German attack. During the same period, again without congressional authorization, the president ordered the U.S. Navy to protect American shipping in the North Atlantic and to "shoot-at-sight" any attackers.[38] This order effectively linked America to Britain's military efforts and brought the nation within a hair's breadth of war with Nazi Germany.

Throughout this prewar period, FDR faced enormous opposition from isolationist and pro-German forces in Congress, including even the congressman from his own home district, Representative Hamilton Fish of New York. Fish actually employed a number of anti-Semitic and pro-German staffers in his congressional office.[39] Despite such obstacles, the president was able to secure the enactment of several important pieces of legislation, in addition to the Lend-Lease Act mentioned above, designed to grant power to the White House in order to promote American security interests. The first was the September 1940 Selective Service Act, which authorized the president to reinstitute military conscription in the form of one year of compulsory military training and service for up to 900,000 men. The draft law faced bitter opposition, especially in the West and Midwest where isolationist sentiment was strongest, but FDR launched an all-out and ultimately successful campaign to woo wavering legislators, promising that conscripts would only defend the shores of the United States and would never be sent outside the Western hemisphere.[40]

The Selective Service Act also reinstated the provisions of the 1917 National Defense Act, which had authorized the president to require plants and factories to suspend other operations if he deemed their facilities necessary for the production of ships, munitions, or other war materiel. Subsequently, Congress authorized the president to establish production priorities for all factories, giving precedence not only to military hardware, but to any goods he deemed necessary to the nation's defense.[41] In summer 1941, the first group of conscripts were nearing the end of their specified year of service. The president asked Congress to formally extend the period of service to two years. Despite the urgency of the times, the extension bill faced strong opposition. Finally, a six-month extension of service passed the House by a margin of only one vote.

A second important piece of prewar legislation was a 1940 act expanding the power of the Reconstruction Finance Corporation (RFC), which had been established earlier as a New Deal effort to spur business investment. In 1940, the RFC was given a new mandate to make government loans and investments aimed at ensuring the acquisition and production of materials and goods the president said were needed for purposes of defense. The RFC was also empowered to create government corporations or other entities for the purpose of producing strategic goods. During the war years, the RFC and its numerous subsidiaries engaged in a variety of economic activities, including rubber production, petroleum distribution, and insurance underwriting.[42]

The 1941 Japanese attack on Pearl Harbor ended debate over the wisdom of American involvement in the war. Pearl Harbor also brought an end to congressional resistance to conferring emergency powers upon the president. Within two weeks of the initiation of hostilities, Congress began to provide the president with an enormous array of economic as well as military powers designed to allow him to mobilize the nation for global war. In December 1941, Congress enacted the first War Powers Act, which, like the World War I Overman Act, gave the president the power to redistribute functions among executive agencies in any manner he saw fit. The act also gave the president authority to regulate international financial transactions and censor private communications with any and all foreign countries.[43] Several months later, Congress enacted the second War Powers Act, which allowed the president complete control over the distribution of scarce materials. This act also gave the Federal Reserve the authority to purchase government securities directly from the U.S. Treasury to finance the government deficits that would almost certainly be brought about by the war.

Another major piece of legislation, the Emergency Price Control Act, was enacted in January 1942, one month after the Pearl Harbor attack. The act established an Office of Price Administration (OPA) with broad authority to control prices and rents. The purpose of the legislation was to prevent wartime inflation so as to make certain that the government could purchase needed goods at a low price. Inevitably, however, price controls produced shortages of many commodities, including gasoline, meat, and coffee. The OPA then instituted a rationing system for such commodities, which was retained throughout the war. In October 1942, Congress augmented the price control act by passing the Economic Stabilization Act, which expanded the president's control over wages and prices and paved the way toward a more comprehensive national economic policy.[44] The president received other emergency economic powers under the War Labor Disputes Act, which granted broad authority to seize companies threatened by strikes; the War Mobilization and Conversion Act; and a host of other pieces of legislation that left the White House in full control of the American economy.

As was true of the Civil War and World War I, the Supreme Court generally acquiesced in the expansion of presidential power during

World War II. In *Yakus v. United States*, for example, the Court ruled that the Emergency Price Control Act was a proper delegation of power to the president.[45] In *Bowles v. Willingham*, the Court upheld the OPA's control of apartment rents.[46] In *Korematsu v. United States*, the Court refused to invalidate Roosevelt's Executive Order 9006 ordering the internment of Japanese-Americans.[47] In a similar vein, the Court ruled that under his powers as commander in chief, the president had the authority to establish a special military commission, outside the ambit of the civilian courts, to try eight Nazi agents, one of them an American citizen, who had entered the United States in 1942 for the avowed purpose of committing acts of sabotage.[48] In times of war, the Court was willing to allow the president broad leeway. Indeed, the war power did not automatically end with the war. In the 1948 case of *Woods v. Miller*, the Court ruled that a 1947 rent control statute was justified by the postwar housing shortage. "The war power," said Justice Douglas, "does not necessarily end with the cessation of hostilities."[49]

The Aftermath of War:
Popular Mobilization and Presidential Retrenchment

In wartime, Congress has been ready to grant enormous powers to the president. After the Second World War, Justice Douglas's assertion to the contrary notwithstanding, Congress generally was able to take back what it had given to the president during the period of national emergency. Sometimes kicking and screaming, the presidential genie was usually returned to its bottle soon after the guns fell silent. To begin with, many of the powers granted to the president were specifically military in character and lost their significance with the war's end. This was true of most of Lincoln's emergency powers, which, as the president said, "would be greatly diminished by the cessation of actual war."[50] After the First World War, Congress moved to revoke the emergency military and economic powers it had granted to President Wilson. Thus by early 1920 the War Industries Board, Fuel Administration, War Trade Board, Grain Board, Shipping Board, Railroad Administration, and a host of other agencies that had been created to implement executive control of the economy had been disbanded. The War Finance

Corporation lasted in attenuated form for another five years before it too was liquidated.[51]

Similarly, after Japan's surrender ended the Second World War, most of the wartime agencies were closed down by congressional and, in some cases, even presidential action. Within little more than a year, the entire structure of wartime wage, price, and production controls was dismantled. Some wartime programs survived. Because of growing concern about the Soviet Union, the system of military conscription instituted in 1940 was retained. Some employment and export programs survived. Generally, World War II promoted increased government intervention in the nation's economy, particularly through macroeconomic management.[52] Yet almost without exception, the instruments through which the president exercised his wartime powers during World War II, like those in past wars, were dismantled soon after the war's end.

In each of these instances, the president lost more than just emergency powers when warfare stopped. In the aftermath of the Civil War and World War I, certainly, and to some extent after World War II as well, Congress laid political siege to the White House. As Arthur Schlesinger has observed, in each case, the president's congressional opponents succeeded in dealing the chief executive a resounding political blow that underscored the Congress's determination to restore the temporarily swollen presidency to its prewar institutional limits.[53] After the Civil War, Congress impeached and very nearly convicted President Andrew Johnson when he sought to thwart congressional reconstruction plans for the defeated South. After the First World War, after a gargantuan struggle with the White House, the Senate refused to ratify the Versailles Treaty, dashing President Wilson's plans for the postwar world order. And, in the aftermath of the Second World War, Congress savaged President Truman's domestic program, recommended passage of the Twenty-second Amendment, limiting the president to two terms, and enacted a number of major pieces of legislation, including the 1947 Taft-Hartley Labor Act and the 1950 McCarran Internal Security Act, over the president's veto. In addition, presidential control over foreign policy came under attack by proponents of the "Bricker Amendment," which stipulated that no treaty or executive agreement could affect U.S. domestic law without action by Congress and, in some instances, the state legislatures. The amendment, which would have curtailed the executive's capacity to negotiate international agreements, ultimately failed but at one point appeared to have majority support in the Congress.[54]

In addition, during this postwar period, conservatives in both houses of Congress also launched major attacks on the presidency through investigations designed to demonstrate that the executive branch had been penetrated by Communist agents. Joseph McCarthy's Senate investigative committee, as well as the House Committee on Un-American Activities (HUAC), charged that Communist spies had penetrated federal agencies, from sensitive positions in the State Department to mundane posts in the Commerce Department. The ultimate target of these investigations was the presidency itself. Some radical critics of the White House asserted that Roosevelt had "sold out" to the Communists during the Yalta conference and that Truman had acquiesced in the appointment of "one-worlders" and Communist sympathizers to high government positions. McCarthy implied that Roosevelt and Truman had been part of an immense conspiracy—"an infamy so black as to dwarf any previous such venture in the history of man"—to undermine the nation.[55] These investigations placed the White House on the defensive, forcing it to devote energy and resources to answer a constantly expanding array of charges. The investigations led, according to political scientist Wilfred Binkley, to a "gravitation of power into the hands of Congress, at the expense of the executive."[56]

And for its part, the Supreme Court, which had championed presidential prerogatives during the Second World War, seemed to agree that the time had come to deflate the powers of the executive. In April 1952, during the height of the Korean War, Truman feared that a threatened nationwide strike would close the steel industry and hamper the war effort. As would have been permissible under now-repealed World War I and World War II legislation, Truman ordered the Secretary of Commerce to seize and operate the mills.[57] In the case of *Youngstown Sheet and Tube v. Sawyer*, the Supreme Court held that the president lacked the power to issue such an order.[58] Nothing could be more sinister and alarming, said Justice Jackson for the Court, than an effort by the president "to enlarge his mastery over the internal affairs of the country" by his commitment of armed forces to a foreign war. Thus the Court now seemed prepared to side with Congress against the White House.

The patterns of postwar congressional assertiveness that we have observed in the three cases reviewed above share a common underlying dimension. Generally speaking, although war initially expands the power of the presidency, war also has social and economic repercussions that can eventually embolden and empower the Congress. In particular, during much of American history, war has resulted in social and political mobilization that gives Congress an opportunity to link itself to newly activated groups in American society and with their backing to do battle with the White House.

WAR AND POPULAR MOBILIZATION

Since colonial times, America has relied upon citizen-soldiers— militiamen, conscripts, and short-term volunteers—to fill out the ranks of its armies in times of war. Until recent years, at least, America has also depended upon a considerable measure of voluntary support from the civilian population to pay for its wars. Sending citizen-soldiers to war and inspiring their fellow citizens to pick up the tab, has led, in turn, to significant levels of popular political mobilization during and in the aftermath of major conflicts.

Colonial militiamen made up the bulk of Washington's Continental army, but their short tours of duty reduced their military effectiveness. Like their French Revolutionary contemporaries, however, American militiamen's enthusiasm for the cause often made up for what they lacked in training and discipline. The colonies' part-time soldiers had other virtues as well. When they returned home, they performed the vital service of holding their communities to the patriot cause, often by intimidation or violence, so that the Continental army had continuing access to its recruitment base and to most of the food produced in the colonies.[59] Once independent, the United States continued to rely primarily on militiamen so as to avoid the dangers that a large professional army entailed for a fledgling democracy. The Federal Militia Acts of 1792 and 1795 provided for the enrollment of able-bodied, free white men between the ages of eighteen and forty-five in the state militias and authorized the president to call the state militias to national service for a period not to exceed three months in any one year. The statutes carried no penalties for failing to enroll in the militia; nevertheless, thousands of Americans signed up and received some measure of military training.[60] The militia produced politicians as well as soldiers. Like Abraham Lincoln, many aspiring officeholders without wealth or social standing brought themselves to the attention of fellow citizens through militia service.

Virtually all the American soldiers who fought in the War of 1812 were militiamen. The vast majority served for six months or less, and the quality of their military performance was spotty. In some instances, rival units refused to cooperate with one another, and battles were lost because militiamen decided to return home in mid-campaign. But militia forces led by able officers like General William Henry Harrison of Kentucky, General Jacob Brown of New York, and, of course, Andrew Jackson, were able to defeat larger, well-trained British forces, thus confirming the American conviction that citizen-soldiers could outfight professionals. After the War of 1812, the organized state militias gave way to local volunteer units who drilled on weekends and paraded in fancy uniforms on patriotic occasions.[61] But some saw military action in civil disturbances, where they often performed effectively. One volunteer regiment in New York City put down major riots in 1834, 1836, and 1837. On the frontier, volunteer units were responsible for much of the violence against Native Americans, and during the Mexican-American War, they accounted for more than 70 percent of the troops mustered. Despite many casualties, primarily from disease and malnutrition, volunteers and militiamen fought well throughout the twenty-one months of the war and distinguished themselves at Buena Vista. Congress was so pleased with the military performance of the volunteers that it slashed the size of the regular army from 30,000 to 12,000 men at the war's conclusion, calculating that volunteers would always be available to satisfy the nation's military needs.

At the outbreak of the Civil War, both the Federal and Confederate governments called the state militias into service. In 1861, President Lincoln asked the states to send 75,000 soldiers to serve for three months under officers appointed by the state governors. As the war continued, the president called for more troops to be raised by the states. The Civil War's bloody consumption of manpower, however, soon outran the supply of state volunteers. In July 1862, facing severe manpower shortfalls, Congress took the unprecedented step of directing the states to draft soldiers to fill their quotas. In 1863, for the first time, the national government, rather than the states and communities, sought to mobilize citizen-soldiers. Congress enacted a conscription law summoning young men directly into the military service of the United States. Those ordered to report were permitted to hire substitutes. Only some 160,000 draftees and substitutes ever served in the Union army, but many tens of thousands of men volunteered in preference to being drafted. Counting militiamen, conscripts, volunteers, and "involuntary volunteers," more than 2 million citizen-soldiers fought in the Union army and another million on the Confederate side.

The American army that fought in World War I was composed primarily of draftees. More than 24 million men registered under the 1917 Selective Service Act, and nearly 3 million were drafted. Another 700,000 young Americans volunteered for service, while 370,000 soldiers were drawn from the National Guard. Guardsmen were drafted by Wilson in August 1917 as individuals, thus formally severing their ties with the states. To reduce anticipated political opposition to conscription, the actual task of selecting draftees was entrusted to 4,600 local boards of citizen volunteers. Additional citizens' committees gave medical and legal advice and assisted inductees until they reported for duty.[62] As a result, the creation of the World War I army was based upon a mix of national recruiting drives aimed at stimulating patriotism and local administration designed to elicit community cooperation for the war effort.

Like the First World War, the Second was fought mainly by an army of conscripted and volunteer citizen-soldiers. Congress, as we saw above, enacted the first peacetime draft in American history in 1940. During the next five years, 10 million men were inducted into the armed forces and another 5 million given deferments for work in war industries. Another 5 million Americans, including more than 300,000 women, volunteered for service, prompted by the same mix of patriotism and anticipation of conscription that produced the original *levée en masse*—that is, mass conscription—in postrevolutionary France. Community boards once again took on the work of conscription and the goal of cultivating grassroots support for the Selective

Service System. This method of recruiting armies continued during the nation's two major postwar conflicts, the wars in Korea and Vietnam.

WARTIME FINANCE

Just as the government depended upon citizen support to raise armies, it relied upon the cooperation of the citizenry to finance wars. After the American Revolution and the construction of the federal government in 1789, the states enacted broadly based property and poll taxes as their major revenue sources. Initially, the federal government financed its limited activities through tariffs and customs duties, supplemented by moderate borrowing in national and international credit markets. During the Civil War, however, the government's need for revenues increased so dramatically that the government could not secure sufficient funds from the traditional sources—domestic banks and financiers. European investors, for their part, had no confidence that the Union would prevail on the battlefield and were reluctant to purchase U.S. securities.[63]

The federal government therefore turned to new ways of raising revenue that relied upon the contributions of millions of ordinary Americans to meet the Union's military expenses, which ultimately totaled more than $4 billion.[64] These included the enactment of a broadly based federal income tax, later declared unconstitutional by the Supreme Court and then reinstated by constitutional amendment in 1913. Another major revenue instrument introduced during the Civil War was the sale of government bonds to small investors. In 1862, Treasury Secretary Chase invited an Ohio Republican banker, Jay Cooke, to attempt to sell $500 million in government bonds that could not be sold to domestic banks or foreign investors. Cooke developed a plan to market these securities to ordinary citizens who had never before purchased government bonds. He thought he could appeal to the patriotism of ordinary Americans, and he believed that widespread ownership of government bonds would give large numbers of ordinary citizens a greater concern for their nation's welfare.[65] Cooke established a network of 2,500 sales agents throughout the North and used the press to promote the notion that purchasing government securities was both a patriotic duty and a wise investment. In every community, Republican party organizations worked hand in hand with Cooke's sales agents, providing what historian Eric McKitrick calls the "continual affirmation of purpose" needed to sustain popular support and the regime's finances through four long years of war.[66] By 1863, all the bonds had been sold, and most were in the hands of private citizens rather than financial institutions.

The financing of World War I also depended upon a mix of compulsory and voluntary contributions from millions of ordinary citizens. First, the income tax played an important role in financing American military efforts. A tax on incomes that by 1918 reached 6 percent on the first $4,000 in income and 12 percent on the remainder generated nearly one-third of the $33 billion in military and related costs incurred by the United States during the war. Citizens were also strongly urged to support their government by buying its bonds.

Using marketing techniques similar to those devised by Jay Cooke during the Civil War, the government urged Americans, through "Borrow and Buy" campaigns, to participate in what were designated "Liberty Loans" and "Victory Loans." Four Liberty and Victory Loan campaigns generated an astonishing $22 billion for the war effort. Bonds were sold in denominations as low as $50, and purchase on an installment plan was allowed. The Liberty and Victory Loan campaigns were conducted by the War Loan Organization, which was organized into sales, speaking, and publicity bureaus. The entire sales network was staffed by tens of thousands of ordinary citizens who volunteered to work in coordination with local banks. Another $1 billion was raised by the sale of thrift stamps, war savings certificates, and small bonds in schools, post offices, and factories to those sufficiently patriotic but too impecunious to participate in the Liberty Loan drive. Stamps cost as little as twenty-five cents each. A sheet of sixteenth thrift stamps could be exchanged for an interest-bearing $5 bond. Stamps and savings certificates were also sold by an army of civilian volunteers.[67]

These same mechanisms helped to finance World War II. During the course of the war, some $50 billion in U.S. savings bonds were sold to individual citizens. Patriotic appeals organized by the War Finance Division of the Treasury Department and backed by mailings of more than 650 million pieces of advertising encouraged workers to enroll in the payroll savings plan. Under this scheme, workers agreed to have approximately 10 percent of their income automatically deducted from their paychecks and invested in savings bonds. As was the case during World War I, government bond drives were marked by a great deal of patriotic hoopla, often centered around appeals by film stars, war heroes, and other celebrities.

The government's reliance upon ordinary citizens to fight as well as finance war efforts has often sparked significant mass political mobilization both in support of and in opposition to presidential war policies. To begin with, the recruitment of troops—especially through conscription—and concomitant efforts to rally citizen support for military undertakings often energizes popular political organization and activity both in support of and opposition to the war effort. For example, as Skocpol has shown, the Civil War and both World Wars prompted the formation of hundreds of patriotic, civic, and service organizations such as the Grange, the Women's Christian Temperance Union, and the Red Cross.[68] Some organizations were sponsored by the government itself. For instance, the American Farm Bureau Federation was organized with federal assistance during World War I to spur food production. Similarly, the Knights of Columbus received government support in exchange for its advocacy of military service for working-class Catholics. Many of these groups became politically active, promoting causes ranging from labor reform to temperance.

At the same time, citizens and groups asked to bear the costs of war often feel emboldened to make new political demands and seek new political rights. For example, in both America and Europe, war has been closely associated with expansion of suffrage. Revolutionary War militiamen called to place their lives at the service of the nation thought themselves just as entitled to vote as their betters who risked only property. Indeed, the Revolutionary militia was known as a breeding ground for radical democrats. In 1776, the Philadelphia Committee of Privates, an organization of Pennsylvania militiamen, advised voters to "Let no man represent you disposed to form any rank above that of Freeman."[69] The sentiments of armed militiamen could not be ignored in the suffrage debates that followed the success of the revolutionary cause. Throughout the colonies, citizen-soldiers pressed for and helped to win expanded voting rights. Organizations of state militiamen demanded an end to property restrictions on suffrage on the ground that those asked to fight should not be barred from voting. In Maryland, groups of armed militiamen went to the polls in 1776 demanding to vote, whether or not they could meet the state's existing property requirements for voters. In some instances, those denied the right to vote threatened to refuse to continue to fight. The result in Maryland and other states was a general expansion of suffrage during the revolutionary period designed to accommodate the demands of those Americans being asked to fight. Subsequently, the War of 1812 led to suffrage reforms in a number of states on the argument that "men who were good enough to fight were good enough to vote."[70] Women's suffrage in the United States, as in England and Canada, was partially brought about by the First World War, on the basis of the notion that women were more likely to support the war effort if they possessed the right to vote.[71] Most recently, the Twenty-sixth Amendment, lowering the voting age to eighteen, was designed in part to bolster support among young men who were then being conscripted for service in the Vietnam War.

While energizing the government's supporters, mobilization for war can also galvanize foes of the government's military efforts. Virtually every American war has engendered opposition from one quarter or another, and often opposition to war has been the basis for passionate rhetoric and intense bouts of organizational activity. Abolitionists, for example, denounced the 1846 Mexican War as a campaign to expand slavery and organized a fierce, if ultimately ineffective, movement to oppose President Polk's policies. Although its opponents failed to block the war, their organizational efforts helped bring about the creation of the Free Soil party, which subsequently became a major component of the Republican coalition.[72] In protracted conflicts, the hardships, casualties, and dislocations suffered by citizen-soldiers and their families can inflame antiwar sentiment and escalate political opposition to continued fighting. Resistance to military conscription often becomes a major focus of these efforts. The Civil War draft was bitterly resisted in many parts of the North and ignited major riots in New York and other cities in 1863.[73] The New York riot lasted four days before it was finally quelled by police and military authorities. So serious was the threat of continuing civil disorder that more than 10,000 soldiers were detached from the Army of the Potomac to garrison New York in the riot's wake.[74] Opposition to the draft and growing popular weariness of the war very nearly led to Lincoln's defeat in the 1864 presidential election. Draft resistance was a major problem during the First World War, when socialist organizers urged draft-age men to refuse induction and thousands of men were arrested for failing to register with their draft boards.[75] During the Vietnam War, liberal foes of American intervention in Indo-China encouraged draft resistance and made conscription a major political issue.[76] Even World War II, a conflict that had overwhelming popular support, saw limited but vocal draft resistance.[77]

Finally, even after the cessation of hostilities, former critics of the war, including even some veterans, search out political vehicles through which to express their alienation, while other Americans who served in the military organize to trumpet their patriotism and to seek recognition for their sacrifices. Thus, many initially politicized by their opposition to the Vietnam War became active in the left-liberal "New Politics" movement of the 1970s.[78] New Politics supporters dominated the Democratic Party convention in 1972 and secured the party's presidential nomination for liberal South Dakota Senator George McGovern. Later New Politics activists played important roles in the consumer, environmental, feminist, and other "postmaterial" political movements.[79] Similarly, many American war veterans joined organizations like the Grand Army of the Republic (GAR) after the Civil War or the American Legion after the two world wars. These organizations became significant actors in American politics, pressing not only for the extensive system of veterans' pensions and benefits made available after the Civil War and World War I and under the post–World War II GI Bill, but for broader political goals as well. The GAR was a powerful force in Republican party politics in the late nineteenth century, and the American Legion became an important conservative pressure group during the twentieth.

These wartime and postwar mobilizations of new political forces in turn created new opportunities for political entrepreneurship on the part of sympathetic or even merely ambitious members of Congress. Occasionally during the war, but most often in the peacetime aftermath of military conflicts, groups in Congress have reached out to the movements energized by the war. Members of Congress have espoused these groups' causes and appealed to their social concerns and material interests—in the case of veterans, for example, associating themselves with veterans' groups and providing pensions, bonuses, and other benefits. In these ways, groups in Congress have been able to link themselves to energetic new political forces which, for their part, now have a stake in supporting congressional power vis-à-vis the executive branch. These alliances with new political forces often allowed postwar congresses to accomplish what the nation's foreign foes could not—take on and defeat the president.

Thus, in the wake of the Mexican War, a number of northern congressional Democrats, including such New York "Barnburners" as David Wilmot, Preston King, and John A. Dix, turned against the national administration.[80] In 1848, these members of Congress aligned themselves with the antislavery forces that had mobilized throughout the North in opposition to the attack on Mexico and subsequent American territorial expansion. This strengthened antislavery coalition became the basis for the Free Soil party and later for the creation of the Republican party. Antislavery forces in Congress harassed and weakened the Fillmore, Pierce, and Buchanan administrations. Although Pierce was able to secure the enactment of the 1854 Kansas-Nebraska Act, repealing the Missouri Compromise, in an attempt to appease both sides in the slavery controversy, the result was to divide irrevocably the Democratic party. During the concluding years of the Buchanan administration, the new Republican party controlled the House of Representatives. Republicans asserted that the power of the presidency should be curbed and established a special committee under the leadership of Representative John Covede of Pennsylvania to investigate the general topic of improper presidential efforts to influence congressional deliberations. The Covede committee charged President Buchanan with using bribes and other unsavory tactics to secure the enactment of legislation he favored and recommended ways of reducing presidential influence in the legislative process.[81]

Likewise, in the aftermath of the Civil War, members of Congress opposed to President Andrew Johnson's reconstruction policies relied heavily upon the political support of the most important Union army veteran's organization, the Grand Army of the Republic, which at its peak enrolled nearly a half million members supported by hundreds of thousands of their family members in its auxiliary organizations. The GAR supported the adoption of the Fourteenth Amendment, which the president opposed, and generally favored the radical Republicans' harsh policies toward the defeated South rather than the conciliatory program espoused by Johnson. Radical Republicans relied upon GAR grassroots support to counter Johnson's efforts to influence the outcome of the 1866 congressional elections. Subsequently in 1867, Johnson attempted to oust Secretary of War Edwin M. Stanton in defiance of the new Tenure of Office act, which required congressional approval for the dismissal of cabinet officers. Many Republican radicals were convinced that Johnson's action was a prelude to some form of coup d'etat and asked the GAR to march a detachment of Union veterans to Washington to protect the Congress. House Speaker Colfax reported that explosives had been stolen in New York and were being brought to Washington to blow up the Capitol. The GAR prepared, unnecessarily as it turned out, to march on Washington at a moment's notice.[82] To emphasize the importance of the alliance between the president's congressional foes and the GAR, during the impeachment proceedings against President Johnson, the GAR's national commander, Congressman John Logan of Illinois, served as one of the House impeachment managers.

A similar pattern of congressional alliances with emergent political forces manifested itself after the two World Wars. After World War I, President Wilson's congressional opponents made common cause with German and Irish Americans and with postwar isolationists to block American participation in the League of Nations and thereby to destroy the Wilson presidency.[83] The Germans and Irish had from the beginning opposed support for Great Britain in the European conflict but had been silenced by the administration's wartime suppression of dissent. Yet even many Americans who had supported the war were shocked by the carnage and disillusioned by the results. Now they opposed having "An American army policing the world and quelling riots in all peoples' back yards."[84] Interestingly, the Versailles Treaty's most vehement foe, Senate Majority Leader Henry Cabot Lodge of Massachusetts, was himself a Rooseveltian internationalist who had supported America's entry into the war. Lodge, however, harbored a deep personal hatred for Wilson and was prepared to align himself with isolationists if to do so would thwart the president. Other Republicans had been angered by Wilson's wartime arrogation of power and were now eager to cut the president down to size and especially to derail any ambitions Wilson might have to seek a third term.[85] After the Second World War, President Truman's congressional foes courted the support of patriotic veterans' groups like the American Legion and the Catholic War Veterans in their investigations of alleged Communist penetration of the executive branch. The American Legion in particular organized nationwide antisubversive seminars publicized and enforced blacklists, supported anti-Communist members of Congress such as Richard M. Nixon, and lent their political clout to the efforts of the HUAC and the McCarthy committee.[86] During the late 1960s, groups in Congress aligned themselves with liberals who mobilized against the Vietnam War to undermine Lyndon Johnson's presidency in the late 1960s. This "New Politics" alliance remained active in American politics during the following decade and played an important role in the ouster of Richard Nixon. During Johnson's second administration, liberals—who had initially supported the war—turned against it largely because military needs began to divert substantial resources from Great Society social programs to which liberal Democrats were strongly committed. Liberals were joined by some civil rights leaders such as Dr. Martin Luther King, who viewed the war as a diversion of national energy and attention from the nation's effort to end segregation.[87] Supported by segments of the national news media, liberals began to criticize not only the administration's war policies, but also practices that had become commonplace in the years since World War II: lax Pentagon procurement practices, Pentagon public relations activities, domestic spying by intelligence agencies, and the hiring of former military officers by defense contractors.[88]

Growing opposition to the war among liberals encouraged some members of Congress, notably Senator J. William Fulbright, chair of the Senate Foreign Relations Committee, along with such senators as George McGovern, Wayne Morse, and Ernest Gruening, to break with the president.[89] Fueling the growth of opposition to the war was the fact that increasing numbers of citizen-soldiers, including conscripts, were being sent to fight in the jungles of Southeast Asia, where they suffered substantial casualties.[90] Initially, the system of deferments and exemptions surrounding military conscription ensured that most draftees would be drawn from working-class and minority households—a segment of society not well represented in the political process or enjoying ready access to the media. They had little defense against wartime exactions. In 1967, however, foes of the war charged that the draft was racist in character because its burden fell so heavily on minority communities. Stung by these charges, President Johnson initiated a set of changes in the draft law that limited student and other upper-middle-class deferments. As critics had hoped, the result was increased opposition to the war from more influential social strata who now saw their children placed at risk. Between 1968 and 1970, tens of thousands of young men claimed conscientious objector status or presented dubious medical excuses, while tens of thousands more refused to register, or destroyed or returned their draft cards.[91] Others clogged the federal courts with challenges to draft orders. Antiwar sentiment among congressional liberals intensified in 1967 and 1968, and Senator Eugene McCarthy launched a bid to deny Johnson the 1968 Democratic nomination. Although he almost certainly would have been renominated despite liberal opposition, Johnson was politically wounded and chose to withdraw from the race. Antiwar Democrats became an important element in the New Politics coalition which in 1974 forced President Richard Nixon from office in the wake of the Watergate scandal. After Nixon's resignation, congressional Democrats enacted a number of pieces of legislation designed to curb presidential power. These included the Budget and Impoundment Control Act to enhance congressional power in the budget process, the Ethics in Government Act to facilitate future prosecution of wrongdoing in the executive branch, and the Freedom of Information Act to open the files of executive agencies to congressional and media scrutiny. Congress also strengthened its own investigative arm, the General Accounting Office. Other legislation to be discussed below specifically struck at presidential war and foreign policy powers.

Thus, in the wake of the Vietnam War as in a number of other instances, important groups within Congress were able to take advantage of war-induced political mobilization to do battle with the White House. The importance of war as an incubator of new political forces has meant that over the decades military action has been a two-edged presidential sword. On the one hand, military exigencies have frequently allowed chief executives to demand—and have compelled congresses to give—vast new powers to the president. On the other hand, however, the political mobilization brought by war has allowed groups in Congress an opportunity to forge political alliances that then enabled them to lay siege to the White House and retrieve some or all of the power that had been surrendered to the president and, perhaps, then some. Recently, however, the importance of this mechanism for keeping presidential power in check has waned, though not completely disappeared. Modern presidents have built institutions for making war that rely less and less on popular mobilization. This is why opposition to President George W. Bush's war in Iraq, while significant, seems a muted thunder that, unlike the protests of the Vietnam era, has had little impact on the presidential determination to "stay the course."

Sharpening the Presidential Sword

America's first wars were fought by citizen-soldiers and financed in part by voluntary popular subscription. America's most recent military actions, by contrast, were fought by professional soldiers—in the case of the Afghan war, mainly special operations troops—utilizing sophisticated military technology and financed by the Federal Reserve System and contributions wrested from America's foreign allies. These conflicts did not stimulate much in the way of popular political mobilization and, for the most part, Congress watched them from the sidelines. The transformation came about in part because of the Cold War and in part because of efforts by successive presidents, beginning most importantly with Harry Truman, to insulate presidential war making from popular politics. The result has been to give presidents enormous freedom of action in the realm of foreign and security policy and perhaps to partially shield presidential power from the historic pattern of postwar retrogression.

PRESIDENTIAL POWER AND THE COLD WAR

The Cold War had an enormous impact upon presidential power. For more than forty years, the United States faced a dire military threat requiring the creation and permanent maintenance of powerful military forces ready to respond to attack at a moment's notice. Indeed, the Cold War blurred the distinction between wartime and peacetime. Against the backdrop of the dangers facing the nation, successive Cold War and post–Cold War presidents were able to expand the power of the executive branch and affirm their own preeminence in security and foreign affairs. In the face of what it perceived to be a threat to the nation's very existence from the Soviet Union, Congress usually acceded to presidential demands as it always had during wartime. Senator J. William Fulbright, who was later to become a major critic of presidential war power, said in 1961, "As Commander-in-Chief of the armed forces, the president has full responsibility, which cannot be shared, for military decisions in a world in which the difference between safety and cataclysm can be a matter of hours or even minutes."[92] Despite congressional deference, successive presidents did not place much trust in Congress or the democratic political process. Instead, they sought to use the dangers facing the nation as a justification for building a set of institutions and procedures that would insulate presidential decision making in the realm of security and foreign policy from public scrutiny and congressional intervention.

Unlike an actual war, moreover, the Cold War did not produce the sort of political mobilization that has historically allowed Congress to confront the White House and restore the antebellum institutional balance. Major conflicts, especially the wars in Korea and Vietnam, were fought during the Cold War era. And, as we saw, particularly in the wake of the Vietnam War, Congress did move to curb presidential power. Unlike the Civil War or the World Wars, however, when the end of the war meant there would be an interlude of peace, however brief, the conclusion of the Vietnam War merely meant a continuation of the underlying superpower confrontation. The continuing threat to American security allowed Presidents Ronald Reagan and George H.

W. Bush to quickly throw off their congressional fetters and resume the onward march of presidential power.

In the immediate aftermath of World War II, the United States moved quickly to demobilize its military forces. Although it helped to bring about the creation of the United Nations, the Truman administration hoped to reduce its international commitments and concentrate on domestic concerns. President Truman had little foreign policy expertise or interest and expected to focus mainly on the domestic social and economic objectives embodied in his "Fair Deal" agenda. As late as October 1945, Truman told the Joint Chiefs to expect sharp cuts in the military budget and steep reductions in the number of American troops stationed in Europe.[93] By 1946, however, crises in the Near East, the Balkans, and Europe forced the president to devote his attention to international and security affairs. Truman's predecessor, Franklin D. Roosevelt, had dominated America's political landscape and governed the nation during a desperate worldwide military struggle. During the war, in historian Arthur Schlesinger's words, Roosevelt "kept the military and diplomatic reins very much in his own hands."[94] The president was confident of his own judgment in these realms and relied upon a cadre of trusted aides such as Harry Hopkins and later "Chip" Bohlen to conduct delicate negotiations.[95] FDR generally bypassed Secretary of State Cordell Hull, whom he saw as useful merely to handle routine diplomatic business.[96] And, while Roosevelt went through the motions of consulting Congress so long as he knew it would support him, he frequently ignored Capitol Hill and regarded legislators, especially senators, "as a bunch of incompetent obstructionists" when it came to matters of national security.[97] Truman lacked the political standing that allowed FDR to ride roughshod over Congress and also lacked FDR's confidence in his own capacity to make unilateral foreign policy decisions. Yet Truman believed strongly in the principle of executive control of foreign policy.[98] Accordingly, he and his advisors moved to create a set of institutions that would give an ordinary mortal like Harry S. Truman powers that once could have been exercised only by a giant like FDR.[99]

Two statutes enacted within less than a year of one another played an important role in institutionalizing the foreign policy and security powers of the presidency. The first, signed into law in August 1946, was the Foreign Service Reform Act, which merged the State Department and the Foreign Service into a single organization. This meant that experienced Foreign Service officers would routinely rotate back to Washington, where they would be available for consultation and policy formation. In 1947, Secretary of State George C. Marshall established the department's policy planning staff, consisting mainly of Foreign Service officers on their Washington tours, to serve as an instrument through which the secretary and the president would be able to evaluate long-term foreign policy goals. From the perspective of Congress, the Foreign Service Act and the development of the policy planning staff would work to reduce the likelihood that future presidents would engage in FDR-style freewheeling diplomacy. But the actual result was to increase rather than curb presidential power. The policy planning staff gave the president a stronger institutional capacity to identify and evaluate foreign policy problems and consider alternative courses of action. The staff's first director, George Kennan, became an important presidential advisor, as did his successor, Paul Nitze, and a number of subsequent directors.

An even more important piece of legislation, the National Security Act, was passed in July 1947. The National Security Act had three major parts. First, it reorganized the military services by separating the air force from the army and abolishing the historic division between the War Department and Navy Department. All three military branches were now placed within a single National Military Establishment, later renamed the Department of Defense (DoD), under the leadership of a civilian cabinet officer—the secretary of defense. Second, the act created the Central Intelligence Agency (CIA) to coordinate the government's information gathering, espionage, and covert operations. Finally, the act established the National Security Council (NSC), chaired by the president and including the major cabinet secretaries, the chairman of the Joint Chiefs of Staff, the three service secretaries, and a number of other high-ranking officials. The NSC was to assist the president in coordinating national security planning and decision making.

Members of Congress brought a mix of motives to the legislation. Some hoped to streamline national security decision making so that the nation could respond more effectively to crises. Others viewed the CIA and NSC as further means of averting a return to Roosevelt-style presidential unilateralism. The CIA's predecessor, for example, the Office of Strategic Services (OSS), had been created by a Roosevelt executive order in 1942 and had operated as a semiautonomous instrument of the White House.[100] From Truman's perspective, however, the National Security Act promised to create important mechanisms for presidential control of American foreign and security policy. Although he was not fully satisfied with all its provisions, Truman made passage of the act a major presidential priority.[101] And subsequent events were to affirm Truman's view as the 1947 National Security Act created the basis for what later critics would call the "imperial presidency."

PRESIDENTIAL CONTROL OF THE MILITARY

To begin with, the 1947 act represented a step in the professionalization of the military services and their subjection to presidential control. As noted above, America's military effort had historically depended upon state militias, which often answered as much to governors, senators, and members of Congress as to the president. During the Civil War, for example, many politicians secured gubernatorial commissions in state militia units, and through them, as well as through the state governors, Congress frequently sought to interfere with Lincoln's military plans. Presidential control of the military was enhanced at the beginning of the Spanish-American War when Congress passed the 1898 Volunteer Act. Under its terms, the general officers and the staffs of all state militia units, now renamed the National Guard, were to be appointed by the president rather than the state governors. The 1903 Dick Act further increased presidential control of the nation's military forces by authorizing the president to dissolve state guard units into the regular army in times of emergency, while the 1916 National Defense Act gave the president authority to appoint all commissioned and noncommissioned Guard officers in time of war. The 1916 Act also began the creation of the national military reserves, which eventually supplanted the state units as the force employed to fill out the military's ranks in time of emergency.[102]

While these pieces of legislation gradually gave the president and the military brass in Washington fuller control over what originally had been primarily state forces, the long-standing division of the military

into two cabinet departments—War (Army) and Navy—also undermined presidential control. Historically, each of the services, as well as
branches within the services, most notably the Marine Corps and more
recently the Army Air Corps, had its own ties to supporters in Congress
and used these to circumvent their nominal superiors. For example,
during the First World War, the Marines mobilized their allies in
Congress to induce the president to accept their participation in the
American Expeditionary Force over the objections of the secretary of
war, the secretary of the navy, and General Pershing, the force's commander.[103] In a similar vein, between the wars, some lawmakers
became enchanted with the idea of military aviation and supported
General Billy Mitchell's quixotic crusade against the War and Navy
Departments. Over the objections of the president and the secretary of
war, Congress enacted the 1926 Air Corps Act, which made the Air
Corps a virtually autonomous entity within the army.[104] Even more
important, the War Department and the Navy Department presented
Congress with separate budgets and competing visions of the nation's
military needs and priorities. The annual struggle for funding between
the two service branches, complete with competing testimony by the
nation's foremost military authorities, opened the way for increased
congressional intervention into military decision making.

The 1947 National Security Act created a single defense secretary
responsible for all defense planning and the overall military budget.
As amended in 1949, the act diminished the status of the individual
service secretaries, who were no longer to be members of the president's cabinet or the National Security Council. Instead, the individual service secretaries were to focus on manpower and procurement
issues and to report to the secretary of defense and his assistant secretaries. To further centralize military planning, the 1949 amendments created the position of chairman of the Joint Chiefs of Staff
(JCS) to denote the officer who was to serve as the principal military
adviser to the defense secretary and the president. By creating a
more unified military chain of command and a single defense
budget, the National Security Act diminished Congress's ability to
intervene in military planning and decision making and increased
the president's control over the armed services and national security
policy. In 1948, under the auspices of the first defense secretary,

James Forrestal, the chiefs of the three military services met at Key West and negotiated a set of agreements on missions and weapons that were expected to mute the interservice squabbles that created openings for congressional intervention.

Initially, of course, some resistance to the newly centralized military regime rose up within the military itself. In 1949, for example, the navy objected strongly to the defense budget developed by Louis Johnson, whom Truman had appointed as defense secretary after Forrestal took his own life. The defense budget was still undergoing postwar contraction and Johnson, believing that large naval forces had been rendered obsolete in the era of the long-range bomber, scrapped plans for the production of new aircraft carriers and announced that the number of existing aircraft carrier battle groups would be reduced from eight to four by fiscal year 1951. At the same time, however, Johnson continued funding for a number of expensive army and air force programs, including production of the costly B-36 intercontinental bomber.

The result was what the press dubbed the "revolt of the admirals." A number of high-ranking naval officers spoke out publicly in defiance of Johnson's directives prohibiting active-duty personnel from so doing. Officers not only argued that Johnson's plans were unsound, but charged both Johnson and the secretary of the air force with a variety of financial improprieties in the procurement of the B-36 long-range bomber. The charges turned out to have been completely fabricated in a propaganda office organized by the navy.[105] The accusations nevertheless led to congressional hearings promoted by Representative James Van Zandt (R-PA), a captain in the Naval Reserve, and opened the way to efforts by members of Congress to play a larger role in military affairs.[106] With the support of JCS chairman General Omar Bradley and the backing of President Truman, Johnson snuffed out the naval revolt. Three admirals, including Chief of Naval Operations Louis Denfeld, along with a number of other officers, were sent into retirement over the protests of their supporters in Congress. Johnson's orders to cut naval strength remained in force, and the principle of centralized control of the military was reaffirmed.[107]

A more serious challenge to the president's control over national security policy was mounted in 1951 by General Douglas MacArthur.

General MacArthur had been the Supreme Commander of Allied forces in the Pacific during the Second World War and after the war had served as America's viceroy in occupied Japan. After the North Korean attack on South Korea in the spring of 1950, MacArthur organized the audacious Inchon landing in September that routed the North Koreans and drove them back across the original line of demarcation at the thirty-eighth parallel. In November 1950, as American forces approached the Chinese border, 250,000 troops of the Chinese People's Liberation Army (PLA) entered the war. Initially, the PLA succeeded in driving American forces back down the Korean peninsula, but by spring 1951, American and allied forces had regained the upper hand and forced the Chinese to retreat to the thirty-eighth parallel.

Asserting "there is no substitute for victory," MacArthur conducted a major political campaign designed to force President Truman to authorize a full-scale attack on Communist China. MacArthur conducted unauthorized press conferences, made contacts with Chinese Nationalist leaders in Taiwan, and mobilized a following among conservative members of Congress. In April 1951, after securing the full support of the secretaries of state and defense, President Truman relieved MacArthur of duty and ordered him to return to the United States. Truman's decision ignited a firestorm on Capitol Hill, where the general's supporters hinted that the president's conduct was nothing short of treasonous and that he should be impeached. Upon his return to Washington, MacArthur appealed to Congress for support against the president, whom he accused of seeking to appease Communism. During lengthy Senate hearings, however, Truman was backed by the military brass as well as the towering figure of General George C. Marshall, who had agreed to return to Washington to serve as defense secretary for one year to deal with the Korean crisis. MacArthur's supporters were unable to overcome the president's decisions to fire the general and to limit the war to the Korean peninsula.[108] After failing to make much headway in the 1952 presidential primaries, MacArthur retired from public life. The principle of presidential control over security policy had been preserved, despite the efforts of an enormously popular general with a vocal following in the Congress. The MacArthur imbroglio would be the last time an American military officer publicly turned to Congress to challenge presidential orders. Suppression of the admirals' revolt and the sacking of MacArthur firmly underscored the principle of unitary presidential command of the nation's military.

While he struggled with MacArthur, Truman also created an enormous standing army. Historically, the United States had built large armies in wartime and quickly disbanded them at the war's end. Opposition to maintaining standing armies in peacetime predated even the birth of the Republic. To meet Korean War needs, Truman was forced to halt the force reductions that had been underway since the end of World War II. By 1951, however, Truman and his advisers were concerned with more than America's immediate military needs. The president had concluded that American security required the construction of a permanent military force capable of deterring military attack from the Soviet Union and its allies anywhere on the globe. This had been the conclusion reached in a planning document known as NSC-68, drafted primarily by Paul Nitze and the State Department's policy planning staff and presented to the National Security Council in April 1950. This document, which became a cornerstone of American security policy, asserted that the principal goal of Soviet policy was the subversion or destruction of the United States. Preventing the Soviet leadership from achieving this goal would require a long-term commitment on the part of the United States to the "containment" of its adversary. This would require the development of enormous military forces—forces so powerful that the Soviets would be deterred from committing acts of aggression against the United States and its allies by the knowledge that the United States had the capacity to retaliate with overwhelming force. In short, the United States must commit itself, for the first time in its history, to the maintenance of powerful peacetime military forces.

Truman did not act on the recommendation of NSC-68 until the next year, when he called for expanded military spending and American rearmament to meet long-term challenges.[109] By 1952, the United States had tripled its military spending, expanded its nuclear weapons programs, begun the deployment of a fleet of heavy bombers capable of attacking the Soviet Union, doubled the size of the army and Marine Corps, and increased rather than diminished the size of its naval forces. To make certain that sufficient manpower would be available to meet military needs, Congress enacted the Universal Military Training and Service Act of 1951 and the Armed Forces Reserve Act of 1952. The first of these pieces of legislation expanded the military draft, which had already been reinstated under the 1948 Selective Service Act. In principle, all eighteenth-year-old men would now be required to undertake military training. However, to mute political opposition, the law allowed the Selective Service System to provide for educational and occupational deferments. In practice, these deferments, like the Civil War commutation fee, which had allowed men to pay $300 in lieu of conscription, permitted individuals wealthy enough to remain in school or resourceful enough to secure occupational deferments from local draft boards to avoid service. Labor leaders like Walter Reuther and African American leaders like A. Philip Randolph objected to the draft's exemptions for the privileged.[110] The system of deferments and exemptions, however, helped to forestall objections from the nation's more influential strata. As Selective Service System Director Lewis Hershey warned, if any effort was made to eliminate the deferments, "All hell will break loose."[111] Those who did serve in the military, whether as conscripts or volunteers, were required under the Reserve Act to remain in the ready reserves, available for call-up in the event of emergency. By 1953, nearly 4 million Americans were on active military service, backed by sizeable National Guard and reserve forces.[112]

To make certain that the nation's military forces had adequate equipment, Congress enacted the 1950 Defense Production Act, which gave the president authority to purchase strategic materials and order industries to give priority to military needs. Three years earlier, the 1947 National Security Act had provided for the creation of a National Security Resources Board to help the president coordinate military and industrial planning in wartime.[113] Rather than attempt to command industry to meet military needs, however, the president opted to expand and institutionalize the World War II contracting system. At the beginning of the Second World War, Secretary of War Henry Stimson had advised Roosevelt to "hire" industrialists by providing them with lucrative military contracts. "If you are going to try to go to war, or to prepare for war, in a capitalist country, you have got to let business make money out of the process or business won't work,"

Stimson said.[114] During the Truman era, this hiring of industrialists became a permanent feature of the American industrial and political landscape. Hundreds of firms received contracts for military equipment, ranging from meals, uniforms, and vehicles to missiles, aircraft, and naval vessels. Most major contracts required subcontracting, so that thousands of firms throughout the nation profited from defense work. For some, like the Lockheed, Northrup, and Grumman aviation companies, military undertakings became the principal source of business. These contractors made themselves virtual arms of the military, usually working closely, if not exclusively, with one particular service branch that, always arguing that the maintenance of a secure industrial base was necessary to promote the nation's security, made certain that its contractors always received a share of military business. The firms' executive ranks, filled with retired admirals, generals, captains, and colonels who now sold weapons to their former services, came to resemble officers' clubs.[115] When existing enterprises did not meet the government's needs, it sponsored the creation of new ones. One of the most important was the RAND Corporation, sponsored by the U.S. Air Force. Formally known as a Federally Funded Research and Development Center or FFRDC, RAND and a number of other corporations were established with the support of the military to engage in weapons research and operational planning.[116] The various corporations linked to the military and dependent upon military contracts and situated in virtually every state and congressional district, but particularly in the South and Southwest, became a powerful constituency for maintaining high levels of military preparedness—and spending—in the years to come.[117] The intense political support of thousands of firms and their unionized workers in what President Eisenhower called the "military-industrial complex" helped successive administrations ensure that the president would always have at his disposal an enormous and powerful military machine.

INTELLIGENCE AND PLANNING

In addition to centralizing military decision making, the 1947 National Security Act increased the White House's capacities for foreign policy and security planning, intelligence gathering and evaluation, and covert intelligence operations. The first of these results stemmed from the creation of the National Security Council. The council was never more than a loose-knit presidential advisory body and seldom had any independent influence. Beginning during the Kennedy presidency, however, the NSC staff became an important presidential instrument. Truman and Eisenhower relied upon the State Department's policy-planning staff and the JCS staff for policy analysis and advice. These groups, however, did not work directly for the president and had other institutional loyalties. Kennedy expanded the NSC staff and designated McGeorge Bundy, a former intelligence officer, to serve as his special assistant for national security affairs and head of the NSC staff. During subsequent presidencies, the NSC staff, eventually consisting of nearly two hundred professional employees organized in regional and functional offices, along with the national security assistant, became an important force in the shaping of foreign and security policy, often eclipsing the State Department and its leadership. For example, when he served as Richard Nixon's national security assistant, Henry Kissinger effectively excluded the secretary of state, William Rogers, from most foreign policy decision making. Similarly, during the Carter administration, the president allowed his national security assistant, Zbigniew Brzezinski, to marginalize Secretary of State Cyrus Vance. Both Rogers and Vance eventually resigned.[118] During George W. Bush's first term in office, the president's close relationship with National Security Adviser Condoleezza Rice gave Rice considerable influence in the Oval Office despite the enormous prestige enjoyed by Secretary of State Colin Powell. Rice's influence continued even after she succeeded Powell at the State Department.

The construction of a national security bureaucracy within the executive office of the president made possible the enormous postwar expansion of presidential unilateralism in the realm of security and foreign policy. Beginning with Truman, presidents would conduct foreign and security policy through executive agreements and executive orders and seldom negotiate formal treaties requiring Senate ratification. Presidents before Truman—even Franklin D. Roosevelt—had generally submitted important accords between the United States and foreign powers to the Senate for ratification and had sometimes seen their goals stymied by senatorial opposition. Not only did the Constitution require senatorial ratification of treaties, but before Truman, presidents lacked the administrative resources to conduct systematic, independent foreign policy. It was not by accident that most of the agreements—particularly the secret agreements—negotiated by FDR concerned military matters, where the president could rely upon the administrative capacities of the War and Navy Departments.[119]

The State Department's policy-planning staff and especially the NSC staff created the institutional foundations and capabilities upon which Truman and his successors could rely to conduct and administer the nation's foreign and security policies directly from the oval office. For example, American participation in the International Trade Organization (ITO), one of the cornerstones of U.S. postwar trade policy, was based on a sole executive agreement, the GATT Provisional Protocol, signed by President Truman after Congress delayed action and ultimately failed to approve the ITO charter.[120] Truman signed some 1,300 executive agreements and Eisenhower another 1,800, in some cases requesting congressional approval and in other instances ignoring Congress. Executive agreements take two forms—congressional-executive agreements and sole executive agreements. In the former case, the president submits the agreement to both houses of Congress as he would any other piece of legislation, with a majority vote in both houses required for passage. This is a lower hurdle than the two-thirds vote required for Senate ratification of a treaty. A sole executive agreement is not sent to Congress at all. The president generally has discretion over which avenue to pursue. All treaties and executive agreements carry the authority of law, although a sole executive agreement cannot contravene an existing statute.[121] During the Truman and Eisenhower presidencies, barely two hundred treaties were submitted to the Senate as stipulated by Article II of the Constitution.[122] The same pattern has continued to the present. In fact, two of the most important recent international agreements entered into by the United States, the North American Free Trade Agreement and the World Trade Organization agreement, were confirmed by congressional-executive agreement, not by treaty.[123]

In a similar vein, the policy-planning staff and NSC opened the way for policy making by executive order in the areas of security and foreign policy. Executive orders issued to implement presidents' military foreign policy goals have been variously called National Security Presidential

Directives (NSPD) and National Security Decision Directives (NSDD) but are most commonly known as National Security Directives or NSDs. These, like other executive orders, are commands from the president to an executive agency.[124] Most NSDs are classified, and presidents have consistently refused even to inform Congress of their existence, much less their content. Generally, NSDs are drafted by the NSC staff at the president's behest. Some NSDs involve mundane matters, but others have established America's most significant foreign and security policies. As mentioned above, NSC 68, developed by the State Department's policy-planning staff in 1950 prior to the creation of an NSC staff, set out the basic principles of containment upon which American Cold War policy came to be based. A series of Kennedy NSDs established the basic principles of American policy toward a number of world trouble spots.[125] Ronald Reagan's 1981 NSD 12 launched the president's massive military buildup and force modernization program, while his 1985 NSD 172 began the development of antimissile programs. President Bush's NSDs authorizing domestic eavesdropping were discussed in the previous chapter. Thus, the creation of new administrative capabilities gave presidents the tools through which to dominate foreign and security policy and to dispense with Congress and what FDR called its "incompetent obstructionists."

Presidential power was further augmented in the 1947 act by the creation of the CIA, which became a centrally important presidential foreign policy tool. The CIA gave the president the capacity to intervene in the affairs of other nations without informing Congress or the public. At the president's behest, the CIA undertook numerous covert operations in foreign countries during the Cold War and afterward. The agency's covert operations branch was established by a top secret presidential order, NSC 10-2, issued in June 1948. These operations were to include propaganda, economic warfare, sabotage, subversion, and assistance to underground movements. The U.S. government was to be able to "plausibly disclaim responsibility" for all covert operations.[126] Carrying out successive secret presidential orders, usually framed as NSDs, the CIA overthrew the Iranian government in 1953 and installed the shah who ruled Iran for the next quarter century. During the 1950s, the CIA also overthrew governments in Guatemala, Egypt, and Laos that were deemed to be unfriendly to the United

States.[127] The CIA helped organize and for a number of years subsidized anti-Communist politicians and political parties in Western Europe. In some instances, of course, CIA operations resulted in embarrassing failures such as the abortive "Bay of Pigs" invasion of Cuba in 1961. Nevertheless, covert CIA operations have been used by presidents to advance American interests in every corner of the globe—literally from Afghanistan to Zaire. For the most part, the nation's new intelligence capabilities were directed outside its own borders. Truman hoped to avoid infringements on the civil liberties of Americans and opposed Director J. Edgar Hoover's efforts to expand the domestic intelligence activities of the FBI.[128] By executive order, however, Truman created a Loyalty Review Board, which brought together a number of World War II programs designed to screen prospective government employees and to investigate charges of treasonable or disloyal conduct. Individual agencies were authorized to develop their own loyalty programs.[129] Truman also issued a number of executive orders establishing a classification system for government secrets that ultimately led to the classification of millions of pages of documents and allowed the president and the various federal agencies to stamp as "secret" almost any information they chose not to reveal to the public and the Congress.[130]

REVENUE EXTRACTION

The construction of America's new standing army and other national security institutions would require the nation to bear, on a permanent basis, levels of military spending previously seen only during wartime emergencies. Stated in constant dollars, President Truman's 1952 defense budget of more than $46 billion represented a twenty-fold increase over America's defense spending in 1940 and approached World War II spending levels. And the nation was expected to sustain these outlays into the indefinite future. To accomplish this Herculean task, however, Truman could rely upon the tremendous capabilities of the federal tax system developed by the Roosevelt administration during World War II. The Second World War marked a watershed in U.S. government finance. First, the Revenue Act of 1942 substantially broadened the nation's tax base, increasing the number of households subject to the income tax from 13 million to 28 million. By 1944, tax rates began at 3 percent on incomes between $500 and $2,000, rose to 20 percent for incomes above $2,000, and climbed steeply to reach a nominal rate of 91 percent on incomes over $200,000.[131] The second important innovation associated with the war was the enactment of the Current Tax Payment Act of 1943. Before 1943, federal income taxes were to be paid quarterly in the year after the income was received. This system depended heavily upon the honesty, good will, and foresight of individual taxpayers. Under the terms of the 1943 act, however, employers were required to withhold 20 percent of wages and salaries and to remit these to the government as the income was earned. The 1943 Current Tax Payment Act partially freed the government from its historic dependence upon the support and integrity of the individual taxpayer. It made the collection of income taxes automatic and involuntary from the perspective of the taxpayer, and, together with higher rates, increased federal income tax revenues from slightly more than $1 billion in 1940 to more than $45 billion by 1945. At the end of World War II, of course, there was considerable political pressure to cut taxes, and Congress did enact a tax cut over the president's veto in 1948.[132] The outbreak of the Korean War, however, produced a series of temporary tax increases, which in many instances became permanent, leading to $65 billion in revenues in 1955 and beginning the march toward today's $2 trillion in federal income tax receipts.

To make this tax burden more palatable to millions of ordinary Americans, the government relied upon the principle of progressivity. Progressivity, enshrined in American tax law since the Revenue Act of 1862, was a concession to the popular sense of justice. According to tax historian Sidney Ratner, progressivity accompanied the extension of new and relative high rates of taxation to citizens with small incomes.[133] In principle, at least, the handful of wealthy Americans had to be taxed at even higher rates in order to convince tens of millions of their less prosperous fellow citizens that the tax system was fair and that they should comply with its demands. At the same time, however, to prevent those very same wealthy and powerful Americans from mobilizing to block the imposition of high tax rates, Congress filled the income tax code with numerous loopholes mainly designed to reduce the tax burdens of upper-income wage earners, investors, and business owners.[134] As in the case of "universal" military conscription, those with sufficient influence to make trouble were bought off.

In addition to taxes, the White House sought to generate financial support for an expanded military effort from two other sources. One was the sale of arms and military equipment to friendly and neutral nations. Allowing American military contractors to sell arms to other countries helped increase the production runs and hence to reduce the unit costs to the American military of expensive weapons, as well as to bring the armies of foreign countries into the American military orbit.[135] At the same time, arms sales would help maintain the vitality of the American arms industry, the so-called defense industrial base, and its contribution to the nation's security.[136] Today, some $20 billion worth of American military hardware is sold abroad every year.[137]

A second and more important source of financial support for America's military effort was "burden sharing." America expected its allies to share the costs of defense either by contributing financially or by contributing troops and equipment in time of need. Burden sharing was certainly not a novel idea. As long ago as 430 B.C., Periclean Athens supported its fleet by creating the Delian League and requiring the islands of Chios, Lesbos, and Samos to make financial contributions for the maintenance of Athenian military and naval forces.[138] At the end of the Second World War, to be sure, America's chief allies were financially exhausted. Therefore, to ensure that the Western European democracies would possess the means to resist Communism and to bolster America's own security, the United States undertook major programs to promote European economic recovery, including the 1948 Marshall Plan.[139] The success of these efforts in turn made the Europeans worthwhile alliance partners. The British in particular were expected to contribute significantly to the American defense burden and were in return given privileged access to U.S. decision making.[140]

In the 1950s, the United States built a number of military alliances, most notably the North Atlantic Treaty Organization (NATO), which required participants to shoulder a portion of America's military costs. During the 1950s, NATO added some twenty divisions of British, German, and other European troops, along with thousands of aircraft and tanks, to the six American divisions defending Western Europe.[141]

Other American military agreements ultimately involved more than fifty nations in Europe and the Pacific region.[142] Military burden sharing continues to the present day. In the 1950s, America sought troops and material assistance from its allies. Today, as we shall see below, the United States is more likely to demand financial contributions from its allies.

In addition to defraying America's military expenses, treaties and defense pacts served presidential interests in another way as well. Presidents could use the cover of one of America's thousands of treaty obligations to undertake actions, especially in the military realm, that faced significant opposition in Congress. International commitments became a presidential trump card to be used against Congress, even as more and more of these commitments were based on executive agreements made by the president without congressional consultation. Early in the Vietnam War, for example, Secretary of State Dean Rusk explained to the Senate Foreign Relations Committee that American assistance to Vietnam was required under the terms of bilateral assistance agreements. It turned out that all these agreements that the administration now cited as American obligations had been entered into by the White House without the knowledge of Congress. Upon further inquiry, the Foreign Relations Committee uncovered hundreds of American international obligations negotiated by presidents without congressional sanction.[143]

Winning authorization from the United Nations Security Council has been a particularly important presidential ploy. President Truman sought and received Security Council approval to intervene against North Korea before even consulting with congressional leaders and then cited the UN resolution rather than congressional approval as the basis for going to war.[144] Similarly, President George H. W. Bush used UN Security Council Resolution 678, authorizing the use of force against Iraq, to bring pressure on a reluctant Congress to approve the deployment of American forces in the Persian Gulf in preparation for the 1990 war.[145] On numerous occasions, in fact, presidents have ordered American forces on UN peacekeeping missions without seeking any endorsement at all from Congress.[146]

Thus, in the early years of the Cold War, President Truman built a huge, permanent military establishment and solidified the principle of centralized presidential control over the military. The president also laid the foundations for funding this military machine and began to assemble a political constituency that would support high levels of military spending. While levels of military spending would fluctuate with international events and political currents over the next several decades, the maintenance of a huge standing army, once unthinkable, was now taken for granted. Truman, moreover, established a national security staff within the executive office and began the construction of an intelligence service capable of covert operations around the globe. These in turn helped Truman and future presidents circumvent Congress and engage in unilateral management of the nation's foreign and security policies. Possession of institutional capacity does not guarantee its use, but it certainly makes its use possible, and the White House emerged from the Truman era with what Schlesinger and others called "imperial" capabilities.

From the Korean War to the War on Terrorism

The imperial presidency overcame challenges from Congress and from members of its own military, notably General MacArthur, to strengthen its power during the Korean War. In June 1950, when North Korean forces invaded South Korea, President Truman and his advisers believed that if they failed to respond forcefully, they would encourage Soviet aggression throughout Europe and Asia. Uncertain about Congress's mood, the president first secured a UN Security Council resolution authorizing military intervention, as noted previously. He then met with a bipartisan group of congressional leaders, informed them of the UN resolution, and won their support. Congressional leaders expected Truman to ask for a formal resolution approving the use of force, if not for a full-blown declaration of war. Truman, however, influenced by the views of Secretary of State Dean Acheson, decided he would not ask for a congressional vote. Instead, Truman accepted Acheson's view that his constitutional powers as commander in chief, coupled with America's obligation to enforce the UN's resolution, were adequate grounds for ordering American forces into combat. By deploying massive forces without asking congressional approval, even though he had been assured that approval was forthcoming, Truman sought to assert the principle that the president, not Congress, could decide whether and when to go to war. Congress complained, but given the growing sense of national emergency, acquiesced by voting appropriations and extending the draft.[147] A fundamental principle had been established. In the future, even when presidents sought congressional assent to the use of force, there was a tendency to view this as a courtesy rather than a constitutional requirement.

Over the next two years, the war became unpopular as the fighting dragged on inconclusively. The new powers of the presidency, however, proved equal to the task of fighting a war and resisting efforts by Congress and others to interfere with presidential prerogatives. Two factors worked in Truman's favor—the economy and the draft. To begin with, Truman chose to finance the war chiefly through increases in federal income tax rates. Although higher taxes are never popular, the early 1950s were a period of economic growth in the United States, and higher taxes were more than offset by rising incomes. The nation could afford both guns and butter.[148] Korean War tax increases, moreover, were not as substantial as they might have been. Two other sources of revenue also helped support the costs of the war. First, a number of American allies contributed troops and materiel. These included Great Britain, Australia, Turkey, and above all, South Korea. Moreover, under the newly established Breton Woods financial system, the U.S. dollar was the world's reserve currency. During this period, billions of dollars were held by foreign banks and the resulting profit to the U.S. Treasury—called seignoirage—was enormous.[149] At the same time, as we saw earlier, Korean War–era conscription was surrounded by a system of deferments and exemptions that permitted members of influential strata to escape military service if they chose. These economic and social factors helped to mute domestic opposition to the war. The result on the battlefield was a stalemate. At home, however, the White House won a resounding victory, as the exigencies of war made it all the more difficult for Congress to carp about the president's expansion of military power and covert capabilities.

The next two presidents made ample use of the capabilities forged by Truman. Eisenhower further centralized presidential control over the military establishment and continued the Truman-era loyalty program. In 1955 and 1956 President Eisenhower in effect demanded a blank check from Congress for possible military action in the Taiwan Straits and the Middle East and in 1958 sent fourteen thousand Marines into Lebanon without asking Congress for authorization. Eisenhower issued numerous NSDs and made ample use of the CIA's covert capabilities. In 1954, Eisenhower made his own contribution to the enhancement of presidential power when he made a virtually absolute claim of executive privilege in refusing to turn over records to Congress.[150] John F. Kennedy, for his part, shared the same inclinations. Kennedy expanded the executive's capacity for covert operations in 1961 by creating the Special Forces, an elite military corps reporting more fully to the president than to the regular army command. Kennedy sent Special Forces and other American military elements to assist the South Vietnamese without consulting Congress. By the Kennedy era, these sorts of actions on the part of the president were more or less taken for granted by Congress, by the public, and by most scholars.[151]

The expansion of presidential power in the realm of foreign and security policy, however, seemed for a time to be halted and even reversed by the clash between Congress and President Lyndon Johnson over the Vietnam War and later the Watergate struggle between Congress and President Richard Nixon. Unlike the war in Korea, the Vietnam War sparked enormous opposition in the American public and in the Congress. While this opposition had a number of sources, one aspect of the problem was economic. By the late 1960s, America no longer possessed the dominant position in the world economy it had enjoyed during the previous decade. It would not be so easy for a president to assure both guns and butter. America's allies had no interest in helping to defray the costs of the war. And, to make matters worse, a powerful domestic constituency, the liberal wing of the president's own political party, was deeply committed to a set of enormously expensive social programs that President Johnson had defined as the nation's top priorities. Diversion of funds from the president's Great Society programs to pay for the war generated fierce opposition. Later, changes in draft rules made politically potent constituencies more vulnerable to conscription and intensified their opposition to the war. The result was to drive Johnson from office and to compel his successor, Richard Nixon, to withdraw American forces under circumstances that made the victory of Communist forces, led by Ho Chi Minh, all but inevitable.

The end of the Vietnam War represented not only a military defeat for the United States, but also a defeat for the presidency. In the aftermath of the war and in particular after the disintegration and eventual collapse of the Nixon administration, Congress seized the opportunity to enact a number of pieces of legislation designed to curb presidential power in the foreign policy and security domains. These included the 1972 War Powers Resolution, limiting presidential control over the deployment of American military forces; the 1973 Case-Zablocki Act, requiring that Congress be informed of all executive agreements; the 1974 Hughes-Ryan Amendments, regulating foreign military assistance; the 1977 International Emergency Economic Powers Act (IEEPA), regulating the exercise of presidential emergency economic power; the Foreign Intelligence Surveillance Act of 1978 and the Intelligence Oversight Act of 1980, providing for congressional oversight of intelligence operations; and the 1976 Arms Export Control Act, limiting presidential use of proxy forces. Congress also created intelligence oversight committees to monitor the president's use of the nation's intelligence agencies. It appeared that the classic pattern of presidential politics had reasserted itself. Political mobilization induced by war had strengthened the Congress and weakened the presidency.

The post-Vietnam retrogression of presidential power, however, proved to be short-lived. Less than two decades after the last American troops were evacuated from Saigon, Johnson's successors had more than restored presidential power in war and foreign relations. The first steps involved the recruitment and internal structure of the military and its relationship to American society. For two centuries, America had relied upon citizen-soldiers to fill the ranks of its armed forces and spurned the idea of a professional army as inconsistent with democratic values. In the wake of the Vietnam War, however, presidents and military planners realized that dependence on citizen-soldiers could impose serious constraints upon the use of military forces. The risks facing citizen-soldiers provided opponents of the use of military force with a potent issue to use against the government. The casualties and hardships borne by citizen-soldiers, moreover, reverberated through society and might, as the Vietnam case illustrated, fuel antiwar movements and resistance to military conscription. University of Chicago economist Milton Friedman, who served as a member of the Gates Commission, created by President Nixon to examine the elimination of military conscription, argued that three-fourths of the opposition to the Vietnam War was generated by the draft.[152] Citizen-soldiers might be appropriate for a national war in which America was attacked and domestic opposition driven to the margins. Anti–Vietnam War protests, however, convinced President Richard Nixon and his successors that an army composed of professional soldiers would give them greater flexibility to use military power when they deemed it necessary.[153]

Accordingly, Nixon ended the draft in 1973 and began conversion of the military into an all-volunteer force of professional soldiers. The presumption was that sending military professionals into battle would spawn less popular and political resistance than deploying reluctant conscripts, and this supposition seems to have been borne out. Indeed, in 2002, some opponents of President George W. Bush's buildup of American forces for an attack against Iraq argued for a renewal of conscription precisely because they believed that the president would be constrained from going to war if the military consisted of draftees.[154] Members of this new professional force, moreover, especially those recruited for its elite combat units, receive extensive training and indoctrination designed to separate them from civilian society, to imbue them with a warrior ethic, emphasizing loyalty to the group and the military service as primary values, and to reduce their level of integration into the larger society.[155] This training is designed to immunize the military against possible contagion from antiwar and defeatist sentiment that may spring up in civilian America and appears to have produced a military, especially an officer corps, that views itself as a distinct caste.[156] To a significant extent, the current military lives as a state within a state, subject to its own rules, norms, and governance.[157] Many are recruited from families with strong military traditions and from areas of the country, primarily the South and West, where conservative politics and support for the military are widespread.[158] This is a military better prepared for the idea that war is a normal state of affairs, and whose members are less likely to complain to the media and members of Congress about the hardships they may endure in their nation's service.

The active-duty, all-volunteer force is backed by approximately one million reservists and National Guard troops who train on a regular basis but are called into service only when needed. Reservists make up a large percentage of troops trained in a number of support specialties—such as water supply, medical specialties, and chemical warfare—that are usually needed only in actual combat situations.[159] Tens of thousands of reservists were mobilized during the 1990 Persian Gulf War, for the various military operations conducted during the Clinton years, and again in 2002–03 in preparation for a second war with Iraq. Although the reservists are volunteers and many are veterans of the regular military, calling them up for service can disrupt the civilian economy and society and sometimes produces hardship and resentment among the reservists, their families, and their employers. During the Vietnam War, both Lyndon Johnson and Richard Nixon refrained from calling up the reserves, believing that such an order would intensify political opposition to the war. Because of these problems, in 2003 Defense Secretary Donald Rumsfeld ordered military planners to find ways of diminishing or even eliminating the armed force's reliance upon reserve troops. This will entail some expansion of the size of the active-duty military as well as training regular forces to take over the specialties currently dominated by reservists.[160] Although both steps will add to defense costs, lessening the government's dependence upon the last of its citizen-soldiers would create a military force even more readily available for use whenever and wherever it was deemed to be needed. Consistent with Rumsfeld's wishes, defense budgets since 2004 have been providing for the conversion of thousands of civil affairs, psychological operations, and special operations slots from reserve to active-duty forces.[161]

In the aftermath of Vietnam, the military was not only professionalized, it was also further centralized. The 1986 Defense Reorganization Act (Goldwater-Nichols) significantly increased the power of the JCS chairman, the defense secretary, and the president to determine military missions and set procurement policies.[162] This change not only promised to improve military effectiveness, but also further reduced the opportunity for the individual services to air their squabbles publicly and open the way for congressional intervention. Interservice squabbles had been a continuing albeit muted problem since the struggles of the Truman era and had broken out anew during the Vietnam War, when the army publicly accused the air force of failing to provide adequate close air support for its ground combat troops.[163]

While a more professional and centralized military might diminish the political constraints on presidential war making, it could not fully eliminate them. Many Americans might be willing to accept the idea of sending professional soldiers into harm's way, especially if their own children were not subject to conscription. But even professional soldiers are Americans with home towns, parents, relatives, and friends, and the Vietnam conflict had demonstrated that American casualties could become a political liability and ultimately a constraint on the use of military force. This problem was one of the factors that led successive administrations to search for means of waging warfare that would minimize American casualties. After the carnage of the Civil War, American military doctrine had already begun to emphasize technology and maximum firepower in order to keep casualties low and maintain public support.[164] In the years after the Vietnam War, the military services invested tens of billions of dollars in the development of cruise missiles, drone aircraft, precision-guided munitions, and a multitude of other advanced weapons systems capable of disabling or destroying America's opponents while reducing the risks to which American troops were exposed.[165] Thus in the 1990 Persian Gulf War and even more so in the 2001–02 Afghan campaign, precision-guided weapons inflicted enormous damage on enemy forces and gave U.S. troops all but bloodless victories. In the 2003 Iraq War, pilotless aircraft, precision-guided munitions, battlefield computers, and new command-and-control technology helped bring about a rapid victory over substantial Iraqi forces with what once might have been seen as impossibly low casualties.[166] Military analysts have pointed to these developments—sometimes called a revolution in military affairs—as indicative of a technological revolution in the conduct of war. Like past transformations in military tactics, however, this one has been caused as much by political as technological or exclusively military factors.[167] At any rate, to the extent that U.S. losses can be limited to smart bombs and pilotless aircraft, popular opposition to the use of military force is less likely to become a political problem. After one Predator drone aircraft was downed in 2002, an air force officer involved in the program said, "It was on page six of the *Washington Post*. If that had been a [manned] F-16, it would have been page one."[168]

While the destruction of Iraqi military forces was accomplished with few American casualties, Iraqi resistance to the subsequent American occupation produced a steady stream of casualties over the next several years. Opponents of the president's policies pointed to American deaths as a reason for withdrawing U.S. forces. President Bush, however, responded to his critics by launching a public relations offensive in 2005–06. The administration's poll data seemed to show that Americans would support continued military operations in the Middle East if they believed America would eventually achieve victory. The president's speeches began to emphasize this theme, and support for his policies increased, at least temporarily.[169] Bush was able to achieve at least a temporary public relations success largely because most Americans' insulation from the war's actual effects left them more vulnerable to presidential persuasion.

Presidents and the military learned two other lessons from the Vietnam War. These concerned media and money. Most military officers and defense officials were convinced that negative media coverage played an important role in the erosion of popular support for America's intervention in Southeast Asia. Stories of atrocities and casualties and a steady diet of media accounts questioning or contradicting official views of the war undoubtedly played a role in turning public opinion against the war during the mid-1960s.[170] After the war, all the services sought to devise procedures and tactics designed to prevent negative media coverage in future conflicts. On the one hand, the services developed rules restricting media access to combat theaters. In the Persian Gulf, Grenada, Panama, Afghanistan, and the other regions in which American forces were sent into battle, reporters were restricted to pool coverage and were strictly prohibited from making unescorted visits to war zones. In general, the press was able to show only what the military wanted the public to see. At the same time, defense brass made a major effort to cultivate reporters and media personalities and assigned only the most articulate military and media-savvy civilian defense officials—Generals Colin Powell and Norman Schwartzkopf in 1990 and Defense Secretary Donald Rumsfeld in 2001—to brief the media and answer questions.

In preparation for an attack on Iraq in 2003, reporters were sent to military "boot camps" where they were prepared for the rigors of combat and given a chance to absorb military perspectives. Some reporters were attached to particular combat units in the hope that they would file favorable stories about the soldiers with whom they lived and worked on a daily basis. One journalist observed that the purpose of this practice was to induce reporters "to bond, to feel part of a unit, and to get the military good press."[171] This program of "embedding" reporters with military units was extremely successful. Many journalists clearly identified with their units and typically used the pronoun "we" when describing military actions undertaken by those units. Such press criticism as was heard during the war generally came from reporters far from the front or from military analysts in New York and Washington. These critics, however, could not compete with the enthusiastic "embeds" who provided dramatic real-time combat photos and coverage via satellite. Simultaneously, experienced and able White House communications staffers such as former deputy communications director James Wilkinson were temporarily assigned to serve as information managers for senior military officers.[172] This was to prevent generals who might lack communications skills from making statements that were inconsistent with White House views or that might be deemed politically incorrect. The combination of restriction and astute public relations had a generally positive effect on media coverage of U.S. military action. In addition, the networks themselves engaged in a good deal of self-censorship. Stung by Republican charges that they lacked patriotism, the major news networks generally made a point of treating Americans to favorable coverage of America's war effort. CNN went so far as to assign a more upbeat anchor team for its domestic broadcasts than for its international service. International audiences heard critical coverage from a team consisting of Jim Clancy, Michael Holmes, and Becky Anderson, who consistently questioned the claims of American officials. American viewers, by contrast, saw the team of Paula Zahn, Aaron Brown, and Wolf Blitzer, who seemed to find considerably more to praise than to question in their review of America's military effort.[173]

As to money, the U.S. government learned two lessons during the Vietnam War. One lesson was that attempting to buy both guns and butter with funds extracted from its own taxpayers could be politically harmful. The second was that Congress might employ its power of the purse to interfere with military operations. During the course of American history, Congress has seldom refused to provide funding for military action when asked to do so by the president. In 1973, however, Congress voted to cut off funding for combat operations in Cambodia, a move that hastened the end of the Vietnam War.[174] Two years later, moreover, Congress voted to block the use of any funds for U.S. military intervention in Angola.[175] In order to make themselves less dependent upon taxpayers and the Congress, post-Vietnam presidents redoubled their efforts to induce American allies and others to share the military burden. This tactic first became apparent during the Reagan administration, when the White House solicited funds from the Sultan of Brunei to pay for military aid to the Nicaraguan Contras. Apparently, the funds were placed in the wrong Swiss bank account and never actually reached the Contras.[176] Despite this fiasco, the ploy of turning to foreigners to fund America's military efforts has been increasing in importance. In the 1990 Persian Gulf War, for example, the Bush administration made much of the fact that the United States had organized a coalition of nations to liberate Kuwait. But with the exception of Great Britain, which contributed valuable combat forces, America's coalition partners provided only token military units. Instead, members of the coalition were expected to contribute financially to the American military effort. Thus, Saudi Arabia, Kuwait, the United Arab Emirates (UAE), Germany, Japan, and France—nations threatened by Iraq or dependent upon Middle Eastern oil— collectively paid the United States some $54 billion as their contribution to the war effort. This sum was actually slightly more than the final cost of the war.[177]

The president had wanted the payments to be tendered as "gifts" directly to the Defense Department, which could then spend the money as the administration saw fit. Congress, however, insisted that the funds be paid to the treasury, where any subsequent disbursements would require a congressional appropriation.[178] The importance of fiscal considerations in the Persian Gulf war is one reason the United States was anxious to keep in its coalition nations such as Saudi Arabia and the UAE that had money but virtually no military forces. Militarily potent but impecunious nations like Israel were not invited to participate. The United States had enough firepower; it needed cash.

From Vietnam to Afghanistan and Beyond

The White House had learned the lessons of Vietnam. The chief lesson was that presidents could wage war on their own initiative so long as influential segments of the public were not inconvenienced. Successive presidents, most notably Ronald Reagan and George H. W. Bush, worked to break the legal fetters through which Congress sought to constrain presidential war making. Some of these fetters proved illusory. For example, the 1980 Intelligence Oversight Act lacked sanctions or penalties and seemed to assume that the president would cooperate with Congress.[179] No subsequent president, however, showed any intention of cooperating, and indeed, beginning with President Reagan, the White House interpreted the act as authorizing the executive to conduct covert operations.[180]

Other encumbrances were removed by the courts. For example, Congress drafted IEEPA to narrow the president's emergency powers and attached a legislative veto provision to ensure its ability to control presidential actions under the act. The U.S. Supreme Court, however, in the 1981 case of *Dames and Moore v. Regan,* stemming from President Carter's handling of the Iranian hostage crisis, construed the president's emergency powers broadly.[181] And in the 1983 case of *INS v. Chadha,* the Court invalidated legislative veto provisions such as those in IEEPA.[182] The result was to leave the president with broader emergency economic powers and less congressional control than he had faced before Congress attempted to limit executive discretion.[183] The *Chadha* case also undermined the 1976 National Emergencies Act, which had provided that an emergency declared by the president could be terminated by a congressional resolution. As a result, an emergency today can be ended only by a joint resolution, which is, of course, subject to presidential veto.[184] The president is still required under the act to notify Congress every six months of the continuation of an emergency situation once it has been declared, but this reporting requirement is hardly a limit on the president's power.

A third presidential fetter was broken by aggressive executive action beginning in the early Reagan years. The 1973 War Powers Resolution provided that presidents could not use military forces for more than ninety days without securing congressional authorization. Many in Congress saw this time limit as a restraint on presidential action although, as has often been observed, it gave the president more discretion than had been provided by the framers of the Constitution. President Gerald Ford carefully followed the letter of the law when organizing a military effort to rescue American sailors held by Cambodia in 1975. But this was the first and last time that the War Powers Resolution was fully observed.[185] The demise of the resolution began during the Reagan administration. President Reagan and his advisers were determined to eliminate this restriction, however negligible, on presidential war power.[186] Accordingly, between 1982 and 1986, Reagan presented Congress with a set of military faits accomplis that undermined the War Powers Resolution and, in effect, asserted a doctrine of sole presidential authority in the security realm. In August 1982, Reagan sent U.S. forces to Lebanon, claiming constitutional authority to do so.[187] After terrorist attacks killed a number of Marines, Congress pressed Reagan to withdraw American forces. To underscore its displeasure, Congress activated the sixty-day War Powers clock, but after the administration accused lawmakers of undermining America's military efforts, Congress extended the president's authority to deploy troops to Lebanon for another eighteen months.

The president essentially ignored Congress but withdrew American forces in February after further casualties and no prospect for success. In October 1983, while American forces were still in Lebanon, President Reagan ordered an invasion of the Caribbean island of Grenada after a coup had led to the installation of a pro-Cuban government on the island. Once again, the president claimed that his position as commander in chief gave him the power to initiate military action on a unilateral basis. Congress threatened to invoke the War Powers Resolution, but Reagan withdrew American troops before the Senate acted. The invasion of Grenada was quick, virtually without casualties, and quite popular, especially after the president claimed to have rescued a group of American medical students attending classes on the island. Also generating considerable popular approval was the

1986 bombing of Libya in response to a terrorist attack in Berlin that the administration blamed on Libyan agents. Again Reagan acted without consulting Congress and claimed that his authority had come directly from the Constitution.

President Reagan was thus able to use American military forces on three separate occasions while denying that he was required to seek congressional authorization for his actions. Congress threatened and grumbled but in each instance was outmaneuvered by the president. Of course, in 1987 several of the president's aides were prosecuted for violations of federal law when it was revealed that the administration had transferred arms to Nicaraguan "Contra" guerillas then fighting against the Sandanista regime in that nation, despite specific congressional prohibitions. Nevertheless, Reagan's successor, George H. W. Bush, resumed using American military forces on his authority as commander in chief. In December 1989, Bush ordered an invasion of Panama designed to oust Panamanian strongman General Manuel Noriega. Bush claimed that American citizens living in the Canal Zone were in danger and charged that Noriega had become involved in drug trafficking. Since drugs are shipped to the United States from many nations, often with the connivance of high-ranking officials, this seemed a rather flimsy pretext. Congress nevertheless made no official response to the invasion. A nonbinding House resolution expressed its approval of the president's actions but urged Bush not to use drug smuggling as a reason to invade Mexico or the remainder of Latin America.[188]

In 1990–91, of course, the Bush administration sent a huge American military force into the Persian Gulf in response to Iraq's invasion and occupation of Kuwait, actions which posed a substantial threat to American economic and political interests. Consistent with the tactics devised by Harry Truman, the administration secured a UN Security Council resolution authorizing member states to use "all necessary means"—i.e., military force—to compel Iraq to restore Kuwaiti independence. The president's spokesmen, in particular Defense Secretary Richard Cheney, asserted that the UN resolution was a sufficient legal basis for American military action against Iraq. Given the UN resolution, said Cheney, no congressional authorization was required.[189] After House Democrats expressed strong opposition to unilateral action by the president, Bush asked Congress for legislation supporting the UN resolution. Both houses of Congress voted to authorize military action against Iraq—the Senate by the narrowest of margins—but the president made it clear that he did not feel bound by any congressional declaration and was prepared to go to war with or without Congress's assent. Indeed, the president later pointed out that he had specifically avoided asking Capitol Hill for "authorization," since such a request might improperly imply that Congress "had the final say in . . . an executive decision."[190] President Clinton continued the Truman and Bush practice of securing authorization to use military force from a compliant international body and then presenting Congress with a fait accompli. Thus in 1994 Clinton planned an invasion of Haiti under the cover of a UN Security Council resolution. The president hoped to oust the military dictatorship that had seized power in a coup and to reinstall President Jean-Bertrand Aristide. Congress expressed strong opposition to Clinton's plans, but he pressed forward nonetheless, claiming that he did not need congressional approval. The invasion was called off when the Haitian junta stepped down, but Clinton sent ten thousand American troops to occupy the island and help Aristide secure power. Congress was not consulted about the matter. In a similar vein, between 1994 and 1998, claiming to act under UN and NATO auspices, the administration undertook a variety of military actions in the former Yugoslavia, including an intensive bombing campaign directed against Serbian forces and installations, without formal congressional authorization. The air campaign lasted some seventy-nine days, involved more than thirty thousand American troops and more than eight hundred aircraft, and was conducted exclusively on the president's own authority.[191] The War Powers Resolution seemed to have entered the same legal limbo as archaic state laws prohibiting blasphemy.

By the end of the Clinton administration, it was no longer clear what war powers, if any, remained in the hands of Congress. Ronald Reagan, George H. W. Bush, and Bill Clinton had all ordered American forces into combat on their own authority, outmaneuvered, bullied, or ignored Congress, and repeatedly asserted the principle that the president controlled security policy and especially the use of military force. Early in the administration of President George W. Bush, Islamic terrorists destroyed the World Trade Center and damaged the Pentagon. The president organized a major military campaign designed to eliminate terrorist bases in Afghanistan and to depose the Taliban regime that sheltered the terrorists. Congress, for its part, quickly authorized the president to use America's armed forces to prevent future acts of terrorism. The congressional resolution was little more than a blank check, barely mentioned by the press and ignored by the public. Both were by now fully aware that, whatever its rhetoric, Congress had very little real control over the use of American military might. Subsequently, President Bush issued a variety of executive orders establishing military tribunals to try suspected terrorists, freezing the assets of those suspected of assisting terrorists, and expanding the authority of the CIA and other intelligence agencies. America's allies were also asked to contribute materiel and financial support for the endeavor, though only Great Britain made a substantial contribution.

Although the president was prepared to act without congressional assent, Congress seemed happy to accede to every White House demand. Within a month of the terrorist attacks, the White House had drafted and Congress had quickly enacted the USA Patriot Act, expanding the power of government agencies to engage in domestic surveillance activities, including electronic surveillance, and restricting judicial review of such efforts. The act also gave the attorney general greater authority to detain and deport aliens suspected of having terrorist affiliations.[192] The following year, Congress created the Department of Homeland Security, combining offices from twenty-two federal agencies into one huge new cabinet department that would be responsible for protecting the nation from further acts of terrorism. The new agency, with a tentative budget of $40 billion, was to include the Coast Guard, Transportation Safety Administration, Federal Emergency Management Administration, Immigration and Naturalization Service, and offices from the departments of Agriculture, Energy, Transportation, Justice, Health and Human Services, Commerce, and the General Services Administration. The actual reorganization plan was drafted by the White House, but Congress weighed in to make certain that the new agency's workers would enjoy civil service and union protections.

In October 2002, Congress voted to authorize the president to attack Iraq, which the administration accused of supporting terrorism and constructing weapons of mass destruction. As had become customary, the congressional resolution gave the president complete discretion, and the president, while welcoming congressional support, asserted that he had full power to use force with or without Congress's blessing. As was noted in Chapter 1, only Senator Byrd even bothered to object to the now obvious political if not constitutional truth of Bush's claim. In a reversal of the usual pattern, however, the president used his congressional resolution to pressure the United Nations Security Council to approve the use of force. Without such a resolution, an attack on Iraq would appear politically less legitimate and, more important, some of the nations expected to bankroll the war might well refuse, fearing their own domestic political repercussions.

The Security Council, however, stopped short of the authorization sought by President Bush, agreeing only to return UN weapons inspectors who had been ousted from Iraq some years earlier. Members of the council, especially France and Russia, argued that Iraq should be given an opportunity to disarm before being attacked. While the inspectors shuffled aimlessly around the suburbs of Baghdad, the president mobilized land, sea, and air forces in preparation for a military assault. And once again, American diplomats worked to build a coalition. The president called it a "coalition of the willing," and said different nations would play different roles in it according to their abilities. Presumably, this meant that the British were expected to provide military support, while Kuwait and Quatar, among others, were expected to provide bases for American forces. Several other nations, including Japan and Germany, nominally opposed to the war, signaled their willingness to help finance the postwar reconstruction of Iraq in exchange for access to Iraqi oil. American officials indicated that even without financial contributions from America's allies, the war would not impose a burden on the American economy. America expected to have privileged access to Iraqi oil after the war, if that nation's oil facilities could be repaired and operated successfully.[193]

Return of the Imperial Presidency

Franklin D. Roosevelt is often credited with the creation of the modern presidency. And indeed, during the Great Depression and the

Second World War, FDR greatly expanded the executive branch and increased the powers of the oval office. In the realm of foreign and security policy, however, it was Harry S. Truman who laid the foundations for presidential supremacy. Roosevelt had been a wartime president who made use of his personal dynamism and political skill to fashion a series of ad hoc arrangements to control the national security arena. Truman, however, built the institutions and invented the procedures that allowed a rather inexperienced legislator from Missouri and his successors of varying abilities, backgrounds, and political persuasions to manage the foreign and security policies of what became a great imperial power. Through the mix of military and civil institutions developed by Truman, the United States contained the Soviet Union and ultimately prevailed in the Cold War. Through these same institutions, however, the presidency came to dominate the realm of national security and Congress was gradually relegated to a secondary position.

Part of the problem was the Cold War itself. Historically, as we saw, presidential power had waxed in wartime and waned afterward as Congress, in alliance with the forces inevitably mobilized by the effects of war, moved to reassert its role. The Cold War erased the distinction between war and peace. The emergency, and presidential demands for emergency powers, were constant, and unfortunately, with the conclusion of the Cold War, new emergencies have arisen. The growth of presidential power, however, was not inevitable, despite the Cold War.

Presidential power expanded because successive presidents devised institutions that bolstered their power at the expense of Congress. And when Congress managed to rein in presidential power after the Vietnam War, presidents did not respond by passively submitting to legislative authority. Instead, they licked their wounds, learned from past mistakes, and introduced institutional innovations intended to restore and enhance the authority of the Oval Office in the realm of security affairs. Among the most important of these has been the end of the nation's dependence upon citizen-soldiers and the construction of a military force and military tactics designed to reduce political constraints on the presidential use of military power.

Increased presidential control of security policy has had implications for presidential power in domestic affairs as well. Since the Civil

War, presidents have demanded and received the power to regulate civilian production in wartime. Since the early years of the Cold War, moreover, military contracts have been a major factor shaping domestic industrial production and priorities. But presidential national security powers unavoidably impinge upon domestic matters going far beyond the economic realm. This has become especially evident since the initiation of President Bush's War on Terror. The Patriot Act and the Homeland Security Department have suddenly brought the president's national security powers home, much as the loyalty and security classification systems of the Cold War era once did. And, since the threat of terrorism is not likely to end in the foreseeable future, the War on Terror promises to become as permanent a part of American political life as the Cold War was for so many years. As the distinction between foreign policy and domestic policy diminishes, the president's growing foreign policy powers are certain to take on ever greater domestic importance.

But life may not become any easier for the president. The domestic intrusions of the War on Terror have helped to re-create problems similar to the ones that the executive branch has been trying to sidestep ever since the Vietnam War. America's military ventures abroad now rely on a relatively small and insulated force of volunteers and professional soldiers whose deployment and casualties produce barely a ripple on Main Street. But if snooping and security measures generate uneasiness and suspicion in the civilian population here at home, they will also produce protests and political inconveniences that challenge the presidential monopoly over national security policy.

In fact, even the attempt to insulate hometown America from the bloody facts of Ramadi and Fallujah may backfire for the president's policies, if not for the presidency itself. The Bush administration's secretive and ideologically restrictive deliberations about going to war in Iraq admitted no dissenting views concerning the consequences that were likely to follow the overthrow of Saddam Hussein. As a result, the White House was clearly unprepared for roadside explosives that would greet our troops in Iraq, expecting instead the floral tributes of a grateful, liberated people. The attempt to limit the scale of our military venture only made things worse. Then Defense Secretary Rumsfeld responded dismissively to professional military advisers such as General Eric Shinseki, who argued that we needed twice as many troops in Iraq as the administration was willing to send. Troop commitments on that scale might have carried the consequences of the Iraq War into so many American households that the domestic political repercussions of call-ups and casualties would have distracted the administration from its objectives. Instead the administration sent too few troops to achieve those objectives. Eventually, its miscues cost the administration dearly in the 2006 national elections, when Democrats won control of both houses of Congress.

The politics of presidential aggrandizement can result in disastrous policy decisions abominably executed. Narrow executive control of national security policy excludes views that ought to be heard and considered. Efforts to limit the political fallout of military mobilization can cripple the effective use of force. In the case of Iraq, the result has been the biggest failure of American power and diplomacy since Vietman, maybe the worst ever. Will it undermind the power of the presidency? Probably not. Presidents fail, but the presidency adapts. Unfortunately, the adjustments that strengthen the presidency do not reliably produce policies that strengthen the country.

7

Congressional Government:
Its Rise and Fall

The Most Popular Branch

IN THE EARLY REPUBLIC, when there were no mass-membership political parties to mobilize the voters, the presidency seemed to be the preeminent institution of American government. George Washington, John Adams, and Thomas Jefferson, along with the key cabinet officials such as Alexander Hamilton, Albert Gallatin, and James Madison, were the dominant figures in the political life of the nation. During Washington's administration, Alexander Hamilton created a national bank and a national currency and put the country's finances in order. Adams built a navy and new army, energetically enforced the Alien and Sedition Acts, and conducted delicate negotiations with France without consulting Congress or even his own cabinet.[1] Jefferson launched a war against the Barbary Pirates, purchased the Louisiana Territory by executive fiat, and proclaimed an embargo on American trade with Britain and France—a decisive stroke of executive energy, but ill-fated.

Jefferson himself was above electioneering, but in the late 1790s his managers (chiefly James Madison) built a network of political clubs and partisans who formed the Democratic Republicans, the progenitor of today's Democrats and the world's first political party. The Federalists became the second. Although they found the whole business distasteful, Federalists recognized that to survive they must organize to electioneer.[2] The Jeffersonians generally appealed to groups further down in the class structure than their Federalist rivals and so worked to reduce the property requirements that limited voting rights in most states. Jefferson himself asserted that all men who paid taxes or served in the militia should have the right to vote, and under Jeffersonian pressure, property requirements were weakened or dropped altogether in a number of states.[3] The chief consequence of the Jeffersonian mobilization was to make Congress the arbiter of presidential nominations. King Caucus, as we have already seen, reigned from the era of Jefferson to that of Jackson. Political mobilization empowered Congress.

The Jacksonians expanded on their Jeffersonian legacy by recruiting an even larger and less privileged part of the male population for electoral politics. Jacksonian influence eliminated most of the remaining property restrictions on voting, and the Jacksonian practice of spoilsmanship helped to solidify and expand the proto-party organization created by the Jeffersonians. The Jacksonian mobilization carried presidential turnout for the first time toward a majority of the eligible voters.[4] The party not only replaced Congress as the mechanism for nominating presidents, but also provided structure for organizing Congress itself.

The framers thought that sooner or later Congress would gain power from what they called its "popularity," that is, its close connection to groups and forces in civil society. And after Jackson, the framers seemed to be correct. Congress grew in stature, while most presidents were little more than clerks. Unlike members of Congress, presidents had distant and indirect connections with the electorate. They presided over a miniscule administrative apparatus. Congress controlled the agencies' budgets and eventually dictated the president's political appointments.[5] The great men of American politics became great in Congress—Henry Clay, John C. Calhoun, Daniel Webster, Stephen Douglas. Only in warfare did presidents seem to rise to leadership, and not always then. It was Clay and the congressional "war hawks" who pushed Madison into war with Great Britain in 1812. Madison's conduct of the war was not distinguished. The army, of which he was commander in chief, consisted of a small professional nucleus fleshed out by state militia units. The officers who commanded these state forces had usually been appointed by governors, not the president. President Polk was more bellicose than Madison. He fabricated a border incident to start the Mexican War. The congressional response reflected a sensitive regard for legislative prerogatives. Congress first censured Polk for acting beyond his authority, then declared war.[6] It took Abraham Lincoln and the special circumstances of the Civil War to elevate the presidency above Congress.

But it was Congress that negotiated the crucial compromises responsible for postponing that war. The Missouri Compromise of 1820, which temporarily settled the question of slavery in the territories, was the creation of Congress. President James Monroe was not a party to the deliberations that produced it, and he expressed no public views on the issue until it was settled.[7] Thirty years later Congress once again staved off the inevitable conflict with the Compromise of 1850, which fixed the boundary between future slave and free states. It was the work of a congressional select Committee of Thirteen that included Clay, Calhoun, and Webster. Beside them, President Millard Fillmore was hardly luminous. He gave his blessing to the agreement, but nothing else. Congress had clearly displaced the presidency as the institution that addressed and resolved the most important issues disturbing the peace of the Republic. And its preeminence was acknowledged. During the process of deliberation leading up to the Missouri Compromise, Supreme Court Justice Joseph Story observed that "The Executive has no longer a commanding influence. The House of Representatives has absorbed all the popular feelings and all the effective power of the country."[8]

The Senate may have had a less direct claim on popular feelings than the House. Until the ratification of the Seventeenth Amendment in 1913, senators were elected by state legislatures. But after the 1830s, the men who could command the support of their state legislatures were usually state party leaders. They were likely to be key figures in the political organizations that orchestrated the political mobilization of the electorate. Senators were the ambassadors whom state party organizations sent to Washington. Perhaps because they were the foreign ministers of nearly sovereign powers, senators were accorded privileges not granted to mere members of the House—unlimited debate and the practice of senatorial courtesy, giving individual members a virtual veto power over measures and appointments affecting their states. The growing stature of the Senate at mid-century led several prominent members of the House, including Clay, Calhoun, and Webster, to secure legislative appointment to the upper chamber.

When Congress and the president clashed, it was Congress that could count on popular reinforcements. House Speaker Henry Clay drew the backing of newspapers, mass meetings, political clubs, and business groups when he sparred with President Monroe on questions of internal improvements or American recognition of Spain's rebellious colonies in Latin America. After visiting Monroe in March 1818, Secretary of State John Quincy Adams wrote in his diary that the president was furious about the "violent, systematic opposition that Clay is raising against his Administration."[9] So much for the so-called Era of Good Feeling, when partisan conflict was allegedly muted. Empowered by their popular support, members of Congress waged what Adams called "a perpetual struggle . . . to control the Executive—to make it dependent upon and subservient to them."[10]

The rise of the Whigs and the development of party competition during the latter part of the Jacksonian era added to the congressional advantage over the president. In the first place, party competition stimulated an expansion of the electorate as rival parties sought the strength to overpower one another. By the end of the nineteenth century, voter turnout was typically over 80 percent and exceeded 90 percent in some areas outside the South.[11] And once politicized, new voters would almost certainly find their own members of Congress more familiar, accessible, and sympathetic than the dim, drab, and distant nonentity who lived in the White House. Competition expanded the popular base for congressional power.

Second, party organization within Congress increased the effectiveness of the legislature as a governing institution. After the Civil War and Reconstruction, voting in Congress increasingly followed party lines.[12] Powerful congressional leaders such as House Speakers Schuyler Colfax, "Czar" Thomas B. Reed, and Joseph G. Cannon, as well as Senate leaders such as Nelson Aldrich, regulated the flow of legislative business, the power of recognition, committee assignments, and patronage. Local party bosses, for their part, controlled nominations and the distribution of campaign funds and workers to the

284 / PRESIDENTIAL POWER

party's favored candidates. As a result, party discipline was a potent force, particularly in the House, allowing party leaders to act decisively on legislative matters. The upshot was that the House Speaker could confront the president with a unified congressional majority and was widely regarded as a more powerful leader than the chief executive.[13]

Party organization also contributed to congressional power in a third way. Because of the decentralized American electoral system, political parties were built from the bottom up rather than the top down. In other words, parties were organized at the municipal, county, and state levels, not the national level. The so-called national parties had never been much more than confederations of state and county organizations. With the exception of a charismatic party founder such as Andrew Jackson, or a wartime party leader such as Lincoln, nineteenth-century party leadership was firmly in the hands of state and local politicians whose interests tended to be quite parochial, focusing on local patronage, appointments, and power.

Presidential power was at odds with party decentralization. While southern political leaders had particular reasons to guard state sovereignty and resist the intrusions of the federal government, all state politicians were partial to the regime of "dual federalism," which left most authority over domestic matters in state government, while national government collected the customs and managed the postal system, the public lands, and what there was of foreign relations. State and local party politicians had more use for Congress than for the executive. Congressional representatives gave them access to power at the national level and to federal patronage in the local customhouses, post offices, and land offices of the national government. Some state party bosses found that they could defend their provincial fiefdoms most effectively by serving in the House or Senate themselves. Senator Roscoe Conkling of New York was an outstanding example of the species, and his struggle with President Hayes for control of the New York Customhouse was a classic manifestation of the clash between presidential power and party bosses.[14]

State party organizations put their friends in Congress; they tried to put harmless figureheads in the White House. Aggressive, energetic presidents with ideas of their own were a menace to the standing order. The great leaders of Congress—men such as Henry Clay or

James G. Blaine—were sometimes able to win the presidential nomination, but never the presidency. As we have already seen, nineteenth-century party conventions preferred dark horses, favorite sons, or military heroes with no discernible political opinions. Their nominations reflected and reinforced the low prestige of the presidency.

Even when compelled to retreat in the face of demands for civil service reform, party politicians protected their provincial interests. The Pendleton Act of 1883 applied only to presidential appointments, not the state and local jobs that were the essential building blocks of state party organization,[15] and even where federal appointments were concerned, the Pendleton Act established a system of state-by-state quotas for federal civil service positions, preserving the principle that civil service appointments should be shared out among the provinces and assuring that state parties would have access to the appointment process, even inviting their participation. The budget of the Civil Service Commission created by the act was of course subject to congressional approval.[16]

Later in the nineteenth and early twentieth centuries, Congress created other agencies to regulate railroads and trade practices. These functions were housed in "independent regulatory commissions" beyond the scope of presidential direction but subject to the budgetary authority of Congress.[17] Congress cast its shadow over the executive branch because its authority acquired substance from the mass mobilization of the electorate and structure from the party organizations that engineered the mobilization. The same political parties that turned out the electorate for parades, rallies, mass meetings, and balloting also gave Congress the organizational solidarity needed to confront the chief executive with a force almost as unified as that of the presidency itself.

In 1896, however, the presidential candidates of both major parties won nomination by campaigning against their parties' established leaders. William Jennings Bryan and William McKinley imposed themselves on their parties, and McKinley rode to the White House on the back of a campaign organization controlled not by party notables but by his personal associates. In a sense, the president had created a party of his own. Or at least the voters no longer chose their presidents strictly on the basis of party labels. Just who stood at the top of the ticket now made a significant difference to them. At the same time, the rest of the ticket became somewhat more responsive to central control. Antiparty progressive reformers may have supported the introduction of an official, state-printed ballot and the primary election because they seemed to undermine bossism. But the measures succeeded, in part, because many bosses and other politicians found that the reforms served their purposes too. Officially printed ballots made it more difficult for local bosses to defy state bosses by modifying the party ticket to suit their parochial preferences or to extort tribute from state party organizations. The direct primary would not have a significant impact on presidential elections for many years, but it did affect state, local, and congressional contests. Primaries served the purposes not just of progressive reformers, but also of ambitious politicians with popular appeal who sought some way to get around the bosses, caucuses, conventions, and political brokers who stood between them and election, and who might demand tribute of them if they won. Primaries promoted candidate autonomy from party control and therefore held virtues for both reform and nonreform candidates.[18]

Though little affected by primaries, presidents did benefit from changes in the mass media. The emergence of national wire services, along with publishers Hearst and Pulitzer, signaled the development of a national media market, for which the nation's chief executive provided an obvious focal point. The McKinley administration, as we have seen, made a concerted effort to cultivate the press and to transfer its attention from the Capitol to the White House. McKinley's frequent presidential tours made him more visible to his public than any of his predecessors. Theodore Roosevelt and Woodrow Wilson kept up the practice. Warren G. Harding, a former newspaper editor, met with reporters on an almost daily basis and introduced the "photo opportunity" as a public relations device.[19] Even the taciturn Coolidge used the newly introduced medium of radio to speak to the nation on important issues.[20]

As presidents became more popular figures, popular participation in elections subsided. Progressive electoral reforms may have been partly responsible for this paradox. New requirements for voter registration systems probably inhibited the entry of immigrants and working-class citizens into the electorate. Civil service reform advanced the conception that bureaucratic institutions were or should be nonpolitical, staffed on the basis of expertise, not political loyalty. As civil service systems penetrated the state and local levels of government, they may have reduced the supply of patronage available to sustain parties.

Perhaps just as important, one result of the 1896 realignment was to reduce party competition in northern states and congressional districts, and when elections become less competitive, mobilizing the electorate may seem a less urgent imperative for state and local party organizations. In the early twentieth century, many of them ignored opportunities to recruit new groups in the electorate. The northward migration of African Americans gained strength in the 1890s, and its volume had increased sharply by World War I. In most cities, parties made little effort to incorporate them. Organized labor was recovering from the reverses of the late nineteenth century, but its past political misfortunes—troops called out to quell strikes, labor legislation overturned by the courts—inclined its leaders to steer clear of politics, at least at the national level.[21] These politically neglected groups would later be recruited to the president's popular constituency. Franklin Roosevelt's New Deal helped to politicize the labor movement once again and mobilized many of the eastern and southern European ethnic voters ignored by urban machines.[22] John Kennedy and Lyndon Johnson would reach out to African Americans.

The Capitol in Twilight

Congress felt the most immediate effects of the more sedentary party organizations and declining voter turnout. It was the popular branch of government. When the parties missed opportunities to mobilize constituents, Congress lost opportunities for power. Samuel Huntington called Congress's failure to secure the allegiance of organized labor and African Americans in the early twentieth century an "adaptation crisis" that deprived the legislative branch of future public support and political influence.[23] The greatest political advantage that Congress held over the other branches of government was its accessibility to important social and economic groups. Groups denied access by progressive reforms or the shortcomings of party would not regard

Congress as a useful institution and would therefore have little stake in the enhancement of congressional power.

The electoral changes of the early twentieth century may have had their most profound impact on the internal operations of Congress itself. Party primaries challenged the political parties' monopoly of ballot access and nominations for office. Now candidates could get elected to Congress on their own. And by the time they took their seats, they had learned that they could get themselves nominated, build their own campaign organizations, and finance their campaigns without becoming the vassals of the parties whose standards they carried. The obvious result was that party leaders in Congress exercised less control over their members than they had in the era of sovereign Speakers. The new order revealed its outlines in the 1910 revolt against Speaker Cannon's autocratic control over House procedures.[24] The uprising ostensibly challenged only the Speaker's hold over the powerful House Rules Committee, but the insurgents' victory pointed toward the end of the late nineteenth-century party discipline that had forged the congressional majority into a unified force. After 1910, members were less inclined to follow party leadership and more inclined to follow instead the promptings of ideology, interest groups, or the parochial imperatives of getting reelected.

The erosion of party discipline undermined congressional power. It meant that Congress could no longer confront the unity of the presidency with a unity of its own. Strong party leadership had once helped Congress to overcome its collective action problem. As we observed in the first chapter, one of the current congressional handicaps in conflicts with the president is that most members are more concerned with their own reelection or their constituency's interests than they are with the long-term institutional power of Congress.[25] The collective welfare of Congress as an institution usually has less weight in their voting decisions than their own immediate political interests. As one contemporary observer put it, few members are prepared to "speak up for the institutional interests of Congress."[26]

For congressional leaders, on the other hand, the power of the institution is almost indistinguishable from personal power, and they have a stake in defending it. Although exceptions can occur when congressional leaders have presidential aspirations, a Congress controlled by party leaders is more likely to defend its institutional prerogatives than is a more decentralized legislative body. Speaker Cannon refused to budge when President Taft sought to expand presidential budget authority at the expense of Congress. But after 1920, the members of more individualistic congresses allowed presidents to appropriate the power of the purse, possibly because the presidential mechanisms for budget-making appeared more disciplined, and deferring to them made members of Congress seem more fiscally responsible to their constituents.

The decline of party discipline also meant that Congress operated with less efficiency and dispatch. The decomposition of party organization makes a large and politically diverse legislature less manageable.[27] In the absence of party discipline, majority support must be assembled anew for each vote, a process that is time-consuming, not only because opponents can throw up obstructions, but also because some members want to extort political compensation in exchange for their support. A bipartisan proposal to overhaul the bankruptcy code introduced in 1996, for example, spent six years in legislative limbo because a variety of legislators demanded a variety of concessions on unrelated matters before they would give their votes to the measure. The bill seemed close to passage in July 2002, after its sponsors agreed to add language demanded by pro-choice senators to prevent antiabortion protesters from declaring bankruptcy to avoid fines for protests at abortion clinics.[28] In October, however, a vote on the proposed legislation was blocked in the House of Representatives, this time by antiabortion forces angered by the provision added to mollify pro-choice legislators.[29] It was not until 2005 that bankruptcy reform survived its congressional ordeal and finally made it to the desk of a waiting president.

A dispersion of power within House and Senate exacerbated the relaxation of party discipline. Its expression was a steady increase in the power of the standing committees and a multiplication of subcommittees in both houses. In the nineteenth century and first years of the twentieth, power over the flow of legislation was concentrated in the hands of the House Speaker and Senate majority leader. By the 1920s, however, with more members seeking a share of power, the authority of committee chairmen was strengthened and the number of subcommittees increased sufficiently to allow most members of the majority party to control their own capsules of congressional power. The 1946 Legislative Reorganization Act added to the power of the committees by greatly increasing their staffs and giving each committee defined oversight powers.[30] While members welcomed the opportunity to exert additional influence, the resulting dispersion of power aggravated the general erosion of party discipline and added to the difficulty of accomplishing anything in Congress. More and more bills ended their legislative histories "bottled up in committee."

Once members overcame the power of party leadership, they could develop rules, norms, and procedures serving the individual interests of the members, not the collective interests of Congress as a whole. The seniority rule was one of these. In the nineteenth century, seniority had been a significant factor in the designation of committee chairs, but it was only one consideration. The House leadership exercised its discretion in weighing a number of factors, including party loyalty, before allocating chairmanships. But after the successful revolt against the Speaker in 1910, seniority became the decisive criterion in the appointment of committee chairs, and it is seldom overridden even today.[31] Since 1994, House Republicans have heeded self-imposed, six-year term limits for committee chairmen. In virtually every case, however, retiring committee chairmen have been replaced by their party's most senior committee member.

The seniority rule appeals to members of Congress—as it does to members of labor unions—because it guarantees eventual promotion and perquisites to any member who manages to remain in Congress long enough, regardless of job performance.[32] But the seniority rule does not necessarily reward party loyalty or expertise, and it limits the discretion of the congressional leadership while granting authority to members who hold the safest seats, rather than those whose views reflect mainstream public opinion. In the 1950s and 60s, for example, the seniority system ceded control of committees to a disproportionate number of conservative southern Democrats whose views prevented Congress from responding to the demands of the civil rights movement, leaving the initiative in this matter to the executive and judicial branches while diminishing the reputation and status of the legislature.[33]

When the leadership of Congress enforced party discipline, the composition of Congress changed with the shifting fortunes of the major parties. Today it hardly changes at all. In the 2002 elections, for example, 98 percent of all incumbent House members seeking reelection were returned to their seats. The figure was a bit higher than usual, but not by much. The overwhelming majority of the victors won with at least 60 percent of the vote.[34] Close competition is not characteristic of congressional elections. A Congress organized around the interests of its individual members rather than the parties to which they belong operates to enhance their job security. When their party takes positions that may hurt their reelection chances, they can vote with their districts rather than their parties. In fact, they can withdraw from the contentious business of debate and legislation to ingratiate themselves with the voters in their districts through constituency casework. Combined with the fundraising advantages that incumbents have over their challengers, these assets should guarantee a long career in Congress, and it can be lengthened further if members can induce their friends in their state legislatures to draw incumbent-friendly congressional districts. Today it is not voters who cause most turnover in Congress, but retirements and deaths.[35]

Incumbency may mean institutional stability, but a legislature that has insulated its members from popular political currents sacrifices institutional influence. Congress still changes, of course. Today's ideologically polarized Congress is a far cry from the post–World War II body, when a moderately conservative bipartisan coalition dominated legislative leadership.[36] But today's Congress changes more slowly than its predecessors. It is responsive to people who have problems with their Social Security benefits or questions about their immigration status, but groups that seek to advance collective demands are more likely than they used to be to bypass Congress and take their problems to the executive branch or even the courts.

CONGRESS AND THE RISE OF PRESIDENTIALISM

Presidential power is not simply a product of congressional abdication. The conjunction of personality and circumstance that occurred during Franklin D. Roosevelt's twelve-year tenure amounted to a rendezvous with destiny for the executive branch.[37] During his first two years in office, FDR created sixty-five new executive agencies to administer such programs as banking relief, public works, farm policies, secu-

rities regulation, home loans, and farm credit.[38] From his inauguration to the start of his final term, federal employment quintupled. The
new agencies and employees meant that the federal bureaucracy per-
meated and engaged the society more fully than ever before.

Congress did not simply roll over for Roosevelt. It dug in to resist
some of the features of his initial reorganization plans for the executive branch that augmented the already considerable powers of the
presidency. They rejected his plan to fold the independent regulatory
agencies into cabinet departments. They also blocked his proposal
that the independent audit of executive agencies by the comptroller
general, a congressional official, should be surrendered to the Budget
Bureau along with his power to disallow agency expenditures. FDR
also wanted to replace the Civil Service Commission with a single personnel director whom he would appoint.[39] Congress blocked that
move as well. But the congressional will to resist could not stand firm
against a popular president who was the chief source of reassurance to
a public that feared unemployment and destitution even more than
fear itself. More often than not, Congress acquiesced to the diminution of its own power and the augmentation of the president's. Its sub-
mission did not end with Roosevelt. The familiar mobilization of
executive power in wartime did not give way to normalcy once World
War II had ended. The Cold War provided President Truman with the
warrant to create a permanent national security establishment under
presidential authority.

DELEGATION OF POWER

Although congressional stature was a casualty of circumstance,
Congress itself was also an accomplice in its own disempowerment. It
voluntarily delegated lawmaking power to the executive branch.
Delegation allowed the members of Congress to concentrate on constituency service instead of legislation. But perhaps the most compelling incentive for delegation was the difficulty that Congress often
faced in reaching agreement. The weakening of congressional leadership and the relaxation of party discipline compounded the difficulty
of reaching consensus on the details of legislation. Congress reduced
the burdens imposed on its capacity to agree by legislating in more
general terms. It was easier to achieve agreement on broad purposes

while leaving the details of implementation to bureaucratic agencies. Then the members could win the gratitude of constituents by helping them navigate the bureaucratic maze whose creation Congress had authorized.

Some delegation of power was inevitable as Congress authorized complex programs that would require years of planning and substantial scientific or technical expertise. Congress was not equipped to fix detailed air quality standards or draw up rules for drug testing or legislate the ballistic properties of artillery rounds for a new army tank. But administrative complexity and the need for expertise can explain only so much of the congressional shift from closely drawn legislation to broad delegations of authority.

Detailed legislation was one instrument of a Congress whose leadership was determined to exercise minute control over the executive branch. In the more individualistic Congress that emerged after the revolt against Speaker Cannon, it was not only more difficult to achieve agreement on detailed legislation. Members could gain credit with constituents and with the larger public by sponsoring legislation that seemed to promote general public interests. It was not only easier to get broadly sketched legislation through Congress; it was probably easier to arouse public support for vague expressions of good intentions than for detailed prescriptions. It was simpler and safer for legislative sponsors to bask in the warm glow of a diffuse but laudable principle. Delegating the details to bureaucratic agencies also allows legislators to shift the responsibility for implementation and the costs of failure from themselves to administrators.[40] Even after the New Deal, Congress continued to enact statutes setting out general objectives without specifying how the government was supposed to achieve them. The federal bureaucracy is left to fill in the blanks. Today, as policy analyst Jerry L. Nashaw has observed, "Most public law is legislative in origin but administrative in content."[41]

Simply comparing the total volume of congressional output with the gross bureaucratic product provides a rough indication of where lawmaking now occurs in the federal government. The 106th Congress (1999–2000) was among the most active in recent years. It passed 580 pieces of legislation, 200 more than the 105th Congress and nearly twice as many as the 104th. Some, such as campaign finance reform, were significant, while many others were not. But the legislative legacy of this congressional session was judged by most observers to be relatively slight. Partisan and ideological divisions as well as ineffective leadership prevented most major items, such as needed revisions of federal budget rules, from even coming to the floor.[42]

During the same two years, executive agencies produced 157,173 pages of new rules and regulations in the official *Federal Register.*[43] The Occupational Safety and Health Administration, for example, introduced new regulations affecting millions of workers and thousands of businesses; the Environmental Protection Agency drafted new air quality standards, and the Securities and Exchange Commission and Commodities Futures Trading Commission announced significant revisions of futures trading rules affecting billions of dollars in transactions. In principle, agency rules and regulations are designed merely to implement the will of Congress as expressed in statutes. In fact, agencies are often drafting regulations based upon broad statutory authority granted years or even decades earlier by congresses whose actual intent has become a matter of political interpretation.

During the 1960s and 70s, Congress tried to police the bureaucracy's exercise of discretion by providing for a legislative veto that would enable the legislature to invalidate administrative regulations issued under statutes that delegated congressional authority to the executive branch. Although Congress appended such provisions to more than two hundred pieces of legislation that granted rule-making authority to administrative agencies, it actually exercised its veto in only a handful of cases. The record prompted one Senator to declare that the idea of controlling administrative discretion through the legislative veto was "hogwash."[44] At least one version of the legislative veto was eventually struck down by the Supreme Court as an unconstitutional violation of the separation of powers.[45]

THE NEW DELEGATION

The mere volume of congressional delegation to the executive branch tells only part of the story. In the late 1940s, Congress took another step to change the character of the powers that it transferred to administrative agencies. It began to transfer the very source of its power—its representative legitimacy—to the federal bureaucracy.

With the enactment of the Administrative Procedure Act in 1946 and Taft-Hartley in 1947, Congress began to require executive agencies to make rules according to representative processes. Agencies were to give public notice of proposed regulations, invite public comment, and hold public hearings. The congressional regulations for the regulators reflected a postwar conservative reaction against the New Deal, an effort to curb the authority of FDR's regulatory agencies by holding them to formal standards of rule making and adjudication. The purpose, in particular, was to prevent the interest groups under regulation from "capturing" the agencies that regulated them by assuring that other groups had access to the agencies' decision-making processes. The principal target of congressional conservatives was the privileged status of labor unions with the National Labor Relations Board. To counter such interest-group influence in the regulatory process, Congress tried to open the administrative rule making to the public at large by requiring public notice and comment. To avoid bias in particular cases, the Administrative Procedure Act attempted to construct a firewall between the agency rule makers and its administrative law judges. And finally, Congress decreed that an agency's decisions could be appealed to the courts.[46]

While conservatives saw these reforms as limiting the power of administrative agencies, liberals had a somewhat different agenda. As law professor Martin Shapiro has argued, congressional liberals viewed the APA and its offshoots as strengthening the New Deal and the postwar expansion of government by legitimating the delegation of law-making power to the executive branch.[47] The APA created procedures within the executive branch that mimicked elements of the legislative process and the adjudication processes of the courts. Affected interests were to be allowed an opportunity to make their views known; agencies were supposed to take those views into account. The effect—unanticipated by the conservatives—was to blunt criticism of the bureaucracy by making it seem accountable to the public. Congress later adopted legislation that gave the administrative process an even more representative spin. The 1972 Advisory Committee Act, for example, attempted to ensure that government agencies could not stack the deck in favor of a particular interest or point of view when soliciting policy advice from outside groups.[48] In 1990 Congress passed the Negotiated Rulemaking Act to encourage administrative agencies to engage in direct and open negotiations with affected interests when developing new regulations.[49]

These regulatory reforms were eminently democratic, at least in a formal sense.[50] They opened government more fully to the participation of its citizens. The Taft-Hartley Act was explicitly justified as a measure that would protect individual workers from undemocratic labor unions as well as from the unfair labor practices of their employers. But the unintended consequence of the new regulatory regime was to reduce the uniqueness of Congress as a representative institution. If interests and organizations could secure full and fair representation in the executive branch, what stake would they have in the power of Congress? Their congressional connections would diminish as policymaking through congressional legislation was displaced by agency rule making. Congress had contributed to its own marginalization.

While Congress was delegating power and legitimacy to the executive branch, it also embarked on the expansion of its own staff and resources. In 1930, members of the House of Representatives employed a staff of fewer than one thousand, and senators barely two hundred. By 1945, both chambers had doubled their staffs. Today, House members employ nearly eight thousand, and Senate offices are supported by roughly four thousand professional employees.[51] The curious conjunction of staff growth with increasing delegation of congressional powers to the federal bureaucracy reflected the fact that most new staff members were engaged in constituency service rather than legislation. The demand for constituency service grew with the bureaucratic expansion that resulted from congressional delegation and the proliferation of rules and regulations that followed. Constituents needed congressional intercession to find their way through the regulatory forest. Constituency service was also suited to the capabilities of Congress. Unlike legislation, it does not require leadership and organization, both of which have become scarce commodities in the contemporary Congress. Each member can now enhance the prospects of reelection through individual effort and staff resources instead of debate and lawmaking.[52] While the members of Congress were reduced to the status of elected ombudsmen, the executive branch governed the country and, to an increasing extent, it did so single-handedly.[53]

THE JUDICIARY

The representative requirements imposed on administrative agencies by the APA and the Taft-Hartley Act were extended in the 1960s and 70s to broad new regions of public policy—civil rights, occupational health and safety, environmental protection, and consumer protection.[54] Groups dissatisfied with the outcome of agency procedures can and do go to Congress for redress, but they are more apt to turn to the courts. That is the remedy offered by the Administrative Procedure Act, and one that does not require interested parties to enlist supportive constituencies in their causes.[55] Since the 1960s Congress and the judiciary have also made the courts more accessible to a wider range of litigants. The Supreme Court, for example, has relaxed the rules governing justiciability—the circumstances under which the courts will accept a case for adjudication. It has liberalized the doctrine of standing so that it can hear challenges to the actions of administrative agencies, enable associations to appear as representatives of their members, and permit taxpayers' suits in which First Amendment issues are involved.[56] It has also amended the Rules of Civil Procedure to facilitate class action suits. The class action is a legal device that permits a court to combine the claims of many individuals and to treat them as a single group during a lawsuit.[57] In the past, a class could be almost any aggregation of plaintiffs deemed by a court to share a common interest. Recent rules have narrowed the standards for the certification of classes. In 1996, for example, congressional Republicans enacted a prohibition against class actions brought by advocates for immigrants against the Immigration and Naturalization Service (INS) and by Legal Services lawyers on behalf of indigents. For more privileged classes, however, class litigation remains an important political tool.[58]

While increasing opportunities for class action suits, the Supreme Court has also tacitly rescinded the abstention doctrine, under which federal courts declined to hear cases not yet resolved by the state courts. It has relaxed the rules governing the determination of when a case is moot, or no longer relevant, and has in practice abandoned the political questions doctrine, which once kept the courts out of policy disputes. Stretching the legal concept of justiciability has broadened the range of issues subject to judicial settlement.

But the courts have also made a wider range of remedies available to those litigants. In the past, for example, a federal court might have ruled that a government agency had violated a plaintiff's rights and then ordered the agency to devise appropriate remedies. Today's federal courts can issue detailed decrees specifying how the agency must conduct its business in the future. Suits challenging conditions in state prisons, for example, have generated an extensive array of court orders detailing the living space, recreational programs, and counseling services that must be provided to all prisoners. Judges have also made use of special masters, officials appointed by the court to supervise the day-to-day operations of institutional defendants such as the Boston school system, the Alabama state prison system, and the Baltimore public housing authority. In short, the federal judiciary can now offer private litigants remedies that were once provided to the public at large only through the executive and legislative branches.[59]

The legislative branch itself has encouraged a shift in interest-group politics from lobbying to litigation. In Title II of the 1964 Civil Rights Act, for example, Congress designated the plaintiffs who filed suit under the act as "private attorneys general," because they were contributing to the enforcement of federal law, and the legislation made them eligible to collect attorneys' fees from defendants if they prevailed at trial. This "fee-shifting" provision was endorsed by the Supreme Court in 1968.[60] In 1976, Congress passed the Civil Rights Attorneys' Fee Awards Act, which allowed for the recovery of attorneys' fees for actions brought under all civil rights laws enacted since 1876. The 1990 Americans With Disabilities Act gave the handicapped protection from discrimination in employment and required that public services be accessible to those with disabilities. The legislation created a cause of action that opened the way for extensive litigation by groups championing the rights of the disabled. Likewise, the 1991 Civil Rights Act, which prohibited job discrimination against women as well as minorities, opened the federal courts to litigants claiming to have been the victims of gender bias.

A number of regulatory statutes enacted during the 1970s contain "citizen suit" provisions that give public interest groups the right to challenge the decisions of executive agencies in environmental and consumer fraud cases. Virtually every federal environmental statute authorizes individual citizens and groups to sue private parties for failure to comply with the provisions of federal statutes and regulations and to collect legal fees and expenses if they succeed. Such citizen-enforcers act not so much as injured parties seeking to redress a wrong done to them but as private attorneys general serving a public interest.[61] By the mid-1980s, more than 150 federal statutes contained fee-shifting provisions.[62] The Supreme Court has limited the standing of private attorneys general by ruling that litigants must have a demonstrable stake in the outcome of the case and that the remedy sought must be within the court's power to grant.[63] Nevertheless, citizen suits continue to be important mechanisms through which public interest groups can simultaneously achieve policy goals and finance their operations.[64]

Their success was noted and imitated by a coalition of small business groups that won the right to collect attorneys' fees for some cases in which small firms were defending themselves against government regulations. The Equal Access to Justice Act of 1980 (EAJA) allows for the collection of attorneys' fees when individual citizens or business firms successfully defend themselves against "overreaching government actions." Though intended to protect small businesses from the ravages of giant regulatory bureaucracies, the act is often used by trade associations representing giant industrial corporations.[65]

Taken together, these statutory and jurisprudential changes have opened the way for groups and even citizens acting alone to use the courts to achieve policy goals that might once have required collective political action and congressional legislation, if they could have been achieved at all. Litigation has played a significant role in the development of important public policies regarding employment discrimination and voting rights, consumer and worker protection, women's rights, protection of the environment, the rights of the disabled, and the exercise of religious freedom.[66] On issues such as racial segregation and women's rights, the federal courts have taken action that we now recognize as essential to democratic fairness but went far beyond what could have been won at the time in the arena of popular politics.[67] These are victories of principle for which the judiciary is revered. On the other side, however, opening the courts to organized interests has further increased the authority of the judiciary at the expense of the legislative branch. Congress, though flawed, is still more immediately representative than the judges behind their benches. But today's organized interests, represented and consulted by administrative agencies and free to take their problems to the courts, have limited use for Congress. And Congress has helped to make it so.

Legislative Investigations

Congress still flexes its muscles occasionally. More often than not, it does so through legislative investigations rather than legislation, especially when there are allegations of misconduct by high-ranking executive branch officials, up to and including the president. Fifty years ago, the McCarthy committee publicized and investigated sensational charges of Communist activity in the Departments of State and Defense. During the 1960s, Senator William Fulbright led an investigation of policy decisions leading to the Vietnam War. Ten years later, the Watergate hearings not only drove President Nixon from office, but also dominated network television coverage and set the dramatic structure to be followed by congressional investigations of the future. During the Reagan administration, the Senate Iran-Contra hearings failed to do in the president but yielded criminal indictments of high executive officials and made some relatively obscure officials such as Oliver North into television personalities. With the hearings on President Clinton's impeachment, Congress went into direct competition with the supermarket tabloids but turned somber again in the congressional 9/11 Commission's 2004 investigation of government precautions leading up to the September 11, 2001, attacks on the Pentagon and World Trade Center. It turned what had been seen as an example of presidential leadership into a possible political vulnerability. More recently, Congress has investigated a possible White House leak of the identity of a covert CIA operative, Valerie Plame, to get even with her husband, Ambassador Joseph Wilson, who criticized the administration's policies in Iraq.

The great congressional investigations of the past fifty years have shifted from a focus on policies and institutions to a preoccupation with scandal and individual wrongdoing. McCarthy smeared individual executive branch officials, but aside from advancing the insatiable ambition of Senator McCarthy, the investigations were about American foreign policy and the reliability of the institutions charged with its formation and execution. Fulbright had little interest in establishing individual blame but sought to expose flaws in the policymaking process developed by the executive branch. The Watergate investigation was sparked by the administration's efforts to expand presidential power.[68] During the course of the probe, however, Congress and the national news media focused mainly on the question of Nixon's personal misconduct in ordering a break-in at the Democratic party's headquarters and paid little or no attention to such institutionally important matters as the president's efforts to reorganize the executive branch without obtaining congressional approval. By the time of the Clinton investigation, institutional and policy issues lost their place on the agenda entirely and were replaced by the ultimately trivial matter of the president's sexual misconduct with a White House intern.

In the case of the 9/11 Commission, congressional Democrats hoped that a probe of the Bush administration's failure to anticipate the 9/11 attacks might turn the defining moment of the Bush presidency into a seed of doubt about the president's determination and ability to protect the country against terrorism. Since the Democrats did not control either house of Congress, they could not use the formal powers of investigation held by the House or the Senate. By mobilizing public opinion, however, they forced Republicans to accede to the creation of an ad hoc, bipartisan panel to be appointed by the congressional leaders of the two parties. Some of those chosen to serve could claim expertise in matters of national security, as might have been expected. In the spirit of Watergate, perhaps, the Democrats appointed two members to the panel whose specialty was not policymaking but prosecution, one of whom, Richard Ben-Veniste, had actually played a significant part in the Watergate investigation. Their métier was the determination of guilt and innocence, not national security. Recognizing the president's peril in such an investigation, the Republicans insisted that the inquiry be completed and its report released by July 2004, four months before the 2004 election. In spite of the time limit, commission hearings in

March and April 2004 suggested that the Bush administration had not been sufficiently attentive to the terrorist threat prior to September 2001 and deeply embarrassed the president. Disclosure of a national intelligence briefing report prepared for the president lent a familiar tone to the hearings. Although the questions may have been worded differently, they echoed the Watergate refrain, "What did the president know and when did he know it?"

The president was not the sole target of criticism. The 9/11 Report also targeted intelligence agencies and practices and offered a number of recommendations. The hearings themselves, however, spotlighted the acts and omissions of the president and top administration officials. Long before the publication of the official report, members of the Commission, Ben-Veniste in particular, made numerous public and media appearances to present their own views critical of the president.

Long ago, the courts and the federal bureaucracy were supposed to concern themselves with the details of individual cases. Congress was not only the popular but also the policymaking branch of government. In today's Congress, there is evidence of a reversal of roles. The courts now respond to the collective demands of organized interest groups, and administrative agencies legislate. Congress occupies itself with matters of individual guilt and innocence and constituency service. As Congress prepares for a new round of investigations in 2007, it remains to be seem whether lawmakers have learned any lessons from their past failures.

A Presidential Republic?

For its recent occupants, the presidency has been a path of thorns. Ronald Reagan, the closest approximation to a happy warrior, retired to applause. But to get there, he had to endure a recession that ravaged his popularity and the Iran-Contra investigation. His best year in office was probably the first. The only other president to serve for two full terms since 1960 was Bill Clinton. His other distinction was his impeachment, the second in the history of the presidency. George H. W. Bush rose to heights of popular approval after liberating Kuwait but was ejected from office the following year. The president's lot is not a happy one. But the presidency flourishes.

The political contradictions of the presidency are mirrored in Congress. Congressional elections can no longer bring out as many voters as presidential contests. But the emergence of the popular presidency has accompanied the decline of popular participation in politics. That decline deprived Congress of its most potent resource. Congressional strength derived from its status as the only truly representative institution in national government; its power grew when the American public mobilized to demand representation. But voter turnout in recent congressional elections suggests a loss of public concern about representation in Congress. Many citizens seek representation in the courts and the bureaucracy. If not superfluous, Congress has lost its uniqueness as a representative institution, its determination to mobilize the electorate, its role as the crucible of public policy. But as Congress has declined, individual members of Congress have flourished. They are almost always reelected, usually by large margins. The public has little confidence in Congress as a whole but is generally satisfied with its own representatives. Congress in turn attends less to the collective interests of its constituency as a whole, but its individual members usually respond with alacrity to the concerns of particular constituents.

At the other end of Pennsylvania Avenue, by contrast, beleaguered presidents, often turned out of office before completing two terms, have become the dominant figures in setting the government's course. The presidency thrives in an era of popular disengagement from politics. Presidents control armies and bureaucracies to execute their decisions. Their institutional rivals depend on the executive's capacity to get things done. Presidents can benefit from popular support and may actively seek it, but they can govern without it.

Consider George W. Bush. He lost the popular vote in a low-turnout election by 550,000 ballots. He was named to the presidency only after the United States Supreme Court, in a 5–4 decision, handed him Florida's electoral votes. Most pundits predicted that, lacking a popular mandate, Bush would be a cautious, moderate president.

But once installed in the Oval Office, Bush proved that he did not need the public in order to govern. Even before the 9/11 terrorist attacks boosted Bush's popularity and left Congress floundering in the president's wake, the president was pushing a sharply defined and aggressive domestic and foreign policy agenda. He issued a cascade of executive orders reversing the decisions of his predecessor and pre-vailed on a Congress not fully under his party's control to enact major tax cuts whose principal beneficiaries accounted for a tiny percentage of the electorate.[69] Lacking an electoral mandate and without strong popular support, the president governed. Bush did not need a mandate—he had the presidency.

8

How the Courts Reinforce
Presidential Power

T HESE ARE THE CIRCUMSTANCES of American politics at the
beginning of the twenty-first century—a weak Congress, demobilized electorate, flaccid political parties, and a White House typically
occupied by the nation's most aggressive and ambitious politicians in
command of the bureaucratic means to legislate on their own. The
description itself is enough to raise doubts about the prospects of our
constitutional republic. But it leaves out of account the courts, whose
independence from public opinion, popular mobilization, and the
executive branch should leave them unmoved and unbowed.

Congress, in fact, has turned to the federal courts to defend its prerogatives from presidential incursion. In the 1970s, for example,
members of Congress filed suit in federal court to challenge a variety
of presidential actions, including the use of military force without congressional authorization.[1] In the 1979 case of *Goldwater v. Carter*, the
Supreme Court said in effect that it was up to Congress to fight its own
battles with the president.[2] And in 1997, the Supreme Court effectively halted such suits by limiting them to instances in which the president had clearly nullified a legislative act and no other legislative
remedy was available.[3] Legislators have continued to file amicus briefs
in suits involving the exercise of presidential power and have cheered
from the sidelines when other litigants have challenged the president
in federal court.[4]

But the cheering is infrequent. The federal courts have not stood

306 / PRESIDENTIAL POWER

firm against the expansion of the chief executive's power. On the contrary, the judiciary has generally reinforced the role of the executive and sanctioned the contraction of congressional authority. At least since the New Deal and the Second World War, the courts have upheld most assertions of presidential power, especially in the fields of foreign policy, war, and emergency powers. In view of the country's expanded international role and its engagement in nearly continuous warfare—cold and hot—perhaps these decisions should have been expected. But the courts have gone further. They have taken extraordinary claims for presidential power made for limited purposes and rationalized them so that presidents could employ them more generally and routinely.

Consider, for example, Richard Nixon's sweeping claims to executive privilege. In *U.S. v. Nixon*, the Court rejected the president's refusal to turn over tapes to congressional investigators. But instead of leaving matters there, the Court proceeded to recognize, for the first time, the validity of the principle of executive privilege, and its opinion discussed the situations in which such claims might be appropriate.[5] The justices granted judicial recognition to a previously questionable principle, so that Presidents Bill Clinton and George W. Bush could later make broad claims of executive privilege with the Court's apparent blessing.[6]

This judicial tilt toward the executive branch caught the attention of such constitutional scholars as Edward Corwin, who explains that the courts tended to defer to the president because presidential exercises of power often produced changes in the world that the judiciary felt powerless to negate.[7] Political scientists Terry Moe and William Howell, on the other hand, ascribe the courts' goodwill toward the executive to their reliance on the executive's goodwill to get judicial decisions enforced.[8] Other scholars emphasize the reluctance of the courts to risk their prestige in disputes with popular presidents.[9]

While all of these explanations have merit, another factor that may incline the courts toward the president is the process of judicial appointment. Presidents obviously seek to appoint judges who will support them, but their expectations are frequently disappointed. Since federal judges have lifetime tenure, the presidential hope of reciprocity is equivalent to an unenforceable contract.[10] There is no guarantee that federal judges will repay their patrons, and justices such as Earl Warren or David Souter have surprised or disappointed the presidents who appointed them.

Presumably, presidents have always appointed judges whom they found politically congenial. What has changed is that presidents no longer choose judicial appointees with legislative backgrounds, and the political milieu in which judges originate presumably affects their institutional affinities and sympathies. During the nineteenth century, federal judges typically emerged from the country's electoral and representative systems. They were active in party politics, and many of them had run for office and served in state legislatures or even the U.S. Congress. Chief Justice John Marshall, for example, had been a member of both the Virginia House of Delegates and the U.S. House of Representatives. His successor, Roger Brooke Taney, had served in the Maryland House of Delegates and state senate. A comprehensive survey of the two hundred district court judges appointed between 1829 and 1861 shows that in addition to being veterans of electoral and legislative politics themselves, more than 60 percent of the appointees had fathers with similar political backgrounds.[11]

Some federal judges in the nineteenth century served as elected legislators even while they sat on the federal bench. U.S. District Court Judge Charles L. Benedict of New York served as a judge for the Eastern District of New York from 1865 until his retirement in 1897. During this entire period, Benedict also served as a member of the New York State Assembly to which he had been elected by his Brooklyn constituency in 1863.[12] Even before the advent of legal and ethical prohibitions, such simultaneous legislative and judicial service was unusual. Quite commonly, however, federal judges returned to electoral and legislative politics after a stint on the bench. William Wilkins of Pennsylvania had served as a member of the Pittsburgh City Council and the Pennsylvania House of Representatives before being named to the U.S. District Court for the Western District of Pennsylvania by President James Monroe in 1824. After seven years on the federal bench, Wilkins resigned to serve a term in the U.S. Senate. His subsequent career included terms in the U.S. House of Representatives and the Pennsylvania state senate.[13] Even when they did not sit in legislative bodies, some federal judges remained active in legislative affairs. Chief Justice Salmon P. Chase, for example, a Republican senator from Ohio before President Lincoln appointed him to the high court, often provided his former colleagues in the Congress with drafts of bills in which he was interested and actually wrote major pieces of Reconstruction legislation.[14]

This ongoing exchange of personnel between the courts and legislative bodies reflected the central place of electoral politics and especially representative assemblies in nineteenth-century America. It was also the age of "dual federalism," when governing the United States was mostly the business of the states, and state legislatures often exercised considerably more influence than governors. Until the Constitution was amended in 1913 to require the popular election of U.S. senators, state legislatures had a direct connection with the upper house of the U.S. Congress, whose members they elected.

Lincoln appointed Salmon Chase to replace Chief Justice Taney after the latter's death because Chase was a leader of the Republican radicals in the Senate and would, it was hoped, help the administration retain the support of this powerful group.[15] Martin Van Buren made similar political calculations after his election to the presidency in 1836. He used federal judicial appointments to bolster his political support in states where personal or partisan opponents appeared to threaten his chances for reelection. Given the prominence of legislators in nineteenth-century party politics, it is understandable that several of Van Buren's judicial appointees were drawn from state legislatures, and some returned there after resigning from the bench.[16]

The fact that many federal judges had served, continued to serve, and often would serve again as legislators helped to reinforce legislative primacy by ensuring that the federal bench would have a certain respect and partiality for legislative institutions. Prior legislative service is certainly no guarantee that a judge will always rule in favor of legislative supremacy, but the importance of legislatures and the close relationship between legislatures and courts in the nineteenth century reinforced one another when it came to judicial decision making. As a matter of practical necessity, judges had to take account of the fact that legislatures were the most powerful institutions of the period. The U.S. Congress, in particular, was capable of undermining judicial power.[17] Perhaps this is one of the reasons why the U.S. Supreme Court struck down only two acts of Congress during the first eighty years after the ratification of the Constitution.

In any case, nineteenth-century courts deferred to the Congress on matters they viewed as political in nature. In contrast to the two laws invalidated by the antebellum Supreme Court, the Rehnquist court alone invalidated more than three dozen congressional enactments.[18] Today, expressions of judicial deference to Congress, when they occur, are regarded as stratagems to keep the courts out of political minefields.[19] In the nineteenth century, however, the idea that courts should defer to legislatures was taken quite seriously.[20] Consider, for example, John Marshall's decision in *McCulloch v. Maryland*.[21] This case helped to establish the foundations of national power vis-à-vis the states. But it is important to recall which institution of the national government was empowered by the Court's decision. As legal scholar Rachel Barkow observes, Marshall's interpretation of the Constitution's "necessary and proper" clause emphasizes Congress's power to determine what is necessary to carry out its express constitutional powers. Marshall is careful not to claim for the judiciary the capacity to decide what is necessary under Article I, Section 8. Indeed, Marshall says an attempt by the Court to make such a decision would "pass the line which circumscribes the judicial department, and tread on legislative ground."[22] It is, he says, the "national legislature" that must possess the discretion, "with respect to the means by which the powers it confers are to be carried into execution, which will enable that body to perform the high duties assigned to it, in the manner most beneficial to the people."[23]

Luther v. Borden is another case in point. Decided by the Supreme Court in 1849,[24] it arose out of Dorr's Rebellion in Rhode Island. In 1841 two competing groups had claimed to be the lawful government of the state. One was the so-called charter government, operating under the state's original colonial charter. The other government claimed legitimacy on the basis of a new constitution approved in a series of mass meetings convened by one Thomas Dorr. The defendants in the case, members of the charter government's state militia led by Borden, had been accused of trespass by the plaintiff, Martin Luther, a Dorr adherent. The militiamen, however, claimed to have entered Luther's home for the purpose of placing Luther under arrest for participating in an insurrection. They claimed further to be acting under the authority of the lawful government of Rhode Island, which had proclaimed martial law to defend itself from insurrection. The case raised several issues, most importantly whether the government on whose behalf the defendants claimed to be acting was indeed the legitimate government of the state and hence competent to declare martial law. This issue became a federal question because of the Constitution's "Guarantee Clause." Article IV of the U.S. Constitution provides that the United States shall guarantee to every state a republican form of government and protect each of them against invasion and domestic violence. This constitutional provision at least suggested that the federal courts might determine whether or not Borden's actions had been lawful.

In his decision for the Court, Chief Justice Taney asserted that the issue of which Rhode Island government to recognize was a political question that could not be determined by the judiciary. Though best remembered for his notorious decision in *Dred Scott,* one of the two pre–Civil War decisions to declare acts of Congress unconstitutional,[25] Taney was regarded by Congress as a chief justice who understood the proper limits of judicial power and who respected legislative primacy.[26]

In the Luther case, Taney did not disappoint his congressional supporters. When he declared the question of which Rhode Island government to recognize a political matter, the chief justice did not simply throw up his hands and leave matters up in the air. He assigned to the Rhode Island state legislature the responsibility for resolving the issue. "In relation to the act of the Legislature declaring martial law," Taney wrote, "it is not necessary . . . to inquire to what extent, nor under what circumstances, that power may be exercised by a State." Second, according to Taney, identifying the rightful government in a particular state and determining whether or not it is republican in character are matters for Congress to decide. "Under this article of the Constitution [Article IV] it rests with Congress to decide what government is the established one in a state. . . . And its decision is binding on every other department of the government, and could not be questioned in a judicial tribunal." The political questions raised by the Luther case were to be resolved by legislative bodies—the Rhode Island legislature and the U.S. Congress.

The most striking example of nineteenth-century judicial obeisance to the legislative branch is the Supreme Court's 1869 decision in *Ex Parte McCardle*.[27] This case arose from the political struggles between Congress and President Andrew Johnson over Reconstruction policy. Under a series of Reconstruction acts, Congress had imposed military governments upon a number of the former Confederate states. McCardle was a Mississippi newspaper editor who had been arrested by the army and held in the stockade without formal charges for publishing articles critical of the military government. Seeking to secure his release, McCardle brought a habeas corpus proceeding under an 1867 act of Congress, which was intended to expand the power of the federal courts in the South by authorizing them to grant habeas corpus to anyone restrained "in violation of the Constitution." The act also authorized appeals to the Supreme Court.[28] The circuit court denied McCardle's petition, and he appealed to the Supreme Court. Fearing that the high court would grant the petition and invalidate military Reconstruction, Congress quickly enacted legislation over the president's veto, withdrawing the Supreme Court's appellate jurisdiction under the 1867 act.

The Court, in an opinion written by Chief Justice Chase, denied McCardle's habeas petition. The chief justice claimed to be powerless to act in the wake of Congress's action. Chase acknowledged the power of Congress to regulate the appellate jurisdiction of the federal courts, even if it made exceptions to the jurisdiction defined in the Constitution. The Court therefore decided that it did not have jurisdiction in McCardle's case. To do otherwise might have been to invite retaliation from the most powerful branch of government. At the time of the McCardle case, radical Republicans in the Congress were trying to impeach the president and cement their grip on the national government. The chief justice realized that a decision in favor of McCardle's petition would be seen by Congress as a direct challenge to its power and would be sure to result in further attacks on the judiciary. Nineteenth-century judges not only had close relationships with legislatures, but also had ample reason to respect their power.

Shifting Institutional Alignments

Judicial deference to legislative power has practically disappeared today. Congress still has the power to control the courts' budgets; it has power over their jurisdiction and over judicial procedure.[29] The exercise of these powers, however, would require a level of organization, consensus, and energy that today's Congress rarely achieves, especially on issues of institutional prerogative that do not directly serve constituency interests. Congressional powers do not arouse as much apprehension in the courts as they once did. When Congress enacted the Religious Freedom Restoration Act (RFRA) to invalidate a Supreme Court decision that angered some conservative religious groups, the Court soon responded with a ruling in *City of Boernie v. Flores* that invalidated RFRA.[30] Members of Congress grumbled, but they did not retaliate.

Congress is not what it used to be. At the same time, judges no longer possess the legislative backgrounds that once gave them a measure of familiarity with and respect for representative institutions. Table 1 reports the percentage of federal judges appointed during the roughly four successive half centuries between the founding of the Republic and the present who served in Congress or the state legislatures before being named to the federal bench. As the data indicate, during the nineteenth century a legislative background was the norm for federal judges and a significant percentage returned to Congress or the legislatures after a stint on the bench. During the first half of the twentieth century, prior legislative service diminished in importance and few federal judges left the bench to pursue legislative careers. In the most recent half century, only a small percentage of federal judges served in representative assemblies before receiving their commissions, and only one seems to have served in Congress or the state legislatures after leaving the bench. This singular exception was former U.S. District Court judge Alcee Hastings of the Southern District of Florida, who was removed from the bench after being impeached and convicted in 1989 on charges of official corruption. Hastings was vindicated when he won election to the U.S. House of Representatives from Florida's twenty-third congressional district in 1993.

Table 8.1

Percentage of Federal Judges with Legislative Experience

Judges Appointed in	Total Number of Judges Appointed	Percentage with Legislative Experience
1790–99	44	75.0
1800–09	18	72.0
1810–19	19	78.9
1820–29	25	68.0
1830–39	26	80.8
1840–49	23	60.9
1850–59	26	61.5
1860–69	45	55.6
1870–79	48	54.2
1880–89	44	43.2
1890–99	72	43.1
1900–09	78	38.5
1910–19	95	28.4
1920–29	130	26.9
1930–39	129	25.6
1940–49	146	22.6
1950–59	170	20.0
1960–69	278	16.2
1970–79	404	9.4
1980–89	397	7.8
1990–99	457	3.9
2000–05	142	4.2

Source: Federal Judicial Center. Biographical Directory of Federal Judges

The decline of legislative experience among federal judges does not mean that political criteria no longer play a role in court appointments. Federal judges continue to be appointed at the recommendation of senators, members of Congress, party leaders, or other prominent politicians. "You can't get on the federal bench in this country without a political claim," says one federal appeals court judge.[31] One former federal judge, Griffin Bell, who later served as attorney general in the Carter administration, said of his own appointment, "Becoming a federal judge wasn't very difficult. I managed John F. Kennedy's presidential campaign in Georgia. Two of my oldest friends were the senators from Georgia. And I was campaign manager and special counsel for the governor."[32]

What has changed in recent decades is the character of the judges' political and governmental experience. Few recent or contemporary federal judges have ever served in a legislative body, but many have served in executive agencies or in federal or state judicial institutions as prosecutors, public defenders, state and municipal judges, or other functionaries of the court system. Today's judges are recruited primarily from executive and judicial positions, not from legislatures.

In the twentieth century, the political importance of parties and legislatures declined, and presidents were more likely to seek the favor of important interest and constituency groups such as environmentalists and consumer activists (if Democrats), or antiabortionists and pro-business forces (if Republicans). These new political notables are often to be found in the executive and judicial branches, where such movements have sought and won privileged access. Lately, interest groups have shifted their operations from legislatures to bureaucratic politics and litigation, where they have been able to achieve satisfactory results without the need to mobilize popular constituencies.[33]

Do the institutional origins of judges make a difference for their behavior on the bench? Conclusive proof is difficult, but everyone who has lived and worked in Washington soon learns that most employees of the executive and judicial branches of the government are disdainful of Congress and dismissive of the state legislatures. To many officials of executive and judicial branches of government, the nation's elected representatives are meddlers and bunglers who almost invariably place political considerations ahead of important national priorities. The late Harold Seidman, one of the nation's greatest scholars of governmental organization and for twenty-five years a senior executive branch official in the Bureau of the Budget, drew an unflattering portrait of the legislative branch. "Within the Congress," Seidman asserts, "words are sometimes equated with deeds ... [and] ... concern ... is focused principally on those elements [of public policy] that directly affect constituency interests or committee jurisdictions. ... Legislative proposals are seldom debated from the viewpoint of their administrative feasibility [and] if things go wrong, failure can always be attributed [to others]."[34] Seidman's views probably reflect the Washington consensus. Senator Robert Byrd (D-WV) felt the consensus as it emanated from the White House staff. "Some of these people," he said, "have complete disdain for Congress. They are contemptuous of Congress."[35]

Contemporary judges are recruited from a political milieu in which legislatures are disdained by the political cognoscenti and during an era when executive power has in fact become more and more pronounced, while that of Congress has gradually diminished. Contemporary judges are not even accustomed to viewing legislatures as institutions capable of taking sound and decisive actions. Perhaps the most significant exception to this rule was former Supreme Court justice Sandra Day O'Connor, who was also the principal author of a number of decisions seeking to return power to the state legislatures. Perhaps it is no coincidence that Justice O'Connor was among the rare federal judges with state legislative experience, having served as a member and majority leader of the Arizona State Legislature during the 1970s.

Many federal judges have come to embrace a set of beliefs that, as discussed in Chapter 2, were first fully articulated in the United States during the Progressive era. In the Progressive vision, only the judiciary and the executive branch are capable of dealing effectively with important national problems. Legislatures, by contrast, are inefficient, fit only to represent parochial interests, as opposed to broad public interests, and are often corrupt. As one prominent federal appeals court judge observed, many contemporary federal judges, influenced by Progressive modes of thought, seek "rationality" in public policy and have an attitude of "hostility to a pluralist, party-dominated, political process."[36] Such views are of course likely to find expression in distaste for legislatures and a preference for decision making by courts and the executive—the nation's "rational" institutions. For a number of years, for example, federal judges objected vigorously to legislative efforts to control sentencing of convicted felons. Congress sought to diminish judges' discretionary power over sentences by creating the United States Sentencing Commission in 1984. Congress authorized the commission to establish a series of rules governing the sentences judges could mete out to those convicted of federal crimes. Although setting the appropriate penalties for violations of statutes would seem to lie within the purview of the nation's legislature, many federal judges regarded congressional efforts to establish sentencing rules as wholly misguided and illegitimate. Not surprisingly, in 2004 and 2005 the U.S. Supreme Court struck down the mandatory sentencing principle and restored judicial discretion in this realm.[37]

For its part, Congress is quite aware of the disdain many judges feel toward the legislative process. This became apparent during the 2005 confirmation hearings for Chief Justice John Roberts. After perfunctory and desultory questioning about abortion and other putatively "hot-button" issues, members of the Senate Judiciary Committee turned to their real concern. Led by Senator Arlen Specter (R-PA), the committee's chairman, members grilled Roberts on the Court's lack of deference to Congress. "I take umbrage at what the court has said, and so do my colleagues," said Specter. Robert's failure to reply clearly annoyed Specter. "Do we have your commitment that you won't characterize your method of reasoning as superior to ours?" the senator asked. Roberts gave a noncommittal reply.[38]

Taken together, these considerations help to explain why in recent decades the federal courts have regularly intruded into a number of areas that once would clearly have been considered political—more specifically, congressional—domains. For example, in the 1962 case of *Baker v. Carr*, the U.S. Supreme Court held that legislative apportionment, a matter the Court had previously said was left by the Constitution to Congress and the state legislatures, could in fact be determined by the federal courts.[39] Similarly, in the 1969 case of *Powell v. McCormack*, the Court heard on the merits former Representative Adam Clayton Powell's claim that he had been improperly denied his seat in Congress.[40] The House had voted to exclude Powell after it found that he had misappropriated congressional funds for personal use. Article 1, Section 5 of the U.S. Constitution, of course, states explicitly that each house of Congress is empowered to judge the qualifications of its own members. The Supreme Court, nevertheless, held that it, rather than the Congress, should determine whether Powell was entitled to his seat.

Perhaps the most striking example of judicial intervention into the political arena in recent years was the Supreme Court's decision in the case of *Bush v. Gore,* one of several state and federal cases arising from the 2000 presidential election in the state of Florida. Here the Court, de facto if not de jure, awarded Florida's electoral votes to George W. Bush in the disputed 2000 Florida presidential vote count.[41] On its face, the issue of whether Florida's electoral votes belonged to Bush or Gore seems to be precisely the sort of political question that the Luther court assigned to Congress and the state legislatures 170 years earlier. Though dismissed by the mainstream media—one national columnist referred to the state's legislative proceedings as "off-the-wall"—the Florida legislature claimed to be prepared to resolve the issue as might have appeared to be its constitutional and legal right.[42] Alternatively, Congress might have settled the outcome. In a similar situation following the disputed 1876 presidential election, the U.S. Congress devised a procedure that ultimately awarded disputed electoral votes to the Republican candidate, Rutherford B. Hayes. In 2000, however, neither the Florida Supreme Court nor the U.S. Supreme Court saw any reason to even consider deferring to meddlesome "off-the-wall" legislative bodies.

If the federal courts simply failed to bow to any other governmental institution, this might be taken as evidence for the judicial imperialism thesis once propounded by some conservative writers.[43] This imperialism, however, seems limited in scope—indeed, mainly confined to wearing away the prerogatives of Congress. When it comes to the actions of the executive branch, however, the federal courts have been far more tolerant. Indeed, as judicial deference to Congress has waned, so has its solicitude for the presidency grown. This duality of outlook is reflected in the views of the Supreme Court's newest justice, Samuel Alito. As a young Justice Department lawyer in the 1980s, Alito bemoaned a congressional effort to ease the Supreme Court's workload. "Our only hope," Alito wrote, "is that Congress will continue to do what it does best—nothing."[44] But when it comes to the presidency, Justice Alito has a different view. "The president has not just some executive powers, but the executive power—the whole thing," Alito said in a 2000 speech to a conservative legal society.[45] It seems that Congress does nothing while the president should do everything. Let us examine four areas—foreign policy, war and emergency powers, legislative powers, and administrative authority—in which the federal courts have acceded to and encouraged the expansion of presidential power.

FOREIGN POLICY

Foreign policy has come to be seen as a presidential preserve, but of course the Constitution assigns important foreign policy powers to the Congress. And, from the birth of the Republic through the early years of the twentieth century, the federal courts recognized Congress's role in shaping American policy toward other nations. For example, in the 1795 case of *Penhallow v. Doane,* the Supreme Court specifically held that the Constitution required the president and the Congress to share foreign policymaking authority.[46] Over the ensuing decades, the courts continued to emphasize congressional power. In the 1829 case of *Foster v. Neilson,* the Court indicated that Congress had the ultimate power to interpret the meaning of language in treaties between the United States and other nations.[47] In the 1850 case of *Fleming v. Page,* the Court held that only Congress, not the president, had the power to annex territory to the United States.[48] In the 1893 Chinese Exclusion Cases, the Court reaffirmed the dominance of Congress in the realm of international relations. Justice Gray, for the Court, said, "The power [in this instance, to exclude aliens] is vested in the political departments of the government, and is to be regulated by treaty or by Act of Congress."[49] In a similar vein, the 1901 Insular Cases conceded to Congress the power to determine the constitutional rights of the inhabitants of America's territories.[50]

This nineteenth-century deference to Congress in the realm of foreign relations gave way, in the twentieth century, to a distinct judicial presumption in favor of executive power in foreign affairs. The turning point was the 1936 case of *U.S. v. Curtiss-Wright Export Corporation.*[51] The company had been charged with conspiring to sell fifteen machine guns to Bolivia. This sale violated a May 1934 presidential proclamation issued pursuant to a congressional resolution authorizing the president to prohibit arms sales to Paraguay and Bolivia, which were then engaged in a cross-border conflict. Attorneys for the company argued that the congressional resolution allowing the president discretion in the matter of arms sales was an unlawful delegation of legislative power to the executive branch.

As we shall see below, in two earlier cases, *Schechter Brothers Poultry v. U.S.* and *Panama Refining Co. v. Ryan,* the Court had struck down acts of Congress on the grounds that they represented unconstitutionally broad delegations of legislative power to the executive branch.[52] Both decisions had prompted severe criticism from the White House and from congressional Democrats. Perhaps for that reason, the Court seemed anxious to distinguish the present case from the earlier decisions without seeming to retreat from its former position. The Court might have accomplished this objective merely by asserting that the discretion allowed the executive branch under the 1936 act was more narrowly defined than the president's authority under the earlier acts. However, the author of the Court's opinion, Justice George Sutherland, had long believed that America should pursue an active foreign policy guided by the president and the judiciary and free from the parochial concerns that, in his view, often dominated congressional policymaking. In essence, Sutherland thought politics should stop at the water's edge.[53]

Writing for the Court, Justice Sutherland made a sharp distinction between internal and external affairs. The congressional resolution delegating power to the executive, said Sutherland, might have been unlawful if it had "related solely to internal affairs." In the realm of foreign affairs, however, different standards and rules applied, permitting Congress to delegate powers to the president with only very general standards or even leaving "the exercise of power to his unrestricted judgment." The difference between foreign and domestic affairs, moreover, did not end here. In the realm of foreign policy, the powers Congress could appropriately exercise and presumably delegate to the president were not limited to the express and implied powers granted in the Constitution. This limitation was said to apply "only in respect of our internal affairs." Finally, in the realm of foreign affairs, said the Court, the president exercised "plenary and exclusive power," independent of any legislative authority, as "the sole organ of the federal government in the field of international relations."

Taken together, these three principles laid the legal groundwork for many of the claims of executive power made by presidents and sustained by the federal courts in subsequent years. The *Curtiss-Wright* decision implied that Congress, through action or inaction, could grant nearly any legislative authority to the president.[54] The president, moreover, possessing "plenary" powers, might in some instances act on his own authority without legislative authorization, or even contrary to the express will of Congress. In particular, *Curtiss-Wright* helped to set the stage for presidential arrogation of one of Congress's most important foreign policy instruments—the treaty power—as well as the notion that presidential foreign policy actions not specifically prohibited by Congress had been tacitly approved through congressional acquiescence to the president's decisions.

With regard to the treaty power, Article II of the U.S. Constitution provides that proposed treaties between the United States and foreign states must be ratified by a two-thirds vote in the Senate before having the effect of law. On numerous occasions the Senate has exercised its Article II powers by refusing to ratify treaties negotiated and signed by the president. In recent years, the Senate has been especially unwilling to ratify human rights treaties and conventions, which Senate Republicans have regarded as impositions on American sovereignty. These include the 1979 Convention to Eliminate All Forms of Discrimination Against Women, the 1989 Convention on the Rights of the Child, the 1978 Convention on Human Rights, and the 2000 treaty creating a Permanent International Criminal Court. After President Clinton signed the latter agreement, Senator Jesse Helms, who then chaired the Senate Foreign Relations Committee, announced it would be "dead on arrival" in the U.S. Senate.[55] In order to circumvent the Senate's Article II treaty powers, as we saw in Chapter 6, presidents have turned to the device of executive agreements with other nations. Largely at the president's discretion and based mainly on political considerations, these may be executive-congressional agreements, requiring a simple majority vote in each house of Congress, or sole executive agreements that are never submitted for congressional approval.[56] In the nineteenth and early twentieth centuries, executive agreements were most often trade pacts linked to prior congressional legislation.[57] For example, the Tariff Act of 1897 authorized the president to negotiate certain types of commercial agreements with other nations.[58] Although the resulting agreements were not submitted for ratification, their underlying purpose had been affirmed by the Congress and the president's discretionary authority limited.[59] There are, of course, nineteenth- or early twentieth-century examples of executive agreements undertaken by presidents on their own authority, sometimes at least nominally linked to the president's duties as commander in chief. For example, in 1900, without asking for authorization, President McKinley signed an agreement to cooperate with other nations to send troops to China to protect European legations during the Boxer rebellion. Subsequently, in 1901, McKinley signed the Boxer Indemnity Protocol between China and other powers, again without seeking Senate approval. Despite these and other exceptions, however, the norm was that compacts between the United States and foreign nations were submitted to the Senate as required by the Constitution.

After taking office in 1933, President Franklin D. Roosevelt had no intention of allowing a small number of senators to block his foreign policy decisions and initiated what is the now the standard practice of conducting foreign policy via executive agreement rather than Article II treaty. During his first year in office, Roosevelt signed what came to be known as the "Litvinov Assignment," which, among other things, provided for American recognition of the Soviet Union and assigned to the government of the United States all Soviet claims against American nationals. When the U.S. government ordered New York's Belmont Bank to turn over certain Russian assets, the bank refused to comply, asserting that the executive agreement upon which the government's claim was based was not the equivalent of an Article II treaty and did not have the force of law. The case reached the Supreme Court in 1937 as *U.S. v. Belmont*.[60]

In its decision, the Court not only upheld the government's claim, but also affirmed the president's power to negotiate agreements without Senate approval that for all intents and purposes would have the legal effect of Article II treaties. Justice Sutherland, writing for the Court, reaffirmed his position in *Curtiss-Wright*, asserting that the president possessed the plenary authority to speak as the "sole organ" of the U.S. government in its foreign relations. As such, the president had the power to make binding international agreements that did not require Senate ratification. This decision was reaffirmed four years later in *U.S. v. Pink*, which also dealt with the disposition of Russian assets in the United States.[61]

Beginning with these decisions, the federal courts have nearly always accepted sole executive agreements and executive-congressional agreements as the equivalents of Article II treaties. A handful of cases have qualified executive agreements or limited their scope. In *Swearingen v. U.S.*, for example, an appeals court held that a sole executive agreement could not supersede the tax code.[62] Such cases, however, are the occasional exceptions. For the most part, the courts have held that, like treaties, executive agreements supersede previously enacted federal and state laws, unless they are subsequently disallowed by the Congress. Thus, for example, in *Bercut-Vandervoort & Co. v. U.S.*, the Court of Customs and Patent Appeals ruled that a provision of the Internal Revenue Code must be interpreted in a manner consistent with GATT, although the latter was a sole executive agreement.[63] And in *Coplin v. U.S.*, the Court of Claims ruled that an executive agreement exempting some Americans working in the Panama Canal Zone from U.S. income taxes effectively repealed prior portions of the internal revenue code with which it was inconsistent. Interestingly, the court reached this conclusion even though attorneys for the government actually conceded that the president had exceeded his authority.[64] Congress can, through the ordinary legislative process, seek to repeal or qualify an executive agreement. When Congress fails to take action and specifically prohibit a presidential initiative, the Supreme Court has held that inaction constitutes a form of congressional acceptance or acquiescence.[65] The U.S. Constitution may be the last remaining limit on executive agreements. In *Reid v. Covert*, at least, the Supreme Court held that an executive agreement could not abridge the constitutional rights of Americans whether living at home or abroad.[66]

At the same time that they have allowed presidents to substitute executive agreements for treaties when doing so suited the chief executive's purposes, the federal courts have also given the president broad latitude in interpreting existing treaties.[67] In one important case, moreover, the Supreme Court declined to intervene to block the president from unilaterally terminating a treaty.[68] When President Jimmy Carter decided to recognize the People's Republic of China, he also recognized China's claim to sovereignty over Taiwan and accordingly withdrew American recognition from the Taiwan government and terminated America's mutual defense treaty with the island's regime.[69] This precedent was, of course, cited by the Bush administration in support of the president's decision in 2001 to unilaterally terminate the 1972 Anti-Ballistic Missile Treaty.[70] If one common theme unites the numerous cases affirming the president's dominance in the realm of foreign policy, it is the theme of expertise. In case after case, the federal courts are moved to declare that the president, and by implication only the president, possesses adequate knowledge, information, and judgment to make foreign policy decisions. Legal historian Joel R. Paul calls this often-expressed judicial presumption "the discourse of executive expediency."[71] Thus in *Curtiss-Wright*, Justice Sutherland refers to the special information the president may have and to the "unwisdom" of requiring too much congressional involvement in decision making. In *Pink*, Justice Douglas writes that presidential primacy in the realm of external relations is necessary to promote "effectiveness in handling the delicate problems of foreign affairs." In *Dames & Moore*, Chief Justice Rehnquist is concerned that Congress continue to allow the president the discretion he needs to conduct the nation's foreign policies and to meet the "challenges" with which he must deal. The courts plainly see that they cannot conduct the nation's foreign policy and so they turn—as they see it—of necessity to the president. "The conduct of foreign relations is not open to judicial inquiry" and must be left to the president, Justice Sutherland said in *Belmont*, and Justice Douglas reiterated in *Pink*.

But what of the Congress? Reflecting the ideological legacy of Progressivism coupled perhaps with a sheer lack of first-hand legislative experience, contemporary courts do not seem to take seriously the notion that Congress should play a major role in conducting the nation's foreign affairs. What would the Congress contribute, besides its parochial perspectives and "unwisdom," to delicate foreign policy matters? As we shall see below, this judicial perspective is even more pronounced when contemporary federal courts consider issues of war and emergency power.

WAR AND NATIONAL EMERGENCY

Contemporary presidents often behave as though they alone possess the authority to deploy military forces and lead the nation into war. Article I of the Constitution, however, seems to assign Congress the central role in this area. The framers gave Congress the power to declare war, to raise and support armies, to maintain a navy, to make rules for the conduct of the army and navy, to call out the militia, and to grant letters of marque and reprisal. Only Congress, moreover, can appropriate funds for the support of military forces. Article II, by contrast, appears to assign the president a lesser role. The president is to serve as commander in chief of the nation's military forces and to see to it that the nation's laws are faithfully executed. On the basis of the Constitution's text and from the debates at the Federal Convention, it appears that most of the framers intended Congress to decide whether, how, and when to go to war. The president's role as commander in chief would consist mainly of implementing congressional decisions by organizing actual military campaigns.[72] In addition, the president's duty to see to the faithful execution of the laws might include the task of responding to civil disorder or to foreign attack when Congress could not be convened in a timely manner.[73] This was certainly the view expressed by James Madison to the Constitutional Convention's committee on drafting when he moved to give Congress the power to declare war while leaving to the executive only the power to "repel sudden attacks."[74] Thomas Jefferson saw Madison's handiwork as an important means of preventing the nation from becoming embroiled in conflicts. "We have already given in example," Jefferson wrote to James Madison, "one effectual check to the Dog of war by transferring the power of letting him loose from those who are to spend to those who are to pay."[75]

The early decisions of the federal courts supported this original conception of the distribution of war powers under the Constitution. In the 1800 case of Bas v. Tingy, the Supreme Court affirmed that only Congress had the power to commit the United States to war either by a formal declaration, which the justices called "perfect war," or to limited military engagements without a formal declaration of war (imperfect war) when, "popular feeling might not have been ripe for a solemn declaration of war."[76] The following year, in Talbot v. Seeman, Chief Justice John Marshall, writing for the Court, said the Constitution gave Congress "the whole powers of war."[77] And in Little v. Barreme, the Court held that the president could not go beyond Congress's explicit instructions when exercising his commander in chief powers.[78] The case arose from America's early nineteenth-century conflict with France. Congress had authorized the president to seize armed French vessels sailing to French ports. President Adams, however, had issued orders for the seizure of such ships sailing to or from French ports. An American vessel had captured a French ship when it emerged from a French port, and the French owners sued to recover damages. The Court held that the captain of the American vessel was liable because the presidential orders under which he had acted exceeded the president's authority and were accordingly invalid. Later, in *Brown v. United States*, the Court invalidated an executive seizure of British property that took place after the initiation of hostilities but before the Congress declared the War of 1812.[79]

Even in the early decades of the Republic, presidents sometimes deployed military forces without seeking congressional authorization. President Jefferson, for example, did not consult Congress before sending warships into the Mediterranean to prepare for action against the Barbary pirates. As legal scholar Jeremy Telman notes, however, the early presidents were very well aware of the fact that the Constitution and the courts had reserved to Congress the power to authorize the use of force and that Congress would act to defend its prerogatives. Accordingly, presidents were generally careful to avoid taking actions that Congress would not support, even for defensive operations. In 1793, for example, George Washington refused a request from the governor of Georgia to send troops to protect settlers from Native Americans on the ground that only Congress could authorize such action.[80] Similar examples are numerous. Indeed, as the U.S. State Department's foremost legal adviser, Judge Abraham Sofaer, writes, "At no point during the first forty years of activity under the Constitution, did a President . . . claim that presidents could exercise force independently of congressional control."[81] A similar point is made by David Currie, who indicates that the early presidents viewed only an actual attack on the United States as adequate justification for the use of armed force absent congressional authorization.[82]

In some instances, presidents asked for congressional approval only after the fact. President Polk, for example, asked for a congressional declaration of war against Mexico in 1846, after provoking an armed skirmish between American and Mexican forces. But, even this post hoc request indicated the president's recognition that he could not use force without congressional sanction. And to underline the point, Congress voted to censure Polk for instigating the clash before it voted to declare war on Mexico.[83] Even Lincoln requested and received retroactive congressional approval of his decision to blockade Southern ports and suspend the writ of habeas corpus during the early days of the Civil War while Congress was in recess.

During the course of the war, Lincoln issued numerous executive orders and military regulations without congressional sanction. He declared martial law far from combat zones, seized property, suppressed newspapers, expanded the army, emancipated slaves, and censored the mails. The president sought when possible to claim that his actions were justified not only by prospective congressional approval, but by actual congressional legislation such as the 1795 and 1807 statutes authorizing the president to call out the militia and to use the military to suppress insurrection.

When push came to shove, however, Lincoln justified his actions on his inherent powers as commander in chief and his presidential duty to see to it that the laws were faithfully executed. In part, this was a constitutional claim based upon an expansive reading of Article II as providing the president with powers beyond those delegated to him by the Congress. And in part, this was also a claim of extraconstitutional power similar to English philosopher John Locke's notion of the Crown's prerogative, "the power to act according to discretion for the public good, without the prescription of the law and sometimes even against it."[84] In the two cases arising from Lincoln's actions during the Civil War, the Supreme Court did not accept this broadened conception of the presidential war power. The first test of the president's war power came in 1863 in the so-called Prize Cases challenging Lincoln's 1861 order to blockade Southern ports.[85]

The Supreme Court upheld the validity of the president's order but did so primarily on the basis of the 1795 and 1807 congressional enactments mentioned above. The Court also cited the president's long-standing duty to repel attacks and invasions. In linking the president's actions to congressional authorizations and to well-established constitutional theory, the Court was affirming the traditional constitutional framework and refusing to give its imprimatur to the president's new claims. In effect, the Court refrained from challenging the then current reality of enhanced presidential power but refused to bolster its jurisprudential foundations.

In the second important case growing out of the Civil War, *Ex Parte Milligan*, decided in 1866, the Court firmly rejected the president's claim to possess emergency powers outside the law or Constitution.[86] In 1861 Lincoln had, on his own authority, declared martial law and suspended the writ of habeas corpus even in states far removed from any theater of war. Milligan, a civilian and a citizen of Indiana, was an active "Copperhead," or supporter of the Confederate cause. In 1864 he was arrested at his home, tried by a military commission, and sentenced to be hanged for his seditious actions. At the time of Milligan's arrest, the civil courts in Indiana were functioning normally and could have heard the charges against him under an 1863 statute providing for the civil disposition of cases involving individuals arrested for disloyal activities.[87] Before Milligan's scheduled execution in 1865, the circuit court in Indianapolis issued a writ of habeas corpus, and the case was brought before the Supreme Court. The Court held that the president had no authority to declare martial law in an area where the civil authorities and civil courts were operating without obstruction and where there existed no imminent threat of attack or invasion. Martial law could be declared only in the event of "compelling necessity." The Court, moreover, rejected any notion that in time of emergency the president possessed powers not prescribed by law or the Constitution. "The Constitution of the United Sates is a law for rulers and people, equally in war and in peace," wrote Justice Davis for the Court. "No doctrine, involving more pernicious consequences, was ever invented by the wit of man than that any of its provisions can be suspended during any of the great exigencies of government."[88]

As has often been noted, the Court issued this judgment after the war had ended. During the war, the justices would likely have hesitated to protect a Confederate sympathizer and thwart the president and military authorities. Nevertheless, *Milligan* helped reassert the nineteenth-century principle of limited presidential authority. Indirectly, *Milligan* also cleared the way for the courts to reaffirm congressional power. While the late nineteenth-century Court was anxious to curb presidential war and emergency powers, it allowed Congress much more lee-way. In the 1871 case of *Miller v. U.S.*, the Court carefully distinguished Congress's war powers from those of the president. While presidential war powers derived from congressional authorization, those of the Congress were limited only by the "law of nations."[89] In a number of post–Civil War cases, moreover, the Court invalidated presidential actions on the ground that the emergency had passed, while upholding Congress's right to continue to exercise powers originally created to deal with the emergency.[90] According to legal historian Christopher N. May, at least up to World War I, it was generally agreed that war and emergency powers were primarily possessed by the Congress, not the president.[91]

The question of inherent presidential emergency powers, however, had not been fully settled at the end of the nineteenth century. Two turn-of-the-century domestic cases provided judicial sanction for the Lincolnesque notion that the president's duty to see to the faithful execution of the laws gave him inherent powers beyond those enacted by Congress or specified by the Constitution. In the first of these cases, *In re Neagle*, a U.S. marshal, David Neagle, assigned by the attorney general to protect Justice Stephen Field, shot and killed a disgruntled litigant who threatened the justice, who was riding circuit in California.[92] When Neagle was arrested by state authorities and charged with murder, the federal government demanded his release, claiming that he was lawfully performing his duties as a marshal, even though there was no specific statute authorizing the president to assign bodyguards to judges. The Court ruled that the president's duty to oversee the faithful execution of the laws gave him power that was not "limited to the enforcement of acts of Congress." The Court took this same position in the 1895 case of *In re Debs*.[93] Here the issue was whether to uphold a contempt citation against Debs and other union leaders for violating an injunction against a strike by rail workers. The executive had no statutory authority for seeking such an injunction, but the Court held nevertheless that this action was within the president's inherent powers.

The Two World Wars

World War I might have been expected to produce a profusion of cases involving presidential emergency powers. President Wilson, however, generally sought and almost always received clear statutory authorization for his actions during the war.[94] As a result, while a number of wartime and postwar cases dealt with the government's seizure of factories, mines, and railroads as well as with wartime restrictions on freedom of speech, few if any disputes bore directly on the question of presidential power. For the most part, the courts were asked to review statutes enacted by Congress, rather than unilateral actions undertaken by the president. The courts almost always upheld Congress's emergency and war powers during the war and for several years thereafter, ignoring what normally might have been seen as unconstitutional exercises of governmental power and violations of civil liberties. These included convictions under the 1917 Espionage Act and the 1918 Sedition Law that are often cited today as textbook violations of civil liberties. As Clinton Rossiter once observed, "The Court, too, likes to win wars."[95] Indeed, the Supreme Court rejected every challenge to emergency wartime legislation until long after the Armistice. In 1921 the Court invalidated portions of the Lever Act, and in 1924 it struck down the District of Columbia emergency rent law.[96] At the same time, however, the Court did seek to affirm the principle—if not the immediate fact—that war powers are limited by the Constitution and subject to judicial review.[97]

Emergency and war powers issues arose again during World War II. Franklin D. Roosevelt issued numerous military and emergency orders during the course of the war, generally claiming statutory authorization for his actions. Unlike Wilson, however, FDR was less than fastidious about the clarity of the relationship between his actions and their purported statutory basis. And indeed in many instances the powers delegated by Congress to the executive were so broad as to provide the president with virtually unfettered discretion. For example, the Emergency Price Control Act of 1942 authorized the executive to set "fair and equitable" prices.[98] Like Lincoln a century earlier, Roosevelt saw his role as commander in chief and his duty to see to the faithful execution of the laws as conferring upon his office constitutional and extraconstitutional powers—the Lockeian prerogative—to defend the nation. Pursuant to this view, Roosevelt seized property, declared martial law, established military tribunals, and interned some seventy thousand American citizens of Japanese descent primarily on his own authority.

For example, in May 1941, with Great Britain apparently on the verge of collapse, the president issued a proclamation declaring a state of "unlimited national emergency," supplanting the "limited" emergency he had declared in 1939. As authority for these proclamations, the president vaguely cited some ninety-nine statutes, many forgotten for more than a century, as well as additional powers "not enumerated in the statutes," which could not be specifically defined but might require the president to take action.[99] A month after proclaiming the emergency, FDR ordered the seizure of a North American Aviation plant in Inglewood, California, that had been closed by a strike. This was the first of many such plant seizures retroactively ratified by the Congress in the 1943 War Labor Disputes Act, which authorized the president to seize mines or plants producing materials required for the war effort. In a similar vein, Roosevelt created a host of new executive agencies without consulting Congress under his authority as "Commander in Chief in time of war."[100] And in 1942, the president told Congress that if it refused to repeal a particular provision of the Emergency Price Control Act, he would be left with "an inescapable responsibility" to prevent domestic economic factors from impeding the war effort. "In the event that the Congress should fail to act," said the president, "I shall accept the responsibility and I will act."[101]

During the course of World War II, the Court, as it had during World War I, upheld the constitutionality of every statute enacted by the Congress for wartime purposes.[102] Because many of these statutes, however, gave the executive branch broad discretionary authority, the Court's decisions, in effect, broadened the president's war and emergency powers. As Sheffer observes, the war powers of the nation became during World War II the war powers of the president, regardless of the "linguistic label."[103] Take, for example, the case of *Yakus v. U.S.*, involving decisions of the Office of Price Administration (OPA) under the Emergency Price Control Act of 1942.[104] A principal issue raised by the plaintiff, a wholesale butcher charged with selling beef for a higher price than allowed by the OPA, was whether the statute entailed an unconstitutional delegation of legislative power to the executive branch. The Supreme Court ruled that Congress clearly had the constitutional power to prescribe prices in a time of emergency. However, since the executive's power under the statute was so broadly defined, the effect of the Court's decision was to allow the executive to prescribe prices during an emergency that was itself declared by the executive.

In a number of other cases, the federal courts ruled more directly on the matter of presidential war and emergency powers, nearly always deciding in favor of the president's possession and exercise of such powers. One decision enhancing the president's emergency powers came in the 1942 case of *Ex Parte Quirin*.[105] Seven German agents were apprehended by the FBI. The men had been trained in sabotage and brought to the United States by submarine to attack American military facilities. President Roosevelt ordered the creation of a special military commission to try the accused saboteurs. Their attorneys argued that the president had no authority to issue such an order, and that the men should be tried in the civil courts in the states where they had been captured. As we saw earlier, the 1866 *Milligan* court had held that the president could not convene military tribunals where the civil courts were functioning normally and the area in question was not a theater of war. The Supreme Court in 1942, however, without explicitly overruling *Milligan,* distinguished the facts and circumstances of the two cases. The Court held that even where the civil courts were fully available and there existed no immediate threat of war or disorder, the president possessed the authority to create military commissions and to designate individuals as unlawful combatants subject to trial by such commissions. Sixty years later, the *Quirin* decision would be cited by the Bush administration in support of its decision to try terrorist suspects before military tribunals rather than the civil courts. In fact, President Bush intentionally modeled his executive order establishing such tribunals after Roosevelt's Executive Order 2561 authorizing military trials for the German saboteurs.[106]

One additional World War II decision cited by the Bush administration was the Supreme Court's 1950 ruling in *Johnson v. Eisentrager.*[107] Eisentrager was a German spy in China. After Germany's surrender, he continued to work for the Japanese until his capture by the United States. Eisentrager was tried and convicted of various crimes by an American military commission in China and sentenced to life in prison. He was incarcerated in a U.S.-run facility in Bavaria. His request for a writ of habeas corpus was rejected by the Supreme Court on the grounds that constitutional protections do not extend to enemy aliens held on foreign soil. The Bush administration has relied on the Eisentrager precedent to bolster its claim that terrorist suspects held by American forces in Guantánamo, Cuba, are beyond the reach of the civil courts.

Another group of important World War II cases involving the president's military powers stemmed from Roosevelt's February 1942 Executive Order 9066 authorizing the secretary of war and military commanders to establish "military areas" from which "any and all persons" might be excluded to prevent espionage and sabotage. Although the order was stated in general terms, its target was the Japanese-American population of the west coast states.[108] On the basis of this order, military authorities removed seventy thousand Japanese-Americans to camps in Utah and elsewhere, where they were detained for the remainder of the war. Congress subsequently enacted legislation effectively ratifying the president's order. The most important of the cases generated by these events was *Korematsu v. U.S.*, decided in December 1944.[109] Korematsu, a U.S. citizen of Japanese ancestry, had violated a military exclusion order by refusing to leave his home in San Leandro, California, and had been arrested. Korematsu attacked the validity of the exclusion order and the entire evacuation program as an unconstitutional exercise of presidential power. A sharply divided Supreme Court, however, held that the order was valid. In his opinion for the Court, Justice Black wrote, "the military authorities considered that the need for action was great, and time was short. We cannot . . . now say . . . these actions were unjustified." In essence, the Court held that it had no power to question the president's declaration of a military emergency and the actions he ordered pursuant to that declaration. More than any case since the Civil War, Korematsu affirmed the martial powers of the president and the deference shown by the courts in the face of a presidential declaration of military emergency.

Several other World War II cases upheld the president's use of emergency economic powers. One such case was *Employers Group of Motor Freight Carriers v. National War Labor Board,* decided by the Circuit Court of Appeals for the District of Columbia.[110] The National War Labor Board (NWLB) had been created by executive order in 1942 and authorized by the president to issue nominally nonbinding "advisory" orders setting wage rates in a variety of industries. Companies that failed to take the NWLB's advice were inevitably denied government contracts, deprived of fuel and supplies, and in several instances saw their plants and facilities seized by presidential orders under one of several statutes authorizing such action. The plaintiff, a trucking company, sought to appeal an NWLB order advising it to grant a $2.75 per week wage increase to its employees, claiming that the NWLB lacked any statutory standing, much less authority to issue orders. The U.S. district and appeals courts, however, both ruled that the president possessed emergency power to establish executive agencies and declined to review the NWLB's orders. In another major case, the courts affirmed the president's power to seize property on his own authority under his general war powers. This was the case of *Montgomery Ward & Co. v. U.S.*[111] In December 1944, the president ordered the seizure of the plants and facilities of Montgomery Ward and Company after the firm's owner refused to comply with the directives of the NWLB. The government asserted that the seizure was justified under the Labor Disputes act but acknowledged that Montgomery Ward might not be a mine, manufacturing plant, or other facility described in the act. If so, said the government, the seizure was justified under the president's "general war powers." These contentions were rejected by the U.S. District Court but affirmed by the Circuit Court. The properties were returned to their owner before the Supreme Court could hear the case.

Youngstown *and Its Aftermath*

Federal court decisions during World War II seemed to offer strong support to the notion that the president possessed emergency military and economic powers that allowed him to declare martial law, seize property, set wages and prices, and generally act as a constitutional dictator during a time of emergency that the president himself had the power to declare. Thus, the federal courts appeared to underwrite the notion that the president, as commander in chief, exercised a Lockeian prerogative. In 1952, however, the Supreme Court's decision in *Youngstown Sheet & Tube Co. v. Sawyer* placed some limits on these earlier holdings.[112] In 1950, after Chinese troops intervened in the Korean War, President Truman declared a state of emergency reactivating various emergency statutes as well as laying the groundwork for emergency exercise of presidential authority. To halt a strike by steel workers in April 1952, Truman ordered the seizure of the nation's steel plants, asserting that an interruption of steel production would imperil the nation's defense. The steel companies opposed Truman's action and the case was soon considered by the Supreme Court.

The Court struck down Truman's actions, finding no constitutional or statutory basis for the president's seizure of the mills. Justice Hugo Black, author of the decision, noted that Congress had enacted legislation, in particular the 1950 Defense Production Act, that the president might have used as a basis for seizing the mills. Black also noted that the president might have invoked the 1947 Taft-Hartley Act (which had been enacted over Truman's veto) to compel the steel workers to halt their strike. The president had instead relied upon his powers as commander in chief, and on this basis Black found no constitutional justification for the seizure of private property. The *Youngstown* decision appeared to place serious limits on the president's emergency powers and to indicate that the Court had serious doubts about the constitutionality of the numerous property seizures ordered by presidents during previous wars.

In retrospect, however, the most important element of the Court's holding in *Youngstown* was not Black's decision for the Court. In terms of its subsequent importance, Black's opinion was overshadowed by Justice Jackson's concurrence. Jackson asserted that presidential power varied with three sets of circumstances. The power of the president was "at its maximum," he wrote, when the president acted "pursuant to an express or implied authorization of Congress." The president's power was "at its lowest ebb" when, as in the *Youngstown* case, he took action incompatible with the express or implied will of Congress. When, however, the president relied upon his independent powers in the absence of a congressional grant or denial of authority, "there is a zone of twilight" where events and "imponderables" would determine the validity of presidential action. Jackson's three-part test became a standard by which the Court evaluated presidential actions in subsequent years and that upon occasion seemed to provide the basis for limiting presidential powers.[113] For example, in the 1971 case of *New York Times v. U.S.*, the Pentagon Papers case, three justices rested their rejection of the government's effort to enjoin publication of the Pentagon Papers on the ground that Congress had considered but rejected proposals to prohibit the disclosure of such information. Thus the president was acting contrary to the implied will of the Congress.[114] And the next year, in *United States v. United States District Court,* the Court ruled that in the absence of congressional authorization and guidelines, the administration's domestic security surveillance program, involving wiretaps and warrantless searches, violated the Fourth Amendment.[115]

For the most part, however, as Gordon Silverstein has observed, the Court has shrunk the definition of presidential action contrary to the will of Congress while expanding the meaning of congressional approval or acquiescence.[116] In other words, before the Court has been willing to rule that the president's actions were prohibited, it has usually demanded evidence that Congress has formally and explicitly forbidden the action in question. The Court has interpreted anything short of unambiguous formal prohibition as tacit approval. Thus, as we saw earlier in *Dames & Moore,* when it claimed to explicitly rely upon Jackson's *Youngstown* categories, the Court held that the absence of congressional disapproval of the president's actions could be construed as approval.

The Court came to a similar conclusion in the 1981 case of *Haig v. Agee,* when it held that the failure of Congress to give the president authority for his actions, "especially in the areas of foreign policy and national security," does not imply congressional disapproval of the president's actions.[117] Subsequently, in *Crockett v. Reagan,* a case in which several members of Congress claimed that the president was violating the War Powers Resolution (WPR) by supplying military assistance to El Salvador, the district court found that before a court could intervene, Congress must take explicit action to apply the WPR to the matter at hand.[118] Similar conclusions were reached by the court in 1987 in *Lowry v. Reagan* and in 1990 in *Dellums v. Bush.*[119] In 1999, several members of Congress brought suit against President Clinton, seeking to compel an end to the air war in Yugoslavia on the grounds that it had not been authorized by Congress and that the president's actions violated the WPR. Here again, both the district and appellate courts held that in the absence of clear-cut evidence of congressional disallowance of the president's actions, no action could be taken by the judiciary.[120]

The War on Terror

Thus, despite the *Youngstown* decision, the clear trend of case law since at least World War II and most markedly since the Vietnam War has been to support the president's use of emergency and war powers.[121] The scope of this discretion has become especially evident in the response of the federal courts to President George W. Bush's "war on terror." Since September 11, 2001, the president has issued numerous executive orders relating to the deployment of military and security forces and to the detention of captured terrorist suspects. While the president sought and received congressional support for many of his actions against terrorist groups, the White House did not concede that its policies with regard to the amount, character, and timing of the force to be used to combat terrorism were subject to congressional approval.[122]

In June 2004, the Supreme Court ruled in three cases involving the president's antiterror initiatives and claims of executive power and in two of the three cases appeared to place some limits upon presidential authority. Indeed, the justices had clearly been influenced by revelations that U.S. troops had abused prisoners in Iraq and sought in these cases to make a statement against the absolute denial of procedural rights to individuals in the custody of American military authorities. But, while the Court's decisions were widely hailed as reining in the executive branch, they actually fell far short of stopping presidential power in its tracks.

The first case decided by the Court was *Hamdi v. Rumsfeld*.[123] Hamdi, apparently a Taliban soldier, was captured by American forces in Afghanistan and brought to the United States, where he was incarcerated at the Norfolk Naval Station. Hamdi was classified as an enemy combatant and denied civil rights, including the right to counsel, despite the fact that he had been born in Louisiana and held American citizenship. A federal district court scheduled a hearing on Hamdi's habeas petition and ordered that he be given unmonitored access to counsel. This ruling, however, was reversed by the Fourth Circuit Court of Appeals.[124] In its opinion the court, quoting *Curtiss-*

Wright, held that in the national security realm, the president wields "plenary and exclusive power." This power was even greater, said the court, citing *Youngstown*, when the president acted with statutory authority from Congress. The court did not indicate which statute, in particular, might have authorized the president's actions, but went on to affirm the president's constitutional power, as supported in the Prize Cases, *Quirin*, and other rulings, to conduct military operations, decide who is and who is not an enemy combatant, and to determine the rules governing the treatment of such individuals. In essence, said the court, the president had virtually unfettered discretion to deal with emergencies, and it was inappropriate for the judiciary to saddle presidential decisions with what the court called the "panoply of encumbrances associated with civil litigation."

In June 2004, the Supreme Court ruled that Hamdi was entitled to a lawyer and "a fair opportunity to rebut the government's factual assertions." However, the Supreme Court affirmed that the president possessed the authority to declare a U.S. citizen an enemy combatant and order such an individual held in federal detention. Several of the justices intimated that once designated as an enemy combatant, a U.S. citizen might be tried before a military tribunal with the normal presumption of innocence suspended. One government legal adviser indicated that the impact of the Court's decision was minimal. "They are basically upholding the whole enemy combatant status and tweaking the evidence test," he said.[125]

A second case decided by the Court in June 2004 was *Rasul v. Bush*.[126] In March 2003, the Circuit Court of Appeals for the District of Columbia had deferred to the White House with regard to the status of the 650 suspected terrorists and Taliban fighters held by the United States at the Guantánamo Bay naval base in Cuba. The government had never filed charges against any of the detainees and took the position that they could be held indefinitely "under the law of war" without legal process or access to counsel. In rejecting attorneys' motions for writs of habeas corpus, the circuit court, citing the *Eisentrager* precedent, ruled that the detainees had no legal rights in the United States because technically they were being held on Cuban soil. The Supreme Court, however, reversed the lower court ruling, holding that Guantánamo Bay was territory under American jurisdiction, entitling the prisoners to habeas corpus hearings. It was not clear how the decision would affect the thousands of foreigners detained by the United States in such places as Iraq and Afghanistan, and at least one justice, Antonin Scalia, vehemently rejected the idea that habeas corpus could be extended throughout the world.

The third June 2004 case involved an American citizen, José Padilla, suspected by the government of conspiring with Islamic terrorists to explode a radiological "dirty bomb" in the United States. Padilla had been arrested at O'Hare Airport and had subsequently been declared an enemy combatant by President Bush. As an enemy combatant, Padilla was subject to indefinite detention and possessed no legal rights. The Supreme Court declined on procedural grounds to rule on the Padilla case.[127] In September 2005, the U.S. Court of Appeals for the Fourth Circuit ruled that President Bush indeed possessed the authority to detain Padilla as an enemy combatant.[128] In reaching this conclusion, the circuit court relied heavily upon the Supreme Court's decision in *Hamdi*. The circuit court did not address the issue of the type of tribunal to which Padilla might now be entitled. That issue was never fully resolved in the *Hamdi* case, since Hamdi was deported to Saudi Arabia soon after the Supreme Court's decision in his case.

Thus, in its June 2004 rulings, the Supreme Court did assert that presidential actions were subject to judicial scrutiny and placed some constraints on the president's unfettered power. But at the same time, the Court affirmed the president's single most important claim—the unilateral power to declare individuals, including U.S. citizens, "enemy combatants" who could be detained by federal authorities under adverse legal circumstances. This hardly seems to threaten the foundations of the imperial presidency. Indeed, whatever the fate of Hamdi and the others, future presidents are likely to cite the Court's decisions as precedents for, rather than limits upon, the exercise of executive power.

The same is likely to be true of the Court's June 2006 decision in the case of *Hamdan v. Rumsfeld*.[129] Salim Hamdan, a Taliban fighter captured in Afghanistan in 2001 and held at Guantánamo since 2002, was slated for trial by a special military tribunal. These tribunals, operating outside both the civilian and military court systems, were created by the Bush administration to deal with captured terrorists in the wake of September 11 and the U.S. invasion of Afghanistan. In its decision, the Supreme Court said that special military tribunals must either be established by statute or, if created by presidential order, must follow rules and procedures consistent with the Uniform Code of Military Justice (UCMJ) and the Geneva conventions. The Court found that President Bush's tribunals were not authorized by statute and operated under procedures providing defendants with fewer rights and safeguards than they would receive under the UCMJ. Hence, the tribunals were invalid.

However, while invalidating these particular tribunals, the Supreme Court accepted the principle that the president could order those he deemed to be unlawful combatants tried by military tribunals so long as the tribunals were lawfully constituted. Accordingly, President Bush asked Congress to authorize the creation of special tribunals that would operate under essentially the same rules and procedures as those declared unconstitutional by the Supreme Court.[130] Congress acceded to the president's request and enacted the Military Commissions Act, which Bush signed into law in October 2006. The act authorized the creation of military tribunals to try terror suspects and made few changes in the procedures originally specified by the administration. The act also authorizes "aggressive interrogation methods" of terror suspects and permits information obtained by such methods to be introduced into evidence. Given this congressional authorization, the *Hamdan* case does not seem to pose a challenge to presidential power.

Declarations of National Emergency:
The Impact of INS v. Chadha

Not only have the federal courts shown enormous deference to presidential power, but they have also undermined congressional efforts to curb the emergency powers of the executive. A very important Supreme Court decision had the unintended effect of undermining a congressional effort to rein in presidential emergency powers. This was the Court's 1983 decision in *INS v. Chadha,* which held that statutory legislative veto provisions were unconstitutional violations of the Presentment Clause.[131] At the time of the decision, numerous statutes contained provisions allowing Congress to veto presidential actions. Two of the most important of these laws were the National Emergencies Act of 1976 (NEA) and the International Emergencies Economic Powers Act of 1977 (IEEPA).[132]

Generally speaking, when the president declares a state of national emergency, he does so under the authority of these pieces of legislation that attempt to define the extent and limits of presidential emergency powers. The statutory origins of presidential emergency powers can be traced to the 1917 Trading With the Enemy Act (TWEA).[133] This World War I–era statute authorized the president to declare a national emergency following a congressional declaration of war if he believed the safety of the nation required it. In the wake of an emergency declaration, the president was authorized to exercise virtually unlimited control over transactions involving any property in which a foreign country had an interest. During the war, this act became part of the statutory basis for property seizures, military conscription, and even suspension of the gold standard.[134]

TWEA had been viewed as an act designed to be used in time of war. In 1933, however, during the depths of the Great Depression, Congress broadened the notion of national emergency to include peacetime crises. The amended act authorized the president to declare a state of emergency to deal with any situation that threatened the nation's well-being.[135] President Roosevelt used this expanded power in a number of instances, including his famous 1933 "Bank Holiday" proclamation, which ordered the temporary suspension of all retail banking activities in the nation. Subsequent presidents cited TWEA as the statutory basis for a number of executive orders. President Truman's 1950 seizure of the nation's steel mills followed his declaration of a state of emergency. President Nixon used a state of emergency to break a 1970 postal strike and in 1971 declared a state of emergency to raise tariffs on certain imported goods.[136]

During its protracted struggle with Nixon during the early 1970s, Congress became quite concerned with presidential emergency powers. In 1973 a Senate Special Committee found that TWEA gave the president unlimited authority to declare an emergency and to "seize property; organize and control the means of production; seize commodities; assign military forces abroad; institute martial law; seize and control all transportation and communication; regulate the operation of private enterprise; restrict travel; and, in a plethora of particular ways, control the lives of all American citizens."[137] Once declared, moreover, a state of emergency persisted until the president chose to end it. Several of the emergencies declared by President Wilson still formally existed. Congress subsequently enacted the NEA and IEPPA to place limits upon presidential emergency powers. The NEA established a two-year sunset provision for presidentially declared national emergencies unless they were renewed by the president. For its part, the IEPPA amended the TWEA by delimiting the president's authority to declare emergencies during peacetime. Under the IEPPA, the president is authorized "to deal with an unusual and extraordinary threat, which has its source in whole or substantial part outside the United States, to the national security, foreign policy, or economy of the United States."[138]

Essentially, under IEPPA, emergency powers are reserved for emergencies linked to international threats, as was the original TWEA before its 1933 amendment. Once an emergency has been declared, the president's powers are defined broadly as under TWEA. Congress, however, introduced an important safeguard into IEPPA that had been lacking in TWEA. IEPPA requires congressional consultation and review whenever the president plans to declare a state of emergency. Moreover, the president is required to report to Congress with regard to any and all actions he is undertaking to deal with the emergency. These consultation and reporting requirements were enforced by legislative veto provisions. Under NEA and IEPPA, Congress could, via concurrent resolution of both houses, terminate any national emergency declared by the president and/or any actions taken by the president pursuant to his emergency declaration. This legislative veto provision replaced the TWEA's provision allowing Congress to terminate an emergency through a joint resolution. The difference, of course, is that a concurrent resolution does not require the president's signature, while a joint resolution is subject to a presidential veto.

Members of Congress thought that this concurrent resolution provision would, on the one hand, allow the president sufficient latitude to protect the nation in the event of emergency but would, at the same time, give legislators ample opportunity to intervene if they felt that the president was acting improperly. Indeed, this seemed to be a reasonable position. In 1983, however, as a result of the Supreme Court's *Chadha* decision, the legislative veto provisions of both NEA and IEPPA became invalid. In response to *Chadha*, Congress was forced to rewrite both the NEA and the IEPPA. The amended statutes provide that instead of a concurrent resolution, Congress can terminate a declaration of national emergency or invalidate presidential actions pursuant to such a declaration by passing a joint resolution supported by a two-thirds majority in both houses. The supermajority requirement was adopted because of the near certainty of a presidential veto of such a resolution.[139] Given the likely difficulty—if not impossibility—of mustering such a supermajority, especially in a time of crisis, the effect of *Chadha* is to substantially weaken the constraints that Congress can impose upon the president's use of emergency powers.

At the present time, sixteen presidential declarations of national emergency, some dating back more than thirty years, are still in force.[140] These include Carter's emergency declarations stemming from the Iranian hostage crisis, Reagan's emergency decrees in response to Libyan terrorism, and George H. W. Bush's declaration asserting that the proliferation of chemical and biological weapons constituted a national emergency. President Clinton declared three national emergencies, all related to Middle Eastern terrorism, which remain in effect. And, of course, President George W. Bush declared an emergency, still in effect, in response to the September 11, 2001, terrorist attacks in New York and Washington.

THE PRESIDENT'S LEGISLATIVE POWERS

The Constitution assigns the president significant legislative power in the form of the right to veto bills of which he disapproves. Over time, presidents have acquired additional legislative power. To begin with, presidents often recommend bundles of programs and policies such as Roosevelt's "New Deal" or Johnson's "War on Poverty" that shape Congress's legislative agenda. Second, under the terms of the 1921 Budget and Accounting Act, the president develops and submits to the Congress a unified executive budget.[141] Although Congress may revise the president's estimates, the executive budget usually becomes the template from which Congress works. Third, Congress is usually compelled to delegate considerable legislative power to the president to allow the executive branch to implement congressional programs. For example, if Congress wishes to improve air quality, it cannot possibly anticipate all the conditions and circumstances that may arise over the years with respect to its general goal. Inevitably, Congress must delegate to the executive substantial discretionary power to make judgments about the best ways to bring about congressional aims in the face of unforeseen and changing circumstances. Thus, over the years, almost any congressional program will result in thousands and thousands of pages of administrative regulations developed by executive agencies nominally seeking to implement the will of Congress.

Such delegation is inescapable in the modern era. Congress can hardly administer the thousands of programs it has enacted and must delegate power to the president and to a huge bureaucracy to achieve its purposes. Delegation of power to the executive, however, also poses a number of problems for Congress. If Congress delegates broad and discretionary authority to the executive, it risks seeing its goals subordinated to and subverted by those of the executive branch.[142] If, on the other hand, Congress attempts to limit executive discretion by enacting very precise rules and standards to govern the conduct of the president and the executive branch, it risks writing laws that do not conform to real-world conditions and that are too rigid to be adapted to changing circumstances.[143]

The issue of delegation of power has led to a number of court decisions over the past two centuries, generally revolving around the question of the scope of the delegation. As a legal principle, the power delegated to Congress by the people through the Constitution cannot be redelegated by the Congress. This principle implies that directives from Congress to the executive should be narrowly defined and give the latter little or no discretionary power. A broad delegation of congressional authority to the executive branch could be construed as an impermissible redelegation of constitutional power. A second and related question sometimes brought before the courts is whether the rules and regulations adopted by administrators are consistent with Congress's express or implied intent. This question is closely related to the first, because the broader the delegation to the executive, the more difficult it is to determine whether the actions of the executive comport with the intent of Congress.

With the exception of three New Deal–era cases, the Court has consistently refused to enforce the nondelegation doctrine.[144] In the nineteenth century, for the most part, Congress itself enforced the principle of nondelegation by writing laws that contained fairly clear standards to guide executive implementation.[145] Congressional delegation tended to be either contingent or interstitial.[146] Contingent delegation meant that Congress had established a principle defining alternative courses of action, and the executive was merely authorized to determine which of the contingencies defined by Congress applied to the circumstances at hand and to act accordingly. For example, the Tariff Act of 1890 authorized the president to suspend favorable tariff treatment for countries that imposed unreasonable duties on American products. In *Field v. Clark,* the Court held that this delegation was permissible because it limited the president's authority to ascertaining the facts of a situation. Congress had not delegated its lawmaking authority to him.[147] The Court also accepted what might be called interstitial rule making by the executive—this meant filling in the details of legislation where Congress had established the major principles. In the 1825 case of *Wayman v. Southard,* Chief Justice Marshall said Congress might lawfully "give power to those who are to act under such general provisions to fill up the details."[148] In 1928 the Court articulated a standard that, in effect, incorporated both these doctrines. In the case of *J. W. Hampton & Co. v. U.S.,* the Court developed the "intelligible principles" standard. A delegation of power was permissible "If Congress shall lay down by legislative act an intelligible principle to which [the executive] is directed to conform. . . ."[149]

As presidential power expanded during the New Deal era, one measure of increased congressional subordination to the executive was the enactment of laws that contained few, if any, principles limiting executive discretion. Congress enacted legislation, often at the president's behest, that gave the executive virtually unfettered authority to address a particular concern. For example, the Emergency Price Control Act of 1942 authorized the executive to set "fair and equitable" prices without offering any indication of what these terms might mean.[150] The Court's initial encounters with these new forms of delegation led to three major decisions in which the justices applied the "intelligible principles" standard to strike down delegations of power to the executive. In the 1935 *Panama* case, the Court held that Congress had failed to define the standards governing the authority it had granted the president to regulate the interstate shipment of oil. In the *Schechter* case, also decided in 1935, the Court found that the Congress failed to define the "fair competition" that the president was to promote under the National Industrial Recovery Act. In a third case, *Carter v. Carter Coal Co.*, decided in 1936, the Court concluded that a delegation to the coal industry itself to establish a code of regulations was impermissibly vague.[151]

These decisions were seen, with considerable justification, as a judicial assault on the New Deal and helped spark President Roosevelt's court-packing plan. The Court retreated from its confrontation with the president and, perhaps as a result, no congressional delegation of power to the president has been struck down as impermissibly broad in the more than six decades since *Carter*. Instead, the Court has effectively rewritten the nondelegation doctrine in the form of the so-called *Chevron* standard. This standard emerged from a 1984 case called *Chevron v. Natural Resources Defense Council*.[150] An environmental group had challenged an Environmental Protection Agency (EPA) regulation as contrary to the intent of the statute it was nominally written to implement. Although a federal district court sided with the environmentalists against the agency, the lower court's decision was reversed by the Supreme Court. In its decision, the Supreme Court declared that, so long as the executive developed rules and regulations "based upon a permissible construction" or "reasonable interpretation" of the statute, the judiciary would accept the views of the executive branch. This standard implies that considerable judicial deference should be given to the executive rather than to Congress. Indeed the courts now look to the agencies to develop clear standards for statutory implementation, rather than to Congress to develop standards for the executive branch to follow.[153] In the 2001 case of *U.S. v. Mead Corp.*, the Court partially qualified the *Chevron* holding by ruling that agencies were entitled to *Chevron* deference only when they were making rules carrying the force of law and not when they were merely issuing opinion letters or undertaking other informal actions.[154] Despite this qualification, *Chevron* still applies to the most important category of administrative activity.

Two other cases concerning delegation of powers should be mentioned. These involve the legislative veto and the line-item veto. As we saw, the legislative veto was one device often used by Congress to maintain some control over the executive's use of delegated powers. Numerous statutes have contained legislative veto provisions, allowing one or both houses of Congress to reject actions by the president or executive agencies as inconsistent with congressional intent. The *Chadha* case, noted above, struck down the one-house veto and raised serious questions about two-house veto provisions. Since the Court ruled that legislative veto provisions were separable from the statutes to which they were appended, the result was to remove restrictions on executive discretion in more than two hundred statutes that contained such provisions. As Silverstein observes, in its decisions the Court has effectively ruled that virtually any delegation of power to the executive branch is constitutional, while devices designed to control delegation are unconstitutional.[155]

The major exception to this rule might appear to be the case of the line-item veto, invalidated by the Court in the case of *Clinton v. City of New York*.[156] Throughout the 1980s and 1990s, Republicans argued that a line-item veto power would allow the president to delete fiscally irresponsible provisions of bills while preserving worthwhile legislation. The line-item veto became an important element in the GOP's "Contract With America," which served as the party's platform in the 1994 congressional elections. After Republicans won control of both houses of Congress that year, the party leadership felt compelled to enact a line-item veto, even though the immediate effect of doing so would be to hand additional power to Democratic president Bill Clinton. Many Republicans breathed a sigh of relief when the Court invalidated the measure. The actual impact of the line-item veto and the Court's decision was minor, primarily because the United States of America does not employ a line-item budget. In most states, each budgetary outlay is by law a line item. In the federal budget, by contrast, Congress is free to lump together items as it sees fit and could prevent line-item vetoes by linking items the president opposed with those he strongly supported. Thus what appears to be the major exception to the rule of judicial support for increased presidential discretion is not as important an exception as is sometimes thought.

For the past century, the federal courts have strengthened the legislative powers of the executive while showing scant concern for those of the legislature.

ADMINISTRATIVE POWER

A fourth realm in which the courts have helped to enhance the authority of the president is that of the president's power as the nation's chief administrator. Three issues in particular have been important—these are executive privilege, the appointment and removal power, and executive orders. As to executive privilege, we noted at the beginning of the chapter that this concept had no firm standing in law until the Court's decision in *U.S. v. Nixon*. The actual term "executive privilege" was coined by President Eisenhower, who frequently refused to provide information to Congress when to do so in his view would violate the confidentiality of deliberations in the executive branch.[157] But long before Eisenhower introduced the phrase, presidents claimed the power to withhold materials from Congress and from the courts.[158] George Washington, for example, refused congressional requests for information about a disastrous campaign against the Indians in 1792 and about the circumstances surrounding the negotiation of the Jay Treaty between the United States and Britain in 1796. In the course of presiding over the criminal case against Aaron Burr, Chief Justice John Marshall gave some standing to such claims. Marshall indicated that in criminal cases the president could not be treated like an ordinary individual and might be compelled to produce evidence only if it was clearly shown by affidavit to be essential to the conduct of the case.[159] Because of the Watergate affair, the term executive privilege has developed a bad odor, and subsequent presidents have used other phrases to deny congressional or judicial requests for information. For example, in refusing to allow the director of Homeland Security to testify before Congress in March 2002, President Bush asserted a claim of "executive prerogative."[160]

In *U.S. v. Nixon* the Court for the first time explicitly recognized executive privilege as a valid presidential claim to be balanced against competing claims. The Court indicated that, where important issues were at stake, especially foreign policy questions as well as military and state secrets, presidential claims of privilege should be given great deference by the courts. Finding no such issues in the present case, however, the Court ruled against Nixon. In a subsequent case, *Nixon v. Administrator of General Services,* the Court held that the former president's records were not privileged communications and could be transferred to the General Services Administration.[161] Once again, however, the Court recognized the existence of executive privilege and said it could be used to protect the president's communications "in performance of [his] responsibilities . . . and made in the process of shaping policy and making decisions." Thus, in both Nixon cases, precedents were established for claims of privilege, and in subsequent years the federal courts have upheld several such claims made by the president and other executive branch officials acting at the president's behest. For example, in *U.S. v. American Telephone & Telegraph,* in response to a presidential claim of privilege, the district court enjoined AT&T from providing a congressional subcommittee with the contents of a number of wiretaps conducted by the FBI.[162] Similarly, in *United States v. House of Representatives,* the district court refused to compel EPA administrator Anne Gorsuch to hand over what she claimed were privileged documents to a House subcommittee.[163]

In a series of recent decisions, federal courts have held that the strongest presumption in favor of privilege arises when national security interests are said to be at stake.[164] Both presidential deliberations and those of presidential advisers and their staffs have been held to be privileged, at least in judicial proceedings.[165] In a recent case, the vice president claimed privilege. This is the case of *Walker v. Cheney,* decided by the U.S. District Court for the District of Columbia in December 2002.[166] In this case, the director of the General Accounting Office (GAO), Congress's chief investigative arm, sought to obtain the records of an energy task force led by Vice President Dick Cheney in 2001. The task force was formed to make recommendations to the administration regarding federal energy policy. The GAO sought the records at the request of two Democratic members of Congress, who charged that the task force gave inordinate influence to energy producers at the expense of consumer and environmental interests. The case was dismissed on the ground that absent a congressional subpoena, the GAO director lacked standing to bring the case to court.

Another administrative realm in which the Court has generally shown deference to the president in recent decades is the area of appointment and removal. The president's appointment powers are defined in the Constitution and have produced little litigation. One important recent case, however, is *Buckley v. Valeo,* in which the Court ruled that Congress was not entitled to give itself the power to appoint members of the Federal Election Commission, an agency of the executive branch.[167] The removal power, by contrast, is not defined in the Constitution and has been a topic of some conflict between the president and Congress. In 1833, Congress censured President Jackson for removing the secretary of the treasury. In 1867, Congress enacted the Tenure of Office Act, which required Senate consent to the removal of cabinet officers, over Andrew Johnson's veto. Johnson's subsequent attempt to remove Secretary of War Stanton played a major role in the president's impeachment. Congress enacted legislation in 1872 and 1876 requiring Senate consent for the removal of postmasters but did, however, repeal the Tenure of Office Act in 1887.[168] The Supreme Court has made a number of decisions regarding the removal power, which for the most part have supported the president. In the 1926 case of *Myer v. U.S.,* the Court struck down the 1876 law, ruling that the power to remove executive officials "is vested in the president alone."[169]

In the 1935 case of *Humphrey's Executor v. United States,* however, the Court ruled against Franklin D. Roosevelt's efforts to remove a Federal Trade Commission (FTC) member before his term had expired. The Court noted that the FTC Act required the president to show cause for such actions and upheld Congress's right to impose such a requirement.[170] More recently, however, in the case of *Bowsher v. Synar,* the Court struck down a portion of the Gramm-Rudman-Hollings Deficit Reduction Act which authorized the comptroller general, an official removable only by Congress, to review executive decisions.[171] And in *Mistretta v. U.S.,* the Court upheld the president's power under the Sentencing Reform Act to remove members of the U.S. Sentencing Commission, including federal judges.[172] In recent years, only in the politically charged cases involving special prosecutors have the courts significantly restricted presidential removal powers. In *Nader v. Bork,* the district court held that President Nixon's firing of Watergate special prosecutor Archibald Cox was illegal.[173] And in *Morrison v. Olson,* the Supreme Court held that restrictions on the president's power to remove a special prosecutor did not invalidate the appointment.[174]

Finally, as to executive orders, it is sufficient to note that of the thousands of such orders issued from the birth of the republic through 1999, the overwhelming majority since 1933, one systematic study found that only fourteen were actually overturned by the courts. Of these fourteen, the federal judiciary struck down portions of twelve orders and overturned two others in their entirety.[175] One additional executive order was invalidated by a lower court in 2001.[176] Another 239 orders were modified or revoked by Congress between 1789 and 1999. One executive order overturned in its entirety was Truman's directive seizing the nation's steel mills, which was of course struck down in the *Youngstown* decision. A second was President Clinton's order prohibiting the federal government from hiring permanent replacements for striking workers. This order, which contradicted both a Supreme Court ruling and specific federal legislation, was invalidated in the 1996 case of *Chamber of Commerce v. Reich*.[177] For the most part, the courts have been reluctant to examine executive orders, often ruling that the plaintiff lacked standing or that the dispute involved a political question. And when they have heard the case, they have almost always upheld the president's directive.[178]

The Judiciary and Executive Power

Thus for the past century, the federal courts have bolstered the power of the executive branch and of the presidency in particular. To a considerable extent, the courts have reflected the changing realities of American political life. In the nineteenth century, Congress and the state legislatures were the dominant institutions of American government. Judges were typically recruited from the legislative arena and had reason to be confident that legislatures could govern. In the twentieth century, by contrast, the power of Congress waned, judges had little or no legislative experience and increasingly viewed the executive as the only branch of government capable of managing the nation's affairs. Congress may have looked to the courts for help in constraining presidential power, but the courts viewed Congress as incompetent to manage the nation's affairs and protect its interests, especially in the realms of foreign policy and security affairs. So, rather than delimit the power of the president, the courts have generally acted to expand the power of the presidency at the expense of Congress. Perhaps the only realm in which the federal courts have served as a check on the White House is the area of the president's personal conduct. The Supreme Court has held, for example, that the president is not immune from civil suits relating to his person, as opposed to official actions.[179] But, while the courts recognize limits on the conduct of the president, they have done much to remove those limits from the conduct of the presidency.

9

Conclusion: Upsizing the Presidency and Downsizing Democracy

FOR MOST OF THE nineteenth century, the presidency was an institution on the periphery of national politics. In unusual circumstances, a Jefferson, a Jackson, or a Lincoln might exercise extraordinary power, but most presidents held little influence over the congressional barons or provincial chieftains who actually steered the government. The president's job was to execute policy, rarely to make it. Policymaking was the responsibility of legislators, the leaders of the House and Senate. A few commanding presidents, such as Jackson, were famous for their vetoes, but most deferred to Congress and rarely presumed to speak their minds to the nation. It was considered bad form. The annual message on the state of the Union, required by the Constitution and transmitted to Congress in writing, was the principal occasion on which the president had a speaking part in American politics.

Today, however, the president has most of the lines, and the presidency has become the engine of national policy formation, especially where money and war are concerned. We are long past the time when the House of Representatives monopolized the power of the purse, doling out dollars down to the level of petty cash. The president is practically master of the nation's budget. And, while Congress may retain the constitutional power to declare war, the power has not been exercised in sixty-five years. The country's military forces have been engaged in conflicts all over the world, but we never declare war.

352

Before invading Iraq in 2003, President Bush demanded and received from Congress what Senator Byrd called a "blank check" from the Congress, "to employ the full military might of the United States wherever he pleased."[1]

For a generation or more, the power of the White House has grown during Republican and Democratic administrations alike. Congressional investigations, personal scandals, and impeachment may have slowed but never halted its advance. Even as presidential approval ratings plummet, presidential power continues to function and grow. The phenomenon is one of the wonders of contemporary national politics.

The political ascent of the presidency was neither accidental nor inevitable. It was contingent on an intersection of presidential motives, means, and opportunities that began to emerge no later than the early decades of the twentieth century. The *motives* of presidents grew more aggressive as the business of becoming chief executive demanded more drive—the "fire in the belly" that modern politicians must feel before they dare commit themselves to the rigors of the presidential quest. The party-centered mode of presidential selection characteristic of the nineteenth century usually propelled to the White House politicians posing no threat to the state and local party bosses who met in national convention to decide who would run for the presidency. The decline of the party convention as a decision-making forum and the rise of a candidate-centered nominating process favored a new kind of presidential contender—not a party workhorse, but a candidate driven by ambition of world-historical dimensions. Roosevelt, Kennedy, Nixon, and Clinton were men who made a career of pursuing the presidency. They sought election not just to hold the office, but to make history, and the office as it stood was usually not enough to satisfy them. They were impatient with its bounds and limits, and their efforts to overcome them provided much of the animating force that drove the expansion of presidential power.

If the president's personal ambition proved insufficient for the modern presidency, the functionaries of the institutional presidency, including cabinet secretaries and key members of the executive office staff, are usually prepared to promote their own "presidential" agendas. This has been true especially since the Cold War reorganization of the presidency, which institutionalized ambition by providing the president with a regiment of assistants and associates interested in expanding and using the powers of the office. As Dean Acheson hoped, these associates—the Haldemans, Roves, Rumsfelds, and Powells—can compensate for the fact that not every president is a Franklin D. Roosevelt.[2] Outside the cabinet and White House staff are the backers and investors who have a stake in presidential power. They attach themselves to presidential aspirants to advance particular causes or interests. Their aspirations add to the scope of the presidency's institutionalized ambition.

Executive *opportunity* grew with the retreat of Congress. When Wilson wrote *Congressional Government,* presidents faced a powerful legislative branch whose leaders jealously guarded its prerogatives and were quick to rein in presidents who overstepped their bounds. But today's Congress is weak, because growing civic disengagement saps its power. The framers knew that representative institutions drew their strength from a mobilized public. In a polity with a demobilized public, executives rule. Congress was also undermined because the same decay of political parties that paved the way for the candidate-centered presidential campaign also reduced the national legislature's organizational coherence and institutional capacity. Congress was a more vigorous institution when political party leadership gave it an organizational backbone. When they commanded disciplined party caucuses, the leaders of the House and Senate were willing and able to fight for institutional interests and to check presidential encroachment upon their powers. In the absence of party discipline, Congress usually lacks the organizational coherence to slug it out with the imperial president on policy issues.

Congressional weakness gives motivated presidents almost all the opportunity they need to project their power across the country. But a cooperative judiciary is usually ready to oblige if presidents need legal or constitutional warrant to achieve their policy objectives. Today's federal judges rarely have legislative experience. They are much more likely to have been prosecutors, attorneys general, or executive branch attorneys, and they are generally more sympathetic to executive claims than to legislative prerogatives.

Finally come the *means.* The expansion of the administrative state created a powerful mechanism of presidential governance, but it did not do so immediately or automatically. Early in the twentieth century, Congress sought to delegate power not to the president, but to administrative agencies. Its budgetary authority and oversight function made it the president's rival for control of the executive branch, and bureaucratic agencies were as likely to serve Congress as the president. Beginning in the 1920s, however, the White House shouldered Congress aside to become headquarters of the executive branch. Expansion of the president's authority over the budget made him master of agency air supply. Meanwhile, congressional oversight deteriorated as Congress lost its cohesion and its members learned to look after themselves. The tedious business of overseeing bureaucratic agencies gave way as legislators preoccupied with constituency service became clients of the agencies, seeking favorable treatment for the voters who had elected them.[3]

While Congress looked the other way, ambitious presidents gradually gained control of the bureaucracy and learned to use it to circumvent the legislative process. Recent presidents have implemented many of their policy goals through executive orders and regulatory review. While facing impeachment and unable to command congressional support for his agenda, President Clinton used the techniques of executive legislation to enact much of his program without bothering to consult the legislative branch. The executive branch itself now provides presidents with the means to make domestic policy unilaterally.

Foreign policy is even more subject to executive initiative than domestic. Presidents have all but abandoned the constitutional process by which the Senate ratified treaties. Executive agreements now serve the same purposes without the inconvenience of consulting the Senate. Foreign policy itself has contributed in obvious ways to the expansion of presidential power. It is one arena in which the nation's need to speak with one voice and to act with one will is plainly essential. Constitutional doctrine and the imperatives of national security both give primacy to the unitary executive. During the twentieth century, America's engagement with the world made the presidency the focal institution for the nation's international ventures. Congress and the courts are usually more than willing to cede powers to the president in moments of international crisis. Presidents, for their part, are seldom eager to return these powers when the emergency has passed. Since the beginning of the Cold War, the military and national security bureaucracy has been presidential territory, and successive presidents have sought to expand it and defend their control of it. Since the opening of the war on terror, the national security apparatus has been transformed into an instrument of domestic government. The Department of Homeland Security is a multi-tentacled agency that stands ready to respond to tornadoes, floods, and Al-Qaeda. The national security state once focused on external threats. It now lives among us.

Presidentialism: Myths and Realities

The shift of institutional power toward the White House has its defenders. Law professor Steven Calabresi has called them the "presidentialists."[4] Often presidentialism is difficult to distinguish from partisanship. As long as the New Deal Coalition remained sufficiently strong to elect Democratic presidents, Democrats predictably promoted presidential authority, while Republicans became advocates for Congress and even states' rights. Since the Vietnam War initiated the era of Republican presidents, the parties' positions have reversed. Republicans rediscovered the virtues of executive power, while many Democrats lost some of their enthusiasm for presidential activism, a partisan change of heart undoubtedly reinforced by George W. Bush's unusual election and subsequent administration.

EMERGENCY POWER

Whatever their party affiliations, the advocates of presidential power have typically advanced three arguments for deferring to the White House. The first, which echoes themes articulated by Alexander Hamilton and others among the nation's founders, is that executive power is needed to deal with emergencies and to ensure the nation's security.[5] While no one could argue with this position in the abstract, particularly in an age of global terrorism, the problem is that presidents may see emergencies that others might question, or they may attempt to manufacture or magnify emergencies to enhance their discretionary power and freedom from scrutiny. The framers of the

Constitution gave Congress, and not the president, the power to make war precisely because they feared that presidents might be too quick to commit the nation to armed conflicts. Madison wrote:

> The strongest passions and most dangerous weakness of the human breast, ambition, avarice, vanity, the honorable or venial love of fame, are all in a conspiracy [within the executive branch] against the desire and duty of peace. Hence it has grown into an axiom that the executive is the department of power most distinguished by its propensity to war.[6]

But if the president is too anxious to go to war, it does not follow that Congress is slow to respond to emergencies. It would be difficult to identify an instance during the past half century in which the nation's security was compromised because the Congress refused to act, although there have been a number of cases, including perhaps the recent Iraq War, in which the president was, as Madison feared, too quick to take vigorous action. When the nation has faced actual emergencies, Congress has seldom refused to grant appropriate powers to the president. Indeed, the legislative branch has generally been too pliable, granting presidents powers to deal with emergencies of their own making, as in the case of the Gulf of Tonkin Resolution that President Lyndon Johnson used as the legislative basis for his Vietnam War policies.

If executive power were held in reserve for urgent crises, the case for presidential primacy might be more persuasive. But presidents exploit the advantages of their office on a routine basis, often to enact elements of their legislative programs that lack both urgency and sufficient support in Congress. President Clinton, for example, used the power of regulatory review to launch an environmental program that had been blocked in the Congress. President Bush used an executive order to place limits on stem cell research, a decision that pleased religious conservatives but could never have achieved majority support in the House and Senate. Right or wrong, these decisions were hardly responses to national emergencies. In both instances, the president was simply asserting his policy preferences and using his executive powers to override or ignore those of his opponents.

THE PUBLIC INTEREST

A second argument for expanded presidential power is that the president speaks for the national interest while Congress is unable to speak with one voice because it represents a multiplicity of parochial or special interests. The argument was popular with Progressives at the turn of the twentieth century who saw the presidency as a political institution that stood above the seediness of partisan politics, a trust-worthy steward of the entire nation's collective good.[7] Similar arguments circulate today, especially when legislative scandals disclose a Congress unable to liberate itself from the tentacles of lobbyists.[8] Administrative theorists who see virtue in the "unitary executive" lend support to presidential control of bureaucratic agencies.[9] Steven Calabresi is one of them. He makes the case for a "President who is alone vested with all of the executive power and is elected by all of the people, can be lobbied to rein in special interests. . . . He can be urged to prevent special interest groups or ideologues from diverting public policy into immoderate or non-public-interested directions."[10]

Presidents, it is true, are unitary actors. As such they may find it more difficult than members of Congress to escape responsibility for their conduct or avoid blame for inaction. To this extent, the presidentialist argument may have some merit. In practice, however, presidents seem no more resistant to parochial interests than members of the House or Senate. Presidents often enough seem to promote programs designed mainly to reward important political backers and contributors, even when these programs clearly do not serve the larger public interest. What public interest was served by President Clinton's decision to pardon fugitive financier Marc Rich? Vice President Cheney's consultations with energy industry executives were shielded from public scrutiny by the White House's claim of executive privilege. In both instances, personal or political calculations appear to have outweighed presidential concern for the public interest.

At least Congress tends to embody a broad range of special interests, and the particular interests promoted by individual members do not automatically become law. Precisely because presidents are unitary actors, presidential prejudice and partiality pass much more easily into public policy. Even more than the interests of influential supporters, presidents are likely to act in the interest of enhanced presidential power, which they often equate with the public interest. Consider, for example, the peculiar case of the Bush administration's decision to oppose federal court challenges to a Clinton-era executive order declaring millions of acres of western lands to be wilderness areas closed to development. During the 2000 campaign, Bush and his supporters had asserted, and doubtlessly believed, that Clinton's actions represented unwarranted intrusions upon property rights and the nation's economic development. Once in office, however, Bush saw court challenges to Clinton's order as threats to the institutional power of the presidency. Accordingly, Solicitor General Theodore Olson appeared in federal court to argue on behalf of the propriety of Clinton's decision.

Presidents, like members of Congress, pursue special and parochial interests and, more than members of Congress, have an institutional stake in policy outcomes. There seems little reason to prefer president to Congress as the guarantor of national interests. Members of Congress may represent special interests, but there is the chance, at least, that their special interests may be checked by the special interests that other members represent, and there are always two parties contending with one another in Congress. The president belongs to only one.

PRESIDENTIALISM AND DEMOCRACY

Beyond the claims that we need strong presidents to act in emergencies and to uphold the public interest, a third presidentialist argument is that the presidency is a more democratic institution than the Congress.[11] This argument has a certain surface plausibility. The president is, of course, the nation's only elected official who can claim to represent all the people. And, although only half of all eligible voters participate in presidential elections, the percentage for congressional races is sharply lower. Issues of gerrymandering, committee structure, seniority, and incumbency also taint Congress's democratic credentials.

But Congress, as we have already suggested, represents a wider range of interests and perspectives than the president, and Congress governs more democratically. Its deliberations are generally open to the public, and its members are not expected to echo the policies of a congressman in chief. True, some members of Congress are venal, inept, or indolent. Incumbents are rarely turned out of office by their constituents. The appearance of public deliberation sometimes masks behind-the-scenes bargains among powerful insiders, and legislative rules sometimes allow entrenched minorities to prevail against the interests of the general public. At its core, however, congressional policymaking operates through open hearings, public debate, and vigorous contention among disparate groups. In those rare instances when congressional hearings are closed, it is usually because executive branch witnesses cite national security concerns. Not only are most hearings open to public scrutiny, but members of the public, along with corporations, interest groups, and administrative agencies, have an opportunity to testify.[12] Floor debate, especially in the Senate, can be lengthy and rancorous, and it is by no means an empty exercise in either house. Amendments are frequently offered from the floor and increasingly likely to win acceptance. In short, despite its many imperfections, the U.S. Congress is a democratic decision-making body.

Presidential decision making, on the other hand, takes place in private and often in secret. The agencies of the executive branch are required by law to engage in an extensive process of open consultation with interested parties when they make regulations, and if they choose to make decisions in consultation with groups outside of government, Congress requires them to meet disclosure and public information requirements under the Advisory Committee Act. But presidents have no such obligation. Recent presidents have routinely invoked executive privilege to shield White House deliberations from public view. This was, of course, the Bush administration's position concerning the composition of the task forces with whom Vice President Cheney met in 2001 to plan the administration's energy policies. The Supreme Court supported the administration's position on the grounds that the "energetic performance" of the executive branch's duties required protection from intrusive requests for information.[13] Presidents have also disciplined staff members who revealed information to Congress, and the White House has tried to block legislation that would protect executive branch whistle-blowers. President Clinton, for example, threatened to veto the 1998 Intelligence

Authorization Act because of provisions designed to protect executive branch employees who engaged in unauthorized disclosures to Congress. Clinton said that any bill permitting executive personnel to provide information to Congress without the approval of their superiors represented "an unconstitutional infringement on the President's authority as Commander in Chief and Chief Executive."[14] Congress retreated in the face of the veto threat.

Presidents justify shielding their deliberations from disclosure so that their advisers will feel free to speak their minds, but the secrecy often extends from the deliberations to the decisions that result from them. Even Congress does not learn about some presidential policy choices. Many so-called national security directives issued by presidents have been used to initiate secret missions by intelligence and defense agencies.[15] Presidents have also signed secret executive agreements with foreign governments undertaking commitments on behalf of the United States that were never disclosed to Congress, much less submitted to the Senate under its power to vote on international treaties. In 1972, Congress enacted the Case-Zablocki Act, which required the president to provide it with an annual list of all international agreements entered into during the previous year. Presidents have never fully complied with the terms of this act, claiming that it did not cover national security directives and other sensitive matters.

Even when presidential actions are not shielded by claims of national security or executive privilege, presidential decision making tends to be less transparent and accessible to outside political interests and actors than is the congressional process. Regulatory review, for example, is one arena of presidential policymaking generally open to the participation of groups beyond the bounds of the executive branch. Since Nixon, presidents have tried to take control of agency rule making by insisting that bureaucratic regulations be cleared through the White House or the OMB's Office of Information and Regulatory Assessment (OIRA), originally created by Congress to help business firms limit the quantity of data that government agencies could compel them to provide. Until the Clinton administration, presidents had used OIRA to kill regulations that they did not want. Clinton transformed regulatory review from an exercise in which presidents could eliminate unwanted rules into an affirmative process through which the president could get federal agencies to adopt regulations that he wanted. The executive order creating his administration's regulatory review process included a provision "to ensure greater openness and accountability" by requiring OIRA to keep formal records of all communications regarding proposed rules between its personnel and political actors outside the executive branch.[16] Democrats had charged that the Reagan and Bush administrations allowed special interests to influence the regulatory review process behind closed doors. Before any rule can actually be adopted by a federal agency, of course, it must undergo the lengthy process of publication and consultation required under the Administrative Procedure Act. But critics charged that the Reagan and Bush administrations had used OIRA and the regulatory review process to open a back door to favored interest groups. Clinton hoped that disclosing the identities of groups consulted during the review process would avert similar criticisms of his administration.

In accordance with Clinton's order, OIRA began maintaining logs of all contacts between agency officials and people outside the government concerning proposed regulations. Such contacts included meetings and written communications. OIRA records from 1993 through 2000 were recently compiled and published by Steven Croley.[17] One important finding to emerge from the data is just how infrequently the White House actually consulted outside interests when framing its regulatory agenda. OIRA reviewed nearly four thousand rules during the eight-year period, but the office's records indicate that only about 10 percent of the proposed rules were discussed with outside parties.[18] About half of these meetings involved proposed EPA rules—a reflection, perhaps, of the administration's effort to implement its environmental program through regulatory review rather than congressional action. The meetings were attended by a small number of representatives of several business and environmental groups.[19] The records do not indicate precisely what was discussed, but Croley's analysis found no relationship between group attendance at OIRA meetings and subsequent changes in proposed rules. In other words, there was no indication that the OIRA meetings had a tangible impact in the rule-making process. "The White House," Croley concludes, "clearly has used rulemaking review to put its own mark on particular agency rules."[20]

In other words, White House regulatory review was virtually immune to external influence, and the president was able to use the rule-making process to implement much of his own environmental agenda—something he was unable to achieve through Congress.[21] In Congress, of course, hundreds of interests had been mobilized to do battle for and against the president's programs. The president lost. In a less open forum, however, controlled by White House officials, the president prevailed. Regulatory review seems to have followed the same pattern under Clinton's successor. The Bush administration OIRA has consulted a limited range of interests in a small number of meetings while reviewing thousands of proposed rules.[22] Even when the White House deliberately opens its decision-making processes to outside participation, the results do not reflect much outside influence.

Policy areas in which Congress is active, on the other hand, get considerable media attention and provoke vigorous debate. Publicity and contention help to assure that extensive information enters the public domain about the policy alternatives under discussion, and they contribute to the mobilization of interested parties. This has been the pattern in congressional deliberations about education, health care, banking, and pensions. President Clinton's health care initiative is an excellent illustration of the difference between executive and legislative policymaking. While Hillary Clinton presided over the formation of the proposal in the executive branch, she invited no public participation or discussion of the measure. Once the discussion moved to Congress, it rapidly spread to the mass media, interest groups, and the public at large.

The difference between executive and legislative modes of deliberation was not an accident, not unique to President Clinton's health care proposal. To exert influence, competing factions in Congress must maintain active and ongoing relationships with organizations and interests outside the government. Constituency mobilization is a major source of political power for members of Congress. The role of "special interests" in Congress may occasion the lamentations of editorialists and cynicism among citizens, but congressional ties to organized interests are essential to maintain parity of power between Capitol Hill and the White House. Today Congress must sometimes mobilize constituency pressure just to compel the president to implement its decisions. One of Congress's weaknesses as an institution is that it must depend upon the executive to carry out the legislation that it passes, and recent presidents have asserted with increasing frequency that they are not obliged to carry out statutes of which they do not approve. President Clinton, for example, refused to enforce a statute requiring the armed services to discharge soldiers found to be infected with the HIV virus, and his Justice Department issued a memorandum claiming that the president could refuse to enforce any law he viewed as unconstitutional.[23] President Bush has used signing statements to approve the acts of Congress while reserving to himself the right to ignore whole sections of statutes because he regards them as inconsistent with executive privilege, presidential control of the executive branch, or national security.

Like members of Congress, of course, presidents can also mobilize groups outside the government. Some presidents of the past, such as Andrew Jackson, turned popular mobilization into a decisive political resource that enabled them to overwhelm their opponents. When it comes to routine governance, however, presidents, especially recent presidents, generally prefer processes of policymaking that limit debate and social mobilization. In an open political struggle involving competition among many interests, presidents may win or they may lose. But when decisions are made discreetly in the corridors and offices of the White House with minimal external intervention, then the president remains in charge. And unlike Congress, the president does not have to rely upon an agency outside his sphere of control to implement the decisions that he makes. Modern chief executives control the means to execute policy, not just to make it. The participation of political actors from outside the executive branch may sometimes be a necessary nuisance, but wherever possible, presidents prefer to rely on decision-making processes that restrict the range of participants and limit the scope of political debate.

The differences between the political processes surrounding presidential policymaking and those associated with the congressional process come into focus if we consider the case of tariff policy. During the nineteenth and early twentieth centuries, tariff policy was hammered out in acrimonious congressional debates. Prior to the Civil War, the tariff was at the center of the great sectional struggle over the proper course of American political development.[24] After the Civil War, Congress continued to control tariff policy, rejecting presidential efforts to intervene on the grounds that the president had no unilateral constitutional authority to make commercial agreements with other nations.[25] Tariff policy remained among the most divisive and contentious issues in American politics, a magnet for lobbyists and interest groups, the grist for a legion of editorialists and letter writers.

The era of lively tariff politics came to an end in 1934 when Congress passed the Reciprocal Trade Agreements Act delegating to the president authority to negotiate trade agreements with other governments. The reasons behind this change in trade policy continue to be debated by scholars, but however murky the causes of the 1934 change, the consequences are clear. Shifting the locus of tariff policy to the chief executive led to the development of procedures that made it difficult for members of Congress or interest groups to know precisely which industries would or would not be affected by future tariff changes.[26] Judith Goldstein calls this a "veil of ignorance."[27]

Two things happened behind this veil. The first was a gradual reduction in tariff barriers as presidents negotiated freely with foreign governments. The second was a diminution of political conflict and mobilization. Presidents used their negotiating authority to bundle import losses with export gains for states and congressional districts. Senators and representatives found themselves cross-pressured by competing constituency claims and were less likely to respond to demands from either side. In short, presidents developed a formula for making tariff policy quietly and with a minimum of outside interference. The tariff lost its place at the center of national political debate and virtually disappeared from public view.[28] Shifting tariff policy from Capitol Hill to the White House had the effect of demobilizing contending political forces and transforming the tariff from an annual bone of political contention into a routine exercise of presidential power.

The development of tariff policy shows how patterns of decision making change when an issue moves into the orbit of the White House. In national security policy, presidents have almost always had the upper hand, but their hand has grown stronger over time, and they now make these life-and-death decisions largely on their own authority.

During the nineteenth and early twentieth centuries, as we saw in Chapter 5, Congress played a coordinate role in the making of national security policy. Congress not only determined budgets and planned force structures; the legislature shared in deciding whether the nation should go to war and how wars should be fought. When Congress dominated the realm of security policy, it exercised power by encouraging and participating in struggles among the rival services and among advocates of alternative force structures, armaments, and military strategies. As recently as the 1930s, officers representing rival services and military perspectives commonly took their differences to Congress. General Billy Mitchell, in fact, organized publicity stunts designed to sway popular and congressional sentiment. Congress listened to heated debates among advocates and opponents of tanks, air power, and aircraft carriers. Public discord and contestation among and between bureaucrats and soldiers served Congress's interests by offering numerous openings for legislative intervention in the security policy realm.

Over the course of the twentieth century, however, presidents moved gradually but decisively to take control of security policy. Congress's role has been sharply diminished. Since the Second World War, as presidents have assumed control of national security policy, they have also changed the way in which national security policy is made. Rather than encourage open debate about security issues, they have tried to bring them under the peremptory authority that the president exercises as commander in chief. The possibilities for political debate, interest group conflict, and popular mobilization are all sharply diminished. The consolidation of the national security establishment after World War II helped to reduce the interservice rivalries that provide opportunities for congressional intervention in military affairs, and in the process also reduced challenges to the president's control of the military.

The turmoil triggered by the Vietnam War induced the White House to push for an end to conscription and the creation of a fully professional military. Successive presidents and their military planners reasoned that a force composed of professional soldiers recruited mainly from military families and living on military bases set apart from civilian society could be sent into combat without engendering the popular clamor that created opportunities for rival politicians and members of Congress to attack presidential policies during the Vietnam era. For the same reason, the White House also developed a host of schemes to prevent the news media from presenting unfavorable accounts of military campaigns. These efforts have been at least partially successful and help to explain why popular opposition to President Bush's Iraq policy was muted despite a steady stream of casualties, uncertain war objectives, and substantial evidence of mismanagement and duplicity on the part of the White House.

Congress exercised power in the national security issues by encouraging public debate among rival agencies and interests. Presidents have exercised power by preventing just such debate. Presidents Reagan, Bush I, Clinton, and Bush II led the nation into significant armed conflicts without substantial prior debate—and not always wisely. In matters of national security, at least, the presidentialist claim that the executive is a more democratic institution than the Congress lacks credibility.

The Rise of the Presidency and the Waning of American Democracy

The expansion of presidential power is both symptom and source of an ongoing decay in America's democratic processes. It is a symptom of that decay because the decline of popular political involvement weakens the Congress and strengthens the presidency. Congressional influence depends on a politically engaged and active civil society. Once elected, presidents only occasionally need such support. In command of armies and bureaucracies, the president can govern according to his own lights, so long as mobilized constituents do not enable Congress to interfere. Contemporary America, with its weak political parties, its partially demobilized electorate, and its citizens transformed into mere "customers" of government, is made to order for presidentialism.

At the same time, the expansion of presidential power is itself a source of democratic decay, because presidents diminish American democracy by being presidential.[29] When presidents rule by decree in even the most routine matters, they diminish democracy. When they and their subordinates ignore, circumvent, and express disdain for legislative processes, they diminish democracy. When they create decision-making processes designed to mute debate and discussion in order to enhance their own power, presidents diminish democracy. In these ways, the onward march of presidentialism makes citizenship superfluous and contributes to what we have elsewhere called the "downsizing" of democracy in America.[30]

In 1793, George Washington issued an "Impartiality Proclamation" asserting American noninvolvement in the war between Britain and France. In the less presidential America of 1793, many believed that such matters of war and peace should be decided by Congress, not the executive acting unilaterally. James Madison declared that if the powers of "war and treaty" were allowed to become the sole province of the executive, then "all powers not less executive in their nature than those powers" might be claimed by the executive. In the end, Madison said, no citizen would even be able to "guess at the character of the government under which he lives."[31] Madison was wrong about one thing. We can guess.

Notes

Chapter 1. From Republican Government to Presidentialism

1   Mike Allen and Juliet Eilperin, "Bush Aides Say Iraq War Needs No Hill Vote," *Washington Post*, August 26, 2002, A1.

2   Robert C. Byrd, "The War Debate," *Los Angeles Times*, October 9, 2002, Part 2, 15; also Jules Witcover, "Byrd Leads but Too Few Follow Him," *Baltimore Sun*, October 11, 2002, 23A.

3   Elizabeth Drew, "War Games in the Senate," *New York Review* 49, no.19 (November 2002), 66–68.

4   Charles G. Sellers, *James K. Polk, Continentalist, 1843–1846* (Princeton: Princeton University Press, 1966).

5   John H. Schroeder, *Mr. Polk's War: American Opposition and Dissent, 1846–1848* (Madison, WI: University of Wisconsin Press, 1973), 10–11.

6   Donald W. Riddle, *Congressman Abraham Lincoln* (Urbana, IL: University of Illinois Press, 1957), 32–34.

7   See, for example, "What Will This Nation Be in Years to Come?" *Salon.com*, March 24, 2003.

8   Benjamin Ginsberg and Martin Shefter, *Politics by Other Means: Politicians, Prosecutors and the Press From Watergate to Whitewater*, 3rd rev. ed. (New York: W. W. Norton, 2002).

9   See L. Gordon Crovitz and Jeremy A. Rabkin, eds., *The Fettered Presidency: Legal Constraints on the Executive Branch* (Washington, DC: American Enterprise Institute, 1989).

10 Louis Fisher, "War and Spending Prerogatives: Stages of Congressional Abdication," *19 St. Louis University Public Law Review* 7 (2000). Also, Louis Fisher, *Congressional Abdication on War and Spending* (College Station, TX: Texas A&M University Press, 2000).

11 Edward Corwin, *The President: Office and Powers, 1787–1957*, 4th rev. ed. (New York: New York University Press, 1957), 234–42.

12 Sidney M. Milkis and Michael Nelson, *The American Presidency: Origins and Development, 1776–2002* (Washington, DC: CQ Press, 2003), 242.

13 Leonard D. White, *The Republican Era, 1869–1901: A Study in Administrative History* (New York: Macmillan, 1958), 55–56.

14 Kenneth Mayer and Thomas Weko, "The Institutionalization of Power," in Robert Y. Shapiro et. al., eds., *Presidential Power* (New York: Columbia University Press, 2000), 195.

15 Ibid., 195–96.

16 Ibid., 197.

17 Charles Dawes, *The First Year of the Budget of the United States* (New York: Harper, 1923).

18 Peri E. Arnold, *Making the Managerial Presidency: Comprehensive Reorganization Planning, 1905–1996,* 2nd ed. (Lawrence, KS: University Press of Kansas, 1998), 114.

19 John B. Gilmour, *Reconcilable Differences? Congress, the Budget Process and the Deficit* (Berkeley: University of California Press, 1990), 229.

20 Allen Schick, *The Federal Budget: Politics, Policy, Process* (Washington, DC: Brookings Institution, 2000), 94–95.

21 Fisher, *Congressional Abdication*, 128.

22 Ginsberg and Shefter, 74–75.

23 Fisher, "War and Spending Prerogatives," 22–26.

24 Robert G. Kaiser, "Congress-s-s: That Giant Hissing Sound You Hear Is Capitol Hill Giving Up Its Clout," *Washington Post*, March 14, 2004, B4.

25 Arthur Schlesinger, Jr., *The Imperial Presidency* (Boston: Houghton Mifflin, 1973), 132–33.

26 Fisher, "War and Spending," 13.

27 For a complete inventory of presidential instruments see Harold C. Relyea, "Presidential Directives: Background and Overview," Congressional Research Service Report 98–611 GOV, November 9, 2001.

28 Charles Lane, "In Terror War, 2nd Track for Suspects: Those Designated 'Combatants' Lose Legal Protections," *Washington Post*, December 1, 2002, 1.

29 Elena Kagan, "Presidential Administration," *Harvard Law Review* 114 (June 2001), 2245–383.

30 See Steven M. Teles, *Whose Welfare?: AFDC and Elite Politics* (Lawrence, KS: University Press of Kansas, 1996), 161–62.

31 Aristide Zolberg, "International Engagement and American Democracy," in Ira Katznelson and Martin Shefter, eds., *Shaped By War and Trade: International Influences on American Political Development* (Princeton: Princeton University Press, 2002), 24–54.

32 See Steven J. Rosenstone and John Mark Hansen, *Mobilization, Participation, and Democracy in America* (New York: Macmillan, 1993).

33 See Grant McConnell, *The Modern Presidency*, 2nd ed. (New York: St. Martin's Press, 1976), 104–5.

34 James Madison, "Federalist 48," in Clinton Rossiter, ed., *The Federalist Papers* (New York: Mentor, 1961), 309.

35 Ibid., 423.

36 Ibid., 435–36.

37 Ibid., 441–47.
38 Milkis, *The President and the Parties*, 97.
39 Jeffrey Tulis, *The Rhetorical Presidency* (Princeton: Princeton Unviersity Press, 1987), 79.
40 Ibid., Ch. 4.
41 George Creel, *How We Advertised America* (New York: Harper and Brothers, 1920).
42 George Brown Tindall, *America: A Narrative History* (New York: W. W. Norton, 1992), 1013.
43 Fred I. Greenstein, *The Hidden-Hand Presidency: Eisenhower as Leader* (Baltimore: Johns Hopkins Press, 1992), 19.
44 David Garrow, *Protest at Selma: Martin Luther King and the Voting Rights Act of 1965* (New Haven: Yale University Press, 1978).
45 Tulis, *Rhetorical Presidency*, 168–72.
46 Lou Cannon, *President Reagan: The Role of a Lifetime* (New York: Public Affairs Press, 1991), 32.
47 David Alpern, "The Second Hundred Days," *Newsweek*, May 11, 1981, 23.
48 Tulis, *Rhetorical Presidency*, 147.
49 Ibid., 161.
50 Theodore J. Lowi, *The Personal President: Power Invested, Power Unfulfilled* (Ithaca, NY: Cornell University Press, 1985).
51 Ibid., 11.
52 Benjamin Ginsberg and Martin Shefter, *Politics by Other Means: Politicians, Prosecutors and the Press From Watergate to Whitewater,* rev. ed. (New York: W. W. Norton, 1999), 35–39.
53 Joseph Lelyveld, "In Clinton's Court," *New York Review of Books* 50, no. 9 (May 29, 2003), 11–15.
54 Jill Abramson, "Washington's Culture of Scandal Is Turning Inquiry into an Industry," *New York Times*, April 26, 1998, 1.
55 Quoted in Robert Shogan, *The Double-Edged Sword: How Character Makes and Ruins Presidents from Washington to Clinton* (Boulder, CO: Westview Press, 1999), 224.
56 Michael Grossman and Martha Kumar, *Portraying the President: The White House and the News Media* (Baltimore: Johns Hopkins Press, 1981).
57 Ginsberg and Shefter, *Politics by Other Means*, 39–46.
58 Samuel Kernell, *Going Public* (Washington, DC: CQ Press, 2006), 114.

Chapter 2. Choosing Presidents

1 Theodore Lowi, *The Personal Presidency: Power Invested, Promise Unfulfilled* (Ithaca, NY: Cornell University Press, 1986).
2 Marc Landy and Sidney Milkis, *Presidential Greatness* (Lawrence, KS: University Press of Kansas, 2001).
3 James N. Ceaser, *Presidential Selection: Theory and Development* (Princeton: Princeton University Press, 1979), 10–11.

4   Clinton Rossiter, ed., *The Federalist Papers* (Harmondsworth, England: Mentor Books, 1999), 382.

5   Ibid., 380.

6   Max Farrand, ed., *The Records of the Federal Convention of 1787*, rev. ed., 4 vols. (New Haven: Yale University Press, 1966), II, 109.

7   Ibid.

8   Joseph J. Ellis, *Founding Brothers: The Revolutionary Generation* (New York: Vintage Books, 2002), 162–63.

9   Richard Shenkman, *Presidential Ambition: Gaining Power at Any Cost* (New York: HarperPerennial, 2000), 3.

10   Quoted in David McCullough, *John Adams* (New York: Simon & Schuster, 2002), 47.

11   Quoted in Ellis, *Founding Brothers*, 213.

12   Quoted in McCullough, *John Adams*, 213. On the driving ambition of Adams and the other founders, see also John A. Schutz and Douglass Adair, eds., *The Spur of Fame: Dialogues of John Adams and Benjamin Rush, 1805–1813* (San Marino, CA: Huntington Library, 1966).

13   McCullough, *John Adams*, 447.

14   Joseph J. Ellis, *American Sphinx: The Character of Thomas Jefferson* (New York: Vintage Books, 1998), 190.

15   Benjamin Ginsberg and Martin Shefter, *Politics by Other Means* (New York: W. W. Norton, 2002).

16   Michael Kelly, "President/Monsters," *Washington Post*, May 22, 2002, A37.

17   See, for example, Jules Witcover, *No Way to Pick a President* (New York: Farrar, Straus and Giroux, 1999), 5.

18   Had Hamilton been born after the ratification of the Constitution, he would have been ineligible for the presidency under the provision that limits the office to native-born Americans; Hamilton was born on the island of Nevis in the West Indies. But the Constitution also opened the presidency to residents who were citizens "at the time of the adoption of this constitution," and Hamilton would have qualified by that standard. On the constitutional qualifications for the presidency, see Michael Nelson, "Qualifications for President," in Thomas E. Cronin ed., *Inventing the American Presidency* (Lawrence, KS: University Press of Kansas, 1989), 13–32.

19   James T. Callender, *The Prospect Before Us* (Richmond, VA: H. Pace, 1801), 76.

20   See James Rogers Sharp, *American Politics in the Early Republic: The New Nation in Crisis* (New Haven: Yale University Press, 1993), 219.

21   Seymour Martin Lipset, *The First New Nation: The United States in Historical and Comparative Perspective* (New York: W. W. Norton, 1979), 42–43.

22   William Safire, *Scandalmonger* (New York: Simon & Schuster, 2000).

23   Lewis Lapham, "Uncommon Sense," *Harper's Magazine* 305 (July 2002): 7–9.

24   Ellis, *Founding Brothers*, 47.

25   Robert F. Jones, *George Washington: Ordinary Man, Extraordinary Leader* (New York: Fordham University Press, 2000), 109.

26 Quoted in Lucius Wilmerding, Jr., *The Electoral College* (New Brunswick, NJ: Rutgers University Press, 1958), 45.

27 Richard P. McCormick, *The Presidential Game: The Origins of American Presidential Politics* (New York: Oxford University Press, 1982), 101–2; Charles A. O'Neil, *The American Electoral System* (New York: G. P. Putnam, 1887), 106.

28 Arthur M. Schlesinger, Jr., ed., *History of American Presidential Elections, 1789–1968*, 4 vols. (New York: Chelsea House, 1972), I, 109; O'Neil, *American Electoral System*, 34.

29 McCormick, *Presidential Game*, 61.

30 Ibid., 110–14; see also O'Neil, *The American Electoral System*, 126; M. J. Heale, *The Presidential Quest* (London: Longman, 1982), 32.

31 McCormick, *Presidential Game*, 61, 208; Noble E. Cunningham, "Election of 1800," in Schlesinger, ed., *History of American Presidential Elections*, I, 105.

32 James Ceaser, *Presidential Selection*, 81.

33 McCormick, *Presidential Game*, 109.

34 Ibid., 49, 154.

35 Quoted in Edmund S. Morgan, *The Genius of George Washington* (New York: W. W. Norton, 1980), 4.

36 Quoted in Ellis, *Founding Brothers*, 7.

37 Morgan, *Genius of George Washington*, 25.

38 Marvin Kitman, *The Making of the President 1789* (New York: Harper Perennial, 1989), 24–25.

39 Morgan, *Genius of George Washington*, 6.

40 Jones, *George Washington*, 18–20.

41 Forrest McDonald, *The American Presidency: An Intellectual History* (Lawrence, KS: University Press of Kansas, 1994), 217.

42 Freeman, *George Washington*, VI, 192–93.

43 Ibid., VI, 240.

44 Tulis, *The Rhetorical Presidency*, 69.

45 Quoted in Hannah Arendt, *On Revolution* (New York: Viking Press, 1965), 63–64.

46 McCullough, *John Adams*, 59–61, 101–3, 374, 421.

47 Ibid., 99.

48 Ellis, *American Sphinx*, 33, 58–59.

49 Ibid., 228–29.

50 Noble E. Cunningham, Jr., *The Jeffersonian Republicans: The Formation of Party Organizations, 1789–1801* (Chapel Hill: University of North Carolina Press, 1957), 13–19.

51 Ralph Ketcham, *James Madison: A Biography* (Charlottesville, VA: University Press of Virginia, 1990), 329.

52 Ibid., 404; Cunningham, *The Jeffersonian Republicans*, 128, 151.

53 Noble Cunningham, Jr., "The Election of 1800," in Schlesinger, ed., *History of American Presidential Elections*, I, 101–34.

54 Quoted in Irving Brant, "The Election of 1808," in Schlesinger ed., *History of American Presidential Elections*, I, 187.

55 Ellis, *American Sphinx*, 245; David N. Mayer, "Thomas Jefferson and the Separation of Powers," in Phillip G. Henderson, ed., *The Presidency Then and Now* (New York: Rowman and Littlefield, 2000), 26.

56 Cunningham, *The Jeffersonian Republicans*, 148.

57 David N. Mayer, "Thomas Jefferson and the Separation of Powers," in Philip G. Henderson, ed., *The Presidency Then and Now* (Lanham, MD: Rowman and Littlefield, 2002), 24–25.

58 Moise Ostrogorski, "The Rise and Fall of the Nominating Caucus, Legislative and Congressional," *American Historical Review* 5 (December 1899): 256.

59 Quoted in Brant, "The Election of 1808," 195.

60 Ceaser, *Presidential Selection*, 119.

61 Brant, "The Election of 1808," 194.

62 Lyman H. Butterfield, ed., *The Adams Papers: Diary and Autobiography of John Adams* (Cambridge: Belknap Press of Harvard University Press, 1961), I, 238; see also Ostrogorski, "Rise and Fall of the Nominating Caucus," 261.

63 Quoted in Marcus Cunliffe, "Elections of 1789 and 1792," in Schlesinger, ed., *History of American Presidential Elections*, I, 9.

64 Richard Hofstadter, *The Idea of a Party System: The Rise of a Legitimate Opposition in the United States, 1780–1840* (Berkeley: University of California Press, 1969), 28, 38, 94.

65 Ellis, *Founding Brothers*, 193.

66 Bruce Miroff, "John Adams and the Presidency," in Cronin, ed., *Inventing the American Presidency*, 304–25.

67 Ellis, *American Sphinx*, 144–45.

68 Garry Wills, *James Madison* (New York: Times Books, 2002), 3; Brant, "The Election of 1808," 185.

69 Quoted in Irving Brant, *James Madison*, 6 vols. (Indianapolis: Bobbs-Merrill, 1941–1961), V, 233, 33.

70 Mayer, "Jefferson and the Separation of Powers," 22–23.

71 Robert V. Remini, *Henry Clay, Statesman for the Union* (New York: W. W. Norton, 1991), 88–89; Harry Ammon, *James Monroe: The Quest for National Identity* (New York: McGraw-Hill, 1971), 382.

72 Hofstadter, *The Idea of a Party System*, 23, 194–99; Harry Ammon, *James Monroe*, 369–79, 437–38.

73 Ammon, *James Monroe*, 384–85.

74 Robert V. Remini, *Henry Clay: Statesman for the Union*, 235.

75 James F. Hopkins, "Election of 1824," in Schlesinger, ed., *History of American Presidential Elections*, I, 361–64.

76 Ostrogorski, "Rise and Fall of the Nominating Caucus," 270.

77 Everett S. Brown, "The Presidential Election of 1824–1825," *Political Science Quarterly* 40 (September 1925): 393–94.

78 Quoted in Andrew Burstein, *The Passions of Andrew Jackson* (New York: Alfred A. Knopf, 2003), 152.

79 M. J. Heale, *The Presidential Quest* (London: Longman, 1982), 49.

80 McCormick, *Presidential Game*, 120.

81 Ostrogorski, "Rise and Fall of the Nominating Caucus," 255.

82 Robert V. Remini, "Election of 1828," in Schlesinger, ed., *History of American Presidential Elections*, I, 418, 421.

83 Ceaser, *Presidential Selection*, 135–40.

84 See, for example, Douglas W. Jaenicke, "The Jacksonian Integration of Party into the Constitutional System," *Political Science Quarterly* 101 (March 1986): 87–88.

85 Remini, "Election of 1828," 425.

86 Quoted in ibid., 419.

87 Burstein, *The Passions of Andrew Jackson*, 195–96.

88 Ibid., 138; Heale, *Presidential Quest*, 73–74; Noble Cunningham, Jr., *Popular Images of the Presidency from Washington to Lincoln* (Columbia, MO: University of Missouri Press, 1991), 149.

89 Heale, *Presidential Quest*, 58.

90 Mayer, "Thomas Jefferson and the Separation of Powers," 20; Gary L. Gregg II, "Whiggism and Presidentialism: American Ambivalence toward Executive Power," in Henderson, *Presidency Then and Now*, 71–72.

91 Robert V. Remini, *The Life of Andrew Jackson* (New York: Harper and Row, 1988), 192, 203–4.

92 Richard B. Latner, "The Kitchen Cabinet and Andrew Jackson's Advisory System," *Journal of American History* 65 (September 1978): 378; Richard P. Longaker, "Was Jackson's Kitchen Cabinet a Cabinet?" *Mississippi Valley Historical Review* 44 (June 1957): 94–108.

93 Donald B. Cole, *The Presidency of Andrew Jackson* (Lawrence, KS: University Press of Kansas, 1993), 41–42.

94 James D. Richardson, ed., *Messages and Papers of the Presidents*, 10 vols. (Washington, DC: Government Printing Office, 1899), II, 448–49.

95 Ibid., 449.

96 Lynn Marshall, "The Strange Stillbirth of the Whig Party," *American Historical Review* 72 (January 1967): 455–57.

97 Matthew A. Crenson, *The Federal Machine: Beginnings of Bureaucracy in the Age of Jackson* (Baltimore: Johns Hopkins University Press, 1975), 3.

98 Ibid., 4.

99 Michael F. Holt, *Political Parties and American Political Development from the Age of Jackson to the Age of Lincoln* (Baton Rouge, LA: Louisiana State University Press, 1992), 43.

100 Jaenicke, "Jacksonian Integration of Parties into the Constitutional System," 86.

101 Robert V. Remini, "The Election of 1832," in Schlesinger, ed., *History of American Presidential Elections*, I, 501, 504.

102 McCormick, *Presidential Game*, 189–90.

103 Quoted in Joel Silbey, "The Election of 1836," in Schlesinger, ed., *History of American Presidential Elections*, I, 585.

104 McCormick, *Presidential Game*, 169.

105 Quoted in Michael F. Holt, *The Rise and Fall of the American Whig Party: Jacksonian Politics and the Onset of the Civil War* (New York: Oxford University Press, 1999), 105.

106 Joel H. Silbey, *Martin Van Buren and the Emergence of American Popular Politics* (Lanham, MD: Rowman and Littlefield, 2002), 122–23.

107 Heale, *Presidential Quest*, 91.

108 Ibid., 134.

109 Charles Sellers, "Election of 1844," in Schlesinger, ed., *History of American Presidential Elections*, I, 772; McCormick, *Presidential Game*, 194–95.

110 Stephen Skowronek, *The Politics Presidents Make: Leadership from John Adams to Bill Clinton* (Cambridge, MA: Belknap Press of Harvard University Press, 1997), 157.

111 Michael P. Riccards, *The Ferocious Engine of Democracy: A History of the American Presidency*, 2 vols. (Lanham, MD: Madison Books, 1995), I, 162–63.

112 Holt, *Political Parties and American Political Development*, 63–64.

113 Norman A. Graebner, "James K. Polk: A Study in Federal Patronage," *Mississippi Valley Historical Review* 38 (March 1952): 623.

114 Ibid.

115 Skowronek, *The Politics Presidents Make*, 162–68.

116 Allan Nevins, ed., *Polk: The Diary of a President, 1845–1849* (New York: Capricorn Books, 1968), 324.

117 McCormick, *Presidential Game*, 203.

118 Quoted in Heale, *Presidential Quest*, 114.

119 Riccards, *Ferocious Engine of Democracy*, 171; quoted in Heale, *Presidential Quest*, 125; Holt, *Rise and Fall of the Whig Party*, 270–71.

120 Sidney Milkis and Michael Nelson, *The American Presidency: Origins and Development, 1776–1998*, 3d. ed. (Washington, DC: CQ Press, 1999), 130–32.

121 Roy and Jeannette Nichols, "Election of 1852," in Schlesinger, ed., *History of American Presidential Elections*, II, 939; Shenkman, *Presidential Ambition*, 87–88.

122 See Michael J. Birkner, "Introduction: Getting to Know James Buchanan Again," in Michael J. Birkner, ed., *James Buchanan and the Political Crisis of the 1850s* (Selinsgrove, PA: Susquehanna University Press, 1996), 17–36.

123 Skowronek, *The Politics Presidents Make*.

124 Ibid., 449.

125 See David F. Lewis and James Michael Strine, "What Time Is It? The Use of Power in Four Different Types of Presidential Time," *Journal of Politics* 58 (August 1996): 697.

126 The term is Skowronek's.

Chapter 3. War and Peace and Parties

1 Richard McCormick, *The Presidential Game: The Origins of American Presidential Politics* (New York: Oxford University Press, 1982), 206.

2 Ibid., 203.

3 Don Fehrenbacher, "The Republican Decision at Chicago," in Norman A. Graebner, ed., *Politics and the Crisis of 1860* (Urbana, IL: University of Illinois Press, 1961), 34; Glenn C. Altschuler and Stuart M. Blumin, "Limits of Political Engagement in Antebellum America: A New Look at the Golden Age of Participatory Democracy," *Journal of American History* 84 (December 1997): 855–85.

4 Only in Rhode Island and New Jersey were the rival Democratic slates able to cooperate to modify the winner-take-all rule and divide the states' electoral votes. See William B. Hesseltine, *Lincoln and the War Governors* (New York: Alfred Knopf, 1955), 73.

5 Michael P. Riccards, *The Ferocious Engine of Democracy: A History of the American Presidency*, 2 vols. (Lanham, MD: Madison Books, 1994), I, 218; Elting Morison, "Election of 1860," in Arthur M. Schlesinger, Jr., ed., *History of American Presidential Elections, 1789–1968*, 4 vols. (New York: McGraw-Hill, 1971), II, 1152; David M. Potter, *Lincoln and His Party in the Secession Crisis* (New Haven: Yale University Press, 1962), 112.

6 Quoted in John C. Waugh, *Reelecting Lincoln: The Battle for the 1864 Presidency* (Cambridge, MA: Da Capo Press, 1997), 136.

7 Potter, *Lincoln and His Party in the Secession Crisis*, 113; J. G. Randall, *Lincoln the President*, 4 vols. (New York: Dodd, Meade, 1945–1955), I, 209.

8 William E. Basinger, "The Republican Triumph," in Graebner, ed., *Politics and the Crisis of 1860*, 100; Potter, *Lincoln and His Party in the Secession Crisis*, 135.

9 Stephen Skowronek, *The Politics Presidents Make: Leadership from John Adams to Bill Clinton* (Cambridge, MA: The Belknap Press of Harvard University Press, 1993), 199, 205; Sidney M. Milkis and Michael Nelson, *The American Presidency: Origins and Development, 1776–1998*, 3d. ed. (Washington, DC: CQ Press, 1999), 144; John J. Nicolay and John Hay, eds., *Complete Works of Abraham Lincoln* (New York: Lamb Publishing Company, 1904), I, 17.

10 Quoted in J. David Greenstone, *The Lincoln Persuasion: Remaking American Liberalism* (Princeton: Princeton University Press, 1993), 12.

11 Richard P. McCormick, *The Second American Party System: Party Formation in the Jacksonian Era* (Chapel Hill: University of North Carolina Press, 1966), 286–87; quoted in Stephen L. Hansen, *The Making of the Third Party System: Voters and Parties in Illinois, 1850–1876* (Ann Arbor, MI: UMI Research Press, 1980), 90. Italics in original.

12 McCormick, *The Second American Party System*, 287; Hansen, *The Making of the Third Party System*, 204–6.

13 Skowronek, *The Politics Presidents Make*, 200, 202.

14 David Herbert Donald, *Lincoln Reconsidered: Essays on the Civil War Era* (New York: Vintage Books, 2001), 133–47, 171–72.

15 Quoted in David Herbert Donald, *Lincoln* (New York: Simon & Schuster, 1995), 514.

16 Stephen B. Oates, "Abraham Lincoln: Republican in the White House," in John L. Thomas, ed., *Abraham Lincoln and the American Political Tradition* (Amherst: University of Massachusetts Press, 1986), 98–110.

17 Brooks D. Simpson, *The Reconstruction Presidents* (Lawrence, KS: University Press of Kansas, 1998), 53–55, 61.

18 Ibid., 69–71, 79.

19 William S. McFeely, *Grant, a Biography* (New York: W. W. Norton, 1981), 279.

20 John Hope Franklin, "Election of 1868," in Arthur M. Schlesinger, ed., *The History of American Presidential Elections* (New York: Chelsea House, 1971), II, 1251.

21 James Bryce, *The American Commonwealth*, 2 vols. (New York: Macmillan, 1895), I, Ch. 8.

22 Stanley I. Pomerantz, "Election of 1876," in Schlesinger, ed., *History of Presidential Elections*, I, 1397–98; Ari A. Hoogenboom, *The Presidency of Rutherford B. Hayes* (Lawrence, KS: University Press of Kansas, 1988), 15–16.

23 Quoted in Simpson, *Reconstruction Presidents*, 155.

24 Mark Wahlgren Summers, *Rum, Romanism, and Rebellion: The Making of a President 1884* (Chapel Hill: University of North Carolina Press, 2000), 35–36.

25 Homer E. Socolofsky and Allan B. Spetter, *The Presidency of Benjamin Harrison* (Lawrence, KS: University Press of Kansas, 1987), 31.

26 Quoted in White, *The Republican Era*, 96.

27 Quoted ibid., 24.

28 Robert D. Marcus, *Grand Old Party: Political Structure in the Gilded Age, 1880–1896* (New York: Oxford University Press, 1971), 26.

29 Sean David Cashman, *America in the Gilded Age: From the Death of Lincoln to the Rise of Theodore Roosevelt*, 3d ed. (New York: New York University Press, 1993), 249.

30 Summers, *Rum, Romanism, and Rebellion*, 70.

31 Allan Nevins, *Grover Cleveland: A Study in Courage* (New York: Dodd, Mead, 1932), 57–62, 95–101; H. Paul Jeffers, *An Honest President: The Life and Presidencies of Grover Cleveland* (New York: William Morrow, 2000), 34–35, 41–46; Mark D. Hirsch, "Election of 1884," in Schlesinger, ed., *History of American Presidential Elections*, II, 1568; Summers, *Rum, Romanism, and Rebellion*, 117–18.

32 Jeffers, *An Honest President*, 132; Schlesinger, ed., *History of American Presidential Elections*, II, 1611; Summers, *Rum, Romanism, and Rebellion*, 198–201.

33 Leonard Dinnerstein, "Election of 1880," in Schlesinger, ed., *History of American Presidential Elections*, II, 1496–97; Allan Peskin, *Garfield* (Kent, OH: Kent State University Press, 1978), 473–74, 479–80.

34 Summers, *Rum, Romanism, and Rebelliion*, Ch. 7; Morgan, *From Hayes to McKinley*, 206; "Democratic Platform," in Schlesinger, ed., *History of American Presidential Elections*, II, 1583–88.

35 Ibid., 255–57, 274–75; Summers, *Rum, Romanism, and Rebellion*, 73–74; H. Wayne Morgan, *William McKinley and His America*, rev. ed. (Kent, OH: Kent State University Press, 2003), 84.

36 Jeffers, *An Honest President*, 235–36; Marcus, *Grand Old Party*, 6–8, Ch. 5.

37 Richard Jensen, *The Winning of the Midwest: Social and Political Conflict, 1888–1896* (Chicago: University of Chicago Press, 1971), 164–65.

38 Ibid., 15, 166–67.

39 Morgan, *From Hayes to McKinley*, 420.

40 Currency was so scarce after the Panic of 1893 that Pillsbury flour mills had to purchase wheat with scrip. Southern farmers were unable to sell cotton because cash was not available to purchase it. Cleveland's use of troops in the Pullman strike seems to have provoked violence rather than prevented it. Much of this disorder is thought to have originated with federal marshals who were employed and paid by the railroad companies. See Nevins, *Grover Cleveland*, 536, 622.

41 Morgan, *From Hayes to McKinley*, 270, 327; Socolofsky and Spetter, *The Presidency of Benjamin Harrison*, 51, 54; Alyn Brodsky, *Grover Cleveland: A Study in Character* (New York: St. Martin's Press, 2000), 224.

42 Morgan, *From Hayes to McKinley*, 217.

43 Ibid., 93–94.

44 On changes in the nature of party identification, see Paul Kleppner, *The Cross of Culture: A Social Analysis of Midwestern Politics, 1850–1900* (New York: Free Press, 1970); Glenn C. Altschuler and Stuart M. Blumin, *Rude Republic: Americans and Their Politics in the Nineteenth Century* (Princeton: Princeton University Press, 2000).

45 Elisabeth S. Clemens, *The People's Lobby: Organizational Innovation and the Rise of Interest Group Politics in the United States, 1890–1925* (Chicago: University of Chicago Press, 1997), 35, 85; Stanley L. Jones, *The Presidential Election of 1896* (Madison, WI: University of Wisconsin Press, 1964), 24, 30.

46 Jones, *The Presidential Election of 1896*, 101.

47 Morgan, *William McKinley and His America*, 127–28.

48 Louis W. Koenig, *Bryan: A Political Biography of William Jennings Bryan* (New York: G. P. Putnam, 1971), 100–101.

49 M. J. Heale, *The Presidential Quest: Candidates and Images in American Political Culture, 1787–1852* (London: Longman, 1982), 4, 21; Jeffrey K. Tulis, *The Rhetorical Presidency* (Princeton: Princeton University Press, 1987), 65–67, 89–91.

50 Gilbert C. Fite, "Election of 1896," in Schlesinger, ed., *History of American Presidential Elections*, II, 1808; Jones, *Presidential Election of 1896*, 186, 190.

51 See Jones, *Presidential Election of 1896*, Ch. 11.

52 Quoted in Kevin Phillips, *William McKinley* (New York: Henry Holt, 2003), 71–72.

53 Ibid., 238–39; Koenig, *Bryan*, 200.

54 Jones, *Presidential Election of 1896*, 185–86.

55 Morgan, *William McKinley*, 161.

56 Ibid., 176–77; Jones, *Presidential Election of 1896*, 284–85.

57 Ibid., 279; Morgan, *William McKinley*, 173; Margaret Leech, *In the Days of McKinley* (New York: Harper and Brothers, 1959), 109, 127.

58 Morgan, *William McKinley*, 171.

59 Koenig, *Bryan*, 241–42; Robert W. Cherny, *A Righteous Cause: The Life of William Jennings Bryan* (Boston: Little, Brown, 1985), 66.

60 An important exception was the *New York Morning Journal* of William Randolph Hearst. The *Journal* was the newest addition to Hearst's chain. One of its reporters relayed to Hearst Bryan's observation that the *Journal* might become the leading Democratic paper in the Northeast by endorsing his campaign. Since virtually all the newspapers of the region sided with McKinley, a *Journal* endorsement of Bryan would give it a monopoly of Democratic and Populist readers. Hearst not only accepted the offer; he and the *Journal* made sizeable contributions to Bryan's campaign treasury. Later they would contribute scurrilous cartoons of Marcus Hanna (McKinley was too likeable for caricature) and help to build the enduring myth that Hanna was the evil genius behind the pliable McKinley. Koenig, *Bryan*, 204; Cherny, *A Righteous Cause*, 65–66.

61 Koenig, *Bryan*, 155.

62 Phillips, *William McKinley*, 110.

63 Morgan, *William McKinley*, 223–25; Leech, *In the Days of McKinley*, 213.

64 Phillips, *William McKinley*, 116.

65 Morgan, *William McKinley*, 193, 223.

66 Ibid., 275, 287, 333.

67 Ibid., 308.

68 Wilfred Binkley, *President and Congress* (New York: Alfred A. Knopf, 1947), 187.

69 Phillips, *William McKinley*, 143–44; Lewis L. Gould, *The Presidency of William McKinley* (Lawrence, KS: University Press of Kansas, 1980), 215; Leech, *In the Days of McKinley*, 529–30.

70 Schlesinger, ed., *History of American Presidential Elections*, II, 1845.

71 Edmund Morris, *The Rise of Theodore Roosevelt* (New York: Modern Library, 2001), 258–59.

72 Quoted in John Morton Blum, *The Republican Roosevelt* (Cambridge, MA: Harvard University Press, 1954), 22; Walter LaFeber, "Election of 1900," in Arthur M. Schlesinger, Jr., and Fred Israel, eds., *History of American Presidential Elections*, 4 vols. (New York: McGraw-Hill, 1971), III, 1888.

73 Blum, *The Republican Roosevelt*, 40.
74 Ibid., 64–65; William H. Harbaugh, "Election of 1904," in Schlesinger and Israel, eds., *History of American Presidential Elections*, III, 1986–87.
75 Edmund Morris, *Theodore Rex* (New York: Modern Library, 2002), 140.
76 Ibid., 165.
77 Ibid., 169; Blum, *The Republican Roosevelt*, 61, 110.
78 Harbaugh, "Election of 1904," 1968–69.
79 Morris, *Theodore Rex*, 358.
80 Ibid., 319.
81 Blum, *The Republican Roosevelt*, 122.
82 David H. Burton, *Theodore Roosevelt, American Politician: An Assessment* (Madison, NJ: Fairleigh Dickinson University Press, 1997), 125–26.
83 Lewis L. Gould, *The Presidency of Theodore Roosevelt* (Lawrence, KS: University Press of Kansas, 1991), 157–58.
84 Blum, *The Republican Roosevelt*, 78; Burton, *Theodore Roosevelt, American Politician*, 107.
85 Gould, *The Presidency of Theodore Roosevelt*, 161–62.
86 Matthew Josephson, *The President Makers* (New York: Harcourt Brace, 1940), 235; Richard Hofstadter, *The American Political Tradition* (New York: Vintage Books, 1954), 233–34.
87 Morris, *Theodore Rex*, 422; quoted in Blum, *The Republican Roosevelt*, 91.
88 Theodore Roosevelt, *An Autobiography* (New York: Da Capo Press, 1985 [1913]), 367.
89 Morris, *Theodore Rex*, 485–87; Roosevelt, *Autobiography*, 378–79.
90 Theodore Roosevelt, *The New Nationalism*, eds. William Leuchtenberg and Bernard Wishy (Englewood Cliffs, NJ: Prentice Hall, 1961), 21–39. "New Nationalism" was an ideological label borrowed from Herbert Croly's *The Promise of American Life* (1909), but the book was less an inspiration to Roosevelt than Roosevelt was the inspiration for the book.
91 Blum, *The Republican Roosevelt*, 122, 143–44; Hofstadter, *American Political Tradition*, 232–33.
92 Quoted in Louis Auchincloss, *Theodore Roosevelt* (New York: Henry Holt, 2002), 119.
93 William E. Leuchtenberg, "Introduction," in Theodore Roosevelt, *The New Nationalism*, 16; James Chace, *1912* (New York: Simon & Schuster, 2004), 57–58; Kathleen Dalton, *Theodore Roosevelt: A Strenuous Life* (New York: Vintage Books, 2002), 372–73, 378.
94 James W. Davis, *Presidential Primaries: Road to the White House* (Westport, CT: Greenwood Press, 1980), 42–43; Alan Ware, *The American Direct Primary: Party Institutionalization and Transformation in the North* (Cambridge: Cambridge University Press, 2002), 248. Press accounts mention twenty-seven states in which there were presidential primaries. The inflated figure results, in part, from the fact that in some states only one of the two parties held primaries. In addition, there was considerable uncertainty about what constituted a primary. Texas, for example, held "precinct primary

conventions." The boundary between primaries and other nominating procedures was fuzzy. See Kathleen E. Kendall, *Communication in the Presidential Primaries: Candidates and the Media, 1912–2000* (Westport, CT: Prager, 2000), 30–31.

95 Roosevelt, *The New Nationalism*, 16, 36; George E. Mowry, "Election of 1912," in Schlesinger and Israel, eds., *History of American Presidential Elections*, III, 2139–40.
96 Ibid., 26.
97 Francis L. Broderick, *Progressivism at Risk: Electing a President in 1912* (Westport, CT: Greenwood Press, 1989), 62–63; Arthur S. Link, *Wilson: The Road to the White House* (Princeton: Princeton University Press, 1947), 6, 10–11.
98 Quoted in Chace, *1912*, 40; Broderick, *Progressivism at Risk*, 62.
99 Ray Stannard Baker, *Woodrow Wilson: Life and Letters* (New York: Doubleday, Doran, 1931), III, 4.
100 Link, *Wilson: The Road to the White House*, 141–42.
101 Ibid., 311, 359–63.
102 Louise Overacker, *The Presidential Primary* (New York: Macmillan, 1925), 165; Broderick, *Progressivism at Risk*, 83–84, 92; Chace, *1912*, 142.
103 Broderick, *Progressivism at Risk*, 88–89.
104 Ibid., 87–101; Chace, *1912*, 150–58.
105 Mowry, "Election of 1912," 2152; Chace, *1912*, 195.
106 Quoted in John Milton Cooper, Jr., *The Warrior and the Priest: Woodrow Wilson and Theodore Roosevelt* (Cambridge, MA: Belknap Press of Harvard University Press, 1983), 206.
107 Tulis, *The Rhetorical Presidency*, 182–83.
108 Kendrick A. Clements, *The Presidency of Woodrow Wilson* (Lawrence, KS: University Press of Kansas, 1992), 22–23; Richard L. McCormick, *The Party Period and Public Policy: American Politics from the Age of Jackson to the Progressive Era* (New York: Oxford University Press, 1986), 222–23.
109 Quoted in Cooper, *The Warrior and the Priest*, 231.
110 For a discussion of traditional limitations on presidential speech, see Tulis, *The Rhetorical Presidency*, Chs. 2–3.
111 Robert Alexander Kraig, *Woodrow Wilson and the Lost World of the Oratorical Statesman* (College Station, TX: Texas A&M Press, 2004), 132.
112 Marshall I. Dimock, "Woodrow Wilson as Legislative Leader," *Journal of Politics* 19 (February 1957): 15–16.
113 Ibid., 5, 9, 12.
114 George Juergens, *News from the White House: The Presidential-Press Relationship in the Progressive Era* (Chicago: University of Chicago Press, 1981), 46–47, 140; Elmer E. Cornwell, Jr., *Presidential Leadership of Public Opinion* (Bloomington, IN: Indiana University Press, 1965), 36–37.
115 Clements, *The Presidency of Woodrow Wilson*, 53, 58.
116 Wilson had 248 delegates at the beginning of the Democratic convention. Of those, 146 had been won in primaries. Clark had 436 pledged

delegates, of whom 156 had been won in primaries. See Chace, *1912*, 142; Overacker, *The Presidential Primary*, 165.

Chapter 4. From Normalcy to Primacy

1   S. D. Lovell, *The Presidential Election of 1916* (Carbondale, IL: Southern Illinois University Press, 1980), 26–38; Arthur S. Link and William M. Leary, Jr., "Presidential Election of 1916," in Schlesinger and Israel, eds., *History of American Presidential Elections*, III, 2248–49.

2   James W. Davis, *Presidential Primaries* (Westport, CT: Greenwood Press, 1980), 45; Charles Edward Merriam and Louise Overacker, *Primary Elections* (Chicago: University of Chicago Press, 1928), 96–107; James W. Ceaser, *Presidential Selection: Theory and Development* (Princeton: Princeton University Press, 1979), 227; Alan Ware, *The American Direct Primary: Party Institutionalization and Transformation in the North* (Cambridge: Cambridge University Press, 2002), 251.

3   Quoted in John W. Dean, *Warren G. Harding* (New York: Times Books, 2004), 51; Eugene P. Trani and David L. Wilson, *The Presidency of Warren G. Harding* (Lawrence, KS: The Regents' Press of Kansas, 1977), 22; Andrew Sinclair, *The Available Man: The Life Behind the Masks of Warren Gamaliel Harding* (New York: Macmillan, 1965), 119, 133.

4   Donald R. McCoy, "Election of 1920," in Schlesinger and Israel, eds., *History of American Presidential Elections*, III, 2353, 2360–61.

5   Trani and Wilson, *The Presidency of Warren G. Harding*, 56–59; Murray, *The Harding Era*, 125–26.

6   Ibid., 185–86.

7   See Robert H. Ferrell, *The Presidency of Calvin Coolidge* (Lawrence, KS: University Press of Kansas, 1998), 13.

8   Michael E. Parrish, *Anxious Decades: America in Prosperity and Depression, 1920–1941* (New York: W. W. Norton, 1992), 67.

9   David Burner, "Election of 1924," in Schlesinger and Israel, eds., *History of American Presidential Elections*, III, 2462–64; Ferrell, *The Presidency of Calvin Coolidge*, 59.

10   Quoted in Parrish, *Anxious Decades*, 52.

11   Elmer E. Cornwell, Jr., *Presidential Leadership of Public Opinion* (Bloomington, IN: Indiana University Press, 1965), 92, 100–101; William Allen White, *Puritan in Babylon* (New York: Macmillan, 1938), 353.

12   Martin L. Fausold, *The Presidency of Herbert C. Hoover* (Lawrence, KS: University Press of Kansas, 1984), 15; Ferrell, *The Presidency of Calvin Coolidge*, 64, 66; Herbert Hoover, *The Memoirs of Herbert Hoover: The Cabinet and the Presidency, 1920–1933* (New York: Macmillan, 1952), 36.

13   White, *A Puritan in Babylon*, 363, 368.

14   Lawrence H. Fuchs, "Election of 1928," in Schlesinger and Israel, eds., *History of American Presidential Elections*, III, 2603–04; Donald R. McCoy, "To the White House: Herbert Hoover, August 1927–March 1929," in

Martin L. Fausold and George T. Mazuzan, eds., *The Hoover Presidency: A Reappraisal* (Albany: State University of New York Press, 1974), 34; Hoover carried twelve of the seventeen states that held Republican primaries in 1928.

15 Jordan A. Schwarz, *The Interregnum of Despair: Hoover, Congress, and the Depression* (Urbana, IL: University of Illinois Press, 1970), 6–7.

16 Fausold, *The Presidency of Herbert C. Hoover*, 49–52; Richard Norton Smith, *An Uncommon Man: The Triumph of Herbert Hoover* (New York: Simon & Schuster, 1984), 107.

17 Fausold, *The Presidency of Herbert C. Hoover*, 49; Hoover, *Memoirs*, 216.

18 Fausold, *The Presidency of Herbert C. Hoover*, 56–57; David B. Burner, "Before the Crash: Hoover's First Eight Months in the Presidency," in Fausold and Mazuzan, eds., *The Hoover Presidency*, 55–57.

19 Fausold, *The Presidency of Herbert C. Hoover*, 59, 84; Burner, "Before the Crash," 57–58; Hoover, *Memoirs*, 281.

20 Albert U. Romasco, *The Poverty of Abundance: Hoover, the Nation, and Depression* (New York: Oxford University Press, 1965), 36–38; Schwarz, *Interregnum of Despair*, 12.

21 Romasco, *Poverty of Abundance*, 30, 47–51; Fausold, *Presidency of Herbert Hoover*, 76.

22 See Ellis W. Hawley, "Herbert Hoover and American Corporatism, 1929–1933," in Fausold and Mazuzan, eds., *The Hoover Presidency*, 101–19.

23 Romasco, *Poverty of Abundance*, 51.

24 Ibid., 92–93; Fausold, *The Presidency of Herbert C. Hoover*, 151–52.

25 Smith, *An Uncommon Man*, 134.

26 Herbert Hoover, *Individualism* (New York: Doubleday, Page, 1922).

27 Ibid., 10, 15, 22–23.

28 Ibid., 27–28, 41–42, 44, 54.

29 Craig Lloyd, *Aggressive Introvert: A Study of Herbert Hoover and Public Relations Management, 1912–1932* (Columbus, OH: Ohio State University Press, 1972), 10.

30 Sidney M. Milkis, *The President and the Parties: The Transformation of the American Party System Since the New Deal* (New York: Oxford University Press, 1993), 9.

31 Sean J. Savage, *Roosevelt: The Party Leader, 1932–1945* (Lexington, KY: University Press of Kentucky, 1991), 4–6; Arthur Schlesinger, Jr., *The Crisis of the Old Order, 1919–1933* (Boston: Houghton Mifflin, 1957), 377.

32 Frank Freidel, *Franklin D. Roosevelt: A Rendezvous with Destiny* (Boston: Little Brown, 1990), 51–52.

33 Conrad Black, *Franklin Delano Roosevelt, Champion of Freedom* (New York: Public Affairs, 2003), 180.

34 Elliot A. Rosen, *Hoover, Roosevelt, and the Brains Trust: From Depression to New Deal* (New York: Columbia University Press, 1977), 27–28; Roy V. Peel and Thomas C. Donnelly, *The 1928 Campaign, An Analysis* (New York: Richard E. Smith, 1931), 47, 50.

35 Schlesinger, *The Crisis of the Old Order*, 127; Savage, *Roosevelt: The Party Leader*, 106–7; Rosen, *Hoover, Roosevelt, and the Brains Trust*, 28.

36 Rosen, *Hoover, Roosevelt, and the Brains Trust*, 32–37; Freidel, *Franklin D. Roosevelt*, 71; Black, *Franklin Delano Roosevelt*, 221.

37 Douglas B. Craig, *After Wilson: The Struggle for the Democratic Party, 1920–1934* (Chapel Hill: University of North Carolina Press, 1992), 208, 214; Black, *Franklin Delano Roosevelt*, 221.

38 Craig, *After Wilson*, 212; Frank Freidel, *Franklin D. Roosevelt: The Triumph* (Boston: Little, Brown, 1956), 252–55, 270.

39 Ibid., 200–201, 215–16; Schlesinger, *The Crisis of the Old Order*, 273, 277; Freidel, *The Triumph* (Boston: Little, Brown, 1956), 176–77.

40 Craig, *After Wilson*, 216–17; Rosen, *Hoover, Roosevelt, and the Brains Trust*, 30.

41 The intraparty fight over Prohibition was not just an opportunity for Roosevelt to polish his image with voters and activists outside the Northeast. It was a struggle for the soul of the party and control of its agenda. Smith, Raskob, and their allies recognized that by making much of Repeal, they could sideline economic issues that might arouse sentiment for an activist government. See Peel and Donnelly, *The 1932 Campaign*, 67; Schlesinger, *The Crisis of the Old Order*, 277.

42 Peel and Donnelly, *The 1932 Campaign*, 60; Black, *Franklin Delano Roosevelt*, 230; Freidel, *The Triumph*, 205, 243.

43 Peel and Donnelly, *The 1932 Campaign*, 64; Rosen, *Hoover, Roosevelt and the Brains Trust*, 134.

44 Peel and Donnelly, *The 1932 Campaign*, 72–79; Schlesinger, *The Crisis of the Old Order*, 293–94; Craig, *After Wilson*, 246; Rosen, *Hoover, Roosevelt, and the Brains Trust*, 245–46, 262–63.

45 Black, *Franklin Delano Roosevelt*, 239.

46 Savage, *Roosevelt: The Party Builder*, 80–81, 84.

47 Freidel, *Franklin D. Roosevelt*, 98.

48 Savage, *Roosevelt: The Party Builder*, 15, 25.

49 James MacGregor Burns, *Roosevelt: The Lion and the Fox* (New York: Harcourt Brace, 1956), 143; Freidel, *Franklin D. Roosevelt*, 77.

50 Broadus Mitchell, *Depression Decade: From New Era through New Deal, 1929–1941* (New York: Rinehart, 1947), 57, 69–71, 76; see also Bernard M. Klass, "The Federal Farm Board and the Antecedents of the Agricultural Adjustment Act, 1929–1933," in Carl E. Krog and William R. Tanner, eds., *Herbert Hoover and the Republican Era, A Reconsideration* (Lanham, MD: University Press of America, 1984), 191–219.

51 Carl Degler, "The Ordeal of Herbert Hoover," *Yale Review* 52 (Summer 1963): 569–71.

52 John D. Hicks, *The American Nation: A History of the United States from 1865 to the Present*, 2nd ed. (New York: Houghton Mifflin, 1949), 673 and Ch. 27 passim.

53 John D. Hicks, *Republican Ascendancy, 1921–1933* (New York: Harper and Brothers, 1960), 216.

54 Rosen, *Hoover, Roosevelt, and the Brains Trust*, Ch. 3; Albert U. Romesco, "Hoover-Roosevelt and the Great Depression: A Historiographic Inquiry into a Perennial Comparison," in John Braeman, Robert H. Bremner, and David Brody, eds., *The New Deal: The National Level* (Columbus, OH: Ohio State University Press, 1975), 25; Skowronek, *The Politics Presidents Make*, 262–63.

55 Quoted in Leuchtenberg, *Franklin D. Roosevelt and the New Deal*, 13; Arthur M. Schlesinger, Jr., *The Coming of the New Deal, 1933–1935* (Boston: Houghton Mifflin, 1958), 1.

56 Black, *Franklin Delano Roosevelt*, 271; Schlesinger, *The Coming of the New Deal*, 10–11; Leuchtenberg, *Franklin D. Roosevelt and the New Deal*, 43–47.

57 On radical movements in the early New Deal, see Leuchtenberg, *Franklin D. Roosevelt*, Ch. 5; Arthur M. Schlesinger, Jr., *The Age of Roosevelt: The Politics of Upheaval* (Boston: Houghton Mifflin, 1960), Chs. 6–10.

58 Leuchtenberg, 147.

59 Burns, *Roosevelt: The Lion and the Fox*, 222–26; Freidel, *Franklin D. Roosevelt*, 157–58.

60 Milkis, *President and the Parties*, 70–71.

61 Ibid., 68–69; Schlesinger, *The Politics of Upheaval*, 425.

62 Freidel, *Franklin D. Roosevelt*, 202–3; Schlesinger, *The Politics of Upheaval*, 559–60.

63 Schlesinger and Israel, eds., *History of American Presidential Elections*, III, 2785; Milkis, *President and the Parties*, 42.

64 Kristi Andersen, *The Creation of a Democratic Majority, 1928–1936* (Chicago: University of Chicago Press, 1979), Ch. 4.

65 Martin Shefter, *Political Parties and the State: The American Historical Experience* (Princeton: Princeton University Press, 1994), 82–83; Savage, *Roosevelt: The Party Leader*, 114.

66 Savage, *Roosevelt: The Party Leader*, 113; William E. Leuchtenberg, "Election of 1936," in Schlesinger and Israel, eds., *History of American Presidential Elections*, III, 2835.

67 Leuchtenberg, *Franklin D. Roosevelt and the New Deal*, 195–96.

68 Milkis, *President and the Parties*, 75–76.

69 Ibid., 80; Peri E. Arnold, *Making the Managerial Presidency: Comprehensive Reorganization Planning, 1905–1996*, 2nd ed. (Lawrence, KS: University Press of Kansas, 1998), 108; Samuel Kernell, *Going Public: New Strategies of Presidential Leadership* (Washington, DC: CQ Press, 1986), 101.

70 Leuchtenberg, *Franklin D. Roosevelt*, 261–62; Milkis, *President and the Parties*, 83–84; Sidney M. Milkis, "Franklin D. Roosevelt and the Transcendence of Partisan Politics," *Political Science Quarterly* 100 (Fall 1985): 486.

71 Milkis, "Roosevelt and the Transcendence of Party Politics," 498; *President and the Parties*, 103.

72 See David K. Nichols, *The Myth of the Modern Presidency* (University Park, PA: Pennsylvania State University Press, 1994).

73 Lewis L. Gould, *The Modern American Presidency* (Lawrence, KS: University Press of Kansas, 2003), 7–15. For other accounts of Franklin Roosevelt's role in the creation of the modern presidency, see James P. Pfiffner, *The Modern Presidency* (New York: St. Martin's Press, 1994); Fred I. Greenstein, "Change and Continuity in the Modern Presidency," in Anthony King, ed., *The New American Political System* (Washington, DC: American Enterprise Institute, 1978), 45–53; Milkis, *President and the Parties*, Ch. 6.

74 William E. Leuchtenberg, *In the Shadow of FDR: From Harry Truman to George W. Bush* (Ithaca, NY: Cornell University Press, 2001), 209–11.

75 Skowronek, *The Politics Presidents Make*, 294–95.

76 Richard E. Neustadt, *Presidential Power and the Modern Presidents: The Politics of Leadership from Roosevelt to Reagan* (New York: Free Press, 1990), 6, 26–28.

77 Ibid., 47, 52.

78 See John Gunnell, "Richard Neustadt in the History of Political Science," in Robert Y. Shapiro, Martha Joynt Kumar, and Lawrence R. Jacobs, eds., *Presidential Power: Forging the Presidency for the Twenty-First Century* (New York: Columbia University Press, 2000), 16–27.

79 Neustadt, *Presidential Power*, 6.

80 Ibid., 68, 79, 128.

81 Milkis, *President and the Parties*, 142.

82 Paul T. David, Ralph Goldman, and Richard C. Bain, *The Politics of National Party Conventions* (Washington, DC: Brookings Institution, 1960), 273, 277.

83 James W. Davis, *Presidential Primaries: Road to the White House* (Westport, CT: Greenwood Press, 1980), 46.

84 Theodore Lowi, *The Personal Presidency: Power Invested, Promise Unfulfilled* (Ithaca, NY: Cornell University Press, 1985), 71–74; Larry M. Bartels, *Presidential Primaries and the Dynamics of Public Choice* (Princeton: Princeton University Press, 1088), 14.

85 Paul T. David, Malcolm Moos, and Ralph M. Goldman, *Presidential Nominating Politics in 1952: The National Story* (Baltimore: Johns Hopkins Press, 1954), 27; Stephen E. Ambrose, *Eisenhower: Soldier and President* (New York: Simon & Schuster, 1990), 229, 259, 264.

86 David, Goldman, and Bain, *The Politics of National Party Conventions*, 278, 298.

87 Lowi, *The Personal President*, 72–73.

88 Ibid., 73–74; Leon D. Epstein, *Political Parties in the American Mold* (Madison, WI: University of Wisconsin Press, 1986), 109.

89 Theodore H. White, *The Making of the President 1960* (New York: Atheneum, 1967), 55.

90 James W. Davis, *National Conventions in an Age of Party Reform* (Westport, CT: Greenwood Press, 1983), 34.

91 Ceaser, *Presidential Selection*, 240.

92 Milkis, *President and the Parties*, 214–15. The abolition of the unit rule applied only to the 1968 convention. It implemented one of the recom-

mendations of a Commission on the Democratic Selection of Presidential Nominees headed by Governor Harold Hughes of Iowa. The Hughes Commission had not been established under the auspices of the Democratic party, but its review of state procedures for delegate selection and its recommendations for change provided the starting point for the official McGovern-Fraser Commission that followed.

93 Nelson Polsby and Aaron Wildavsky, *Presidential Elections: Strategies and Structures of American Politics*, 10th ed. (New York: Chatham House, 2000), 123–24.

94 Austin Ranney, *Curing the Mischief of Faction: Party Reform in America* (Berkeley: University of California Press, 1975), 206; Bartels, *Presidential Primaries*, 22–23.

95 Epstein, *Political Parties in the American Mold*, 99.

96 White, *The Making of the President 1960*, 47.

Chapter 5. Making the President Imperial

1 Peri E. Arnold, *Making the Managerial Presidency: Comprehensive Reorganization Planning, 1905–1996*, 2nd ed. (Lawrence, KS: University Press of Kansas, 1998), 24.

2 Cited in Clinton Rossiter, *The American Presidency*, 2nd ed. (New York: Harcourt Brace, 1960), 129.

3 Peter H. Argersinger, "The Transformation of American Politics: Political Institutions and Public Policy, 1865–1910," in Byron E. Shafer and Anthony J. Badger, eds., *Contesting Democracy: Substance and Structure in American Political History, 1775–2000* (Lawrence, KS: University Press of Kansas, 2001), 120; Leonard D. White, *The Republican Era: A Study in Administrative History, 1869–1901* (New York: Free Press, 1958), 98–103.

4 John P. Burke, *The Institutional Presidency* (Baltimore: Johns Hopkins University Press, 1992), 4–5.

5 Fred I. Greenstein, "Change and Continuity in the Modern Presidency," in Anthony King, ed., *The New American Political System* (Washington, DC: American Enterprise Institute, 1979), 50.

6 Quoted in Leonard D. White, *The Republican Era: A Study in Administrative History, 1869–1901* (New York: Free Press, 1958), 103.

7 Quoted in Sidney Milkis, *The President and the Parties* (New York: Oxford, 1993), 128.

8 Burke, *The Institutional Presidency*, 4–5; Greenstein, "Change and Continuity in the Modern Presidency," 50–51; Samuel Kernell, "The Evolution of the White House Staff," in James P. Pfiffner, ed., *The Managerial Presidency*, 2nd ed. (College Station, TX: Texas A&M Press, 1999), 39; Frank Freidel, *Franklin D. Roosevelt: A Rendezvous with Destiny* (Boston: Little, Brown, 1990), 121.

9 Harold W. Stanley and Richard G. Niemi, *Vital Statistics on American Politics, 2001–2002* (Washington, DC: CQ Press, 2001), 250–51.

10 Arnold, *Making the Managerial Presidency*, 53; John Hart, *The Presidential Branch from Washington to Clinton*, 2nd ed. (Chatham, NJ: Chatham House, 1995), 32.

11 Stephen Hess, *Organizing the Presidency*, rev. ed. (Washington, DC: Brookings Institution, 1988), 35.

12 Ibid., 36.

13 Quoted in Hart, *The Presidential Branch*, 29.

14 Bert A. Rockman, "Staffing and Organizing the Presidency," in Shapiro, Kumar, and Jacobs, eds., *Presidential Power: Forging the Presidency for the Twenty-First Century* (New York: Columbia University Press, 2000), 165.

15 David McCullough, *Truman* (New York: Simon & Schuster, 1992), 473–74, 477.

16 Quoted in Hess, *Organizing the Presidency*, 44.

17 Milkis, *President and the Parties*, 160.

18 Hart, *The Presidential Branch*, 68–69. The secretary of the navy and the other service secretaries lost their seats on the National Security Council under the 1949 amendments to the National Security Act. See Hess, *Organizing the Presidency*, 52.

19 Ibid., 54; Arnold, *Making the Managerial Presidency*, 129, 148–49.

20 Fred I. Greenstein, *The Hidden-Hand Presidency: Eisenhower as Leader* (New York: Basic Books, 1982), 106.

21 Ibid., 114–16; Edward S. Corwin, *The President: Office and Powers, 1787–1957*, 4th ed. (New York: New York University Press, 1957), 301, 303; Hess, *Organizing the Presidency*, 60–61.

22 Arnold, *Making the Managerial Presidency*, 162–64; Greenstein, *Hidden-Hand Presidency*, 110.

23 Ibid., 111.

24 Arnold, *Making the Managerial Presidency*, 189–90.

25 Ibid., 164, 173, 176.

26 James P. Pfiffner, *The Strategic Presidency: Hitting the Ground Running*, 2nd ed. (Lawrence, KS: University Press of Kansas, 1996), 71; Robert Maranto, *Politics and Bureaucracy in the Modern Presidency: Careerists and Appointees in the Reagan Administration* (Westport, CT: Greenwood Press, 1993), 32–33.

27 Stephen Hess with James Pfiffner, *Organizing the Presidency*, 3rd ed. (Washington, DC: Brookings Institution, 2002), 65–66.

28 Hess and Pfiffner, *Organizing the Presidency*, 71–73; Andrew Rudalevige, *Managing the President's Program: Presidential Leadership and Legislative Policy Formulation* (Princeton: Princeton University Press, 2002), 49; Shirley Anne Warshaw, *The Domestic Presidency: Policymaking in the White House* (Needham Heights, MA: Allyn and Bacon, 1997), 8.

29 Maranto, *Politics and Bureaucracy*, 35.

30 Kennedy apparently overcame his aversion to organizational machinery in the case of congressional relations because of his experience with the House Rules Committee early in his administration. The president and

his staff belatedly realized that their legislative program could be shelved by the committee unless its largely conservative membership could be expanded to give it a majority favorable to the administration and independent of the Committee's obstructionist chairman, Representative Howard Smith of Virginia. The successful but difficult battle to enlarge the committee convinced the White House that it could not afford an ad hoc approach to congressional relations. Kenneth E. Collier, *Between the Branches: The White House Office of Legislative Affairs* (Pittsburgh: University of Pittsburgh Press, 1997), 66–67.

31 Charles E. Walcott and Karen M. Hult, *Governing the White House from Hoover through LBJ* (Lawrence, KS: University Press of Kansas, 1995), 27.

32 Quoted in John Hart, "Staffing the Presidency: Kennedy and the Office of Congressional Relations," *Presidential Studies Quarterly* 13 (Winter 1983): 105.

33 Hess, *Organizing the Presidency*, 29.

34 Collier, *Between the Branches*, 2, 37–39, 55; Walcott and Hult, *Governing the White House*, 39; George C. Edwards III and Stephen J. Wayne, *Presidential Leadership: Politics and Policy Making*, 3rd ed. (New York: St. Martin's Press, 1994), 312.

35 Hart, "Staffing the Presidency," 106; Walcott and Hult, *Governing the White House*, 37.

36 Hess, *Organizing the White House*, 85.

37 Terry M. Moe, "The Presidency and the Bureaucracy: The Presidential Advantage," in Michael Nelson, ed., *The Presidency and the Political System* 4th ed. (Washington, DC: CQ Press, 1995), 416–17; Samuel Kernell, *Going Public: New Strategies of Presidential Leadership* (Washington, DC: CQ Press, 1986), 25–26.

38 Walcott and Hult, *Governing the White House*, 47. Matthew Dickinson has argued more generally that the expansion of the White House staff may actually interfere with effective presidential bargaining. See Matthew J. Dickinson, *Bitter Harvest: FDR, Presidential Power and the Growth of the Presidential Branch* (New York: Cambridge University Press, 1997).

39 Quoted in Collier, *Between the Branches*, 102.

40 Ibid., 100.

41 Edwards and Wayne, *Presidential Leadership*, 313–14.

42 Collier, *Between Branches*, 109, 115, 119–20.

43 A complete inventory is provided by Harold C. Relyea, "Presidential Directives: Background and Review," Library of Congress, Congressional Research Service Report 98-611, November 9, 2001.

44 Terry M. Moe and William G. Howell, "The Presidential Power of Unilateral Action," *Journal of Law, Economics and Organization* 15/1 (January 1999): 133–34.

45 Todd F. Gaziano, "The Use and Abuse of Executive Orders and Other Presidential Directives," *Texas Review of Law and Politics* 5 (Spring 2001): 267–315.

46   Kenneth R. Mayer, *With the Stroke of a Pen: Executive Orders and Presidential Power* (Princeton: Princeton University Press, 2001), 71.

47   Ibid., 72–73.

48   Louis Fisher, *Constitutional Conflicts Between Congress and the President*, 4th ed. (Lawrence, KS: University Press of Kansas, 1998), 110.

49   Philip J. Cooper, *By Order of the President: The Use and Abuse of Presidential Direct Action* (Lawrence, KS: University Press of Kansas, 2002), 13–14, 86.

50   Moe and Howell, "The Presidential Power of Unilateral Action," 164.

51   Mayer, *With the Stroke of a Pen*, Ch. 6.

52   346 U.S. 579 (1952).

53   *Chamber of Commerce v. Reich*, 74 F. 3rd 1322 (D.C. Cir. 1996).

54   Cooper, *By Order of the President*, 22.

55   Ibid., 24.

56   *Dames & Moore v. Regan*, 453 U.S. 654 (1981).

57   Quoted in Kenneth R. Mayer and Thomas J. Weko, "The Institution-alization of Power," in Shapiro, Kumar, and Jacobs, eds., *Presidential Power*, 181.

58   Cooper, *By Order of the President*, 17.

59   Mark Killenback, "A Matter of Mere Approval: The Role of the President in the Creation of Legislative History," 48 University of Arkansas Law Review 239 (1995); Cooper, *By Order of the President*, 201.

60   Edward S. Corwin, *The President: Office and Powers*, 4th rev. ed. (New York: New York University Press, 1957), 283.

61   Cooper, *By Order of the President*, 201, 203.

62   Ibid., 216.

63   Ronald Reagan, Statement on Signing a Veterans' Benefit Bill, November 18, 1988, Public Papers of the President, 1988–1989 (Washington, DC: Government Printing Office, 1990), Book 2, 1558.

64   Ronald Reagan, Public Papers, Statement on Signing the Bill Prohibiting the Licensing or Construction of Facilities on the Salmon and Snake Rivers in Idaho, November 17, 1988, Book 2, 1525.

65   *AMERON, Inc. v. U.S. Army Corps of Engineers*, 610 F. Supp. 750 (D.N.J. 1985).

66   *Lear, Siegler v. Lehman*, 842 F. 2nd 1102 (1988).

67   Cooper, *By Order of the President*, 206–7.

68   Ibid., 217; Kristy Carroll, "Whose Statute Is It Anyway? Why and How Courts Should Use Presidential Signing Statements When Interpreting Federal Statutes," 16 Catholic University Law Review 475 (1997).

69   Andrew Sullivan, "We Don't Need a New King George: How can the President interpret the law as if it didn't apply to him?" *Time*, January 24, 2006, 27–28.

70   Gaziano, "Use and Abuse of Executive Orders," 283.

71   Quoted in Rudalevige, *Managing the President's Program*, 159.

72   Tara L. Branum, "President or King? The Use and Abuse of Executive Orders in Modern-Day America," *Journal of Legislation* 28/1: 1–59.

73 Cooper, *By Order of the President*, 108–9.

74 Frank J. Murray, "Justice Fights to Keep Clinton Monument Edicts Intact," *Washington Times*, July 28, 2003, A3.

75 James Reisen and Eric Lichtblau, "Bush Lets U.S. Spy on Callers Without Courts: Secret Order to Widen Domestic Monitoring," *New York Times*, December 16, 2005, 1.

76 Eric Lichtblau and James Risen, "Legal Rationale By Justice Department On Spying Effort," *New York Times*, January 20, 2006, 1.

77 Joseph Curl, "Legal Scholars Split on Wiretaps," *Washington Times*, January 18, 2006, A4.

78 Scott Shane, "Behind Power, One Principle," *New York Times*, December 17, 2005, 1. Yoo's views are more fully spelled out in his 2005 book, *The Powers of War and Peace* (Chicago: University of Chicago Press, 2005).

79 *Building Construction Trades Department v. Allbaugh*, 295 F. 3rd 28 (2002).

80 Moe and Howell, "The Presidential Power of Unilateral Action," 174; Cooper, *By Order of the President*, 77.

81 Elisabeth Bumiller, "For President, Final Say on a Bill Sometimes Comes After the Signing," *New York Times*, January 16, 2006, A11.

82 Ibid.

83 Ibid.

84 Sullivan, "We Don't Need a New King George," 28.

85 White House, Statement on HR 2673, January 23, 2003.

86 The classic critique of this process is Theodore J. Lowi, *The End of Liberalism* (New York: W. W. Norton, 1969).

87 Kenneth Culp Davis, *Administrative Law Treatise* (St. Paul, MN: West Publishing, 1958), 9.

88 Mayer and Weko, "Institutionalization of Power," 199.

89 James F. Blumstein, "Regulatory Review by the Executive Office of the President: An Overview and Policy Analysis of Current Issues," *Duke Law Journal* 51 (December 2001): 856.

90 Moe, "The President and Bureaucracy," 432.

91 Elena Kagan, "Presidential Administration," *Harvard Law Review* 114 (June 2001): 2262.

92 Moe, "The President and the Bureaucracy," 430–31.

93 Joel D. Aberbach and Bert A. Rockman, *In the Web of Politics: Three Decades of the U.S. Federal Executive* (Washington, DC: Brookings Institution, 2000), 169.

94 Marissa Martino Golden, *What Motivates Bureaucrats? Politics and Administration During the Reagan Years* (New York: Columbia University Press, 2000).

95 Blumstein, "Regulatory Review," 859.

96 Bradley H. Patterson, Jr., *The White House Staff: Inside the West Wing and Beyond* (Washington, DC: Brookings Institution, 2000), 302.

97 Richard H. Pildes and Cass Sunstein, "Reinventing the Regulatory State," 62 *University of Chicago Law Review* 1 (1995).

98 Kagan, "Presidential Administration," 2247.

99 Ibid., 2267.

100 Ibid., 2265.

101 Blumstein, "Regulatory Review," 860.

102 See, for example, Douglas W. Kmiec, "Expanding Executive Power," in Roger Pilon, ed., *The Rule of Law in the Wake of Clinton* (Washington, DC: Cato Institute Press, 2000), 47–68.

103 Blumstein, "Regulatory Review," 854.

104 Stephen Power and Jacob M. Schlesinger, "Bush's Rules Czar Brings Long Knife to New Regulations," *Wall Street Journal*, June 12, 2002, 1.

105 Ellen Nakashima, "Chief Plans Overhaul of Regulatory Process," *Washington Post*, March 20, 2002, A31.

106 Robert Percival, "Presidential Management of the Administrative State," *Duke Law Journal* 51 (December 2001): 1015.

107 John D. McKinnon and Stephen Power, "How U.S. Rules Are Made Is Still a Murky Process," *Wall Street Journal*, October 22, 2003, A6.

108 Jeffrey Tulis, *The Rhetorical Presidency* (Princeton: Princeton University Press, 1987), 79.

109 Kagan, "Presidential Administration," 2351.

110 Clinton Rossiter, ed., *The Federalist Papers*, No. 70 (New York: Signet, 1961), 423–30.

111 Moe, "The Presidency and the Bureaucracy," 416–20.

Chapter 6. Presidential War Powers

1 Edward S. Corwin, *The President: Office and Powers*, 4th rev. ed. (New York: New York University Press, 1957), 171.

2 Clinton Rossiter, ed., *The Federalist*, No. 64 (New York: Mentor, 1961), 390–96.

3 James W. Davis, *The American Presidency* (Westport, CT: Praeger, 1995), 246.

4 Corwin, *The President*, 178–79.

5 Ibid., 182.

6 Leonard White, *The Federalists* (New York: Free Press, 1948), 55.

7 Alexander Hamilton and James Madison, *Letters of Pacificus and Helvidius* (New York: Scholars Facsimiles & Reprints, 1999).

8 *Letters of Pacificus and Helvidius*, 13.

9 Corwin, *The President*, 181.

10 Sidney M. Milkis and Michael Nelson, *The American Presidency: Origins and Development* (Washington, DC: CQ Press, 1999), 91.

11 Leonard White, *The Jeffersonians* (New York: Free Press, 1951), 32.

12 Davis, *The American Presidency*, 242.

13 *U.S. v. Curtis-Wright Export Corporation*, 209 U.S. 304 (1936).

14 *Letters of Pacificus and Helvidius*, 58.

15 Corwin, *The President*, 189.

16 White, *The Federalists*, 64.

17 Louis Fisher, *The Politics of Shared Power*, 4th ed. (College Station, TX: Texas A&M Press, 1998), 186.

18 Rossiter, ed., *The Federalist*, 418.

19 See Max Boot, *The Savage Wars of Peace: Small Wars and the Rise of American Power* (New York: Basic Books, 2002).

20 Corwin, *The President*, 188.

21 Fisher, *Politics of Shared Power*, 209–10.

22 James G. Randall, *Constitutional Problems Under Lincoln* (New York: Appleton, 1926), Ch. 1.

23 Corwin, *The President*, 229.

24 2 Bl 635 (1863).

25 4 Wall. 2 (1866).

26 Corwin, *The President*, 235.

27 Robert Higgs, *Crisis and Leviathan* (New York: Oxford University Press, 1987), 139.

28 Paul Koistinen, *Mobilizing for Modern War: The Political Economy of American Warfare* (Lawrence, KS: University Press of Kansas, 1997), Chs. 10 and 11.

29 Higgs, *Chrisis and Leviathan*, 141.

30 Philip J. Cooper, *By Order of the President* (Lawrence, KS: University Press of Kansas, 2002), 72.

31 *U.S. v. Cohen*, 255 U.S. 81 (1921).

32 *Shenck v. U.S.*, 249 U.S. 47 (1919).

33 Corwin, *The President*, 238.

34 Ibid.

35 Kenneth R. Mayer, *With the Stroke of a Pen* (Princeton: Princeton University Press, 2001), 111.

36 Corwin, *The President*, 243.

37 Davis, *The American Presidency*, 224.

38 Arthur M. Schlesinger, Jr., *The Imperial Presidency* (Boston: Houghton Mifflin, 1973), 110–11.

39 Benjamin Ginsberg, *The Fatal Embrace: Jews and the State* (Chicago: University of Chicago Press, 1983), 118.

40 J. Garry Clifford and Samuel R. Spencer, *The First Peacetime Draft* (Lawrence, KS: University Press of Kansas, 1986).

41 Corwin, *The President*, 240.

42 Higgs, *Crisis and Leviathan*, 204.

43 Ibid., 205.

44 Ibid., 210.

45 321 U.S. 414 (1944).

46 321 U.S. 503 (1944).

47 323 U.S. 214 (1944).

48 *Ex parte Quirin*, 317 U.S. 1 (July Special Term, 1942).

49 333 U.S. 138 (1948).

50 Schlesinger, *The Imperial Presidency*, 66.

51 Higgs, *Crisis and Leviathan*, 154.

52 Bartholomew H. Sparrow, *From the Outside In: World War II and the American State* (Princeton: Princeton University Press, 1996).

53 Schlesinger, *The Imperial Presidency*, 127.

54 Ibid., 151.

55 David Oshinsky, *A Conspiracy So Immense* (New York: Free Press, 1985).

56 Wilfred Binkley, "The Decline of the Executive," *New Republic*, May 18, 1953, 26–28.

57 Maeva Marcus, *Truman and the Steel Seizure Case: The Limits of Presidential Power* (New York: Columbia University Press, 1977).

58 343 U.S. 579 (1952).

59 John K. Mahon, *History of the Militia and the National Guard* (New York: Macmillan, 1983), Ch. 3.

60 D. Christopher Leins, "The American Experience With an Organized Militia," unpublished seminar paper, Johns Hopkins University, 1999.

61 Mahon, *History of the Militia*, 84.

62 Allan Millett and Peter Maslowski, *For the Common Defense: A Military History of the United States of America* (New York: Free Press, 1994), 350.

63 Richard Franklin Bensel, *Yankee Leviathan: The Origins of Central State Authority in America, 1859–1877* (New York: Cambridge University Press, 1990), 248.

64 John F. Witte, *The Politics and Development of the Federal Income Tax* (Madison, WI: University of Wisconsin Press, 1985), Ch. 4.

65 Ellis Paxson Oberholtzer, *Jay Cooke: Financier of the Civil War* (Philadelphia: Jacobs, 1907).

66 Eric L. McKitrick, "Party Politics and the Union and Confederate War Efforts," in William Nisbett Chambers and Walter Dean Burnham, eds., *The American Party Systems*, 2nd ed. (New York: Oxford University Press, 1975), 147.

67 Donald R. Stabile and Jeffrey A. Cantor, *The Public Debt of the United States: An Historical Perspective, 1775–1990* (New York: Praeger, 1990), 79.

68 Theda Skocpol, Ziad Munson, Andrew Karch, and Bayliss Camp, "Patriotic Partnerships: Why Great Wars Nourished American Civic Voluntarism," in Ira Katznelson and Martin Shefter, eds., *Shaped by War and Trade: International Influences on American Political Development* (Princeton: Princeton University Press, 2002), 143–80.

69 Michael D. Pearlman, *Warmaking and American Democracy* (Lawrence, KS: University Press of Kansas, 1999), 57.

70 Chilton Williamson, *American Suffrage From Property to Democracy, 1760–1860* (Princeton: Princeton University Press, 1960), Ch. 6.

71 Benjamin Ginsberg, *The Consequences of Consent* (New York: Random House, 1982), Ch. 1.

72 Eric Foner, *Free Soil, Free Labor, Free Men: The Ideology of the Republican Party Before the Civil War* (New York: Oxford University Press, 1970).

73 Iver Bernstein, *The New York City Draft Riots* (New York: Oxford University Press, 1997).

74 Jack F. Leach, *Conscription in the United States* (Rutland, VT: Charles E. Tuttle, 1952), 296.

75 David M. Kennedy, *Over Here: The First World War and American Society* (New York: Oxford University Press, 1986), 144–67.

76 Stephen Kohn, *Jailed For Peace* (Westport, CT: Greenwood Press, 1986).

77 James Tracy, *Direct Action: Radical Pacifism from the Union Eight to the Chicago Seven* (Chicago: University of Chicago Press, 1996).

78 Martin Shefter, *Political Parties and the State* (Princeton: Princeton University Press, 1994), 88–91.

79 For a discussion of postmaterial politics, see Jeffrey M. Berry, *The New Liberalism* (Washington, DC: Brookings Institution, 1999).

80 Herbert D. A. Donovan, *The Barnburners* (New York: New York University Press, 1925).

81 George L. Mayer, *The Republican Party, 1854–1966* (New York: Oxford University Press, 1967), 71.

82 Ibid., 161.

83 Howard Jones, *Crucible of Power* (Wilmington, DE: SR Books, 2001), 103–5.

84 Senator Hiram Johnson, quoted in Mayer, *The Republican Party*, 354.

85 Ibid., 353.

86 Ellen Schrecker, *Many Are the Crimes* (Boston: Little, Brown, 1998).

87 Herbert Shapiro, "The Vietnam War and the American Civil Rights Movement," in Walter Hixson, ed., *The Vietnam Antiwar Movement* (New York: Garland, 2000), 71–95.

88 Benjamin Ginsberg and Martin Shefter, *Politics by Other Means*, 3rd ed. (New York: W. W. Norton, 2002), 91.

89 Robert D. Johnson, "The Origins of Dissent: Senate Liberals and Vietnam," in Hixson, ed., *The Vietnam Antiwar Movement*, 151–275.

90 Scott Gartner, Gary Segura, and Michael Wilkening, "Local Losses and Individual Attitudes Toward the Vietnam War," in Hixson, ed., *The Vietnam Antiwar Movement*, 193–218.

91 Bartholomew Sparrow, "Limited Wars and the Attenuation of the State," in Katznelson and Shefter, eds., *Shaped by War*, 277–78.

92 Schlesinger, *The Imperial Presidency*, 166.

93 Michael J. Hogan, *Cross of Iron: Harry S. Truman and the Origins of the National Security State, 1945–1954* (New York: Cambridge University Press, 1998), 72–73.

94 Schlesinger, *The Imperial Presidency*, 118.

95 Robert Sherwood, *Roosevelt and Hopkins* (New York: Universal Library, 1950), 636–40.

96 Matthew J. Dickinson, *Bitter Harvest: FDR, Presidential Power and the Growth of the Presidential Branch* (New York: Cambridge University Press, 1996), 178–81.

97 Charles E. Bohlen, *Witness to History* (New York: W. W. Norton, 1973), 210.

98 Milkis and Nelson, *The American Presidency*, 280.

99 Robert D. Schulzinger, *U.S. Diplomacy Since 1900* (New York: Oxford University Press, 1998), 212.

100 Rhodri Jeffreys-Jones, *The CIA and American Democracy*, 2nd ed. (New Haven: Yale University Press, 1998), Ch. 1.

101 Alonzo Hamby, *A Man of the People: A Life of Harry S. Truman* (New York: Oxford University Press, 1995), 309–11.

102 Millett and Maslowski, *For the Common Defense*, Ch. 10.

103 Allan R. Millett, *Semper Fidelis: The History of the United States Marine Corps* (New York: Free Press, 1991), 292–96.

104 Millett and Maslowski, *For the Common Defense*, 366.

105 Hogan, *Cross of Iron*, 187.

106 Jeffrey G. Barlow, *Revolt of the Admirals* (Washington, DC: Ross and Perry, 2001), Ch. 8.

107 Stephen Howarth, *To Shining Sea* (Norman, OK: University of Oklahoma Press, 1991), 485–86.

108 Richard Rovere and Arthur Schlesinger, Jr., *General MacArthur and President Truman: The Struggle for Control of American Foreign Policy* (New Brunswick, NJ: Transaction, 1992), Ch. 3.

109 Millett and Maslowski, *For the Common Defense*, 515.

110 Hogan, *Cross of Iron*, 151.

111 George Q. Flynn, *The Draft* (Lawrence, KS: University Press of Kansas, 1993), 141.

112 Millett and Maslowski, *For the Common Defense*, 517.

113 Aaron L. Friedberg, "American Antistatism and the Founding of the Cold War State," in Katznelson and Shefter, eds., *Shaped by War*, 254.

114 Paul Koistinen, *The Hammer and the Sword: Labor, the Military, and Industrial Production, 1920–1945* (New York: Arno Press, 1979), 580.

115 Ken Silverstein, *Private Warriors* (London: Verso, 2000), Ch. 5.

116 Harold Seidman, *Politics, Position, and Power*, 5th ed. (New York: Oxford University Press, 1998), 208–11.

117 Ann Markusen, Peter Hall, Scott Campbell, and Sabina Deitrick, *The Rise of the Gunbelt: The Military Remapping of Industrial America* (New York: Oxford University Press, 1991), Ch. 10.

118 John P. Burke, *The Institutional Presidency*, 2nd ed. (Baltimore: Johns Hopkins University Press, 2000), 37–40.

119 Joel R. Paul, "The Geopolitical Constitution: Executive Expediency and Executive Agreements," *University of California Law Review* 86 (July 1998): 713–14.

120 Ibid., 720–21.

121 Ibid., Section 3; also Fisher, *Politics of Shared Power*, 190–91.

122 Harold W. Stanley and Richard Niemi, *Vital Statistics on American Politics, 2001–2002* (Washington, DC: CQ Press, 2001), 334.

123 John C. Yoo, "Laws as Treaties?: The Constitutionality of Congressional-Executive Agreements," 99 *University of Michigan Law Review* 757 (February 2001).

124 Cooper, *By Order of the President*, 144.

125 Ibid., 158.

126 Jeffreys-Jones, *The CIA*, 55–56.

127 Schlesinger, *The Imperial Presidency*, 167.

128 Robert J. Donovan, *Conflict and Crisis: The Presidency of Harry S. Truman, 1945–1948* (New York: W. W. Norton, 1977), 296–97.

129 Athan Theoharis, ed., *The Truman Presidency: The Origins of the Imperial Presidency and the National Security State* (Stanfordville, NY: E. M. Coleman, 1979), 257–61.

130 Schlesinger, *The Imperial Presidency*, Ch. 10.

131 Margaret Myers, *A Financial History of the United States* (New York: Columbia University Press, 1970), Ch. 15.

132 Friedberg, "American Antistatism," 250.

133 Sidney Ratner, *American Taxation: Its History as a Social Force in Democracy* (New York: W. W. Norton, 1942), 72.

134 Joseph A. Pechman, *Federal Tax Policy*, 5th ed. (Washington, DC: Brookings Institution, 1987), 355–63; also B. Guy Peters, *The Politics of Taxation* (Cambridge, MA: Blackwell, 1991), 1–15.

135 Todd Sandler and Keith Hartley, *The Economics of Defense* (Cambridge: Cambridge University Press, 1995), Ch. 10; also Michael T. Klare, *American Arms Supermarket* (Austin, TX: University of Texas Press, 1984), 34.

136 David Gold, "The Changing Economics of the Arms Trade," in Ann Markusen and Sean Costigan, eds., *Arming the Future* (New York: Council on Foreign Relations Press, 1999), 249–68.

137 Leslie Wayne, "Polish Pride, American Profits," *New York Times*, January 12, 2003, Section 3, 1.

138 Larry Neal, *War Finance* (Brookfield, VT: Edward Elgar Publishing, 1994), I: 3.

139 Dean Acheson, *Present At the Creation* (New York: W. W. Norton, 1987), Ch. 26.

140 Malcolm Chalmers, *Sharing Security: The Political Economy of Burdensharing* (London: Macmillan, 2000), 33.

141 Millett and Maslowski, *For the Common Defense*, 519.

142 Schlesinger, *The Imperial Presidency*, 165.

143 Ibid., 200–207.

144 Ibid., 132–33.

145 Edward C. Luck, *Mixed Messages: American Politics and International Organization, 1919–1999* (Washington, DC: Brookings Institution, 1999), 61–62.

146 Ibid., Ch. 7.

147 Schlesinger, *The Imperial Presidency*, 132–35.

148 Jonathan Hughes and Louis P. Cain, *American Economic History*, 5th ed. (Reading, MA: Addison-Wesley, 1998), 529.

149 Neal, *War Finance*, 17.

150 Schlesinger, *The Imperial Presidency*, 156–58.

151 Louis Fisher, *Congressional Abdication on War and Spending* (College Station, TX: Texas A&M Press, 2000), 49–52.

152 Flynn, *The Draft*, 265.

153 Douglas Bandow, "Fixing What Ain't Broke: The Renewed Call for Conscription," *Policy Analysis* 351 (August 31, 1999): 2.

154 Charles B. Rangel, "Bring Back the Draft," *New York Times*, December 31, 2002, A21.

155 Thomas E. Ricks, *Making the Corps* (New York: Simon & Schuster, 1997), Ch. 5.

156 Ole R. Holsti, "Of Chasms and Convergences: Attitudes and Beliefs of Civilians and Military Elites at the Start of a New Millennium," in Peter D. Feaver and Richard H. Kohn, *Soldiers and Civilians* (Cambridge, MA: MIT Press, 2001), 15–100.

157 Jonathan Turley, "The Military Pocket Republic," 97 *Northwestern University Law Review* 1 (Fall 2002).

158 David M. Halbfinger and Streven A. Holmes, "Military Mirrors a Working-Class America," *New York Times*, March 30, 2003, 1; also David Shiflett, "An Army That Drawls: Johnny Reb Goes to Iraq and Everywhere Else," *National Review*, May 5, 2003, 29–30.

159 In the aftermath of the Vietnam War, some generals supported placing critical specialties in the reserves to prevent presidents from asking the army to fight without popular support. See Greg Jaffe, "Today, Military Kids Often Say Goodbye to Dad—and Mom," *Wall Street Journal*, March 11, 2003, 1.

160 Thom Shanker, "U.S. Considers Limits on Role of the Reserves," *New York Times*, January 26, 2003, 1.

161 Vernon Loeb, "Rumsfeld Turns Eye to Future of Army," *Washington Post*, June 8, 2003, A12.

162 James R. Locher III, *Victory on the Potomac: The Goldwater-Nichols Act Unifies the Pentagon* (College Station, TX: Texas A&M Press, 2002).

163 Franklin C. Spinney, "Notes on Close Air Support," in Donald Vandergriff, ed., *Spirit, Blood and Treasure: The American Cost of Battle in the 21st Century* (Novato, CA: Presidio Press, 2001), 199–213.

164 Geoffrey Perret, *A Country Made by War* (New York: Random House, 1989), 305–8.

165 George and Meredith Friedman, *The Future of War* (New York: St. Martin's Press, 1996), Ch. 10.

166 Matthew Brzezinski, "The Unmanned Army," *New York Times Magazine*, April 20, 2003, 38–80.

167 MacGregor Knox and Williamson Murray, *The Dynamics of Military Revolution, 1300–2050* (New York: Cambridge University Press, 2001), 188–92.

168 Christopher Palmeri, "A Predator That Preys on Hawks?" *Business Week*, February 17, 2003, 78.

169 "Victory in Iraq or Victory in the Polls," *Editor and Publisher*, December 3, 2005, 1.

170 David Halberstam, "Televising the Vietnam War," in Doris A. Graber, ed., *Media Power in Politics* (Washington, DC: CQ Press, 1984), 290–95.

171 Jennifer Harper, "Journalists Prepare to See War from the Battlefield," *Washington Times*, March 4, 2003, A5.

172 Tim Reid, "Texan Sent to Be Voice of War," *The Times* (London), November 14, 2002, 19.

173 Michael Massing, "The Unseen War," *New York Review*, May 29, 2003, 16–19.

174 John Lehman, *Making War: The 200 Year Old Battle Between the President and the Congress Over How America Goes to War* (New York: Scribner's Sons, 1992), 263.

175 Ibid., 265.

176 Louis Fisher, "The Spending Power," in David Gray Adler and Larry N. George, *The Constitution and the Conduct of American Foreign Policy* (Lawrence, KS: University Press of Kansas, 1996), 234.

177 Ibid., *War Finance*, 18.

178 Fisher, *Congressional Abdication*, 76.

179 Gordon Silverstein, *Imbalance of Powers: Constitutional Interpretation and the Making of American Foreign Policy* (New York: Oxford University Press, 1997), 145.

180 Lori F. Damrosch, "Covert Operations," in Louis Henkin, Michael J. Glennon, and William D. Rogers, eds., *Foreign Affairs and the U.S. Constitution* (Ardsley-on-Hudson, NY: Transnational Publishers, 1990), 87–97.

181 453 U.S. 654 (1981).

182 462 U.S. 919 (1983).

183 Harold H. Koh, *The National Security Constitution* (New Haven: Yale University Press, 1990), 46–47.

184 Christopher N. May, *In the Name of War: Judicial Review and the War Powers Since 1918* (Cambridge, MA: Harvard University Press, 1989), 256.

185 Thomas M. Franck, "Rethinking War Powers: By Law or by 'Thaumaturgic Invocation'?" in Henkin et al., 59.

186 Caspar W. Weinberger, "Dangerous Constraints on the President's War Powers," in L. Gordon Crovitz and Jeremy Rabkin, eds., *The Fettered Presidency: Legal Constraints on the Executive Branch* (Washington, DC: American Enterprise Institute, 1989), 95–116.

187 Fisher, *Congressional Abdication*, 68.

188 Ibid., 75–76.

189 Ibid., 77.

190 George Bush and Brent Scowcroft, *A World Transformed* (New York: Knopf, 1998), 441.

191 Robert J. Delahunty and John C. Yoo, "The President's Constitutional Authority to Conduct Military Operations Against Terrorist Organizations

and the Nations That Harbor Them," 25 *Harvard Journal of Law and Public Policy* 487 (Spring 2002).

192 For an analysis of the act, see Michael T. McCarthy, "USA Patriot Act," 39 *Harvard Journal on Legislation* 435 (Summer 2002).

193 David R. Sands, "Allies Unlikely to Help Pay for Second Iraq Invasion," *Washington Times*, March 10, 2003, 1.

Chapter 7. Congressional Government: Its Rise and Fall

1 Joseph J. Ellis, *Founding Brothers* (New York: Knopf, 2000), 188–95.

2 Henry Jones Ford, *The Rise and Growth of American Politics* (New York: Macmillan, 1898), Chs. 8 and 9.

3 Chilton Williamson, *American Suffrage from Property to Democracy, 1760–1860* (Princeton: Princeton University Press, 1960).

4 See Arthur M. Schlesinger, Jr., *The Age of Jackson* (Boston: Little, Brown, 1945), Ch. 4.

5 Michael J. Gerhardt, *The Federal Appointments Process* (Durham, NC: Duke University Press, 2000), 63–69.

6 John H. Schroeder, *Mr. Polk's War* (Madison: University of Wisconsin Press, 1973), 154.

7 W. P. Cresson, *James Monroe* (Chapel Hill: University of North Carolina Press, 1946), 340–50.

8 William W. Story, *Life and Letters of Joseph Story*, Vol. I, March 12, 1818 (Boston: Little, Brown, 1851), 311.

9 John Quincy Adams, *Memoirs*, Vol. 4, March 28, 1818 (Philadelphia: Lippincott, 1874–77), 70.

10 Ibid., January 8, 1820, 497.

11 Steven Rosenstone and Marc Hansen, *Mobilization, Participation, and Democracy in America* (New York: Longman, 2002), 231–32.

12 See Harold W. Stanley and Richard G. Niemi, *Vital Statistics on American Politics* (Washington, DC: CQ Press, 2001), 211.

13 Mary Follett, *The Speaker of the House of Representatives* (New York: Longman's, 1896), 326.

14 See David M. Jordan, *Roscoe Conkling of New York* (Ithaca, NY: Cornell University Press, 1971).

15 Martin Shefter, *Political Parties and the State* (Princeton: Princeton University Press, 1994), 74.

16 Leonard D. White, *The Republican Era* (New York: Free Press, 1958), 301–22.

17 See Marver H. Bernstein, *Regulating Business By Independent Commission* (Princeton: Princeton University Press, 1955).

18 Alan Ware, *The American Direct Primary: Party Institutionalization and Transformation in the North* (New York: Cambridge University Press, 2002), 28.

19 Sidney M. Milkis and Michael Nelson, *The American Presidency: Origins and Development*, 3rd edition (Washington, DC: CQ Press, 1999), 249.

20 Robert Sobel, *Coolidge* (Washington, DC: Regnery Publishing, 1998), 301–2.

21 Grant McConnell, *Private Power and American Democracy* (New York: Knopf, 1966), 298.

22 Stephen Erie, *Rainbow's End* (Berkeley: University of California Press, 1990).

23 Samuel P. Huntington, "Congressional Responses to the Twentieth Century," in David Truman, ed., *Congress and America's Future* (New York: Prentice Hall, 1965), 5–31.

24 Ronald M. Peters, *The American Speakership* (Baltimore: Johns Hopkins University Press, 1997), 75–91.

25 Terry M. Moe, "The Presidency and the Bureaucracy: The Presidential Advantage," in Michael Nelson, ed., *The Presidency and the Political System* (Washington, DC: CQ Press, 1995), 408–39; also Douglas R. Williams, "Congressional Abdication, Legal Theory, and Deliberative Democracy," *Saint Louis University Public Law Review* 19 (2000): 75–116.

26 Robert G. Kaiser, "Congress-s-s-s: That Great Hissing Sound You Hear Is Congress Giving Up Its Clout," *Washington Post*, March 14, 2004, B1.

27 John Aldrich, *Why Parties?* (Chicago: University of Chicago Press, 1995).

28 Andrew Taylor with Alan K. Ota, "Bankruptcy Bill Set to Clear," *Congressional Quarterly Weekly Report* 60/30 (July 27, 2002): 2026–27.

29 Tom Hamburger and Shailagh Murray, "Bankruptcy Bill Surprisingly Fails over Obscure Abortion Provision," *Wall Street Journal*, November 15, 2002, 1.

30 Huntington, "Responses," 20.

31 Nelson W. Polsby, Miriam Gallaher, and Barry Spencer Rundquist, "The Growth of the Seniority System in the U.S. House of Representatives," in Nelson W. Polsby, ed., *Congressional Behavior* (New York: Random House, 1971), 172–202. The seniority rule is occasionally violated as was the case during the 104th Congress in 1994 when the new Republican majority bypassed two senior members who were deemed insufficiently energetic or conservative to lead committees. Even in these instances, however, the chairmanships went to the next most senior committee members.

32 David Mayhew, *Congress: The Electoral Connection* (New Haven: Yale University Press, 1974), 94.

33 Huntington, "Congressional Responses," 5–6.

34 David J. Garrow, "Running the House," *New York Times*, November 13, 2002, A33.

35 Congressional tactics are discussed in Mayhew, *Congress*. For discussions of incumbent gerrymandering see Mark Monmonier, *Bushmanders and Bullwinkles: How Politicians Manipulate Electronic Maps and Census Data to Win Elections* (Chicago: University of Chicago Press, 2001); also Douglas J. Amy, "How Proportional Representation Would Finally Solve Our Redistricting and Gerrymandering Problems," in Douglas J. Amy, ed., *Real Choices/New Voices* (New York: Columbia University Press, 2002), Ch. 2; also Gary W. Cox and Jonathan N. Katz, *Elbridge Gerry's Salamander: The*

Electoral Consequences of the Reapportionment Revolution (Cambridge: Cambridge University Press, 2002), 128–32. For an excellent discussion of these issues see the recent exchange between Samuel Issacharoff and Nathaniel Persily: Samuel Issacharoff, "Gerrymandering and Political Cartels," 116 *Harvard Law Review* 593 (December 2002); Nathaniel Persily, "Reply: In Defense of Foxes Guarding Henhouses: The Case for Judicial Acquiescence to Incumbent-Protecting Gerrymanders," 116 *Harvard Law Review* 649 (December 2002); Samuel Issacharoff, "Surreply: Why Elections," 116 *Harvard Law Review* 684 (December 2002).

36 Nelson Polsby, *How Congress Evolves* (New York: Oxford University Press, 2004).

37 See Robert Higgs, *Crisis and Leviathan* (New York: Oxford University Press, 1986).

38 Richard Polenberg, *Reorganizing Roosevelt's Government* (Cambridge, MA: Harvard University Press, 1966).

39 Herbert Emmerich, "The Johnson System," in Raymond E. Wolfinger, ed., *Readings on Congress* (Englewood Cliffs, NJ: Prentice Hall, 1971), 225–41.

40 Morris Fiorina, *Congress: Keystone of the Washington Establishment*, 2nd ed. (New Haven: Yale University Press, 1989), 46–47; also Mathew McCubbins and Talbot Page, "A Theory of Congressional Delegation," in Mathew McCubbins and Terry Sullivan, *Congress: Structure and Policy* (New York: Cambridge University Press, 1987), 409–26.

41 Jerry L. Nashaw, *Greed, Chaos and Governance: Using Public Choice to Improve Public Law* (New Haven: Yale University Press, 1997), 106.

42 Andrew Taylor, "The Plan: Go Home, Limp Back After Voters Set the Agenda," *Congressional Quarterly Weekly Report*, 58/43 (November 4, 2000), 2587.

43 Stanley and Niemi, *Vital Statistics*, 262.

44 Jessica Korn, *The Power of Separation: American Constitutionalism and the Myth of the Legislative Veto* (Princeton: Princeton University Press, 1996), 43.

45 *Immigration and Naturalization Service v. Chadha*, 459 U.S. 1097 (1983).

46 Ronald A. Cass, "Models of Administrative Action," 72 *Virginia Law Review* 377 (1986).

47 Martin Shapiro, "APA: Past, Present, Future," 72 *Virginia Law Review* 447 (March 1986).

48 Steven P. Croley and William F. Funk, "The Federal Advisory Committee Act and Good Government," 14 *Yale Journal on Regulation* 451 (Spring 1997).

49 William F. Fox, Jr., *Understanding Administrative Law*, 4th ed. (New York: Lexis Publishing, 2000), 178–81.

50 O'Brien, "Taking the Conservative State Seriously," 50.

51 Stanley and Niemi, *Vital Statistics*, 205.

52 Fiorina, *Congress*, 44–45.

53 Huntington, "Congressional Responses," 26–31.

54 O'Brien, "Taking the Conservative State Seriously," 61; Susan Sterett,

"Legality in Administration in Britain and the United States: Toward an Institutional Explanation," *Comparative Political Studies* 25 (July 1992): 210–11.

55 Matthew A. Crenson and Benjamin Ginsberg, *Downsizing Democracy* (Baltimore: Johns Hopkins University Press, 2002), Ch. 7.

56 Susan Olson, "The Political Evolution of Interest Group Litigation," in Richard Gambitta, Marlynn May, and James Foster, eds., *Governing Through the Courts* (Beverly Hills: Sage Publications, 1981), 225–58; also Karen Orren, "Standing to Sue: Interest Group Conflict in the Federal Courts," *American Political Science Review* 70 (1976): 723–41.

57 Stephen C. Yeazell, *From Medieval Group Litigation to the Modern Class Action* (New Haven: Yale University Press, 1987); also Jack B. Weinstein, *Individual Justice in Mass Tort Litigation: The Effects of Class Actions, Consolidations and Other Multiparty Devices* (Evanston, IL: Northwestern University Press, 1995).

58 Samuel Issacharoff, "Governance and Legitimacy in the Law of Class Actions," 1999 *Supreme Court Review* 337 (1999).

59 Jeremy Rabkin, *Judicial Compulsions* (New York: Basic Books, 1989).

60 *Newman v. Piggie Park Enterprises, Inc.*, 390 U.S. 400 (1968). In the May 2001 case of *Buchannon Board & Care Home v. West Virginia Department of Health and Human Resources* (No. 99-1848), the U.S. Supreme Court placed limits on fee shifting by ruling that a plaintiff could not be awarded fees if a suit achieved its aim by producing "a voluntary change" in a defendant's conduct. Some public interest lawyers asserted that this decision would undermine public interest litigation by discouraging plaintiffs from incurring costs for which they might ultimately not be reimbursed even if they prevailed. Other experts, however, said there were a number of tactics that public interest litigators could use to circumvent the *Buchannon* ruling. For a discussion, see Marci Coyle, "Fee Change is a Sea Change," *National Law Journal*, June 11, 2001, A1.

61 Michael Greve, "The Private Enforcement of Environmental Law," 65 *Tulane Law Review* 339 (1990).

62 Robert Percival and Geoffrey Miller, "The Role of Attorney Fee Shifting in Public Interest Litigation," 47 *Law and Contemporary Problems* 233 (1984).

63 Natalie Bussan, "All Bark and No Bite: Citizen Suits After *Steel Company v. CBE*," 6 *Wisconsin Environmental Law Journal* 195 (1999). Important cases include *Lujan v. Defenders of Wildlife*, 504 U.S. 555 (1992) and *Chicago Steel and Pickling Company v. Citizens for a Better Environment*, 118 S. Ct. 1003 (1998).

64 See Jeremy Rabkin, "Government Lawyering: The Secret Life of the Private Attorney General," *Law and Contemporary Problems* 61 (Winter 1998): 179. See also Karen O'Conner and Lee Epstein, *Public Interest Law Groups* (Westport, CT: Greenwood Press, 1989).

65 Joseph Ward, "Corporate Goliaths in the Costume of David: The

Question of Association Aggregation Under the Equal Access to Justice Act," 26 *Florida State University Law Review* 151 (1998).

66 See Richard Neely, *How Courts Govern America* (New Haven: Yale University Press, 1981); also Michael McCann, "How the Supreme Court Matters in American Politics," in Howard Gillman and Cornell Clayton, eds., *The Supreme Court in American Politics* (Lawrence, KS: University Press of Kansas, 1999).

67 Lee Epstein and Thomas Walker, "The Role of the Supreme Court in American Society," in Lee Epstein, ed., *Contemplating Courts* (Washington, DC: CQ Press, 1995), 315–46.

68 Benjamin Ginsberg and Martin Shefter, *Politics by Other Means*, 3rd ed. (New York: W. W. Norton, 2002), 37–38.

69 Andrew Taylor, "After First Hundred Days, Bush Emerges as Pragmatic Warrior," *Congressional Quarterly Weekly Report* 59/17 (April 28, 2001): 907–8.

Chapter 8. How the Courts Reinforce Presidential Power

1 The first was *Mitchell v. Laird*, 488 F. 2nd 611 (1973), in which thirteen members of Congress asked the court to order the president to bring an end to the Vietnam War on the grounds that it had not been properly authorized by the Congress.

2 444 U.S. 996 (1979).

3 *Raines v. Byrd*, 521 U.S. 811 (1997). See also *Campbell v. Clinton*, 52 F. Supp. 2d 34 (D.D.C. 1994). For an interesting discussion of efforts by legislators to use the courts to bring about changes in presidential policies, see Anthony Clark Arend and Catherine Lotrionte, "Congress Goes to Court: The Past, Present and Future of Legislator Standing," 25 *Harvard Journal of Law and Public Policy* 209 (Fall 2001).

4 For an example of a congressional amicus brief see Roy E. Brownell, "The Unnecessary Demise of the Line-Item Veto Act," 47 *American University Law Review* 1273 (June 1998).

5 *U.S. v. Nixon*, 418 U.S. 683 (1974).

6 On Clinton, see Jonathan Turley, "Paradise Lost: The Clinton Administration and the Erosion of Executive Privilege," 60 *Maryland Law Review* 205 (2001). On Bush, see Jeffrey P. Carlin, "*Walker v. Cheney*: Politics, Posturing and Executive Privilege," 76 *Southern California Law Review* 235 (November 2002).

7 Edward Corwin, *The President: Office and Powers*, 4th rev. ed. (New York: New York University Press, 1957), 16.

8 Terry M. Moe and William G. Howell, "The Presidential Power of Unilateral Action," *Journal of Law, Economics and Organization* 15/1 (1999): 151–52.

9 Thomas E. Cronin and Michael A. Genovese, *The Paradoxes of the American Presidency* (New York: Oxford University Press, 1998), 271.

10 Moe and Howell, "Unilateral Action," 150.

11 Kermit L. Hall, *The Politics of Justice: Lower Federal Judicial Selection and the Second Party System, 1829–1861* (Lincoln, NE: University of Nebraska Press, 1979), 152–56.

12 "The Federal Court Judges Biographical Database," *Appellate.net.*

13 "Biographical Database," *Appellate.net.*

14 John R. Schmidhauser, *Judges and Justices: The Federal Appellate Judiciary* (Boston: Little, Brown, 1979), 135.

15 Stanley I. Kutler, *Judicial Power and Reconstruction Politics* (Chicago: University of Chicago Press, 1968), 22–23.

16 Hall, *Politics of Justice*, 29–36.

17 Kutler, *Judicial Power*, Chs. 4 and 5.

18 Cass R. Sunstein, "In Court v. Congress, Justices Concede One," *Washington Post*, December 21, 2003, B3.

19 John A. Ferejohn and Larry D. Kramer, "Independent Judges, Dependent Judiciary: Institutionalizing Judicial Restraint," 77 *New York University Law Review* 962 (October 2002).

20 Rachel E. Barkow, "More Supreme Than Court? The Fall of the Political Question Doctrine and the Rise of Judicial Supremacy," 102 *Columbia Law Review* 237 (March 2002).

21 17 U.S. (4 Wheat.) 316 (1819).

22 Ibid., 423.

23 Ibid., 421.

24 48 U.S. (7 How.) 1 (1849).

25 *Dred Scott v. Sanford*, 19 How. 393 (1857).

26 Kutler, *Judicial Power*, 43.

27 74 U.S. 506 (1869).

28 Gerald Gunther, *Constitutional Law*, 10th ed. (Mineola, NY: Foundation Press, 1980), 48–49.

29 Ferejohn and Kramer, "Independent Judges," 979–84.

30 521 U.S. 507 (1997).

31 J. Woodford Howard, *Courts of Appeals in the Federal Judicial System* (Princeton: Princeton University Press, 1981), 90.

32 Quoted in David M. O'Brien, *Judicial Roulette* (New York: Twentieth Century Fund, 1988), 37.

33 Matthew A. Crenson and Benjamin Ginsberg, *Downsizing Democracy: How America Sidelined Its Citizens and Privatized Its Public* (Baltimore: Johns Hopkins University Press, 2002), 14–19.

34 Harold Seidman, *Politics, Position and Power: The Dynamics of Federal Organization*, 5th ed. (New York: Oxford University Press, 1998), 52.

35 David Baumann, "Budget Debates Leave White House With Foes in Both Parties," *GovExec.com*, February 15, 2002, 1.

36 Ralph K. Winter, "The Activist Judicial Mind," in Mark W. Cannon and David M. O'Brien, *Views From the Bench* (Chatham, NJ: Chatham House, 1985), 291.

37 *U.S. v. Booker*, 04-104 (2005).
38 Linda Greenhouse, "The Court v. Congress," *New York Times*, September 15, 2005, 1.
39 369 U.S. 186 (1962).
40 395 U.S. 486 (1969).
41 531 U.S. 98 (2000). For the background and details of the case see E. J. Dionne and William Kristol, eds., *Bush v. Gore: The Court Cases and the Commentary* (Washington, DC: Brookings Institution, 2001). For a defense of the Court's actions, see Richard Posner, *Breaking the Deadlock: The 2000 Election, the Constitution and the Courts* (Princeton: Princeton University Press, 2001).
42 Benjamin Ginsberg and Martin Shefter, *Politics by Other Means* (New York: W. W. Norton, 2002), Ch. 6. The quoted comment regarding the Florida legislature is from Thomas Oliphant, "Gov. Bush's Cynical End-Around in the Florida Legislature," *Boston Globe*, December 3, 2000, D8.
43 For a critique of the notion of judicial imperialism see Mark Kozloski and Anthony Lewis, *The Myth of the Imperial Judiciary* (New York: New York University Press, 2003).
44 Jo Becker and Brian Faler, "The Cordial Nominee Once Had Choice Words for Lawmakers," *Wall Street Journal*, September 1, 2005, A4.
45 Jess Bravin, "Judge Alito's View of the Presidency: Expansive Powers," *Wall Street Journal*, January 6, 2006, 1.
46 3 Dall. 54 (1795).
47 2 Pet. 253 (1829).
48 50 U.S. 602 (1850).
49 *Fong Yue Ting v. U.S.*, 149 U.S. 698 (1893).
50 182 U.S. 1 (1901).
51 299 U.S. 304 (1936).
52 *Schechter Bros. v. U.S.*, 295 U.S. 495 (1935); *Panama Refining Co. v. Ryan*, 293 U.S. 388 (1935).
53 Gordon Silverstein, "Judicial Enhancement of Executive Power," in Paul Peterson, ed., *The President, the Congress and the Making of Foreign Policy* (Norman, OK: University of Oklahoma Press, 1994), 28–29.
54 Randall W. Bland, *The Black Robe and the Bald Eagle: The Supreme Court and the Foreign Policy of the United States, 1789–1953* (San Francisco: Austin & Winfield, 1996), 172.
55 Sarah H. Cleveland, "Crosby and the 'One Voice' Myth in U.S. Foreign Relations," 46 *Villanova Law Review* 975 (2001).
56 John C. Yoo, "Laws as Treaties?: The Constitutionality of Congressional-Executive Agreements," 99 *Michigan Law Review* 757 (February 2001).
57 Corwin, *The President*, 212–13.
58 Bland, *Black Robe and Bald Eagle*, 177.
59 See *Field v. Clark*, 143 U.S. 649 (1892).
60 299 U.S. 304 (1936).
61 301 U.S. 324 (1937).

62 565 F. Supp. 1019 (D. Colo. 1983).

63 151 F. Supp. 942 (1957).

64 6 Cl. Ct. 115 (1984). The decision was later reversed on appeal by the U.S. Court of Appeals for the Federal Circuit primarily because both the U.S. and Panamanian governments asserted that the executive agreement had not been intended to relieve Canal Zone workers of their federal tax obligations. See 761 F. 2nd 688 (1985).

65 *Dames & Moore v. Regan*, 453 U.S. 654 (1981).

66 354 U.S. 1 (1957).

67 Relevant cases include *Rust v. Sullivan*, 500 U.S. 173 (1991) and *U.S. v. Alvarez-Machain*, 504 U.S. 655 (1992).

68 *Goldwater v. Carter*, 444 U.S. 996 (1979).

69 Victoria M. Kraft, *The U.S. Constitution and Foreign Policy: Terminating the Taiwan Treaty* (New York: Greenwood, 1991), Ch. 3.

70 Joshua P. O'Donnell, "The Anti-Ballistic Missile Treaty Debate: Time for Some Clarification of the President's Authority to Terminate a Treaty," 35 *Vanderbilt Journal of Transnational Law* 1601 (November 2002).

71 Joel R. Paul, "The Geopolitical Constitution," 86 *California Law Review* 671 (July 1998), 672.

72 Ronald J. Sievert, "*Campbell v. Clinton* and the Continuing Effort to Reassert Congress's Predominant Constitutional Authority to Commence, or Prevent, War," 105 *Dickinson Law Review* 157 (Winter 2001).

73 D. A. Jeremy Telman, "A Truism That Isn't True? The Tenth Amendment and Executive War Power," 51 *Catholic University Law Review* 135 (Fall 2001).

74 Max Farrand, ed., *The Records of the Federal Convention of 1787* (New Haven: Yale University Press, 1937), II: 318.

75 Julian C. Boyd, ed., *The Papers of Thomas Jefferson* (Princeton: Princeton University Press, 1950), XV, 397.

76 4 U.S. 37 (1800).

77 5 U.S. 1 (1801).

78 6 U.S. 170 (1804).

79 12 U.S. 110 (1814).

80 Telman, "The Tenth Amendment," 144.

81 Abraham D. Sofaer, "The Power Over War," 50 *University of Miami Law Review* 33 (October 1995).

82 David P. Currie, "Rumors of War: Presidential and Congressional War Powers, 1809–1829," 67 *University of Chicago Law Review* 1 (Winter 2000).

83 Telman, "The Tenth Amendment," 145.

84 John Locke, *Treatise of Civil Government and a Letter Concerning Toleration* (New York: Appleton-Century-Crofts, 1937), 109.

85 67 U.S. 635 (1863).

86 71 U.S. 2 (1866).

87 Martin S. Sheffer, *The Judicial Development of Presidential War Powers* (Westport, CT: Praeger, 1999), 25.

88 71 U.S. 2 (1866), 121, 122.

89 78 U.S. 268 (1871).

90 For example, *Stewart v. Kahn*, 78 U.S. 493 (1871).

91 Christopher N. May, *In the Name of War: Judicial Review and the War Powers Since 1918* (Cambridge, MA: Harvard University Press, 1989), 19.

92 135 U.S. 546 (1890).

93 158 U.S. 564 (1895).

94 Wilson did undertake a number of measures on his own authority as commander in chief, such as the creation of the Committee on Public Information, the War Industries Board and the War Labor Board, but for the most part he relied on statutory authority for his actions. Corwin, *The President*, 237.

95 Clinton Rossiter, *The Supreme Court and the Commander in Chief* (Ithaca, NY: Cornell University Press, 1951), 91.

96 May, *In the Name of War*, 258.

97 For example, see *Hamilton v. Kentucky Distilleries*, 251 U.S. 146 (1919).

98 Corwin, *The President*, 241.

99 Arthur Schlesinger, *The Imperial Presidency* (Boston: Houghton Mifflin, 1973), 111.

100 Corwin, *The President*, 243.

101 Ibid., 250.

102 May, *In the Name of War*, 258.

103 Sheffer, *Judicial Development*, 53.

104 321 U.S. 414 (1944).

105 317 U.S. 1 (1942).

106 Lisa M. Ivey, "Ready, Aim, Fire? The President's Executive Order Authorizing Detention, Treatment and Trial of Certain Non-Citizens in the War Against Terrorism is a Powerful Weapon, But Should it Be Upheld?" 33 *Cumberland Law Review* 107 (2002–2003).

107 339 U.S. 763 (1950).

108 Rossiter, *Supreme Court*, 43.

109 323 U.S. 214 (1944).

110 143 F. 2nd 145 (D.C. Cir. 1944).

111 150 F. 2nd 369 (1945).

112 343 U.S. 579 (1952).

113 Patricia Bellia, "Executive Power in Youngstown's Shadows," 19 *Constitutional Commentary* 87 (Spring 2002).

114 403 U.S. 713 (1971).

115 407 U.S. 297 (1972).

116 Gordon Silverstein, *Imbalance of Powers: Constitutional Interpretation and the Making of American Foreign Policy* (New York: Oxford University Press, 1997), 176.

117 453 U.S. 280 (1981).

118 558 F. Supp. 893 (1982).

119 *Lowry v. Reagan*, 676 F. Supp. 333 (1987); *Dellums v. Bush*, 752 F. Supp. 1141 (1990).

120 340 U.S. App. D.C. 149 (2000).

121 Harold H. Koh, *The National Security Constitution* (New Haven: Yale University Press, 1990), 137.

122 Robert J. Delahunty and John C. Yoo, "The President's Constitutional Authority to Conduct Military Operations Against Terrorist Organizations and the Nations That Harbor or Support Them," 25 *Harvard Journal of Law and Public Policy* 487 (Spring 2002).

123 124 S. Ct. 2633 (2004).

124 296 F. 3rd 278 (4th Cir. 2002).

125 Charles Lane, "Justices Back Detainee Access to U.S. Courts," *Washington Post*, June 29, 2004, 1.

126 2004 WL 1432134.

127 2004 WL 1432135.

128 *Padilla v. Hanft*, 2005 WL 2175946, C.A. 4 (S.C.).

129 05-184, June 29, 2006.

130 Jonathan Weisman and Michael Abramowitz, "White House Shifts Tack on Tribunals," *Washington Post*, June 20, 2006, A3.

131 462 U.S. 919 (1983).

132 National Emergencies Act, 50 U.S.C. 1601; International Emergency Economic Powers Act, 50 U.S.C. 1701.

133 40 Stat. 411 (1917).

134 Frederick Block, "Civil Liberties During National Emergencies," 29 *New York University Review of Law and Social Change* 459 (2005), 462.

135 Pub. L. 73-1, March 9, 1933.

136 Block, 463.

137 S. Rep. No. 93-549 at III (1973).

138 50 U.S.C. 1701(a).

139 Jason Luong, "Forcing Constraint: The Case for Amending the International Emergency Economic Powers Act," 78 *Texas Law Review* 1181 (April 2000), 1200.

140 Block, 466.

141 Several agencies, however, are not subject to presidential budgetary review. See Louis Fisher, *Constitutional Conflicts Between Congress and the President*, 4th ed. (Lawrence, KS: University Press of Kansas, 1997), 201.

142 See Theodore J. Lowi, *The End of Liberalism*, 2nd ed. (New York: W. W. Norton, 1979); also David Schoenbrod, *Power Without Responsibility: How Congress Abuses the People through Delegation* (New Haven: Yale University Press, 1993).

143 Kenneth Culp Davis, *Discretionary Justice* (Baton Rouge, LA: Louisiana State University Press, 1969), 15–21.

144 David M. O'Brien, *Constitutional Law and Politics*, Vol. 1, 4th ed. (New York: W. W. Norton, 2000), 368.

145 Lowi, *The End of Liberalism*, 94–97.

146 Jeffrey A. Wertkin, "Reintroducing Compromise to the Nondelegation Doctrine," 98 *Georgetown Law Journal* 1055 (April 2002), 1012–13.

147 143 U.S. 649 (1892).

148 23 U.S. 1 (1825).

149 276 U.S. 394 (1928).

150 56 Stat. 23 (January 30, 1942).

151 298 U.S. 238 (1936).

152 467 U.S. 837 (1984).

153 See *Whitman v. American Trucking Associations,* 531 U.S. 457 (2001) and *AT&T Corp. v. Iowa Utilities Board,* 525 U.S. 366 (1999).

154 533 U.S. 218 (2001).

155 Silverstein, *Imbalance,* 187.

156 524 U.S. 417 (1998).

157 Archibald Cox, "Executive Privilege," 122 *University of Pennsylvania Law Review* 1383 (1974).

158 Raoul Berger, *Executive Privilege* (Cambridge, MA: Harvard University Press, 1974).

159 *U.S. v. Burr,* 25 F. Cas. 187 (1807).

160 Jeffrey P. Carlin, "*Walker v. Cheney*: Politics, Posturing and Executive Privilege," 76 *Southern California Law Review* 235 (November 2002), 245.

161 433 U.S. 425 (1977).

162 The appeals court, however, developed a procedure that gave the subcommittee limited access to documents under court supervision. 551 F. 2nd 384 (D.C. Cir. 1976).

163 556 F. Supp. 150 (D.D.C. 1983). As in the *AT&T* case, the court developed a procedure providing limited access to the contested documents.

164 See, for example, *Bareford v. General Dynamics Corp.,* 973 F. 2nd 1138 (5th Cir. 1992).

165 See, *In re Sealed Case,* 121 F. 3rd 729 (D.C. Cir. 1997).

166 230 F. Supp. 2nd 51 (2002).

167 424 U.S. 1 (1976).

168 Robert V. Percival, "Presidential Management of the Administrative State: The Not-So-Unitary Executive," 51 *Duke Law Journal* 963 (December 2001), 972.

169 272 U.S. 52 (1926).

170 295 U.S. 602 (1935).

171 478 U.S. 714 (1986).

172 48 U.S. 361 (1989).

173 366 F. Supp. 104 (D.D.C., 1973).

174 487 U.S. 654 (1988).

175 William J. Olson and Alan Woll, "Executive Orders and National Emergencies: How Presidents Have Come to Run the Country By Usurping Legislative Power" (Washington, DC: Cato Institute, 1999).

176 *Building and Construction Trades Department v. Allbaugh,* 172 F. Supp. 2nd 138 (D.D.C., 2001).

177 74 F. 3rd 1322 (D.C. Cir. 1996).

178 Tara L. Branum, "President or King? The Use and Abuse of Executive Orders in Modern-Day America," 28 *Journal of Legislation* 1 (2002), 18.

179 *Clinton v. Jones*, 520 U.S. 681 (1997).

Chapter 9. Conclusion: Upsizing the Presidency and Downsizing Democracy

1 Robert C. Byrd, *Losing America: Confronting a Reckless and Arrogant Presidency* (New York: W. W. Norton, 2004), 167.

2 Dean Acheson, *Present At the Creation* (New York: W. W. Norton, 1969).

3 David Nather, "Congress As a Watchdog: Asleep on the Job?" *Congressional Quarterly Weekly* 61/21 (May 22, 2004): 1190–95.

4 Steven Calabresi, "Some Normative Arguments for the Unitary Executive," 48 *Arkansas Law Review* 23 (1995).

5 A contemporary statement of this position is Harvey C. Mansfield, Jr., *Taming the Prince: The Ambivalence of Modern Executive Power* (New York: Free Press, 1989), Ch. 1.

6 Richard Loss, ed., *The Letters of Pacificus and Helvidius* (Delmar, NY: Scholars Facsimiles and Reprints, 1976), 91–92.

7 Martin Shefter, *Political Parties and the State* (Princeton: Princeton University Press, 1994), 78–79.

8 C. Boyden Gray, "Special Interests, Regulation and the Separation of Powers," in L. Gordon Crovitz and Jeremy Rabkin, eds., *The Fettered Presidency: Legal Constraints on the Executive Branch* (Washington, DC: American Enterprise Institute Press, 1989), 211–23.

9 For example, Lawrence Lessig and Cass Sunstein, "The President and the Administration," 94 *Columbia Law Review* 1 (1994), 85–106.

10 Steven Calabresi, "The Virtues of Presidential Government," 18 *Constitutional Commentary* 51 (Spring 2001), 72.

11 Grant McConnell, *The Modern Presidency* (New York: St. Martin's Press, 1976); also Calabresi, "Some Normative Arguments," 58.

12 William J. Keefe and Morris S. Ogul, *The American Legislative Process* (Upper Saddle River, NJ: Prentice Hall, 2001), 236.

13 *U.S. v. U.S. District Court of the District of Columbia*, 124 S. Ct. 1391 (2004).

14 Kenneth R. Mayer, *With the Stroke of a Pen* (Princeton: Princeton University Press, 2001), 59.

15 Christopher Simpson, *National Security Directives of the Reagan and Bush Administrations* (Boulder, CO: Westview Press, 1995).

16 Executive Order 12866, 3 CFR 638 (1993). President Bush ordered continuation of this procedure in his Executive Order 13258

17 Steven Croley, "White House Review of Agency Rulemaking: An Empirical Investigation," 70 *University of Chicago Law Review* 821 (Summer 2003), 821–85.

18 Ibid., 854.

19 Ibid., 857.

20 Ibid., 883.

21 Elena Kagan, "Presidential Administration," 114 *Harvard Law Review* 2245 (June 2001).

22 A summary of OIRA meetings and their participants since 2001 is posted on the OMB Web site.

23 Dawn E. Johnson, "Presidential Nonenforcement of Constitutionally Objectionable Statutes," 63 *Law and Contemporary Problems* 7 (Winter/Spring 2000), 7–60.

24 Judith Goldstein, "International Forces and Domestic Politics: Trade Policy and Institution Building in the United States," in Ira Katznelson and Martin Shefter, eds., *Shaped By War and Trade: International Influences on American Political Development* (Princeton: Princeton University Press, 2002), 214.

25 Ibid.

26 Ibid., 218.

27 Ibid.

28 Ibid., 219.

29 The phrase "diminished democracy" is, of course, used in a slightly different context by Theda Skocpol in her excellent book, *Diminished Democracy: From Membership to Management in American Civic Life* (Norman, OK: University of Oklahoma Press, 2003).

30 Matthew A. Crenson and Benjamin Ginsberg, *Downsizing Democracy: How America Sidelined Its Citizens and Privatized Its Public* (Baltimore: Johns Hopkins University Press, 2002).

31 Loss, ed., *Letters of Pacificus and Helvidius*, 64–65.

Index